W9-CSQ-773

Jim IFFLANDER
FINANCE DEPT

The Theory of Finance

The
Theory
of
Finance

Eugene F. Fama
Merton H. Miller

Graduate School of Business
The University of Chicago

DRYDEN PRESS
HINSDALE, ILLINOIS

Copyright © 1972 by Holt, Rinehart and Winston, Inc.
All rights reserved
Library of Congress Catalog Card Number: 74–168400
ISBN: 0–03–086732–0
Printed in the United States of America
6 038 987

To Our Wives

PREFACE

This book, in various versions, has been the main text for courses in finance taught by us over the last six years at the Graduate School of Business of the University of Chicago. We have generally supplemented it with other materials, ranging all the way from cases and homework problems, on the one hand, to journal articles and research papers on the other, depending on the level of the course and its place in the curriculum. Even in the most elementary courses, however, we have always assigned some journal articles as supplementary reading. We believe an important function of graduate professional education to be that of acquainting future practitioners with leading scientific journals in their field. From our experience, moreover, students at all levels have generally welcomed this chance to confront the literature of finance directly and especially to plunge into the many controversies that have enlivened, if not always enlightened, the subject. But for students to be able to grapple with the issues effectively or to make independent critical evaluations of contending points of view, they must have a more thorough, systematic, and rigorous grounding in the basic theory of finance than can be obtained from any of the standard, all-purpose texts currently available. Hence, this book.

To make the essential theoretical framework of the subject stand out sharply, we have pruned away virtually all institutional and descriptive material. We also largely pass over such popular standard topics as cash flow forecasting, cash budgeting, ratio analysis, credit management, and similar aspects of managerial finance. We do not deny that these problems are often of great practical importance, but except perhaps for capital budgeting, theoretical work in the area has so far been ad hoc and largely unrelated to the material that we try to cover. In any event, instructors who wish to place more emphasis than we do on these problems of internal financial management and control should have no difficulty in finding suitable supplementary readings.

We have also decided—and here the decision was much more painful—to omit any review or extensive discussion of empirical tests of the theory. So much high-quality empirical work is now being done and with techniques so varied that we despaired of being able to do justice to it without adding excessively to the length of the book and the number of different topics covered. Once again, however, we feel that instructors so inclined can readily supplement the text with journal articles and, where necessary, with selected chapters from texts in econometrics and statistics.

Readers will also note the absence of any detailed examples, of the kind often found in standard texts, purporting to show how to apply the theory, in precise, quantitative terms, to real-world decision problems. This omission is less a move to save space than a reflection of our belief that the potential contribution of the theory of finance to the decision-making process, although substantial, is still essentially indirect. The theory can often help expose the inconsistencies in existing procedures; it can help keep the really critical questions from getting lost in the inevitable maze of technical detail; and it can help prevent the too easy, unthinking acceptance of either the old clichés or new fads. But the theory of finance has not yet been brought, and perhaps never will be, to the cookbook stage.

The cutback that we have made in the amount and kind of material to be covered is also accompanied by a fairly drastic change, as compared with standard texts, in the way the book is organized. Rather than follow the popular practices of structuring by the balance sheet—starting with short-term assets and liabilities and working successively down the right-hand side into longer-term financing—or by the stages in the financial life cycle of a firm—starting with organization and incorporation and working on through to bankruptcy and reorganization—we have tried to present the material in the order of difficulty and logical priority, although this means that we often are forced to spread the discussion of particular applied problems, such as dividend policy, over several chapters.

Because a complete overview is provided at the start of each main part of the book, we need say little more here about the precise organization of the material beyond indicating that Part I covers the case of certainty and Part II that of uncertainty. Our treatment of uncertainty is carried out for the most part within the so-called mean-variance or, better, two-parameter risk-return framework. Empirical research in finance has increasingly been conducted within this framework and, on the whole, quite successfully. Hence we give only passing attention to the more elegant but so far much less operational time-state preference approach.

It is assumed throughout that all securities are traded in perfect markets. Originally, we had hoped to have a third major part in the book in which, after having dropped the assumption of perfect certainty, we went on to drop the assumption of perfect capital markets. After surveying the relevant literature, however, we feel that results in the theory of finance under imperfect capital markets are still too few, too unconnected, and too little tested to justify their incorporation into an introductory textbook. We recognize that there are dangers in arming the student only with comparative static models based on the perfect market assumption, and we have therefore tried to call his attention at various points to some of the pitfalls involved in the unthinking application of these models to real-world problems. But we feel that in the present state of the art, any extended discussion of financing problems under imperfect markets would run the greater danger of deluding the student, and the practitioner, into believing that the profession had found more solutions for such problems than is in fact the case.

Not only are analytical results in the area of imperfect markets relatively meager, except perhaps in the area of models of cash balance management, but at least insofar as concerns the valuation side of finance, there seem to be no very compelling reasons for extending the analysis in the direction of incorporating imperfections and irrationalities. The most striking single impression that emerges from the mass of empirical work that has been done in the last ten years is how robust the perfect and efficient market models are in confrontation with the data, despite what seem to be the outrageous simplifications that have gone into their construction.

Although the discussion to this point suggests, and a glance through the book itself will confirm, that we rely much more heavily on the standard apparatus of economic theory than is typically the case in finance, this book is, nevertheless, intended as a text in finance and not as one in economics. For example, in discussions of decision making, the emphasis throughout is on the microdecision problems of the investor and the corporate manager and not on the macroeconomic problems of social policy that are the main concern of economists. Even at the micro level, we have not hesitated to omit pieces of the standard apparatus that an economist would be likely to regard as essential, such as the distinction between income and substitution effects or between relative and absolute risk aversion, but for which it happens that we have no need. Nor, furthermore, has any very substantial previous acquaintance with economics on the part of the reader been assumed. We have taken as a prerequisite only that amount of introductory economics that has long been the compulsory dosage in MBA and even undergraduate business programs—one course in price theory and perhaps one in macroeconomics. Having issued this disclaimer for the benefit of any economist reviewers, we should like to indicate our belief that this book can also be used effectively as at least a supplementary text in courses in intermediate price theory and capital theory.

We have tried to keep the mathematics requirements as low as possible to avoid excluding those long-since-graduated practitioners of finance who still maintain an active interest in the technical professional literature of their field but who have inevitably become a bit rusty in mathematics. Despite any initial impression to the contrary that might be gained from casually riffling through the pages, only a working knowledge of high school algebra, geometry, and some elementary statistics is really required to be able to follow the main line of the argument. Where more than this assumed minimum is used, we have so indicated by starring the particular section concerned or by putting the material in footnotes. Such sections and footnotes may safely be skipped by readers who lack the requisite mathematical background, but we should strongly urge even them to try at least to skim through this material. To make doubly sure that there is no loss of continuity, we have taken pains to see that each main point is always covered in a variety of ways: mathematically, verbally, graphically, and in a few cases, by numerical examples.

Finally, we should like to emphasize again that this book was written as a textbook, not a treatise. Virtually all the substantive content, except for a number of new proofs that we have felt called on to supply, can be traced directly back to sources that have long since been published and subjected to critical scrutiny by the profession. We have made no attempt to document these sources in detail or to provide any very elaborate history of doctrine. We have, however, added a brief annotated bibliography to the end of each chapter, although it is intended only to indicate some of the high spots and makes no pretense to completeness.

In putting together this book, we have been more than usually fortunate in being able to draw on the thinking and advice of our students and colleagues, some of whom have actually used this book in note form as a text in their own courses. Our sincerest thanks to them and to the many others at Chicago and elsewhere whose comments and criticisms have helped shape this book.

Some of the proofs and related discussions first appeared in articles in the *American Economic Review*, the *Journal of Business*, the *Journal of Finance*, and the *Journal of Political Economy*. We wish to thank these journals and their publishers, the *American Economic Association*, the *American Finance Association*, and the *University of Chicago Press* for permission to draw on and adapt this material for use in the present volume. We also wish to thank Mr. Robert Officer for his help in checking the text and in constructing the index.

Chicago
November 1971

Eugene F. Fama
Merton H. Miller

CONTENTS

I

CERTAINTY MODELS

The theory of finance is concerned with how individuals and firms allocate resources through time. In particular, it seeks to explain how solutions to the problems faced in allocating resources through time are facilitated by the existence of capital markets (which provide a means for individual economic agents to exchange resources to be available at different points in time) and of firms (which, by their production-investment decisions, provide a means for individuals to transform current resources physically into resources to be available in the future).

A central or perhaps the central theme of this book is the role of a capital market that is perfect, in a sense to be defined in detail later, in allowing individuals and firms most efficiently to exchange resources to be available at different points in time.

The procedure in this book is to work from simple models to more complicated ones. Thus, the first part of the book is concerned with a world in which there is no uncertainty about future events; the future consequences of actions taken now are assumed to be perfectly predictable. The second part of the book then moves on to consider models of a world of uncertainty.

The steps to be followed in presenting the theory of finance for a world of perfect certainty are as follows. First, we introduce a model of the problem of resource allocation through time faced by an individual consumer as a special case of the general theory of choice. The two important elements of this model are (1) some presumptions about the individual's tastes in ordering the objects about which decisions must be made, and (2) a specification of the opportunities that are available.

Chapter 1 considers only the opportunities available to the individual when there is a capital market in which current resources can be sold in exchange for resources to be obtained in the future; and vice versa, resources to be obtained in the future can be sold now in exchange for current resources. Chapter 2 expands the opportunity set to include the opportunities for transforming current resources into future resources provided by the investment of current resources in physical production, which production is assumed to be undertaken by firms. Finally, Chapter

3 considers some of the problems of detail involved in implementing the decision rules developed in Chapters 1 and 2, especially the problems that arise in implementing the rules for optimal production-financing-investment decisions by firms.

1

A MODEL OF THE ACCUMULATION AND ALLOCATION OF WEALTH BY INDIVIDUALS

M.S.U.
BOOKSTORE

ᴈ·   19.50 T 108

·TX   00.75 108

ᴈ·   18.75 S 108

:P·   01.80   108

ᴵᴮ·   16.95   108

2971   1 4 Jan 77

NO RETURN
WITHOUT RECEIPT
I

In this introductory chapter to Part I, we present one of the fundamental building blocks of the theory of finance, namely, the model of the accumulation and allocation of wealth over time by individuals under conditions of certainty and perfect capital markets. Once the model itself has been set forth in fairly general and abstract terms, we go on in subsequent chapters to consider its extensions to a variety of problems in finance. The extension of the model to the case of uncertainty is given in Part II.

Because the wealth allocation model itself is merely a special case of the more general economic theory of choice under certainty, we begin by reviewing briefly some of the main concepts and features of this theory.

I. THE ECONOMIC THEORY OF CHOICE

I.A. Opportunities and Preferences

The economic theory of choice, like any other body of theory, aims at establishing empirical generalizations

3

about the class of phenomena under study. For the theory of choice, this means generalizations about the way in which choices change in response to changes in the circumstances surrounding the choice.

The first step in constructing the theory is the simple but important one of classification. We divide the many separate elements bearing on any choice into two classes. One class is called the "opportunity set" or "constraint set." As the name implies, it is the collection of possible choices available to the decision maker. Its content, depending on the context, may be determined by technological limitations, such as the impossibility of constructing a perpetual-motion machine, or by legal restrictions, such as those prohibiting selling oneself into slavery, or by market restrictions, such as the inability to buy a new automobile for $5 because of the absence of sellers at this price.

The other main elements in the decision problem are the decision maker's "tastes" or preferences. For an individual choosing on his own behalf, these tastes depend on personality, upbringing, education, and so forth. The theory does not propose to say precisely how these factors enter separately into the choice but takes the individual and his preferences as given from outside the problem and proceeds from there. For individuals acting as managers, and hence presumably on behalf of others, the question of precisely whose preferences we are talking about, that is, the agent's or the principal's or some combination, must also be faced. We eventually try to do so, but to keep the presentation uncluttered, we defer this issue to Chapter 2. For the remainder of the present chapter, we are concerned only with a single individual acting entirely on his own behalf.

I.B. Representation of Preferences: The Utility Function and Indifference Curves

To develop interesting generalizations about choice behavior, we need a convenient way of representing tastes and opportunities. One possibility is to tabulate the decision maker's choices under laboratory conditions. We could present the subject with a series of bundles or boxes each containing some of the relevant objects of choice, carefully record the contents of each box, and then note which box he actually chose. By suitably varying the contents of the boxes, we could obtain an extensive picture of his likes and dislikes.

Such a table would certainly contain a great deal of information about the subject's tastes, but it would be difficult to work with. Any patterns in it would be too hard to see. The question arises, therefore, whether some simpler and more compact way exists for representing or at least approximating the data in the table. Such a representation is indeed possible, provided that the subject's preferences satisfy certain conditions.

I.B.1. The axioms of choice and the principle of maximum utility

These conditions collectively constitute the axioms of the economic theory of choice. The word *axiom* is not to be taken here in its old-fashioned sense of a self-evident truth. The axioms are to be regarded rather as provisional assumptions, plausible enough, perhaps, as approximations, but whose ultimate justification comes, not from their own truth or plausibility, but from the predictive and descriptive power of the conclusions to which they lead.[1]

In discussing the axioms, we let the letters x, y, and z represent boxes of objects presented to the subject for choice. These objects, whatever their outward form, are referred to as "commodities" to which, instead of names, we assign numbers $1, 2, \ldots, n$. Each box is completely specified by indicating the number of units q of each commodity that it contains; that is, the box x is represented by an n-tuple of the form $(q_1^{(x)}, q_2^{(x)}, \ldots, q_n^{(x)})$.

Axiom 1 (Comparability). For every pair of boxes x and y the decision maker can tell us either (1) that he prefers x to y, or (2) that he prefers y to x, or (3) that he is indifferent to having x or y.

The function of the axiom of comparability is to rule out cases in which the decision maker refuses or is unable to make a choice, because, for example, he may regard the objects of choice as essentially different and hence incomparable.

Axiom 2 (Transitivity). Whenever the decision maker prefers x to y and y to z, he also prefers x to z. Likewise, if he is indifferent to having x or y and to having y or z, he is also indifferent to having x or z. Basically, the subject behaves consistently in making his choices.

If the decision maker's tastes conform to these axioms, the following important proposition holds:

The subject's choice behavior may be characterized by saying that he behaves as if he were maximizing the value of a "utility function." This function assigns a numerical value or "utility index" to each box $x, y, \ldots,$

---

[1] The methodological principle that theories are to be judged by the empirical validity of their consequences rather than by that of their assumptions considered separately has come to be called "positivism." The classical statement of the positivist position in economics is that of Milton Friedman, "The Methodology of Positive Economics," in *Essays in Positive Economics.* Chicago: University of Chicago Press, 1956.

with the quantities of each commodity in the box as the arguments of the function.

To illustrate, suppose that we somehow knew that a utility function for a particular subject took the form

$$U = F(q_1, q_2) = q_1{}^2 + q_2{}^2,$$

where the letter U is the utility index and q_1 and q_2 are the quantities respectively of commodities 1 and 2 in any box. Suppose that we also knew that box x held 6 units of commodity 1 and 4 units of 2 and that box y held 8 units of commodity 1 and 2 units of 2. Which one does he prefer? Substituting the contents of box x into the utility function, we obtain an index of $6^2 + 4^2 = 52$; for the second box we have $8^2 + 2^2 = 68$. The assignment of a higher utility index to the second box is equivalent to saying that the subject prefers box y to box x.

Note that in the statement of the proposition we say that the subject behaves as if he were maximizing the value of a utility function. The economic theory of choice does not assert that the subject performs these calculations on his utility function in making his choices or even that the subject knows that he has a utility function. It says merely that if his preferences are complete and consistent, the utility function provides us, as outside observers, with a way of representing his choices. In what follows we sometimes gloss over this distinction and speak, say, of a decision maker's increasing or decreasing his utility by some action. But this should always be considered a stylistic device and must not be taken literally.

The reasonableness of the proposition in relation to the axioms is easily seen. The axioms of comparability and transitivity permit us to rank all possible boxes in increasing order of preferability. This rank ordering, in turn, can always be expressed by some device that assigns numbers to each box so that higher numbers go with higher ranks. The utility function is just such a device.[2]

It should also be clear that any specific representation of a subject's utility function, such as in this illustration, is not unique. If one such function exists, so do many others, because what matters is whether the number assigned to a box is higher or lower than that of another box. How much higher or lower is of no consequence so long as the ranking is preserved. Thus multiplying by a positive constant or performing any other monotone-increasing transformation of a utility function also yields an

---

[2] The more advanced mathematical treatments in the economics literature are also concerned with the continuity of the utility function and the additional requirements necessary to assure it. Readers interested in a complete and rigorous discussion of these and related issues can find it in the classic treatment of the subject by Gerard Debreu, *The Theory of Value.* New York: Wiley, 1959.

equivalent and perfectly consistent representation of the subject's preferences.[3]

Given the utility function to represent the general structure of preferences, the next step in the search for interesting, and testable, generalizations about choice behavior is to invoke certain additional assumptions with respect to the form and properties of this function. Some of these assumptions are mainly for mathematical convenience and are noted here, in footnotes, only for the sake of completeness.[4] Others, however, are more substantive and merit further discussion. In introducing and explaining them, it is helpful first to show how choices and utility functions can be represented in geometrical or graphical form.

I.B.2. Indifference curves and the geometrical representation of preferences

In representing the utility function $U = U(q_1, q_2, \ldots, q_n)$ graphically, we are, of course, limited to at most three dimensions. Because we must reserve one dimension for U, the value of the utility index, we are thus restricted to only two commodities in making up the boxes between which the subject is to choose. Although this collapsing down from n distinct commodities to only two may seem a very drastic simplification, the loss of generality is actually quite small. For establishing the kinds of propositions that are our main concern, the two-commodity case is almost always adequate.

One way of representing a utility function in three dimensions on a two-dimensional page is with figures of the kind used in solid geometry. Because it is difficult, and expensive, to draw the figures in correct perspective, however, we use a projective method that is considerably simpler but requires, at first, a somewhat greater effort in interpretation on the part of the reader. To see how it works, imagine a three-dimensional solid representation of the utility function $U = U(q_1, q_2)$, with q_1 and q_2 on two axes in a horizontal plane and U measured on a third axis vertical, and perpendicular, to the other two. Imagine now that we pick some particular value

[3] Utility functions with this property are said to be "ordinal" functions, in contrast to "cardinal" utility functions, which are unique up to a "linear" transformation and which hence can convey some indication of how much higher one bundle is on the subject's scale of preferences than another. We have no need for the stronger, cardinal functions until we reach Part II and introduce uncertainty.

[4] In particular, we assume that the arguments of the utility function, q_i, can be represented as continuous variables, that is, that all commodities are infinitely divisible, that the utility function itself is a continuous function of its arguments, and that it has continuous derivatives of whatever order we happen to need.

Another assumption that we have already made implicitly by our distinction between tastes and opportunities is that the two can in fact be separated in the sense that each can be defined independently of the other.

of U, say, $U = 7$, and pass a knife horizontally through the surface at this level. The cut being horizontal, the outline is necessarily always a two-dimensional figure. Now project, that is, drop, this horizontal outline down onto the horizontal q_1q_2 plane. If we repeated this process for many different values of U, we should obtain a whole set of such two-dimensional figures; and by labeling each such figure or contour with its value of U, we could mentally reconstruct the entire three-dimensional figure.

An example of a utility function represented by such contours is shown in Figure 1.1a. From the numbering of the contours it can be seen that the utility surface has the form of an irregular hill rising to a summit at the point labeled $U = 40$. The indentations in the contours on the southwest slope imply a trough or draw at the lower levels running in the northeast-southwest direction. The circular area labeled $U = 20$ lying between the contours $U = 10$ and $U = 15$ implies a small isolated knoll on the northeast face. And so on for the various other curls and wrinkles that have been drawn into the map.

In addition to the utility surface itself, the figure also shows the representation of some boxes offered to the subject for choice and the pattern of his preferences among them. These boxes are indicated by the points labeled w, x, y, and z—the box w containing $q_1^{(w)}$ units of commodity 1 and $q_2^{(w)}$ of commodity 2, and similarly for the others. As drawn, the points w, x, and y lie on the same contour, $U = 10$. That these boxes all have the same utility index is the same as saying that the subject was completely

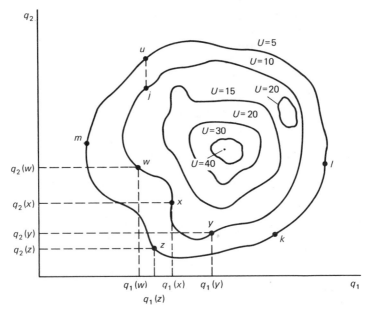

Figure 1.1a Iso-utility Contours

indifferent when presented with a choice between them—hence the term "indifference curves," which is customarily used in the theory of choice to refer to an iso-utility contour line. Box z, however, lies on an indifference curve with a lower utility index, which is to say that it would be rejected by the subject in any choice involving w, x, or y.

I.B.3. The axioms of nonsatiation and convexity

We turn now to the final two axioms or assumptions about choice behavior.

Axiom 3 (Nonsatiation of Wants). The subject would always prefer, or at worst would be indifferent, to have more of any commodity if at the same time he did not have to take less of any other commodity.

This assumption serves to rule out any positively sloped segments of indifference curves, such as the segments mu or kl on curve $U = 5$ in Figure 1.1a. For where such segments exist, there are points, such as j, having the same amount of q_1 as box u but less q_2 and yet preferred to u, as shown by the higher utility index of its indifference curve. A map of a utility surface that does conform to the axiom—a hill with no summit or northeast face—is shown in Figure 1.1b.

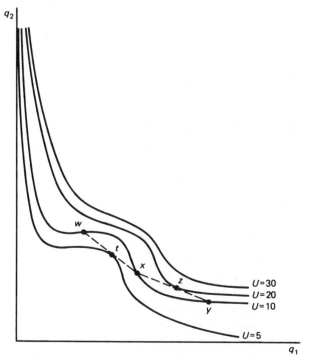

Figure 1.1b Convexity and Concavity of Indifference Curves

Axiom 4 (Convexity). If x and y are two boxes such that $U(x) = U(y)$ and if z is a combination of boxes x and y of the form $z = \alpha x + (1 - \alpha)y$, $0 \le \alpha \le 1$, then $U(z) \ge U(x) = U(y)$. In words, if we have two boxes between which the subject is indifferent, and we construct a new box whose contents, commodity by commodity, are a weighted average of those of x and y, where the weights are positive and sum to unity, the subject never chooses either x or y in preference to the combination box z.[5]

Examples of (local) regions of the utility surface that do and do not meet this convexity assumption are shown in Figure 1.1*b*. If we draw a straight line connecting the points w and x lying on the same indifference curve $U = 10$, this straight line representing all the combination boxes along the line $\alpha x + (1 - \alpha)w$ for $0 \le \alpha \le 1$, we see that a combination box, such as t, would not be preferable to x or w. It lies on a lower indifference curve with index, say, $U = 5$, as we have happened to draw it. In this region, then, the indifference curve does not meet the convexity assumption. By contrast, the intermediate points on a straight line between x and y all lie on higher indifference curves, and in this region the indifference curve for $U = 10$ is convex.

To see in more concrete terms what this assumption of convexity implies about choice behavior, imagine that the boxes contain two commodities, such as books and theater tickets. Suppose that we start with a box containing 20 books and 3 tickets and then withdraw 1 ticket. Books and tickets both being desirable commodities for the subject, we should have to add, say, 2 additional books to the box to keep him on the same indifference curve—the additional books, in effect, compensating for the ticket withdrawn. If now we subtract another ticket from the 2 remaining, the convexity assumption implies that we should have to add at least another 2 books and possibly more, to keep the utility index of the box unchanged. When the removal of the second item requires more compensation than that of the first, the indifference curve is said to be "strictly convex." When the compensation required is the same on successive removals, the curve is linear, which is the limiting extreme case of convexity.[6]

In most subsequent applications of the theory to problems of finance we work with indifference maps of the kind shown in Figure 1.1*c*. Such maps have a number of important features and properties that will be invoked

---

[5] As an illustration of the contruction of z from x and y, suppose that x has 8 units of commodity 1 and 6 units of commodity 2 and y has 6 units of 1 and 10 units of 2; then by taking $\alpha = \frac{1}{4}$, z would be a box with $\frac{1}{4}(8) + \frac{3}{4}(6) = 6\frac{1}{2}$ units of commodity 1 and $\frac{1}{4}(6) + \frac{3}{4}(10) = 9$ units of commodity 2.

[6] For those readers who find it difficult to accept the convexity axiom, even provisionally, it may be well to point out that we use it here mainly to simplify the graphical presentations and to avoid the complication of multiple or "corner" solutions. All the really essential conclusions can be derived from the first three axioms only.

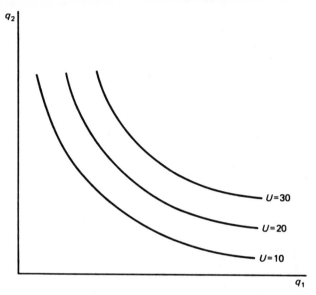

Figure 1.1c   A Standard Indifference Map

repeatedly in deriving propositions about choice behavior. To summarize, the slope of an indifference curve, often called the marginal rate of substitution of q_2 for q_1, is always negative. The marginal rate of substitution rises in algebraic or falls in absolute value as we move from left to right. Curves take on higher utility indexes as we move upward on the map. And there are never any crossings of indifference curves. To test their understanding, readers for whom this apparatus is unfamiliar may find it useful to imagine the contrary of each of these properties and then show that such cases would be inconsistent with one or more of the basic axioms of comparability, transitivity, nonsatiation, or convexity.[7]

[7] Because these concepts are used repeatedly throughout the book, it is well to note more formally here the distinction between convex "sets" and convex and concave "functions" and "curves." A set of points is said to be convex if for any two points x and y in the set, the point $z = \alpha x + (1 - \alpha)y$, $0 \leq \alpha \leq 1$, is also in the set. Geometrically, a set is convex if all points on a straight line between any points in the set are also in the set.

On the other hand, a function f is convex if for any two points x and y in the domain of f

$$f(\alpha x + (1 - \alpha)y) \leq \alpha f(x) + (1 - \alpha)f(y), \qquad 0 \leq \alpha \leq 1,$$

and the function is concave if

$$f(\alpha x + (1 - \alpha)y) \geq \alpha f(x) + (1 - \alpha)f(y), \qquad 0 \leq \alpha \leq 1.$$

Geometrically, a function or curve is convex if a line between any two points on the

I.C. The Opportunity Set

As noted earlier, the class of choice problems of most concern in economics as opposed to, say, psychology or aesthetics is that in which the decision maker's choices are limited by external restrictions. A graphical representation of such restrictions for a two-commodity case is shown in Figure 1.2. As indicated by the shading, the feasible boxes or combinations of commodities 1 and 2 are restricted to those lying within, or on the boundaries of, the irregular figure outlined by OAB. Any box not lying within this opportunity set is excluded from consideration, no matter how desirable it might be for the subject to have it.

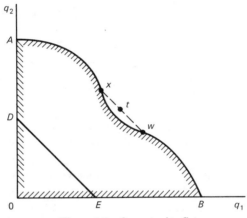

Figure 1.2   Opportunity Sets

The precise content or shape of the opportunity set depends, of course, on the problem at hand. There is, however, one general restriction that is a feature of virtually all those to be considered here, namely, the assumption that the set is convex; that is, if x and y are any two boxes in the opportunity set, all boxes z of the form $z = \alpha x + (1 - \alpha)y, 0 < \alpha < 1$, are also in the set. Thus, in terms of Figure 1.2, the property of convexity of the set

---

function lies everywhere on or above the function; concavity implies that a line between any two points is everywhere on or below the function.

Hence, when added to the nonsatiation axiom, the convexity axiom presented in the text is an assumption that commodity indifference curves are convex. But note carefully that it is not an assumption that the utility function U is convex. This function is still only ordinal; that is, the only restriction on the numbers assigned to successive indifference curves are that they are monotone-increasing, so that the curvature of the function across indifference curves is arbitrary.

rules out segments like that between w and x, where there are boxes like t lying on a line joining x and w, but not part of the allowable choices.[8]

Note that the definition of convexity includes sets with straight-line outer boundaries, such as the set bounded by ODE in Figure 1.2, as the limiting special case. In general, convex opportunity sets with curved boundaries usually arise when the constraints are imposed by "technology" and the curvature represents "diminishing returns" in the physical possibilities of transforming commodity 1 into commodity 2. The straight-line cases usually represent market exchange opportunities, the constant slope implying that the commodities can be exchanged for each other at given, fixed prices. In some cases, we consider problems with both types of constraints operating simultaneously.

I.D. Choice Subject to Constraints

To obtain a representation of a choice in the presence of constraints, there remains now only to bring together the two pieces of the problem, tastes and opportunities, that we have so far considered separately. A graphical illustration for a two-commodity case is shown in Figure 1.3. The

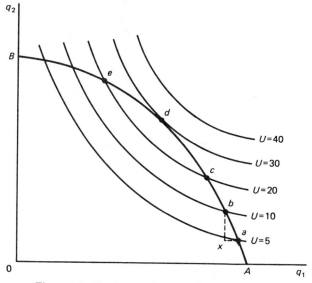

Figure 1.3   Representation of a Constrained Choice

figure shows a subject whose preferences meet the four axioms of choice and can therefore be represented by a utility map with convex indifference

[8] As with the assumption of convexity of indifference curves (see footnote 6 above), the assumption of convex opportunity sets is much stronger than necessary for most of the important conclusions and is used throughout mainly to simplify the presentation.

curves increasing in utility index as one moves up and to the right. The possible boxes available to him lie within the figure OBA. Which one of the immense number of possibilities represents the one that he would actually choose?

We can, first of all, eliminate immediately a large number of boxes as possibilities. In particular, no box such as x in the interior of the opportunity set could possibly be his eventual choice, because the boxes lying between a and b on the boundary all have at least as much of one of the two commodities as x and more of the other. By virtue of the nonsatiation axiom, such dominated interior boxes are ruled out, and only the boxes along the right boundary need be considered. It is for this reason that the right boundary of the opportunity set is often referred to as the "efficiency frontier" or "efficient set".[9]

Having narrowed the range of possibilities to the efficient set, we need only sweep along it in some systematic manner. If, for example, we work up from the lower right-hand corner, steadily decreasing the amount of q_1 in the box and increasing the amount of q_2, we produce a series of choices of the form a versus b, then b versus c, and so on. As drawn, the subject prefers b to a, indicated by the fact that b lies on a higher indifference curve, and prefers c to b. Eventually, by repeating this process, we find a point that is preferred to its neighbors on either side. In the figure as drawn, this is the point d, at which an indifference curve is tangent to the efficiency frontier. All other boxes, whether on the efficiency frontier or within it, lie on lower indifference curves.

This representation of a constrained choice completes our review of the fundamentals of the theory of choice. The importance of this theory for our purposes lies in its simplicity and in the fact that it is both context- and subject-free. No matter what kinds of commodities that we put in the boxes and no matter who the subject or what the details of his personal preferences, his choice can always be represented by a point on the efficiency frontier, provided only that his tastes meet Axioms 1 to 3. If, in addition, his tastes meet Axiom 4 and if the opportunity set is convex, we can narrow the possible choices along the frontier down to the single one where an indifference curve is tangent to the opportunity set. The four axioms plus the convexity of the opportunity set guarantee both that there must be such a point and that there is no more than one.[10]

_____

[9] Because the right boundary of the opportunity set is assumed to be negatively sloping, the assumption that the set is convex implies that this boundary must be a concave curve.

[10] In what follows, we frequently refer to these tangency points as "optimal solutions" or "equilibrium points." As in the case of references to utility, however, such terms are normally to be taken in an as if sense and not as implying that the subject is consciously optimizing or equilibrating.

The task of much of the rest of the book is essentially a filling in of these "empty boxes" and a showing of how the very general and abstract theory of choice can be specialized to obtain meaningful generalizations about financial choices. But before turning to this task, we present for the record a very brief account of how a choice subject to constraints can be represented in mathematical form.

*I.E. The Solution in Mathematical Form[11]

In particular, for an n-commodity case, the subject's choice can be expressed as the solution to the problem[12]

$$\max_{q_1, q_2, \ldots, q_n} U(q_1, q_2, \ldots, q_n)$$

subject to a constraint or opportunity set that may be written in general, implicit form as

$$T(q_1, q_2, \ldots, q_n) = 0,$$

and which represents the points $(q_1, q_2, \ldots, q_n)$ that lie along the efficiency frontier.

With appropriate assumptions about the continuity of the derivatives of the U and T functions, we can use the methods of the differential calculus to study properties of the solution to this problem. Specifically, form the lagrangian function

$$L = U(q_1, q_2, \ldots, q_n) - \lambda T(q_1, q_2, \ldots, q_n), \tag{1.1}$$

and differentiate partially with respect to λ and each of the q_i. Setting these derivatives equal to zero yields the following $n + 1$ equations as first-order or necessary conditions for a maximum:[13]

$$
\begin{aligned}
U_1' - \lambda T_1' &= 0 \\
U_2' - \lambda T_2' &= 0 \\
&\vdots \\
U_n' - \lambda T_n' &= 0 \\
T(q_1, q_2, \ldots, q_n) &= 0,
\end{aligned}
\tag{1.2}
$$

[11] Starred sections here and throughout mark the places in the exposition where some knowledge of the calculus is required. Such sections may safely be skipped by readers lacking the necessary mathematical background, without fear of losing the main thread of the argument. Such readers may nevertheless find it helpful to skim through the sections, because the discussion surrounding the mathematical results may provide additional insights.

[12] The expression

$$\max_{q_1, q_2, \ldots, q_n} U(q_1, q_2, \cdots, q_n)$$

is read "choose values of q_1 to q_n that maximize the utility index."

[13] In general, in the mathematical treatments of various maximization and minimiza-

where U_i' and T_i' are the partial derivatives of U and T with respect to q_i.

To see the relation between this representation and the graphical representation of the two-commodity case, observe that between any pair of commodities we can eliminate λ from the relevant equations of (1.2) to obtain, for example,

$$\frac{U_1'}{T_1'} = \frac{U_2'}{T_2'} \quad \text{or} \quad \frac{U_1'}{U_2'} = \frac{T_1'}{T_2'}. \tag{1.3}$$

The definition of an indifference curve is equivalent to the solution set satisfying the condition on the differential

$$dU = U_1'dq_1 + U_2'dq_2 + \cdots + U_n'dq_n = 0$$

for some specified level of U. Holding q_3 to q_n constant, that is, setting dq_3 to $dq_n = 0$, this condition implies that

$$\frac{dq_2}{dq_1} = -\frac{U_1'}{U_2'}.$$

Or, in words, the slope of an indifference curve at any point is equal to (minus) the ratio of the first partial derivatives evaluated at this point. Similarly, for the opportunity set we have

$$\frac{dq_2}{dq_1} = -\frac{T_1'}{T_2'}.$$

Thus the condition (1.3) is equivalent to the statement that at a maximum of U, the slope of an indifference curve is the same as that of the opportunity set, which is, of course, the familiar tangency condition in the geometric analysis.

II. THE APPLICATION OF THE THEORY OF CHOICE TO THE ALLOCATION OF FINANCIAL RESOURCES OVER TIME

II.A. The Two-Period Case

As noted earlier, the basic application of the theory of choice under certainty to the field of finance is the problem of the allocation of financial resources by individuals over time. The rest of the present chapter is

---

tion problems in this book, we do not present sufficient or second-order conditions, because they usually contribute little in the way of economic insight, which, after all, is the primary concern. Moreover, such "mathematical license" is often characteristic of our mathematical treatments in other ways as well. For example, we ignore, for the most part, the additional complications introduced by nonnegativity conditions on some or all of the variables.

devoted to the development of this application in its most general and abstract form. A number of extensions are then taken up in subsequent chapters.

II.A.1. The objects of choice: standards of living at different points in time

In studying the allocation of financial resources over time, the objects of choice can be defined in several ways, depending on how much detail is to be shown and precisely how the passage of time is to be represented. Taking the question of time first, we assume throughout that the passage of time is not continuous but occurs in discrete jumps one "unit of time" apart. Decisions are assumed to be taken and payments to be made only at the start of these discrete time periods. For generating the kind of qualitative generalizations about behavior that are our concern, no precise statement need be made about the length of a unit time period in terms of calendar time.[14]

As for the objects of choice, we could continue to work in the standard economic framework of individual commodities, giving each commodity a time index to indicate the period in which it was being presented to the subject. The utility function would then be of the form $V(q_{11}, q_{21}, \ldots, q_{n1}, q_{12}, q_{22}, \ldots, q_{n2}, \ldots, q_{1t}, q_{2t}, \ldots, q_{nt}, \ldots)$. But although formally unobjectionable, and really no great complication mathematically, such an approach makes it difficult to focus sharply on the effects of time per se and on the purely financial aspects of the allocation decision. To highlight these aspects of the problem, therefore, we make the following simplifications in the utility function.

First, because the function in its most general form includes in principle commodities that represent income-earning activities, for example, hours of labor, we assume that these can be separated out and that a utility function can be defined over the set of consumer goods; that is, we assume that preferences between boxes of consumer goods depend only on the contents of the boxes and not on the amount or nature of the income-earning activities that might accompany them. This creates some problems with respect to what might be called "leisure goods," but they are minor for our purposes and are neglected. We also neglect the details of the decision with respect to occupational choice and hours of work. The subject's occupation and earnings are taken as given, determined somehow outside the model.

---

[14] Despite assertions to the contrary occasionally encountered in the literature, there is little basis other than taste or convenience in choosing between a discrete-time formulation of the kind to be followed here and a continuous-time formulation of the kind often found in economists' expositions of capital theory. Substantive results that can be developed under the one convention can always be translated into the other under conditions of certainty (see, in this connection, footnote 27, below.)

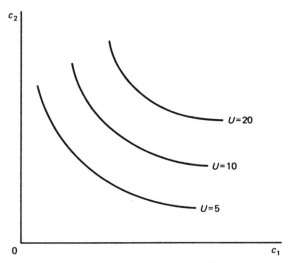

Figure 1.4   Indifference Curves for Patterns of Total Consumption

Second, we replace the individual consumer goods in any period t by a single composite commodity c_t, called the subject's "total consumption" or "standard of living" in period t. This composite commodity is defined as

$$c_t = p_{1t}q_{1t}^* + p_{2t}q_{2t}^* + \cdots + p_{nt}q_{nt}^*,$$

where the p_{it} are the prices of the commodities[15] in period t, assumed to be known and fixed in our perfect certainty framework, and the q_{it}^* are the amounts of the commodities that would be purchased by the consumer, given the prices and a pattern of total resources over all periods that would permit him to spend c_t in period t. Operationally, in terms of the earlier imaginary choice experiments, we now picture ourselves confronting the subject with different patterns of standards of living, such as, say, $10,000 for period 1 and $8000 thereafter versus $6500 for period 1, $6000 for period 2, and $9000 thereafter. The subject decides how he would allocate these amounts among commodities in each period and then announces his

---

[15] Although we speak of prices and commodities, it should be remembered that the q_i represent not stocks of commodities but services rendered by the stocks. In the case of durable goods, for example, the p_{it} are to be interpreted not as the purchase prices but as the one-period rentals for the equipment.

Note also that the p_{it} are to be regarded as being measured in terms of some standard commodity or numéraire whose price per unit is arbitrarily set equal to 1 in period 1 and every period thereafter. We shall often refer to this standard commodity as "money" and hence speak of dollars of income or consumption. It is important to keep in mind, however, that this is again only a stylistic device, and the concept of money in our sense should not be equated with money in its more familiar sense, in which it serves as a medium of exchange and a store of value as well as the unit of account.

preference ordering for time sequences of standards of living. This preference ordering over time sequences of standards of living is summarized in a utility function as $U(c_1, c_2, \ldots, c_t, \ldots)$.

It is shown in the next (starred) section that this function, stated in terms of total consumptions optimally allocated, satisfies the axioms assumed for the underlying utility function defined in terms of the commodities q_{it}. This implies that the indifference map for such a utility function for a two-period case must have the general properties shown in Figure 1.4. In particular, the nonsatiation axiom implies that any given indifference curve for total consumption must be negatively sloped and that utility must increase as we move upward and to the right onto higher indifference curves. The axiom of transitivity implies that indifference curves cannot cross; the axioms of nonsatiation and convexity together imply convex indifference curves.

*II.A.2. The properties of $U(c_1, c_2, \ldots, c_t, \ldots)$

For simplicity, the analysis is carried out for a two-period, two-commodity case. But the method is perfectly general and can readily be extended to the multiperiod, multicommodity case.

If U is a utility function for dollars of consumption and V a utility function for consumption commodities, the relationship between the two functions can be expressed as

$$U(c_1, c_2) = \max_{q_{11}, q_{21}, q_{12}, q_{22}} V(q_{11}, q_{21}, q_{12}, q_{22}) \tag{1.4a}$$

subject to

$$c_1 = p_{11}q_{11} + p_{21}q_{21} \quad \text{and} \quad c_2 = p_{12}q_{12} + p_{22}q_{22}. \tag{1.4b}$$

We first show that if the convexity axiom applies to V, it also applies to U.

Let $(q_{11}^*, q_{21}^*, q_{12}^*, q_{22}^*)$ be the optimal quantities of commodities consumed when the dollar levels of consumption are (c_1, c_2), and let $(\dot{q}_{11}^*, \dot{q}_{21}^*, \dot{q}_{12}^*, \dot{q}_{22}^*)$ be optimal for $(\dot{c}_1, \dot{c}_2)$. Assume in addition that

$$V(q_{11}^*, q_{21}^*, q_{12}^*, q_{22}^*) = V(\dot{q}_{11}^*, \dot{q}_{21}^*, \dot{q}_{12}^*, \dot{q}_{22}^*)$$

so that

$$U(c_1, c_2) = U(\dot{c}_1, \dot{c}_2).$$

Thus (c_1, c_2) and $(\dot{c}_1, \dot{c}_2)$ are on the same indifference curve.

For $0 \leq \alpha \leq 1$, let

$$(\hat{c}_1, \hat{c}_2) = (\alpha c_1 + (1 - \alpha)\dot{c}_1, \ \alpha c_2 + (1 - \alpha)\dot{c}_2)$$

$$(\hat{q}_{11}, \hat{q}_{21}, \hat{q}_{12}, \hat{q}_{22}) = (\alpha q_{11}^* + (1 - \alpha)\dot{q}_{11}^*, \ \ldots, \ \ldots, \ \alpha q_{22}^* + (1 - \alpha)\dot{q}_{22}^*),$$

so that

$$\hat{c}_1 = p_{11}\hat{q}_{11} + p_{21}\hat{q}_{21}, \quad \hat{c}_2 = p_{12}\hat{q}_{12} + p_{22}\hat{q}_{22},$$

and $(\hat{q}_{11}, \hat{q}_{21}, \hat{q}_{12}, \hat{q}_{22})$ is a feasible consumption pattern for $(\hat{c}_1, \hat{c}_2)$.

From the axiom of convexity, the utility function for consumption commodities satisfies

$$V(\hat{q}_{11},\hat{q}_{21},\hat{q}_{12},\hat{q}_{22}) \geq \alpha V(q_{11}^*,q_{21}^*,q_{12}^*,q_{22}^*) + (1 - \alpha) V(\dot{q}_{11}^*,\dot{q}_{21}^*,\dot{q}_{12}^*,\dot{q}_{22}^*).$$

Or, equivalently,

$$V(\hat{q}_{11},\hat{q}_{21},\hat{q}_{12},\hat{q}_{22}) \geq \alpha U(c_1,c_2) + (1 - \alpha) U(\dot{c}_1,\dot{c}_2).$$

Although feasible, the allocation of $(\hat{c}_1,\hat{c}_2)$ implied by $(\hat{q}_{11},\hat{q}_{21},\hat{q}_{12},\hat{q}_{22})$ is not necessarily optimal. The decision maker, if given $\hat{c}_1$ and $\hat{c}_2$ directly, might choose some other allocation among commodities in preference to that of

$$(\alpha q_{11}^* + (1 - \alpha)\dot{q}_{11}^*, \ldots, \ldots, \alpha q_{22}^* + (1 - \alpha)\dot{q}_{22}^*).$$

Because the more constrained choice can never be preferable to the less constrained one, we thus must have

$$U(\hat{c}_1,\hat{c}_2) \geq V(\hat{q}_{11},\hat{q}_{21},\hat{q}_{12},\hat{q}_{22}).$$

Hence $U(\hat{c}_1,\hat{c}_2) \geq \alpha U(c_1,c_2) + (1 - \alpha) U(\dot{c}_1,\dot{c}_2), \qquad 0 \leq \alpha \leq 1,$

which implies that the convexity axiom also applies to $U(c_1,c_2)$.

To show that the nonsatiation axiom also applies to $U(c_1,c_2)$, note that if the dollars available for consumption in either period are increased, consumption of at least one commodity can be increased without reducing consumption of any other commodity in either period. Thus, the nonsatiation of wants assumed in deriving the commodity utility function V must carry over directly to the utility function U. As in the case of commodity indifference curves, the nonsatiation and convexity axioms together imply convexity of the indifference curves.

It is also clear that the axiom of comparability carries over directly from V to U. Establishing that the preference ordering implied by $U(c_1,c_2)$ satisfies the transitivity axiom is left as an exercise for the reader.

Finally, it is well to note that the function $U(c_1,c_2)$, like the function $V(q_{11},q_{21},q_{12},q_{22})$, provides only a rank ordering of consumption boxes; that is, it tells us only whether one box is preferred to another, so that U and V are ordinal utility functions, as distinct from cardinal functions that would also tell us unambiguously by how much one box is preferred to another.

II.A.3. Opportunities: resources and capital markets

The resources that an individual can draw on for his consumption in any period are of several kinds. Most households, for example, carry over stocks of durable consumer goods from previous periods, so that they may either consume the services of these stocks directly or may rent or sell the goods and consume the proceeds. For simplicity, however, we defer all consideration of durable goods until Chapter 2, after we have first sketched the main features of the wealth allocation model. For concreteness, at this stage, the reader may perhaps find it helpful to think of the household as renting its housing, automobile, television set, and any other durables from specialized rental firms.

Also generally available to individuals to support their current consumption are, of course, any wages, salaries, or other similar payments that they receive as compensation for current labor services provided. We denote such payments during any period t as y_t and refer to them, somewhat loosely, as the individual's "income." In addition to his current income, the individual typically can look forward to further income in future years. Future earnings obviously cannot be directly consumed today, but they may still be able to support current consumption, provided that the individual can arrange to transfer them to someone else in exchange for resources to be made available to him immediately.

In what follows, we assume that such exchanges can in fact be made and that they take place in a "capital market." The term *market*, of course, is to be taken, not in the narrow sense of a physical place where buyers and sellers gather, although some real-world capital markets have this property as well, but rather in its broader economic sense of the whole collection of legal, moral, and physical arrangements that make it possible to effect exchanges of current and future incomes.

The precise form that the household's opportunity set takes in the presence of a capital market depends on the additional specifying characteristics that we choose to attribute to the market. An extreme, but particularly fruitful, special set of attributes are those which constitute a "perfect capital market." In such a market we assume the following:

1. All traders have equal and costless access to information about the ruling prices and all other relevant properties of the securities traded.
2. Buyers and sellers, or issuers, of securities take the prices of securities as given; that is, they do, and can justifiably, act as if their activities in the market had no detectable effect on the ruling prices.
3. There are no brokerage fees, transfer taxes, or other transaction costs incurred when securities are bought, sold, or issued.[16]

Needless to say, no such market exists in the real world, nor could it. Rather, what we have here is an idealization of the same kind and function as that of a perfect gas or a perfect vacuum in the physical sciences. Such

---

[16] Although perhaps not strictly an attribute of the market proper, we also assume that there are no income taxes on the earnings from securities; or, if there are, that there are at least no income tax differentials between income in the form of capital gains and dividends or interest.

idealizations permit us to focus more sharply on a limited number of aspects of the problem and usually greatly facilitate both the derivation and statement of the sought-for empirical generalizations. In the nature of the case, however, the generalizations so obtained can never be anything more than approximations to the real phenomena that they are supposed to represent. The question is whether, considered as approximations, they are close enough; and this, of course, is a question that can only be answered empirically and in the light of the specific uses to which the approximations are put.[17]

II.A.4. The opportunity set under perfect capital markets

An immediate implication of a perfect market, and one of the main reasons for using this concept, is that at any one time only one price may rule in the market. For if two different prices ruled simultaneously, no one whose preferences obey the nonsatiation axiom would be willing to sell at the lower of the two prices or buy at the higher. Only when a common, single price had been restored could transactions take place.[18]

In the capital markets the commodities currently being bought and sold are sums of money to be delivered at various future points in time. We regard the delivery contracts for each such future point as a separate (perfect) market and represent the single, current or spot price at the beginning of the τth period for delivery of \$1 at the beginning of the tth period as $_\tau p_t$; that is, $_\tau p_t$ is the amount of money that must be paid at period τ for \$1 to be obtained, for certain, at t. The advantages of the double subscript notation become clear in later extensions of the analysis.[19]

Given these market prices or rates of exchange between future and current resources, what can be said about the form of the opportunity set confronting the decision maker? Let us consider first a two-period case, and ask how much the decision maker can consume in the second of the

---

[17] To make use again of the analogy from physics, laws of motion derived under a perfect-vacuum assumption may be close enough appproximations for many engineering purposes when dealing with heavy objects, but not for some light objects when the neglect of air resistance could lead to a breakdown of the mechanism.

[18] An equivalent, alternative proof often useful in showing the implications of the perfect capital market assumption in more complicated cases involves the notion of "arbitrage" in the sense of a sure profit at no risk or expense; that is, if for ignorance or some other reason there did exist some willing sellers at the lower price and some willing buyers at the higher, knowledgeable arbitragers would buy and resell until one or the other group had been driven from the market.

[19] The prices $_\tau p_t$ are obviously somehow related to interest rates. But to stress the similarity between capital markets and other kinds of markets, it is convenient to present the analysis initially in terms of the $_\tau p_t$. The formal relationships between these prices and interest rates are shown later.

two periods. Because the second period is the "last" period, no resources can be obtained in period 2 by drawing on future periods. The decision maker's resources would be limited to his income for period 2, y_2, plus any financial assets carried over from period 1, a_2, or minus any net liabilities incurred in period 1 that must now be repaid, in which case a_2 would be a negative number; that is, the period 2 consumption would be

$$c_2 = y_2 + a_2. \tag{1.5}$$

Of the two components y_2 is taken for our purposes as a fixed and unalterable amount determined somehow from outside the context of the problem, but a_2, within limits at least, is under the decision maker's control. The less he consumes in period 1, the more funds he can bring to the capital market to purchase funds deliverable at the start of period 2. In particular, his net worth at period 2 will be

$$a_2 = [(y_1 + a_1) - c_1] \cdot \frac{1}{_1p_2} . \tag{1.6}$$

The term in brackets represents the difference between his resources in period 1 and his consumption in this period and is the amount used to purchase resources to be delivered at period 2. The total number of dollars to be received at period 2 is then just the amount invested divided by the price $_1p_2$.[20] Substituting Equation (1.6) for a_2 in the period 2 constraint (1.5), we obtain

$$c_2 = y_2 + (y_1 + a_1) \frac{1}{_1p_2} - c_1 \cdot \frac{1}{_1p_2} \tag{1.7}$$

as the relation describing the allowable, efficient combinations of c_1 and c_2 that can be obtained by an individual whose income plus initial wealth consists of $y_1 + a_1$ in the first period and whose income is y_2 in the second.

In graphical terms (see Figure 1.5) Equation (1.7) is a straight line in the c_1c_2 plane with a slope of $-1/_1p_2$ and running through the "endowment point" x whose coordinates are $((y_1 + a_1), \quad y_2)$. A movement along this efficiency frontier away from this point to point v would represent a purchase of funds for future delivery, that is, lending, and from x to z a sale of future funds, that is, borrowing. The maximum attainable value of c_2, that is,

---

[20] Alternatively, if the amount invested at period 1 is $[(y_1 + a_1) - c_1]$ and the price of a dollar to be delivered at period 2 is $_1p_2$, the number of period 2 dollars purchased at period 1 must be the value of a_2 such that

$$[(y_1 + a_1) - c_1] = _1p_2a_2,$$

from which we easily obtain Equation (1.6). Thus $1/_1p_2$ is the number of dollars at period 2 that can be obtained by investing a dollar at period 1.

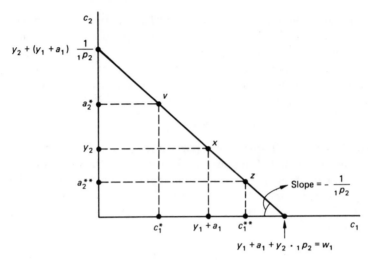

Figure 1.5 Opportunity Set in a Perfect Capital Market

the intercept on the c_2 axis, is

$$y_2 + (y_1 + a_1) \cdot \frac{1}{_1p_2},$$

which occurs when all the resources available at period 1 are used to purchase dollars for delivery at period 2. The maximum attainable value of c_1, that is, the intercept on the c_1 axis,

$$y_1 + a_1 + y_2 \cdot {}_1p_2,$$

occurs when all income to be received at period 2 is sold at the beginning of period 1. This maximum attainable c_1 can also be interpreted as the consumer's wealth w_1 at period 1; it is the market value of all his current and future resources.

II.A.5. Interest rates and present values

We have chosen to express the opportunities for carrying over resources in terms of current market prices for dollars to be delivered in the future partly to stress the fundamental similarity between capital markets and any of the other markets considered in economics and partly to lay the groundwork for future extensions in which this approach is really the only feasible one. For the present class of problems, however, there is another way of expressing the rate of exchange between current and future sums.

Suppose, for example, that we have the current sum of P dollars and ask what will be the number of dollars A that we shall have at the beginning of the next period if we purchase contracts for the future delivery of dollars at the current market price of $_1p_2$. The answer is

$$A = P \frac{1}{_1p_2}. \tag{1.8}$$

But we can always express the terminal amount A as a sum of the initial value P, plus, or minus, the difference between A and P, say, ΔP. Hence we can rewrite Equation (1.8) as

$$\frac{1}{_1p_2} = \frac{A}{P} \equiv \frac{P + \Delta P}{P} = 1 + \frac{\Delta P}{P}. \tag{1.9}$$

The term $\Delta P/P$ is the rate of growth of the capital sum invested during the period, to be denoted by $_1r_2$ and referred to as the one-period, spot rate of interest or, for short, just "rate of interest." The term $1 + \Delta P/P \equiv 1 + _1r_2$ is often referred to in the economics literature as the "force of interest" and in the actuarial literature as the one-period "accumulation factor" at the rate $_1r_2$.[21]

Note that in an equation such as (1.8) we can also perform the inverse

---

[21] Here and throughout, unless otherwise noted, interest rates, such as $_1r_2$, are assumed to be those on securities denominated in the numéraire commodity, which we here call money. Nothing in the analysis, however, rules out the possibility that there might also exist securities denominated in terms of other commodities (or other currencies). If the prices, in terms of numéraire, of such commodities differ in different time periods, the rates of interest on such commodity-denominated securities are not the same as those on numéraire-denominated securities. Nevertheless, we need not take such securities explicitly into account in constructing the opportunity set. As long as the markets for both types of securities are perfect, arbitrage ensures that the effective yield in terms of numéraire is the same on both numéraire- and commodity-denominated contracts; that is, we must have, for any commodity i,

$$(1 + _1r_2{}^i)\left[1 + \left(\frac{p_{i2} - p_{i1}}{p_{i1}}\right)\right] = (1 + _1r_2)$$

or, equivalently,

$$_1r_2 = _1r_2{}^i + \left(\frac{p_{i2} - p_{i1}}{p_{i1}}\right) + (_1r_2{}^i)\left(\frac{p_{i2} - p_{i1}}{p_{i1}}\right),$$

where p_i is the unit price, in terms of numéraire, of commodity i and $_1r_2{}^i$ is the rate of interest on securities denominated in commodity i. The same expression rearranged as

$$_1r_2{}^i = _1r_2 - \frac{p_{i2} - p_{i1}}{p_{i1}}$$

is, of course, familiar to economists as the principle that under certainty, the "real" rate of interest is equal to the money rate minus the rate of change of prices. The cross-product term $(_1r_2{}^i)[(p_{i2} - p_{i1})/p_{i1}]$ is usually omitted, because in the economics literature time is typically treated in continuous rather than discrete terms.

operation and obtain the relation

$$P = A \cdot {}_1p_2 = A \frac{1}{1 + {}_1r_2}. \tag{1.10}$$

Here we are answering the question, What is the market value today of A dollars delivered next period? The sum P is called the "present value" of the deferred payment A, and the term

$$\frac{1}{1 + {}_1r_2} = {}_1p_2,$$

known as the one-period "present value factor" at the rate of interest ${}_1r_2$, provides an alternative interpretation of the price ${}_1p_2$.

These relations between present and future sums are shown graphically in Figure 1.6. The future sum A to which the present P accumulates at the rate ${}_1r_2$ is indicated by the intercept on the period 2 axis of a line drawn through the point P with slope equal to (minus) the accumulation factor. And, in the other direction, passing the line through a point such as A gives us the present value of the point as the point P, the intercept on the period 1 axis. The same procedure can, of course, also be used to find the present value, or, equivalently, current market value, of any combination of period 1 and 2 sums, such as the point x, whose present value is P'.

We can now easily restate the efficient opportunity set in terms of interest rates merely by substituting $(1 + {}_1r_2)$ for $1/{}_1p_2$ in Equation (1.7). We thus obtain

$$c_2 = y_2 + (y_1 + a_1)(1 + {}_1r_2) - c_1(1 + {}_1r_2) \tag{1.11}$$

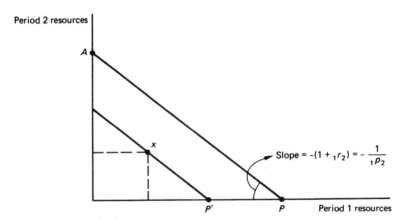

Figure 1.6   Present Value Lines

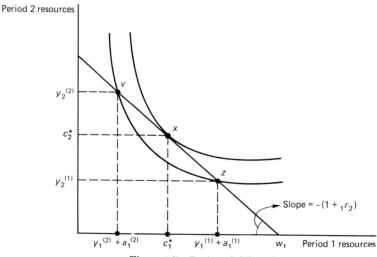

Figure 1.7   Preferred Allocation

or, rearranging,

$$c_1 + \frac{c_2}{(1 + {}_1r_2)} = y_1 + a_1 + \frac{y_2}{(1 + {}_1r_2)}. \qquad (1.12)$$

In words, the efficient combinations of standards of living in the two periods, from among which our subject can and will choose, are those for which the present value of total consumption is equal to the present ($\equiv$market) value of total resources. His actual choice among these possibilities depends on his tastes, as summarized in his utility function and his indifference curves. A geometric illustration of an optimal allocation for a particular set of indifference curves is shown in Figure 1.7.

II.A.6. The preferred allocation

The pattern of standards of living chosen by the decision maker is indicated by the tangency point x, the total consumptions being c_2^* in the first period and c_2^* in the second. If his initial endowment were the point z, with first-period resources of $y_1^{(1)} + a_1^{(1)}$ and second-period income of $y_2^{(1)}$, he would have moved from z to the preferred point x by sacrificing some potential consumption in period 1, lending the proceeds $y_1^{(1)} + a_1^{(1)} - c_1^*$ on the capital markets at the rate ${}_1r_2$, and then adding the matured proceeds plus the interest on them to his second-period income of $y_2^{(1)}$ to reach c_2^*. If he had started from v, where his second-period resources were so much greater than those of the first, he would have moved to the preferred point by borrowing against these future resources to the extent of $c_1^* - (y_1^{(2)} + a_1^{(2)})$. At the start of the next period he would repay his loan plus interest from his income $y_2^{(2)}$ and consume the balance of $c_2^* = y_2^{(2)} - (c_1^* - (y_1^{(2)} + a_1^{(2)}))(1 + {}_1r_2)$.

It is important to note that the decision maker is really indifferent as to whether his initial endowment is the point v or the point z in Figure 1.7. From either starting position, his ultimate consumption combination for the two periods is c_1^* and c_2^*. The initial endowment affects merely the market exchanges that he undertakes to obtain this consumption combination. Indeed, with a perfect capital market, c_1^* and c_2^* are the optimal combination of consumptions for any initial endowment, such as v or x or z, with market value w_1 at period 1. This follows from the fact that in a perfect capital market any endowment with a given market value can be exchanged for any consumption combination with the same market value.

Thus despite, or perhaps because of, the immense simplifications that have gone into its construction, the solution shown in Figure 1.7 does serve to point up one of the crucial functions that the capital markets perform in economic life. In the absence of such markets, the patterns of consumption that individuals could obtain would be rigidly tied to the patterns in which they earned their incomes. When these patterns are very irregular, individuals might find it preferable to shift out of such activities into those offering smoother patterns even at some loss in total earnings for them, and some consequent reduction in the total income potential for society as a whole. Capital markets, however, serve to reduce wastes and inefficiencies of this kind by making it possible, to a considerable extent, to separate the income-earning from the consumption-pattern decisions. Individuals are free to make their earning and occupation decisions largely on other grounds, relying on the capital markets to effect any desired degree of "smoothing" of the standard of living over time.[22]

II.B. Extension to Three or More Time Periods

Although the simple two-period model is adequate for conveying the essence of the allocation problem, there are a number of applications for which it is essential to be able to work with more than two periods. An extension of this kind poses no great difficulty insofar as the utility function is concerned. As long as the subject has a finite planning horizon, which may be, and, in principle normally is, as long as his lifetime, we can simply incorporate into the utility function as many additional c_t as required to

---

[22] This stress on consumption smoothing should also help make clear how transactions in capital assets can arise even without "differences of opinion." Although all households are assumed to have identical and entirely correct expectations as to market returns and might equally well have been assumed to have identical preferences, exchanges would still take place as long as the pattern of endowments is different. Further discussion and illustration of consumption smoothing and its economic significance is given in the appendix to the present chapter.

bring us to the horizon period N. The desire to leave an estate, although the transfer might occur after the individual's lifetime, also poses no difficulty and can be treated simply as an additional consumption term, c_{N+1}.[23]

The extension of the opportunity set to more than two periods, however, does pose, if not difficulties, at least some complications. For when we consider many periods, we also open up for the individual many different strategies for transferring funds between periods. In a three-period case, for example, an individual who wants to carry over funds for two periods might buy a two-period claim; or he might buy a one-period claim this period and then reinvest the proceeds next period in another one-period claim. We also have to admit the existence of "compound claims," such as coupon securities paying specified amounts in each of n time periods plus a further lump-sum amount in the nth period. The opportunity set must somehow allow for these and every other transfer possibility.

II.B.1. The structure of prices for claims

To see how this problem can be solved as well as to gain some additional insight into the structure of prices for claims under perfect capital markets, let us first consider a simple case involving only one- and two-period claims. In particular suppose that the current price of \$1 delivered at the start of period 2 is $_1p_2$ and that the price at the start of period 2 for \$1 to be delivered at period 3 is known to be $_2p_3$; that is, $_2p_3$ is next period's price for a one-period claim, a number to be taken as known now under perfect certainty. What can we say about the price now for a claim for \$1 to be delivered at the beginning of period 3, that is, $_1p_3$?

The answer is that under perfect capital markets we must have

$$_1p_3 = {_1p_2} \cdot {_2p_3}; \tag{1.13}$$

that is, the price of a two-period claim for \$1 must be equal to the product of the prices for one-period claims in the two periods. For suppose that such were not the case and that the price of a two-period claim were greater than this, say,

$$_1p_3 = {_1p_2} \cdot {_2p_3} + \epsilon, \qquad \epsilon > 0. \tag{1.14}$$

Then an individual, no matter what his resources, could always issue a two-period claim for $_1p_3$, that is, promise to repay \$1 at the end of two periods, and immediately invest the proceeds in a one-period claim. The

---

[23] In principle we could also handle cases in which the planning horizon is infinitely long. Where such an approach is taken, however—and it is quite commonly found in economic theory, particularly in connection with macro growth models—it is necessary to impose certain additional restrictions about the individual's "time preference" so as to guarantee a finite solution to the maximization of utility. The concept of time preference is discussed and illustrated in the appendix to the present chapter.

value of the one-period claim at the beginning of period 2 would be[24]

$$\frac{_1p_3}{_1p_2} = \frac{_1p_2 \cdot _2p_3 + \epsilon}{_1p_2}.$$

When these claims came due at the beginning of period 2, he could again reinvest the proceeds in one-period claims, so that at the beginning of period 3 he would receive

$$\left(\frac{_1p_2 \cdot _2p_3 + \epsilon}{_1p_2}\right)\frac{1}{_2p_3} = \left(1 + \frac{\epsilon}{_1p_2 \cdot _2p_3}\right)$$

dollars. This would be sufficient for him to discharge his debt for $1 on the two-period claim that he issued and still leave a net gain of $\epsilon/(_1p_2 \cdot _2p_3)$ dollars as a pure arbitrage profit.

Similarly in the other direction, if $_1p_3 = _1p_2 \cdot _2p_3 - \epsilon$, an individual could buy such a two-period claim, which will yield him $1 at the end of two periods, and finance the purchase by issuing a one-period claim, that is, by promising to pay

$$\frac{_1p_3}{_1p_2} = \frac{_1p_2 \cdot _2p_3 - \epsilon}{_1p_2}$$

at the beginning of period 2. When this claim came due, he could issue a second claim, that is, promise to repay

$$\left(\frac{_1p_2 \cdot _2p_3 - \epsilon}{_1p_2}\right)\frac{1}{_2p_3}$$

at the beginning of period 3. His total liability at period 3 would thus be

$$\left(1 - \frac{\epsilon}{_1p_2 \cdot _2p_3}\right),$$

which he could repay from the proceeds of $1 coming due on his two-period claim and still have $\epsilon/(_1p_2 \cdot _2p_3)$ as a pure arbitrage profit.[25]

---

[24] Recall that when the price is $_1p_2$, the market value at period 2 of $1 invested at period 1 is $1/_1p_2$. Similarly, when the price is $_2p_3$, the value at period 3 of $1 invested at period 2 is $1/_2p_3$.

[25] The ratio of the two "spot prices," $_1p_3/_1p_2$, is often called the "implicit forward price" for a one-period claim, one period from now. The name comes from the fact that, even without making a direct or literal forward contract, an investor with, say, A_2 of funds available at the start of period 2 can always act now to guarantee himself the opportunity to purchase one-period claims with these funds next period at a price $_2p_3^F \equiv {}_1p_3/_1p_2$ by borrowing "short" an amount equal to $(A_2 \cdot _1p_2)$ and lending it "long," thus yielding $(A_2 \cdot _1p_2)/_1p_3$. In terms of the implicit forward prices, an equivalent way of stating the equilibrium condition in Equation (1.13) would be $_2p_3^F = _2p_3$; that is, as the proposition that in perfect capital markets and perfect certainty, the implicit forward rate for any period must equal the spot rate expected to rule for the period.

The same reasoning can be applied to cases of three or four or indeed any number of periods, and starting from any period, so that we can write as the general rule for the price in period τ for an n-period claim for \$1, that is, a claim to be delivered at the beginning of period $\tau + n$,

$$\tau p_{\tau+n} = {}_\tau p_{\tau+1} \cdot {}_{\tau+1} p_{\tau+2} \cdots {}_{\tau+n-1} p_{\tau+n}, \tag{1.15}$$

or, more compactly,

$$\tau p_{\tau+n} = \prod_{t=\tau}^{\tau+n-1} {}_t p_{t+1}. \tag{1.16}$$

Note also that with Equation (1.15) or (1.16) we can immediately obtain the price of any compound claims, because with no transaction costs, any claim to pay or deliver sums in more than one period can always be duplicated by a set of separate one-period contracts. In particular, the market value $V(\tau)$ at the beginning of period τ of any claim, positive or negative, to $X(\tau + 1)$ dollars at the end of one period, $X(\tau + 2)$ at the end of two periods, and so on, down to $X(\tau + n)$ n periods later, can always be expressed under perfect capital markets as the simple sum of the market values of the component claims:

$$V(\tau) = X(\tau + 1)_\tau p_{\tau+1} + X(\tau + 2)_\tau p_{\tau+2} + \cdots + X(\tau + n)_\tau p_{\tau+n}$$

$$= X(\tau + 1)_\tau p_{\tau+1} + X(\tau + 2)_\tau p_{\tau+1} \cdot {}_{\tau+1} p_{\tau+2}$$

$$+ \cdots + X(\tau + n) \prod_{t=\tau}^{\tau+n-1} {}_t p_{t+1}. \tag{1.17}$$

Or, to put it somewhat more dramatically, in a perfect capital market the market value of any set of claims depends only on the amounts of the claims and the prices of one-period unit claims and not at all on how the claims happen to be "packaged."

II.B.2. An equivalent representation in terms of interest rates

Before applying these results to the problem of constructing the opportunity set, it is helpful once again to restate the essentials in terms of the more familiar interest rate and yield formulations in which discussions in finance are typically conducted. In particular, recall that we have previously defined the one-period rate of interest in terms of the price of one-period claims by the relations

$$1 + {}_\tau r_{\tau+1} = \frac{1}{{}_\tau p_{\tau+1}} \tag{1.18}$$

or

$${}_\tau p_{\tau+1} = \frac{1}{1 + {}_\tau r_{\tau+1}}. \tag{1.19}$$

Substituting from Equation (1.19) into (1.17), we obtain for $V(\tau)$

$$V(\tau) = \frac{X(\tau+1)}{1 + {}_\tau r_{\tau+1}} + \frac{X(\tau+2)}{(1 + {}_\tau r_{\tau+1})(1 + {}_{\tau+1} r_{\tau+2})} + \cdots + \frac{X(\tau+n)}{\displaystyle\prod_{t=\tau}^{\tau+n-1}(1 + {}_t r_{t+1})},$$

(1.20)

which is, of course, the familiar expression for the present value of an arbitrary stream of payments $X(\tau+1), X(\tau+2), \ldots, X(\tau+n)$.

Certain special cases of Equation (1.20) are frequently encountered in the literature, mainly because they permit simpler and more easily manipulated valuation formulas. If, for example, we assume that the one-period interest rates are constant over time at some given value r, products of accumulation factors over n periods of the form

$$\prod_{t=1}^{n}(1 + {}_t r_{t+1})$$

can be expressed as powers of the force of interest of the form $(1 + r)^n$ and similarly with the present value factors $1/(1 + r)^n$. If in addition to assuming a constant one-period interest rate, we assume that the payments too have some constant value X over time, we obtain the familiar "annuity factors," and their inverses, the "capital recovery factors." In particular, Equation (1.20) reduces to

$$V = \frac{X}{1 + r} + \frac{X}{(1 + r)^2} + \cdots + \frac{X}{(1 + r)^n}.$$

(1.21)

Multiplying both sides by $1/(1 + r)$ and subtracting the resulting expression from Equation (1.21) yields

$$V - \frac{1}{1 + r}V = \frac{X}{1 + r} + \frac{X}{(1 + r)^2} + \cdots + \frac{X}{(1 + r)^n} - \frac{X}{(1 + r)^2}$$

$$- \frac{X}{(1 + r)^3} - \cdots \frac{X}{(1 + r)^{n+1}} = \frac{X}{1 + r} - \frac{X}{(1 + r)^{n+1}},$$

(1.22)

from which it follows that

$$V = X\left[\frac{(1 + r)^n - 1}{r(1 + r)^n}\right].$$

(1.23)

The expression in brackets in Equation (1.23) is the uniform annuity present value factor for n periods at a rate of $100r$ percent per period. It is sometimes also called the n-period "capitalization factor," because it tells us by how much we have to multiply a given flow of payments to convert them to a stock of capital value, that is, to convert the income statement item to a balance sheet item. The inverse operation

$$X = V\left[\frac{r(1 + r)^n}{(1 + r)^n - 1}\right] \qquad (1.24)$$

converts a capital sum V to an equivalently valued n-period flow of payments X at the rate r, a process familiar to any homeowner with a conventional, equal-payment mortgage. Still another interesting variant on the annuity formula is the case of a perpetual annuity or "perpetuity." In Equation (1.23), if $r > 0$, the term $-1/r(1 + r)^n$ approaches zero as n approaches infinity. Hence the capitalization factor in brackets collapses in this case to the very simple and convenient expression[26]

$$V = \frac{X}{r}. \qquad (1.25)$$

Many other interesting and useful variations on these formulas can be developed, and some of these are in fact introduced at appropriate places in subsequent chapters. For present purposes, the important feature of the analysis is not the formulas themselves. Our concern has rather been to show where the formulas come from, and to call attention to the critical role of the concept of a perfect capital market[27] in their derivation.

---

[26] For many beginners there is something unnatural about a stream of payments supposed to continue forever. It should be emphasized, therefore, particularly because we make heavy use of such perpetuities in later analyses, that there is nothing particularly strange about such securities and that they do exist in considerable numbers and varieties in real-world capital markets. Land, common stocks, and most issues of preferred stocks are the most obvious examples of securities without any specific maturity date, but there are also some bonds of a similar kind, notably the celebrated "consols" issued by the British government in the nineteenth century, and so called because they were a "consolidation" of a series of previously issued debts. Another homely example would be the "perpetual maintenance" agreements assumed by many sellers of cemetery plots.
[27] Some of the reading for which this book is intended to serve as an introduction will be found to run in terms of continuous compounding rather than the discrete compounding that we have chosen to use throughout. Results and formulas developed under one convention for the case of constant interest rates may be easily translated into the other merely by interchanging $(1 + r)^t$ with e^{rt} and interchanging integrals with the corresponding summations. Thus, for example, the annuity formula (1.23) can be obtained in a continuous formulation as

$$V = X\int_0^n e^{-rt}dt = \frac{X(e^{rn} - 1)}{re^{rn}}$$

and similarly for the rest of the family of simple formulas. The perpetuity capitalization factor $1/r$ remains the same, of course, for both cases.

II.B.3. Multiperiod rates of interest and the concept of the term structure

We have shown and made use of the fact that a one-to-one correspondence exists between the one-period rate of interest and the price of one-period claims. We can readily push this correspondence further and obtain, say, a two-period rate of interest that would be the similar equivalent to the price of a two-period claim.

Consider first the case of simple claims. In particular, suppose that we have now in period 1 a claim for \$1 payable at the beginning of period 3, whose current price is $_1p_3$, and suppose further that the period 1 and period 2 one-period interest rates are $_1r_2$ and $_2r_3$. Then from the product rule we have

$$_1p_3 = {}_1p_2 \cdot {}_2p_3 = \frac{1}{(1 + {}_1r_2)} \cdot \frac{1}{(1 + {}_2r_3)} \equiv \frac{1}{1 + {}_1\hat{r}_3},$$

where $_1\hat{r}_3$ is the rate over two periods that corresponds to the price $_1p_3$. We use the new symbol $_1\hat{r}_3$ to emphasize that $_1\hat{r}_3$ cannot be directly compared with one-period rates, such as $_1r_2$ or $_2r_3$, because the period of accumulation for $_1\hat{r}_3$ is twice as long. To obtain this comparability, however, we need merely ask what one-period rate, if earned in two successive periods, would leave the investor indifferent to the actual sequence of $_1r_2$ followed by $_2r_3$. By indifferent we mean, of course, that a present amount P would accumulate to the same amount A under either strategy, or that a future sum A would have the same present value in the two cases. In symbols, if we let $_1r_3$ be the uniform rate, we ask what value of $_1r_3$ satisfies

$$P(1 + {}_1r_3)(1 + {}_1r_3) = P(1 + {}_1r_3)^2 = P(1 + {}_1r_2)(1 + {}_2r_3) = A,$$

or, equivalently,

$$\frac{A}{(1 + {}_1r_3)(1 + {}_1r_3)} = \frac{A}{(1 + {}_1r_3)^2} = \frac{A}{(1 + {}_1r_2)(1 + {}_2r_3)} = P.$$

Solving either expression and keeping only the positive root, we obtain

$$(1 + {}_1r_3) = \sqrt[2]{(1 + {}_1r_2)(1 + {}_2r_3)}$$

or

$$_1r_3 = \sqrt[2]{(1 + {}_1r_2)(1 + {}_2r_3)} - 1.$$

More generally, for an n-period simple claim

$$_1r_{n+1} = \sqrt[n]{(1 + {}_1r_2)(1 + {}_2r_3) \cdots (1 + {}_nr_{n+1})} - 1.$$

In words, the n-period rate of interest that is equivalent to the sequence of n one-period rates is the geometric average of (unity plus) the future one-period rates (minus unity).

The entire set of n-period rates for all values of n in sequence, that is, $_1r_2, {}_1r_3, {}_1r_4, \ldots, {}_1r_{n+1}$, constitutes what is often called the "term structure of interest rates." Some representations of various possible term structures are shown in Figure 1.8. In structure A, for example, the rates rise through-

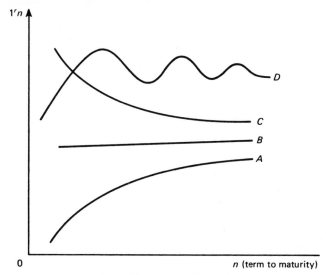

Figure 1.8   Term Structures

out; B is a flat term structure; C falls throughout. Structure D is of an irregularity far more severe than any term structures ever observed, but still entirely conceivable.

In relating the structure of these "long" rates to the one-period "short" rates of which they are averages, a useful concept is that of the "marginal rate," or, as it is sometime called, the implicit forward rate.[28] In particular, the marginal or forward rate for period t, $_t r_{t+1}^m$, may be defined as the rate at which the capital sum invested in a simple claim grows when invested for one more period, that is, when held through the period t. If we let $V(t+1)$ stand for the value at the start of period $t+1$ of \$1 invested at the start of period 1, and $V(t)$ for the value at the start of t, this marginal rate is clearly $V(t+1)/V(t) - 1 = _t r_{t+1}^m$. Under perfect capital markets we can replace the V's by their corresponding accumulation factors and obtain

$$1 + _t r_{t+1}^m = \frac{V(t+1)}{V(t)} = \frac{(1 + _1 r_{t+1})^t}{(1 + _1 r_t)^{t-1}} = \frac{(1 + _1 r_2)(1 + _2 r_3) \cdots (1 + _t r_{t+1})}{(1 + _1 r_2)(1 + _2 r_3) \cdots (1 + _{t-1} r_t)}$$

$$= 1 + _t r_{t+1};$$

that is, not surprisingly, under perfect certainty and perfect capital markets, the marginal or forward rate for any future period is equal to the (known) future spot rate for the period.

---

[28] Compare footnote 25 above. In much of the literature on the term structure of interest rates, the term *implicit* is usually omitted, for simplicity, in referring to forward rates. We stress it here merely to remind students of finance that true explicit forward contracts also exist and in fact are quite common, especially in connection with the financing of residential construction.

The relation between these marginal rates and the (geometric) average n-period, or long, rates of the term structure is the same as that between any other average and the series marginal to it. In particular when the marginal rate exceeds the average rate, the average rises; and when the marginal is below the average, the average falls. In Figure 1.8, for example, the rising yield curve A implies that future one-period spot rates will be higher than both the current one-period spot rate and current long rates, although not necessarily in any uniform or regular way. For curve C, the opposite is the case, and for the flat curve B, all future spot rates are constant and equal to the current rate. For curve D, the pattern is one of substantial fluctuation in the future short rates sometimes rising above and sometimes falling below the current rates.[29]

II.B.4. The equal rate of return principle

Up to this point, we have been discussing yields and interest rates mainly in the context of simple claims, that is, claims in which there is only a single cash payment that occurs at the maturity date. There remains only to show the implications of the results obtained for the case of compound claims. In particular, what can we say about the yields on such claims in relation to those of simple claims?

Consider, for example, an n-period compound security that pays $X(t+1)$ in cash at the beginning of period $t+1$, and suppose that the one-period rate of interest for t is $_tr_{t+1}$. As before, we can define the one-period yield on the compound security during period t as the rate of growth of wealth initially invested in such a security. If we denote this initial investment by $V(t)$, this rate of growth, $_t\rho_{t+1}$, is

$$_t\rho_{t+1} = \frac{X(t+1) + V(t+1) - V(t)}{V(t)}, \qquad (1.26)$$

where $V(t+1)$ is the market value of the claim as of the start of period $t+1$. Under the perfect market assumption we know that this one-period yield or rate of return on any compound security during any period must be exactly the same as what we have been calling the one-period rate of interest on a simple claim for the period. In such a market the investor is free to

---

[29] As drawn, curve D is meant to imply that some marginal rates, and hence future spot rates, will actually be negative. If we interpreted the rates as "real" rates in the sense of footnote 21, there would, of course, be nothing whatever anomalous about such negative rates. Their occurrence would simply mean that the rate of price increase of the commodity exceeded the nominal or money rate of interest. Even for contracts denominated in numéraire, however, there would be nothing in the present framework to prevent negative rates if we expressly ruled out the carry-over of any physical commodity, including, presumably the numéraire commodity itself. Once the carry-over of numéraire is allowed, of course, we do have a floor under money rates of interest. but this floor may still be below zero to the extent that there are storage or other costs of carry-over.

hold any of the securities available during a given time period, and to shift
costlessly among securities from one period to the next. Thus if all securities
are to be held, all must yield the same rate of return during any period.
Equivalently, the existence of differential yields would imply the existence
of costless arbitrage, which is, of course, inconsistent with a perfect market.

Some further insight into the meaning of this result can be obtained by
separating the definitional expression (1.26) into two components as

$$_t\rho_{t+1} = _tr_{t+1} = \frac{X(t+1)}{V(t)} + \frac{V(t+1) - V(t)}{V(t)}. \tag{1.27}$$

The first term $X(t+1)/V(t)$ is often called the "cash yield" and the
second the "capital gain yield." Our analysis implies, in effect, that the
total yield is independent of the packaging. A security with a high cash
yield will have a correspondingly low capital gain yield, or even a capital
loss; but whatever the package, the total is the same and is always equal to
the market rate of interest for the period.

Because $_t\rho_{t+1} = _tr_{t+1}$ for every period t, it also follows that we can define
an n-period holding yield

$$_t\rho_{t+n} = \sqrt[n]{(1 + _t\rho_{t+1})(1 + _{t+1}\rho_{t+2}) \cdots (1 + _{t+n-1}\rho_{t+n})} - 1$$

exactly analogous to, and in terms of its value, exactly equal to, the n-period
rate of interest $_tr_{t+n}$. As it turns out, there is relatively little need for this
more general form of the holding period yield in the class of decision
problems that we examine in this book. Its main function in the finance
literature has been to serve as one basis for the *ex post* evaluation of investments in particular securities—a use in which it is often referred to as the
yield "with reinvestment."[30]

---

[30] To see the origin and justification of this characterization of the n-period yield, suppose
that an investor held n_t units of a given compound security at the start of period t. If he
reinvests its cash payment of $X(t+1)$ per unit at the then ruling market price of
$V(t+1)$ per unit, he will have $n_t(1 + X(t+1)/V(t+1)) = n_{t+1}$ units at the start
of period $t+1$. Hence the total value of his holdings of the security at that time will be

$$n_{t+1}V(t+1) = n_t\left(1 + \frac{X(t+1)}{V(t+1)}\right) \cdot V(t+1)$$

$$= n_t\left(\frac{V(t+1) + X(t+1)}{V(t+1)}\right) \cdot V(t+1)$$

$$= n_t\left(\frac{V(t+1) + X(t+1)}{V(t)}\right) \cdot V(t) = n_tV(t)[1 + _t\rho_{t+1}].$$

At the start of $t+2$, his wealth will be

$$n_{t+2}V(t+2) = n_{t+1}V(t+1)[1 + _{t+1}\rho_{t+2}]$$

$$= n_tV(t)[1 + _t\rho_{t+1}][1 + _{t+1}\rho_{t+2}] = n_tV(t)[1 + _t\rho_{t+2}]^2$$

and so on.

II.B.5. The n-period opportunity set

With these results about the structure of prices and yields in perfect capital markets in hand, we may turn back now to the task of constructing the opportunity set for a decision maker in the multiperiod case. As before, consider first the total consumption possible for the subject during the last period N. Because we permit no carryover of resources to or from later periods, this maximum must be given by

$$c_N = y_N + a_N \geq 0,$$

that is, by the sum of the income for the period plus the proceeds of any securities accumulated from previous periods. The term y_N is taken as somehow given from outside the problem, but a_N can be further decomposed into

$$a_N = [y_{N-1} + a_{N-1} - c_{N-1}](1 + {}_{N-1}r_N).$$

Note that with our perfect market assumption, this expression for a_N applies regardless of the particular financial strategy that he may happen to adopt; that is, whatever may be the particular securities composing a_{N-1} and a_N, we know that the one-period yield on any resources invested during period $N - 1$ will be precisely ${}_{N-1}r_N$. Furthermore this will be the appropriate rate to apply regardless of whether he is a net borrower for the period—the case of $y_{N-1} + a_{N-1} < c_{N-1}$ and hence $a_N < 0$[31]—or a net lender, because with perfect markets the borrowing and lending rates are the same.

By repeated application of the same reasoning we can eliminate all the intermediate values of a_t, obtaining ultimately as the expression for the opportunity set

$$c_1 + \frac{c_2}{1 + {}_1r_2} + \frac{c_3}{(1 + {}_1r_2)(1 + {}_2r_3)} + \cdots + \frac{c_N}{\prod_{t=1}^{N-1}(1 + {}_tr_{t+1})}$$

$$= a_1 + y_1 + \frac{y_2}{(1 + {}_1r_2)} + \frac{y_3}{(1 + {}_1r_2)(1 + {}_2r_3)} + \cdots + \frac{y_N}{\prod_{t=1}^{N-1}(1 + {}_tr_{t+1})};$$

$$(1.28)$$

In addition to the yield with reinvestment, references are sometimes found to a "yield without reinvestment." This yield is the same as that of the so-called "discounted cash flow, internal rate of return," that we consider in Chapter 3. It is also the way in which the so-called "yield to maturity" on a coupon bond is customarily computed and quoted.

[31] Note incidentally that the requirement that c_N be nonnegative implicitly puts a maximum on the amount that can be borrowed during $N - 1$ and, by extension, in all previous periods. Or, to put it another way, no one is allowed to die in debt.

that is, the efficient combinations of standards of living available to the
decision maker under perfect capital markets are only those for which the
present ($\equiv$market) value of the sequence of consumptions is equal to the
present value of his income plus any initial endowment a_1. This set encom-
passes every financial strategy, security package, or portfolio composition
available to the decision maker over the N-period horizon.

*II.B.6. The optimal allocation in the multiperiod case; mathematical treatment

Putting together the expressions for the utility function and the opportunity set, we may now represent the optimal allocation of financial
resources over time as the solution to the problem

$$\max_{c_1,c_2,\ldots,c_N} \quad U(c_1,c_2,\ldots,c_N)$$

subject to the constraint expressed by Equation (1.28). To obtain the
necessary conditions for a maximum, form the lagrangian function

$$L = U(c_1,c_2,\ldots,c_N) - \lambda\left(c_1 + \frac{c_2}{1 + {}_1r_2} + \cdots + \frac{c_N}{\prod_{t=1}^{N-1}(1 + {}_tr_{t+1})} \right.$$

$$\left. - a_1 - y_1 - \frac{y_2}{1 + {}_1r_2} - \cdots - \frac{y_N}{\prod_{t=1}^{N-1}(1 + {}_tr_{t+1})} \right),$$

and differentiate partially with respect to λ and to each of the c_t. Setting
these derivatives equal to zero, the first-order conditions for a maximum are
then the following N equations, plus Equation (1.28):

$$U_1' - \lambda = 0$$

$$U_2' - \lambda \frac{1}{1 + {}_1r_2} = 0$$

$$\vdots$$

$$U_N' - \lambda \frac{1}{\prod_{t=1}^{N-1}(1 + {}_tr_{t+1})} = 0,$$

where U_i' is the partial derivative of U with respect to c_i. Or, equivalently,

$$U_1' = U_2'(1 + {}_1r_2) = \cdots = U_N' \prod_{t=1}^{N-1}(1 + {}_tr_{t+1}) = \lambda.$$

Note that between any pair of periods whether adjacent or not we continue
to have a simple tangency solution of precisely the same kind as in the two-

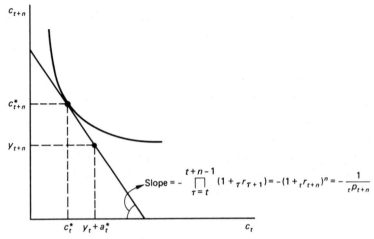

Figure 1.9   Preferred Allocation between Nonadjacent Periods

period case. For example, between periods 1 and 2 we have, after multiplying both sides by -1,

$$-\frac{U_1'}{U_2'} = -(1 + {}_1r_2);$$

between periods 3 and 7,

$$-\frac{U_3'}{U_7'} = -(1 + {}_3r_4)(1 + {}_4r_5)\cdots(1 + {}_6r_7);$$

and for the general term,

$$-\frac{U_t'}{U_{t+n}'} = -\left(\prod_{\tau=t}^{t+n-1}(1 + {}_\tau r_{\tau+1})\right). \tag{1.29}$$

The term on the left-hand side is the slope of the indifference curve in the $(t, t + n)$ plane, that is, dc_{t+n}/dc_t, and the term on the right represents the slope of the opportunity set, which is, of course, (minus) the force of interest over the indicated n periods. A graphical illustration for this n-period solution is shown in Figure 1.9 with c_t^* and c_{t+n}^* as the optimal total consumption in the two periods when a_t^* is the optimal initial assets for period t.

II.C. Conclusion

We now have in hand most of the essential elements of the model of wealth allocation over time under certainty and perfect capital markets. An illustration of how the abstract model can be specialized and adapted to help explain important features of observed savings behavior is given in the appendix to the present chapter. The development of the remaining aspects of the model and in particular its extension to allow for durable goods, real investment, and corporations is the task of Chapters 2 and 3.

REFERENCES

Elementary discussions of the economic theory of choice under certainty, such as in Section I, can be found in many intermediate economics texts. An excellent early advanced treatment, still very much worth reading, is that of
Hicks, John R., *Value and Capital*, 2d ed. Oxford: Clarendon Press, 1946.
The standard advanced mathematical treatments of the theory are those of
Debreu, Gerard, *The Theory of Value*. New York: John Wiley & Sons, Inc., 1959.
Samuelson, Paul, *The Foundations of Economic Analysis*. Cambridge, Mass.: Harvard University Press, 1947.
A lucid introduction to the methodology of economics and especially of the positivist position is in
Friedman, Milton, "The Methodology of Positive Economics," in *Essays in Positive Economics*. Chicago: The University of Chicago Press, 1956.
The original but still surprisingly up-to-date application of the theory of choice to the allocation of resources over time is that of
Fisher, Irving, *The Theory of Interest*. New York: Augustus M. Kelley, Publishers, 1965. Reprinted from the 1930 edition.
A graphical and algebraic exposition of the Fisherian wealth allocation model, touching on many of the same topics covered in Part I, is that of
Hirshleifer, Jack, "On the Theory of Optimal Investment Decision," *Journal of Political Economy* (August 1958).
Further extensive exposition, especially of the general equilibrium implications of the model, is given by the same author in his recent treatise,
Hirshleifer, Jack, *Investment, Interest and Capital*. Englewood Cliffs, N.J.: Prentice-Hall, Inc., 1970.
The Fisherian model has provided the micro foundations, along lines illustrated in the Appendix, for much of the modern theory of aggregate consumption and saving by households. Two of the most influential treatments have been those of
Modigliani, Franco, and Richard Brumberg, "Utility Analysis and the Consumption Function: An Interpretation of Cross-Section Data," in Kenneth Kurihara, Ed., *Post-Keynesian Economics*. New Brunswick, 1954.
Friedman, Milton, *A Theory of the Consumption Function*. Princeton, N.J.: Princeton University Press, 1957.

APPENDIX

An Illustrative Application
of the Wealth Allocation Model:
The Life Cycle of Savings

The specific application of the model of wealth allocation over time that we consider in this appendix is that of savings decisions by individuals. In particular, we try to show how the model, when fleshed out with certain additional specifying assumptions about the structure of tastes and opportunities, can be made to yield propositions about how the level of current savings by an individual varies over his lifetime and how it responds to differences in age, wealth, income, and the rate of interest. Our approach is to start with the simplest possible version and then successively bring in additional complications, pointing up along the way some of the implications of the various models for the field of finance.

I. THE BASIC FRAMEWORK[1]

I.A. Smoothing Irregularities in the Income Stream

In Chapter 1, the general model of wealth allocation was used to show, among other things, how an individual could "smooth" his standard of

[1] The classic statement of the "life-cycle" approach that we take here is in F. Modigliani and R. Brumberg, "Utility Analysis and the Consumption Function: An Interpretation of Cross-Section Data," in K. Kurihara, ed., *Post-Keynesian Economics*, New Brunswick, 1954.

living over time in the face of an unsmooth income stream, for example, by consuming less than his income in periods when it was abnormally high and carrying over the funds saved to periods when it was abnormally low; or by borrowing, that is, "dissaving" during a period of low income to maintain the standard of living in anticipation of repayment of the loan from the proceeds of higher income receipts in the future. A natural way, therefore, to begin any more detailed study of savings decisions is to seek out the major sources of irregularity in income streams that might call for such smoothing. Under our assumptions of perfect certainty and perfect capital markets—which rule out the need to save for unforeseen contingencies, such as illness or unemployment, or to accumulate liquid assets in advance of purchasing large consumer durables—there are still, typically, two major sources of unevenness in his lifetime income experience that an individual attempts to smooth by his saving plan. First, in most occupations, annual earnings can be expected to rise more or less steadily with age, partly as a reflection of increases in skill and experience and partly because of the continued, projected growth of productivity that steadily raises the level of wages and salaries throughout the economy. Second, most wage and salary earners can confidently look forward to compulsory or voluntary retirement, at which point their nonproperty income ceases entirely.[2]

I.B. Some Specifications and Simplifications

The major implications for savings behavior of these irregularities in the income stream can be brought out most sharply by further specifying and simplifying the model in Chapter 1. In particular, we assume that:

1. The individual plans to leave no estate to his heirs at the time of his death and, by the same token, will not be the beneficiary of any bequests during his own lifetime. This unrealistic assumption, we hasten to add, is a good deal stronger than is really necessary for our purposes. In principle, the estate motive can readily be incorporated into the analysis simply by adding an additional "consumption" term to the utility function in the year of death. We omit it completely here, however, partly because so little is known about motives for gifts and bequests and partly to emphasize how much can be said about saving behavior even in the absence of estate motive saving.

2. The individual has no "time preference" for either immediate or deferred consumption. More precisely, if A and B are two fixed levels of resources and t and $t + 1$ are any two time periods, then $U(c_t = A,$

---

[2] A third source of irregularity, even in a certainty framework, would be changes in family size and hence in per capita income within the family. We do not go into such matters here, however, except in passing and as a qualification to certain results obtained from the single-decision-maker models.

$c_{t+1} = B) = U(c_t = B, \ c_{t+1} = A)$. In terms of Figure 1.4 or 1.7, this assumption implies that the indifference curves for standards of living are symmetric around a 45° line through the origin. Like the no-bequest assumption, this too is much stronger than is necessary, but it has the virtue of great simplicity, as well as emphasizing that psychological or cultural preferences for deferred gratification are in no sense essential to the explanation of saving behavior.

3. The market rate of interest is zero. This assumption is introduced only temporarily to facilitate the calculation of specific examples. It is dropped after the main features of the simplest models have been fully explored. In the meantime, it may perhaps also serve as a useful reminder that, although interest is indeed the "reward for saving," the absence of any such reward does not imply the absence of any motive for individual saving.

I.C. Consumption, Saving, and Wealth over the Life Cycle

Given these assumptions and assuming further that the individual is entering his tth year in the labor force, has a further life expectancy of $N - t$ years, a further working-life expectancy of $W - t$ years, and will have no wage or salary income during the $N - W$ years of his retirement, we can express his choice problem as

$$\max_{c_t, \ldots, c_N} U(c_t, c_{t+1}, \ldots, c_N) \tag{A.1}$$

subject to the budget constraint

$$\sum_{\tau=t}^{N} c_\tau = a_t + \sum_{\tau=t}^{W} y_\tau = a_t + (W - t + 1)\bar{y}_t, \tag{A.2}$$

where $\bar{y}_t = \left(\sum_{\tau=t}^{W} y_\tau\right) / (W - t + 1)$ is the average income of the individual over the remainder of the working life as of the start of period t, and a_t is the accumulated value of his financial assets at the start of t.

By virtue of our assumptions of zero time preference and a zero market rate of interest we know that the optimal value of consumption must be the same in every period, that is,

$$c_t^* = c_{t+1}^* = \cdots = c_N^*.^3$$

---

[3] Readers for whom this conclusion is not immediately obvious may find it helpful to portray the decision problem graphically for a two-dimensional case. They should quickly see that the assumption of symmetry of the indifference curves implies that the slope of any indifference curve equals -1 at the point where the indifference curve intersects a 45° line through the origin. But -1 is the slope of an opportunity line when the interest rate is zero. Hence, for this rate, the optimal solutions lie along the 45° line, with equal consumptions in both periods.

We may thus rewrite the resource constraint (A.2) as

$$\sum_{\tau=t}^{N} c_\tau^* = [N - t + 1]c_t^* = a_t + [W - t + 1]\bar{y}_t$$

and, by rearranging, obtain

$$c_t^* = \frac{1}{N - t + 1} a_t + \frac{W - t + 1}{N - t + 1} \bar{y}_t \qquad (A.3)$$

as an explicit "consumption function" for an individual during the tth year of his participation in the labor force.

The economic meaning of this result can perhaps best be appreciated by following a hypothetical individual through a complete life cycle. For concreteness, suppose that his total work expectancy when he enters the labor force at, say, age 20 is 40 years, after which he anticipates a retirement period of an additional 10 years; that is, at age 20, $t = 1$, $W - t + 1 = 40$, and $N - t + 1 = 50$. Suppose, further, that his average annual earnings when he enters employment are expected to be \$10,000 and that he expects to earn exactly this amount in each of the 40 years of employment. (The assumption of a constant annual income is made at this point solely for the purpose of isolating the pure retirement effect.) Because he starts with no inherited or accumulated wealth, his consumption during his first year of entry, that is, at $t = 1$, as given by Equation (A.3), is

$$c_1^* = \frac{1}{50} 0 + \frac{40 - 0}{50} 10{,}000 = 8000.$$

Because his income exceeds his consumption, he is saving and thereby accumulating capital, so that his wealth at the start of the following period is \$2000. Hence, his consumption during the next year is

$$c_2^* = \frac{1}{49} 2000 + \frac{40 - 1}{49} 10{,}000 = \frac{392{,}000}{49} = 8000.$$

Once again, he consumes less than his income, adding a further increment of \$2000 to his wealth. During each of his years in the labor force thereafter the pattern is repeated. His expected total future income from work falls by one year's earnings of \$10,000 each year; but his accumulated wealth rises by an additional \$2000, and the number of years of remaining life over which he must spread his resources falls by one. These forces just balance to maintain his desired consumption at a level of \$8000.

By the time he retires he will have accumulated a retirement fund of \$80,000 (40 years at \$2000 per year). His consumption during his first year of retirement is then

$$c_{41}^* = \frac{1}{10} 80{,}000 = 8{,}000,$$

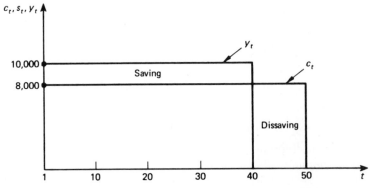

Figure A.1   Life Cycle Profile for the Basic Case

and because his income is zero, this $8000 of consumption represents net dissaving on his part. The decumulation of capital proceeds steadily thereafter until his life and his resources terminate together. (Needless to say, in the real world, the story does not always have such a neat and happy ending.)

The lifetime profiles of earnings, consumption, saving, and wealth implied by this highly simplified model are shown in Figures A.1 and A.2. Several features of these profiles are worth some comment at this point. Note first the implied difference in "investment objectives" between the young and the old—the former being concerned with the growth of their retirement funds and the latter with their orderly liquidation. Note also the obvious tendency of the process to lead to a substantial concentration in the distribution of wealth. If, for example, there were equal total numbers in each age group and if all entered the labor force at age 20, then despite our extreme egalitarian distribution of wage income among those still

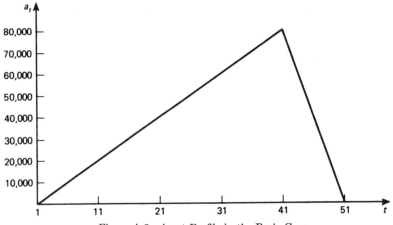

Figure A.2   Asset Profile in the Basic Case

employed, some 55 percent of total wealth would be held by a group amounting to only 40 percent of the total population, that is, the group of relatively elderly persons aged between 50 and 70. Note finally that if the anticipated retirement period is of any sizable length, the volume of wealth necessary to sustain the intergenerational cycle is quite large in relation to total labor income. Assuming again equal numbers in each age group, we find that the ratio of wealth to income is 5 to 1, a figure of about the same order of magnitude as found in modern industrial societies and one that the simple life-cycle model can produce without having to invoke any estate motive for saving.[4]

I.D. Consumption and Saving with a Growing Income

Additional insights into saving behavior are provided when we drop the assumption of a constant annual income during the working years and replace it with one involving the steady rise in income over time anticipated in most occupations. To effect this change, it is convenient to separate current income and average future income in the resources constraint (A.2), rewriting it as

$$\sum_{\tau=t}^{N} c_\tau^* = a_t + \sum_{\tau=t}^{W} y_\tau = a_t + y_t + \sum_{\tau=t+1}^{W} y_\tau \qquad (A.4)$$

$$= a_t + y_t + (W - t)\bar{y}_{t+1},$$

where $\bar{y}_{t+1}$ = average annual income from $t + 1$ on. Because the change in assumptions with respect to the income pattern does not affect the optimal consumption pattern, we still have a solution of the form $c_t^* = c_{t+1}^* \cdots = c_N^*$, and repeating the steps in the previous section, we obtain

$$c_t^* = \frac{1}{N - t + 1} a_t + \frac{1}{N - t + 1} y_t + \frac{W - t}{N - t + 1} \bar{y}_{t+1} \qquad (A.5)$$

as the explicit consumption function and

$$s_t^* = y_t - c_t^* = \frac{N - t}{N - t + 1} y_t - \frac{1}{N - t + 1} a_t - \frac{W - t}{N - t + 1} \bar{y}_{t+1} \qquad (A.6)$$

[4] Readers interested in comparing these and subsequent profiles with profiles actually compiled from survey data can find examples of the latter in "The 'Permanent Income' and 'Life-Cycle' Hypotheses of Saving Behavior," by F. Modigliani and A. Ando, in *Proceedings of the Conference on Consumption and Saving*, vol. 2, Philadelphia, 1960, and in "The Life Cycle in Income, Saving and Asset Ownership," by H. Lydall, in *Econometrica*, April 1955.

The main qualitative discrepancy between these profiles and ours arises from the fact that the family rather than the individual is really the basic decision unit and the family typically changes in size over the life cycle. Thus even for extreme consumption smoothers, family consumption tends to rise as children enter the family, reach a peak as they reach adolescence, and then decline as they leave home to set up new family units of their own. Hence, in practice, saving and wealth holdings tend to be even more concentrated in the upper age groups than our simple models suggest.

as the explicit savings function in terms of wealth, current income, average future income, and the life-cycle parameters W, N, and t.

To facilitate comparison with the simpler model in the previous section, suppose that N and W are 50 and 40 years, as before, and that the individual's average annual income over his entire working lifetime is still \$10,000. But let his starting income at $t = 1$, that is, at calendar age 20, be only \$5125 with a steady annual increment of \$250 a year thereafter, thus reaching a level of \$14,875 in the last year before retirement, 40 years later. Because the total lifetime level of resources is still \$400,000, the actual amount of consumption is also still \$8000 per year, as in the case considered earlier. The pattern of saving and of wealth holdings, however, is quite different.

During the first year of entry into the labor force, the individual's saving is

$$ s_1^* = \frac{49}{50} \cdot 5125 - \frac{1}{50} \cdot 0 - \frac{39}{50} \cdot \frac{394{,}875}{39} = -2875. $$

He is, in short, actually dissaving initially, and financing this excess of consumption expenditures over current income by borrowing, for example, by tuition loans to attend graduate school. During the next period, his income rises by \$250, his net wealth becomes $-$\$2875, and his saving for the year thus becomes

$$ s_2^* = \frac{48}{49} \cdot 5375 - \frac{1}{49} (-2875) - \frac{38}{49} \cdot \frac{389{,}500}{38} = -2625. $$

It is easy to see that with the numerical values assumed, this dissaving will

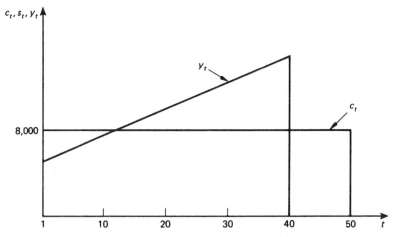

Figure A.3   Savings and Consumption Profiles with Rising Income

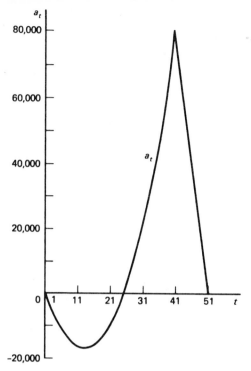

Figure A.4   Asset Profile for the Rising Income Case

continue to diminish steadily by \$250 per year and cease altogether after 12 years. It will take another 13 years until his net wealth reaches zero, that is, until all the debts incurred during the early, low-income years have been repaid. Hence the entire retirement fund of \$80,000 is actually accumulated during the last 16 years of work, with nearly 20 percent of it actually coming during the last 2 years before retirement. The profiles of income, consumption, saving, and wealth for this income growth example are shown graphically in Figures A.3 and A.4.[5]

[5] Note, incidentally, that by introducing anticipated income growth over the working years, we have in effect provided a rationale for the standard Keynesian consumption function as applied to a cross section of income receivers. By a Keynesian consumption function we mean one of the form $c = a + by$, with $a > 0$ and b, the "marginal propensity to consume," positive, but less than unity. These conditions on a and b imply that c/y, the average propensity to consume, falls with y or, conversely, that s/y rises with y. As can readily be seen from Figure A.3, the average propensity to save out of current income, s_t^*/y_t, does indeed rise steadily with income during the working years, although putting the emphasis entirely on income, as is all too often the case in the standard texts, obscures the basic life cycle and hence age-dependent mechanism at work.

I.E. The Effects of Changes in Income and Wealth

The consumption and savings functions in the previous section, with their separate coefficients for current income and expected future income, can also be used to show at least the essential rationale for the distinction between "permanent" and "transitory" changes in income that figures so heavily in recent discussions and controversies over saving behavior.[6]

Consider, for example, an individual somewhere in the working age group, say at age 45, that is, at $t = 26$, for concreteness. Using the previous values of 40 years and 50 years for the work span and life span respectively, his consumption function for the year is

$$c_{26}^* = \frac{1}{50 - 25} a_t + \frac{1}{50 - 25} y_t + \frac{40 - 25 - 1}{50 - 25} \bar{y}_{t+1} \qquad (A.7)$$

$$= 0.04a_t + 0.04y_t + 0.56\bar{y}_{t+1}.$$

Suppose now that the individual received an "unanticipated" raise in salary of $100 per year.[7] Then his permanent labor income has risen by $100 and his current (and future annual) consumption expenditures will rise by $0.04(\$100) + 0.56(\$100) = \$60$. Alternatively and equivalently, of course, we could say that his lifetime level of resources has risen by $1500 ($100 in each of the 15 remaining years of employment); and because he spreads his resources equally over his remaining lifetime—in this case, 25 years—his annual consumption rises by $1500/25 or $60 per year.

Suppose, on the other hand, that the $100 raise were in the form of a bonus that was regarded as purely transitory, that is, as not expected to be repeated in any subsequent year. Then from Equation (A.7) we see that his current (and future annual) consumption will rise by only $4. This much lower marginal propensity to consume out of transitory labor income reflects the fact that his lifetime resources have in this case risen by only $100, with 25 years of life remaining over which consumption is to be spread.

[6] The classic statement of the permanent income hypothesis is in Milton Friedman, *A Theory of the Consumption Function*. Princeton, N.J.: Princeton University Press, 1957.

[7] We are, of course, speaking loosely in referring to "unanticipated changes." Given the certainty assumption of the model, we can really speak validly only of cross-sectional differences as between individuals, not of changes for a given individual. In the present context, however, these loose, although expositionally convenient, references to changes do no great harm, because in these and similar examples in this appendix our concern is really only with the likely signs and rough relative orders of magnitude of the responses. For insights at this level of generality, the certainty models are "good enough."

II. CONSUMPTION, SAVING, AND THE RATE OF INTEREST[8]

II.A. Some Additional Assumptions: Homogeneity and Its Implications

Having explored some of the basic forces molding consumption and savings patterns over the life cycle, we now go on to enrich the picture further by dropping our simplifying assumption that the rate of interest is zero. As before, our goal is to obtain a simple and transparent consumption function, and the first step in its derivation is again that of introducing additional specifications with respect to the utility function. In particular, we assume that preferences have the following property: If

$$U(c_1{}^i,c_2{}^i,\ldots,c_N{}^i) = U(c_1{}^j,c_2{}^j,\ldots,c_N{}^j),$$

then $\qquad U(\lambda c_1{}^i,\lambda c_2{}^i,\ldots,\lambda c_N{}^i) = U(\lambda c_1{}^j,\lambda c_2{}^j,\ldots,\lambda c_N{}^j);$

that is, if the decision maker is indifferent when asked to choose between two patterns of lifetime consumption i and j, he would also be indifferent between two patterns that represent a mere proportionate scaling up or down of i and j.

An illustration for a two-period case is provided in Figure A.5. The points x and y are two particular combinations of c_1 and c_2 that have equal utility indexes and hence lie on the same indifference curve. If we draw a straight line, or ray, from the origin through the point x, any point along the ray represents the same pattern of consumptions in the two periods as the point x, although the absolute amounts differ. At the point x', for example, the total consumption in each period is λ_1 times that of the point x. Our assumption requires that if we now draw the ray through y and find the point $y' = \lambda_1 y$, then y' lies on the same indifference curve as x'. Because what is true for the two points x and y is true for all the points on indifference curve I, our assumption also means that all indifference curves are parallel, radial projections of one another.

The important economic consequences of this property can be seen as soon as we add in the opportunity set. In Figure A.5, for example, the line K_1K_2 represents the opportunities available to an individual, the present value of whose resources is K_1, at a time when the interest rate is $_1r_2$. Because the indifference curves are radially parallel, we know that the slope of the indifference curve II at the point x' must also equal $-(1 + _1r_2)$ and hence that the point x' is the chosen combination for this value of the interest rate and a level of initial resources $K_1' = \lambda_1 K_1$. Thus, under our assumption, all expansion paths of tangency points traced out by varying levels of

---

[8] This section is intended mainly for those readers with a special interest in the micro foundations of aggregate savings functions.

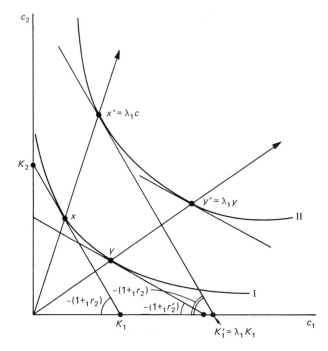

Figure A.5 Homogeneity Postulate

wealth for some given value of r (the analogs of the Engel curves in ordinary consumer demand theory) are straight lines through the origin.

This property, in turn, has some obvious but important implications for the form of the consumption function. The general budget constraint of Equation (1.28) can be written for an individual with a further work expectancy of $W - t$ years and a life expectancy of $N - t$ years as

$$c_t + \sum_{\tau=t+1}^{N} \frac{c_\tau}{\prod\limits_{\alpha=t+1} (1 + {}_{\alpha-1}r_\alpha)} = a_t + y_t + \sum_{\tau=t+1}^{W} \frac{y_\tau}{\prod\limits_{\alpha=t+1} (1 + {}_{\alpha-1}r_\alpha)} \equiv w_t(r),$$

(A.8)

where $w_t(r)$ is the value of lifetime resources as of the start of period t. Because the Engel curves or expansion paths are straight lines through the origin, we have, between consumption in t and any later period $t + \delta$, the proportionality relation

$$c_{t+\delta} = k_{t+\delta}(r)c_t,$$

where the factor of proportionality, which is, of course, the slope of the expansion path, is written as $k_{t+\delta}(r)$ to emphasize its dependence in general on the level of interest rates but independence of the level of wealth.

Substituting into Equation (A.8) and simplifying yields

$$c_t \left[1 + \sum_{\tau=t+1}^{N} \frac{k_\tau(r)}{\displaystyle\prod_{\alpha=t+1}^{\tau} (1 + {}_{\alpha-1}r_\alpha)} \right] = w_t(r) \qquad (A.9)$$

or, equivalently, in consumption function form

$$c_t = \left[1 + \sum_{\tau=t+1}^{N} \frac{k_\tau(r)}{\displaystyle\prod_{\alpha=t+1}^{\tau} (1 + {}_{\alpha-1}r_\alpha)} \right]^{-1} w_t(r) = \gamma_t(r) w_t(r); \quad (A.10)$$

that is, consumption during period t is proportional to lifetime resources at the start of the period—the specific proportion depending on the stage in the life cycle and the level of interest rates.

This property of proportionality or linear homogeneity of the consumption function is one that we have already exploited in the previous examples in Section I, although we arrived at it by a somewhat different route.[9] It is also a property that in one form or another has come to play a central role in many recent theoretical and empirical studies of savings behavior.

II.B. Interest Rates and Consumption Decisions over the Life Cycle

To bring out more sharply some of the main interactions between interest rates and consumption decisions over the life cycle implicit in a consumption function such as (A.10), it is helpful to specialize the utility function still further. In particular, we assume that the utility function can be approximated by a simple, equally weighted product of the standard of living in each year,

$$U(c_t, c_{t+1}, \ldots, c_N) = c_t \cdot c_{t+1} \cdot \ldots \cdot c_N. \qquad (A.11)$$

Given such a function, which satisfies our assumption of linear, homogeneous expansion paths and which also preserves the symmetry or zero time preference of the earlier examples, and given, for further simplicity, that the rate of interest is the same in all periods, so that the lifetime resources constraint becomes

$$c_t + \sum_{\tau=t+1}^{N} \frac{c_\tau}{(1+r)^{\tau-t}} = a_t + y_t + \sum_{\tau=t+1}^{W} \frac{y_\tau}{(1+r)^{\tau-t}} \equiv w_t(r), \quad (A.12)$$

---

[9] Our assumption of zero time preference implies in effect that the Engel curve corresponding to a zero rate of interest is a straight line through the origin. And because zero was the value that we specifically assumed for the rate of interest, we got the proportionality properties over the particular range we were considering.

it can readily be shown that the relation between the optimal value of consumption in year t and that in any subsequent period τ is

$$c_\tau^* = c_t^* (1 + r)^{\tau-t}; \qquad (A.13)$$

that is, for this particular form of the utility function and constraint set

$$k_\delta(r) = (1 + r)^\delta. [10]$$

Substituting once again for the c_τ or the left-hand side of Equation (A.9), the terms $(1 + r)^\delta$ cancel, and we obtain

$$c_t^* + \sum_{\tau=t+1}^{N} \frac{c_t^*(1 + r)^{\tau-t}}{(1 + r)^{\tau-t}} = c_t^*(N - t + 1) = w_t(r) \qquad (A.14)$$

or in consumption function form

$$c_t^* = \left[\frac{1}{N - t + 1}\right] w_t(r). \qquad (A.15)$$

Thus, for the special utility function that we have chosen, the proportionality factor $\gamma_t(r)$ can be stated in terms of the life-cycle parameters N and t as simply $1/[N - t + 1]$, exactly the same factor as in our earlier examples.[11]

As for the income and asset components of $w_t(r)$, assume for simplicity, as well as to provide a direct basis of comparison with earlier examples, that the rate of labor earnings is a constant amount y during each year of employment. If so,

$$w_t(r) = a_t + y_t + \sum_{\tau=t+1}^{W} \frac{\bar{y}_{t+1}}{(1 + r)^{\tau-t}} = a_t + y_t + A(r; W - t)\bar{y}_{t+1}, \qquad (A.16)$$

[10] We leave the proof as an exercise for any student who may feel in need of some further drill.

[11] That $\gamma_t(r)$ is independent of r is a consequence of the particular utility function used—Equation (A.11)—and does not rest on our further simplifying assumption of constant interest rates. Equation (A.15) would continue to hold in exactly that form even if interest rates differed from period to period.

Note also that Equation (A.15) is essentially the Friedman form of the consumption function. For empirical testing, however, and especially for facilitating comparison with the Keynesian form, he prefers to state it not in terms of the stock variable $w_t(r)$ but in terms of a flow variable that he dubbed permanent income (see Section I.E.). In principle, at least, the conversion is simple: let $F(r; N - t + 1) =$ the capital recovery factor for $N - t + 1$ years at the rate r—see Equation (1.24)—and let $y_t^p =$ permanent income at the start of $t = w_t(r) \cdot F(r; N - t + 1)$; and let $\alpha_t' = (1/N - t + 1)/F(r; N - t + 1)$. Then the equivalent permanent income form of Equation (A.15) would be $c_t^* = \alpha_t' y_t^p$.

where the term $A(r; W - t)$ denotes the present value of an annuity of \$1 for $W - t$ years at the rate r—see Equation (1.23)—and $\bar{y}_{t+1}$ is the uniform, and hence also average, labor income from $t + 1$ on. Combining Equations (A.15) and (A.16), we thus have as our explicit consumption function in terms of the life-cycle parameters N, W, and t, labor income, financial assets, and the rate of interest

$$c_t^* = \frac{1}{N - t + 1} a_t + \frac{1}{N - t + 1} y_t + \frac{A(r; W - t)}{N - t + 1} \bar{y}_{t+1}. \quad \text{(A.17)}$$

Note that for the special case of $r = 0$, Equation (A.17) reduces exactly to our earlier consumption functions, such as (A.5), because $A(0; W - t) = W - t$. For $r > 0$, of course, $A(r; W - t) < W - t$.

It is useful to have variants of Equation (A.17) running in terms of total current income, that is, labor income plus interest income, rather than of labor income alone. In particular, if we define w'_{t-1} as the value of any assets carried over before the addition of the interest earned, so that $w'_{t-1}(1 + r) = a_t$, then we can rewrite Equation (A.17) as

$$c_t^* = \frac{1}{N - t + 1} w'_{t-1} + \frac{1}{N - t + 1} [rw'_{t-1} + y_t] + \frac{A(r; W - t)}{N - t + 1} \bar{y}_{t+1}$$

$$\text{(A.18)}$$

and the corresponding saving function as

$$s_t^* = y_t + rw'_{t-1} - c_t^* = \left(r - \frac{1 + r}{N - t + 1} \right) w'_{t-1} + \frac{N - t}{N - t + 1} y_t$$

$$- \frac{A(r; W - t)}{N - t + 1} \bar{y}_{t+1} = - \frac{1}{N - t + 1} w'_{t-1}$$

$$+ \left[\frac{N - t}{N - t + 1} \right] (y_t + rw'_{t-1}) - \frac{A(r; W - t)}{N - t + 1} \bar{y}_{t+1}. \quad \text{(A.19)}$$

For purposes of comparison with the results in Section I, suppose again that N and W are 50 and 40 years, respectively, that y_t is \$10,000 in each year of the working life, and that the annual interest rate is 4 percent. Then, during the first year in which the individual enters the labor force, his consumption is

$$c_1^* = \frac{1}{50} 0 + \frac{1}{50} 10{,}000 + \frac{19.58}{50} 10{,}000 = \frac{20.58}{50} 10{,}000 = 4117,$$

and his saving for the year is

$$s_1^* = \left(0.04 - \frac{1.04}{50} \right) 0 + \frac{49}{50} 10{,}000 - \frac{19.58}{50} 10{,}000 = \frac{29.42}{50} 10{,}000 = 5883.$$

The corresponding figures for the zero interest rate model, it will be recalled, were $8000 for consumption and $2000 for saving. What has happened, of course, is that the prospect of a 4 percent return on savings has led him to reduce his immediate consumption substantially—the loss in utility due to this reduction being compensated for by the higher level of consumption and utility that this abstinence makes possible in subsequent years. During the next year, for example, his income will rise by the $235 of interest earned on his fund of $5883, and his consumption will increase to

$$c_2^* = \frac{(1.04)}{49} 5883 + \frac{1}{49} 10{,}000 + \frac{19.37}{49} 10{,}000 = 4281;$$

and his saving to

$$s_2^* = \left(0.04 - \frac{1.04}{49}\right) 5883 + \frac{48}{49} 10{,}000 - \frac{19.37}{49} 10{,}000 = 5984.$$

By year $t = 18$, his consumption will have regained the $8000 level, and in the first year of retirement at $t = 41$ it will have increased to slightly more than $19,000 for the year. The sum total of his consumption expenditures over his entire lifetime will be more than a million dollars, as compared with only $400,000 in the no-interest case, the entire difference representing

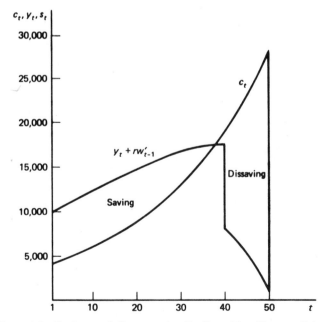

Figure A.6   Savings and Consumption Profiles with a Nonzero Interest Rate

the investment earnings on his accumulated savings. Such is the power of compound interest!

The profiles of earnings, consumption, saving, and wealth are presented graphically in Figures A.6 and A.7.

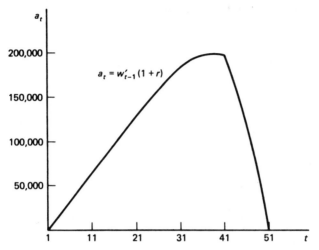

Figure A.7   Asset Profile for the Case of a Nonzero Interest Rate

2

EXTENSION OF THE MODEL TO DURABLE COMMODITIES, PRODUCTION, AND CORPORATIONS

In this chapter we extend the model of wealth allocation introduced in Chapter 1 to allow for commodity storage and production as vehicles, in addition to the purchase of securities, for the carrying of wealth from period to period. This extension is straightforward so long as the firms holding or producing the commodities are taken as owned and managed by a single individual. But serious problems in defining an appropriate criterion function arise as soon as we try to allow for multiowner corporations in which the decision-making power has largely been delegated to managers. Fortunately, however, there are at least some circumstances in which the existence of well-functioning markets for corporate securities permits a simple solution to these problems. And equally important from the present point of view, it turns out that much of the standard theory of valuation and corporate finance emerges naturally in the process of developing and interpreting the solution.

I. DURABLE COMMODITIES AND INVESTMENT

I.A. Representation of the Carry-over Opportunities
Provided by Commodity Storage and Production

Even in simple two-period cases, the number and kind of opportunities for carrying over resources by means of commodities are quite large. The decision maker may choose, for example, to store commodities, such as wheat, in the first period and then either sell or consume them in the second. Or he may purchase a durable good, such as an automobile, and either rent out or consume its services and subsequently dispose of it by resale or scrapping. Or he may own some firm or other productive opportunity that he can exploit by transforming labor services and raw materials in period 1 into some finished product for sale or consumption in period 2.

Despite the differences in outward form, we can represent any such opportunities in general terms by the implicit function $T(K_1,K_2) = 0$, where K_1 represents the dollar value of the consumption possibilities provided by the opportunity in period 1 and K_2 the maximum value of these possibilities in period 2 consistent with having K_1 in period 1. The precise shape and position of T depend, of course, on the nature of the opportunity.

In the case of commodity storage, for example, the relationship between K_2 and K_1 summarized by the function T is a straight line if we assume that the commodity is traded in a perfect market and that the per unit cost of storage is independent of the quantity stored. Such a case is shown in Figure 2.1. The point $K_1^* = p_1 q_j$ is the current market value of a holding

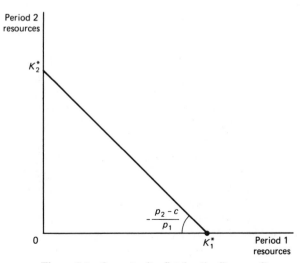

Figure 2.1   Opportunity Set for the Storage Case

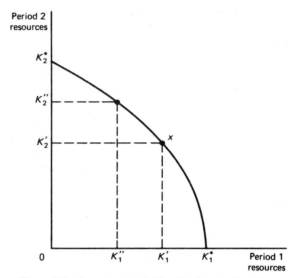

Figure 2.2   Opportunity Set for the Production Case

consisting of q_j units of some storable commodity j with current market price p_1. If the entire stock were carried over to period 2, its value would be $K_2^* = (p_2 - c)q_j$, where c is the unit cost of storage. The straight line through these points shows all the possible intermediate strategies involving both some storage and some immediate liquidation of the stock; an explicit representation of the T function in this case would be

$$K_2 = K_2^* - \frac{p_2 - c}{p_1} K_1.$$

Figure 2.2 shows a T function that might be appropriate where the carry-over was by way of production or where the costs of storage increased with the quantity stored. The point K_1^* represents the current market value of initial resources. For concreteness, we may think of these resources as consisting of a given number of bushels of corn that may be either sold currently or planted to yield a further crop of corn next period. The point x represents a strategy involving the immediate sale of part of the stock yielding K_1' dollars and a planting of the remaining stock, that is, an investment of $K_1^* - K_1'$ dollars. The net value at period 2 of the crop obtained from this investment, after paying for any productive services used, is K_2'.

Note that, as drawn, the slope of the T function—the marginal rate of transformation of K_1 into K_2—falls steadily in absolute value as we advance along the curve from K_1^* toward K_2^*. Or using more context-oriented terms, the marginal rate of yield or marginal rate of return on investment declines steadily as the level of investment increases; that is, an investment of $K_1^* - K_1'$ yields a return of K_2', but a further investment of exactly the same amount $K_1' - K_1'' = K_1^* - K_1'$ yields only $K_2'' - K_2' < K_2'$, and so on.

In drawing the curve with this shape and position, we are, of course, making a number of implicit assumptions about the underlying conditions of production and sale, as well as about the policies followed by the owner in his price and output decisions. Precisely what these assumptions are need not concern us at the moment; in Chapter 3 we take up the relations between the transformation function and the optimal price and output decisions as treated in the standard theory of the firm. For the present, we simply take all this substructure as somehow given and assume that the optimal solution to these decision problems yields a transformation function for the production carry-over case with the concavity property pictured. It is not important for our purposes at this point that we cannot state this function in explicit form.

I.B. The Opportunity Set When Both Commodity Carry-overs and Capital Markets Are Available

The construction of the opportunity set when both commodity carry-overs and capital markets are available is a simple enough matter in the linear storage case. Figure 2.3, for example, shows two such storage possibilities. In the first case, represented by the line $K_1^* K_2^*$, the returns from storage—price change minus storage costs—are less than the returns from

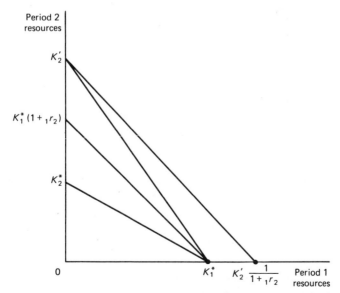

Figure 2.3   Storage and Capital Market Opportunities Combined

securities; that is, the slope of the line $K_1^* K_2^*$ is less in absolute value than that of the present value line $K_1^* K_1^* (1 + {}_1r_2)$. Because the present value line through K_1^* completely dominates the possibilities along the storage line,[1] the combined efficient set is attained by selling out the stock K_1^* immediately and relying on the capital market for any desired carry-over. In the second case, shown by the line $K_1^* K_2'$, the returns from storage are greater than from holding securities, and the reverse policy would be indicated; that is, the entire stock K_1^* should be stored to obtain K_2' at period 2, and any consumption needs during the current period met by borrowing against K_2', that is, by borrowing down the present value line $K_2' K_2' [1/(1 + {}_1r_2)]$. Actually, of course, the latter case is considered for purposes of illustration only; its occurrence is ruled out when capital and commodity markets are perfect. For if it arose, a sure profit could always be made by the time arbitrage, so to speak, of buying the commodity currently—borrowing, if necessary—and reselling one period later. The assumption of perfect capital and perfect commodity markets, in other words, implies that the real returns from storage can never exceed the market rate of interest (but they may fall below the market rate, in which event the commodity is not stored at all).

I.C. The Case of Production and Investment

I.C.1. The double-tangency solution

For the case of productive opportunities, the steps in the construction of the combined opportunity set are shown in Figure 2.4. Consider first the point K_1^*, corresponding to an immediate and complete liquidation of the productive resources. The combinations of c_1 and c_2 that can then be obtained by lending part of K_1^* in the capital market are represented by the present value line $K_1^* K_1^* (1 + {}_1r_2)$, which is obtained by passing a line with slope $- (1 + {}_1r_2)$ through K_1^*. Consider next an investment policy leading to some higher point along the productive efficient set, such as the point x. The consumption combination that could be attained by using the capital market to reallocate the resource combination provided by x is represented by the present value line $K_1^{**} K_1^{**} (1 + {}_1r_2)$ through x, which clearly everywhere dominates that for the policy of complete liquidation, that is, the policy of paying out K_1^* in period 1. By repeating this process for all the possible investment strategies along the productive frontier, we can see that the investment policy that dominates all others is the point y, where the relevant present value line is exactly tangent to the productive efficient

---

[1] The notion of dominance used here is, of course, an implication of the nonsatiation axiom. For a given level of resources in period 1, the consumer always prefers more to less resources in period 2. And similarly, given the level of resources in period 2, more resources in period 1 are always preferred to less.

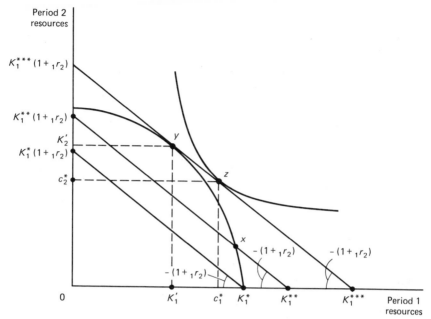

Figure 2.4   Joint Equilibrium of Production and Consumption Decisions

frontier. Or to use the rate terminology, the dominant investment policy is the one for which the marginal internal (one-period) rate of return is exactly equal to the (one-period) market rate of interest.

Given this fundamental result, the complete solution, showing the decision maker's simultaneous choices as to both investment and consumption patterns, can be indicated merely by adding in the consumption indifference curves. In the case shown in Figure 2.4, for example, the preferred position is the point z (for a decision maker assumed to have no other resources than the productive opportunity). This point represents the following combined set of choices:

1. The immediate liquidation and withdrawal of K_1' of the K_1^* dollars' worth of productive resources currently held in the firm
2. The investment of the remaining $K_1^* - K_1'$ dollars' worth of resources in the productive process to yield withdrawable proceeds of K_2' next period
3. The consumption of c_1^* this period and the borrowing of $c_1^* - K_1'$ dollars to finance the gap between consumption and the available proceeds from the immediate withdrawal
4. The consumption of c_2^* next period, repaying the loan plus interest $(c_1^* - K_1')(1 + {}_1r_2) = K_2' - c_2^*$ from the proceeds of the previously scheduled production in the firm

I.C.2. Some remaining issues

We have so far developed the model of allocation over time in terms of a single individual decision maker. To the extent that this individual had opportunities to carry over his resources by investing in productive assets, it was assumed that these opportunities arose in a business firm of which the individual was the sole owner and manager.

A model of a single owner-manager is certainly not devoid of interest in its own right, because the unincorporated business sector of the economy is by no means trivial. But the main concern here is with financial policy and investment decisions in the corporate sector. And before we can come to grips with these problems, we must show how the basic model can be extended or reinterpreted to accommodate two key facts of corporate life: (1) instead of a single owner whose preferences can be described by a single utility function, the typical corporation has many owners whose utility functions must be presumed to be different; and (2) the day-to-day business decisions, including most financial and investment decisions, are made, not directly by the stockholders, but by professional managers. It is true that for some large or important decisions, such as issues of new shares, a plebiscite of the shareholders, weighted by size of holding, may have to be taken; and the dividend decision is technically always made by the board of directors, who are in a legal sense the direct representatives of the shareholders. As a practical matter, however, and despite inevitable exceptions, effective control over decisions in large, widely held corporations is exercised by the management.

The next section in the present chapter focuses on these and related problems and, in particular, attempts to show how an operational criterion for management decisions can be developed within the framework of the model already presented. Before turning to this task, however, we first sketch out the mathematical solution to the two-constraint problem for the general n-period case.

*I.D. The Solution in the n-Period Case

As compared with the n-period choice problem considered in Chapter 1, the major change for the present problem is that we now have two sets of decision variables—the K_t as well as the c_t—and two opportunity sets, one representing borrowing and lending possibilities in the capital markets and the other investment and withdrawal opportunities from the production possibilities. The essence of the latter can be captured effectively by a simple implicit-form constraint written as

$$T(K_1, K_2, \ldots, K_N) = 0. \tag{2.1}$$

To see how the former can be obtained, begin again with the last period, and note that the maximum amount of consumption possible in period

N is now

$$c_N = a_N + y_N + K_N.$$

Working backwards again, we obtain for a_N

$$a_N = (a_{N-1} + y_{N-1} + K_{N-1} - c_{N-1})(1 + {}_{N-1}r_N),$$

and similarly until after the successive substitutions and rearrangements we obtain the following as the general capital market constraint:

$$c_1 + \frac{c_2}{1 + {}_1r_2} + \frac{c_3}{(1 + {}_1r_2)(1 + {}_2r_3)} + \cdots + \frac{c_N}{\displaystyle\prod_{t=1}^{N-1}(1 + {}_tr_{t+1})}$$

$$= a_1 + y_1 + \frac{y_2}{1 + {}_1r_2} + \frac{y_3}{(1 + {}_1r_2)(1 + {}_2r_3)} + \cdots + \frac{y_N}{\displaystyle\prod_{t=1}^{N-1}(1 + {}_tr_{t+1})}$$

$$+ K_1 + \frac{K_2}{1 + {}_1r_2} + \frac{K_3}{(1 + {}_1r_2)(1 + {}_2r_3)} + \cdots + \frac{K_N}{\displaystyle\prod_{t=1}^{N-1}(1 + {}_tr_{t+1})}. \quad (2.2)$$

In words, only those patterns of consumption are efficient for which the present value of the consumption stream exactly equals the sum of the present value of the future earned incomes plus the present value of the withdrawals from the productive firm or from other commodity carry-over opportunities.

The decision maker's preferred choice can then be represented as the solution to the problem

$$\max_{c_1,\ldots,c_N;K_1,\ldots,K_N} U(c_1,c_2,\ldots,c_N) \quad (2.3)$$

subject to the constraints (2.1) and (2.2). To obtain a more explicit characterization, we form the lagrangian expression

$$U(c_1,c_2,\ldots,c_N) - \lambda_1 T(K_1,K_2,\ldots,K_N)$$

$$+ \lambda_2 \left(K_1 + \frac{K_2}{1 + {}_1r_2} + \cdots + \frac{K_N}{\displaystyle\prod_{t=1}^{N-1}(1 + {}_tr_{t+1})} \right.$$

$$- c_1 - \frac{c_2}{1 + {}_1r_2} - \cdots - \frac{c_N}{\displaystyle\prod_{t=1}^{N-1}(1 + {}_tr_{t+1})}$$

$$\left. + a_1 + y_1 + \frac{y_2}{1 + {}_1r_2} + \cdots + \frac{y_N}{\displaystyle\prod_{t=1}^{N-1}(1 + {}_tr_{t+1})} \right),$$

differentiate successively with respect to λ_1, λ_2, and each of the $2N$ decision variables, and obtain as the first-order conditions for a maximum (2.1), (2.2), and the relations

$$U_1' - \lambda_2 = 0$$

$$U_2' - \lambda_2 \frac{1}{1 + {}_1r_2} = 0$$

. . . .

$$U_t' - \lambda_2 \frac{1}{\displaystyle\prod_{\tau=1}^{t-1} (1 + {}_\tau r_{\tau+1})} = 0 \qquad (2.4)$$

. . . .

$$U_N' - \lambda_2 \frac{1}{\displaystyle\prod_{\tau=1}^{N-1} (1 + {}_\tau r_{\tau+1})} = 0$$

and

$$\lambda_2 - \lambda_1 T_1' = 0$$

$$\lambda_2 \frac{1}{1 + {}_1r_2} - \lambda_1 T_2' = 0$$

. . . .

$$\lambda_2 \frac{1}{\displaystyle\prod_{\tau=1}^{t-1} (1 + {}_\tau r_{\tau+1})} - \lambda_1 T_t' = 0 \qquad (2.5)$$

. . . .

$$\lambda_2 \frac{1}{\displaystyle\prod_{\tau=1}^{N-1} (1 + {}_\tau r_{\tau+1})} - \lambda_1 T_N' = 0.$$

The set (2.4) is the same as that obtained for the allocation problem considered in Section II.B.6 in Chapter 1 and leads to the same conclusion; namely, between any two periods, adjacent or not, we have

$$-\frac{U_t'}{U_{t+n}'} = - \prod_{\tau=t}^{t+n-1} (1 + {}_\tau r_{\tau+1});$$

that is, the preferred allocation of consumption between the two periods is characterized by a point of tangency between an indifference curve and the capital market opportunity line given in this case by Equation (2.2). As for the set (2.5), between the same two periods we have

$$-\frac{T'_t}{T'_{t+n}} = -\prod_{\tau=t}^{t+n-1} (1 + {}_\tau r_{\tau+1}),$$

implying that the preferred combination of investment and withdrawals from the productive opportunity between the two periods is characterized by a point of tangency between the productive opportunity set and the capital market opportunity line. As indicated by the analysis of Figure 2.4, however, only by coincidence do the two tangency points coincide.

II. EXTENSION TO THE CASE OF CORPORATIONS

II.A. Management Objectives and Stockholder Preferences

In Chapter 1 it was shown that the general process of choice or decision making could be represented as one of maximizing a given utility function subject to constraints. Managerial decision making is no exception; the problem is, however, that if the decision-making power is considered as having been delegated to management by the shareholders, it is not immediately clear what is the utility function that management should be seeking to maximize or how it could be constructed.

If the firm had only a single owner, it might seem plausible that the appropriate criterion function should be that of the owner. Although hardly to be considered a practical approach, it is at least possible to imagine that the owner might interrogate himself about his preferences and communicate the results, along with a list of all his other transformation opportunities, to his management so as to give an unambiguous decision criterion covering all eventualities. Indeed, on a small scale within organizations today operations researchers and other technicians very frequently assist those responsible for decisions in stating their preferences in the form of explicit utility functions and even sometimes take the initiative in suggesting possible alternative utility functions for the problem at hand subject to final selection by the officer ultimately responsible.[2]

Practicality aside, however, there are also some serious conceptual problems involved. In particular, it is by no means clear how such a direct approach is to be implemented when we allow, as we must, for the possibility of many owners with possibly very different preferences, and other opportunities. To see the nature of the difficulties involved in attempting to construct an aggregate preference function from the separate individual

---

[2] See, for example, C. J. Grayson, "The Use of Statistical Techniques in Capital Budgeting," in *Financial Research and Management Decisions*, A. Robichek, ed. New York: John Wiley & Sons, Inc., 1967.

functions, consider the following simple example. Suppose that we have a firm owned by three shareholders A, B, and C each with an equal one-third interest. Suppose further that the firm faces an investment or other decision that can be reduced to a choice of one among three mutually exclusive proposals 1, 2, and 3. The stockholders, after due reflection, inform management that the order of their preferences among these alternatives is as follows:

Stockholder	First Choice	Second Choice	Third Choice
A	1	2	3
B	2	3	1
C	3	1	2

And suppose finally that management attempted to combine the preferences and make the choice on the basis of "majority rule." If management first considered proposal 1 versus proposal 2, then proposal 1 would be the choice, because it is preferred to 2 by A and C. If the next confrontation is between the previous winner 1 and proposal 3, then the winner is 3, because it is preferred to 1 by C and B. If now one last check is made, comparing 3 with the previously rejected 2, then 2 emerges as the preferred alternative, because it is preferred to 3 by A and B. Thus the results of the majority-rule combination of the individual preference functions of the owners is either indecisive and circular if all two-way comparisons are made or completely capricious and arbitrary if an alternative, once rejected, is not given its second chance, because in this case the final outcome depends entirely on the order in which the comparisons happened to be made.

Nor is this result in any way freakish or merely an artifact of the particular combination rule used. It can be shown, more generally, that if we impose certain minimal standards of sensible behavior for any aggregation rule, there exists no sensible nondictatorial aggregation rule that can guarantee the avoidance of the kind of inconsistency or intransitivity encountered in the example. Or to put it in terms more closely related to the basic framework, there is, in general, no way of directly combining the preference or utility functions of the individual shareholders into a single global preference function which meets all the axioms of choice and hence which a management could use as an unambiguous criterion for making decisions "in the best interests of the owners."[3]

---

[3] The proposition was first presented and proved in Kenneth J. Arrow, *Social Choice and Individual Values*. New York: John Wiley & Sons, Inc., 1951. Note the qualification that "in general" no unambiguous composite utility function exists. It is possible, however, to construct special cases in which all the properties of the individual utility functions do carry through to an aggregate representation of preference.

II.B. The Market Value Criterion

Fortunately, however, there is at least one important class of circumstances in which we can avoid these and related difficulties of constructing a decision criterion for management directly from stockholders' preferences. Where there exist organized capital markets in which shares can be freely bought and sold and where these markets are perfect in the sense defined in Chapter 1, it is possible to develop an objective, operational decision criterion for management that (1) does not involve stockholder utility functions directly but (2) leads to precisely the same investment and operating decisions that each stockholder would make if he were running the firm himself.

Important and fundamental as this result is for the theory of corporation finance, its proof requires little more than a reinterpretation of results that we have already obtained in Section I for the owner-managed firm. Recall that an overall optimum of consumption, saving, borrowing, and investment by a single owner-manager was characterized by the simultaneous satisfaction of two conditions: (1) tangency between the transformation curve of his firm and the capital market opportunity line and (2) tangency between the capital market opportunity line and an indifference curve. The points y and z in Figure 2.4 represent such an optimum, with $K_1^* - K_1'$ the amount invested in the firm, K_1' the amount withdrawn, $c_1^* - K_1'$ the amount borrowed or equivalently the amount of securities sold, and c_1^* and c_2^* the amounts allocated to consumption in periods 1 and 2, respectively.

Note that the achievement of the first of the two optimality conditions—that of tangency between the transformation function and the market opportunity line—does not require any of the "subjective" information summarized in the owner's indifference curves. It involves only the "objective" knowledge of the technology of the firm and of the ruling rate of interest. Hence finding a tangency point, such as y, is a subtask that can in principle be delegated to a manager.

Moreover, this delegation can readily be implemented by a decision rule that conforms directly to the standard model of the theory of choice presented in Chapter 1. Recall that market opportunity lines may also be interpreted as present value lines, or market value lines, because with perfect capital markets, current market value necessarily equals present value; that is, the intercept on the period 1 axis of any such line with slope $-(1 + {}_1r_2)$ shows the value in terms of current resources of any resource combination lying on the line, the value K_1^{**} in Figure 2.4, for example, thus being the present or market value of the point x. Hence the injunction to management to find the point of tangency y is equivalent to the injunction to maximize the current market value of the withdrawals to be provided by the firm to its current owners, subject to the technological constraints imposed by the transformation function. This criterion is henceforth often referred to as the "market value rule."

Having exploited the opportunities of transformation inherent in the firm and thereby having increased the owner's wealth from its initial value of K_1^* to its maximum possible value of K_1^{***}, management can safely leave the rest of the full solution to the owner himself. Given the optimum investment and withdrawal pattern represented by the point y, the owner can then exploit the capital market on his own account, in this case by borrowing $c_1^* - K_1'$ to reach his personal maximum of utility at z.

II.B.1. The case of many owners

Not only does the market value rule provide a utility-maximizing surrogate criterion for the managers of a single-owner firm, but it should be clear from the nature of the argument that the essential reasoning applies to the same extent and with equal force regardless of the number of individual shareholders or the differences in their preferences or other opportunities. To illustrate, consider a firm with two owners each owning a half interest and each with no further outside resources. For each owner, we could draw a figure similar to Figure 2.4, but because we assume their ownership to be equal and the firm to be their sole opportunity beyond those of the capital markets, we can combine them both into a single graph, as in Figure 2.5. As before, each owner, if entrusted with the complete power

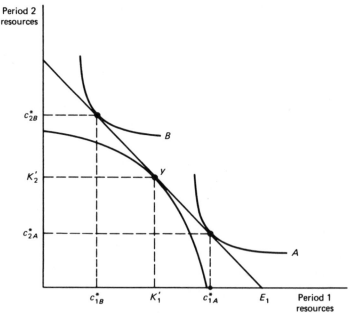

Figure 2.5   Equilibrium Production and Consumption Decisions for the Multiowner Firm

to manage, would choose the point y as the investment-withdrawal combination for the firm, the same point that would be chosen by a separate management following the market value rule. The differences in their tastes show up only in the second stage of the maximization by way of the capital market opportunities. Mr. A, with a strong preference for current consumption, supplements his "dividend" of K'_1 from the firm by borrowing the additional amount $c^*_{1A} - K'_1$; and Mr. B, who prefers to devote more of his wealth to future consumption, supplements the carry-over by way of the firm by investing $K'_1 - c^*_{1B}$ of his dividend in securities in the market. But these subsequent personal details are of no concern to the management. They can regard their obligations to the owners as having been satisfied by having achieved the point y and thereby having maximized the value of the resources available to the owners.

The relevance of the market value criterion for managerial decisions is in no way restricted to the case of two time periods or to the special assumptions that we have been making about the shape of the transformation function. Rather the decisive elements in the argument are the assumption of perfect capital markets and the nonsatiation axiom. It is the former that permits the results of all economically relevant management actions in any time period, current or future, to be expressed in terms of a common denominator, current wealth. More specifically, as we showed in Chapter 1, in a perfect capital market, and for given values of current and future one-period interest rates, a consumer's current wealth is sufficient information to describe all his consumption opportunities over time, because in such a market any sequence of dollar consumptions with a given market value can be exchanged for any other sequence with the same market value. Moreover, in a perfect capital market any changes in the configuration of consumption possibilities K_t that an owner can derive from a firm can be converted uniquely and unambiguously to a present wealth equivalent by discounting at the rates of interest ruling in the capital markets. Thus if the change in the owner's current wealth implied by a given management decision is positive, he must be better off, because he would then be able to increase his consumption in some time periods without having to reduce his consumption in any other period.[4]

---

[4] Although each individual owner always wants the firm to maximize the current market value of his holdings, it is possible to imagine (somewhat artificial) cases in which this does not imply an unambiguous decision rule for the firm. There are no problems as long as there is only one type of security outstanding, so that each unit of the security implies the same proportionate share of payoffs provided by the firm in all periods. Then increasing the current market value of the holdings of one owner always implies increasing the values of the holdings of the others.

But suppose, for example, that instead of a single type of security the firm has issued n different types each of which represents a share only in the payoffs for a given

*II.C. The Market Value Criterion in the General n-Period Case

A more formal proof that maximizing the utility of the owners implies maximizing the market value of their holdings in the firm is easily provided. We consider first a one-owner firm and then generalize the results to the multiowner case.

The choice problem presented by a one-owner firm has already been stated in mathematical form for the n-period case in Section I.D. To restate it for current purposes in more compact and transparent form, let $C = (c_1, c_2, \ldots, c_n)$ represent the entire vector of consumption expenditures per period, K the vector of withdrawals from the firm, $V(C)$ the present value of lifetime consumption, $V(Y)$ the present value of lifetime earnings, plus any initial financial assets, and $V(K)$ the present value of future withdrawals from the firm, or for short, the present value of the firm. The system of Equations (2.1) to (2.3) then can be written

$$\max_{C,K} U(C) \tag{2.6}$$

subject to

$$V(C) = V(Y) + V(K), \tag{2.7}$$

$$T(K) = 0. \tag{2.8}$$

This constrained maximum problem can be written in entirely equivalent form as the unconstrained maximum problem

$$\max_{C,K} \left[U(C) - \lambda_1(V(C) - V(Y) - V(K)) - \lambda_2 T(K) \right], \tag{2.9}$$

where λ_1 and λ_2 are lagrangian multipliers.

Because the utility function $U(C)$ is assumed to be monotone-increasing, by virtue of the nonsatiation axiom, the multipliers λ_1 and λ_2, which measure the effect on the utility index of loosening the constraints, must be strictly

---

period with no share in the payoffs of other periods. Then it is easy to imagine situations in which a production decision increases the total current market value of the firm, which in this case is best thought of as the sum of the market values of the payoffs in each period, but reduces the market values of the payoffs for some periods. Thus some of the firm's security holders are better off but others are worse off with the decision. As long as the total market value of the firm has increased, however, those who are better off receive more than enough to compensate in turn those who are worse off and so induce the latter to go along with the decision.

As indicated above, such problems are somewhat artificial in the context of a perfect certainty model. They will be less artificial, however, when we come to a world of uncertainty where multisecurity firms, for example, bonds and common stock, are common and the firm can undertake (unforeseen) actions that sacrifice the interests of one group to those of another.

positive. Hence we may regroup the C and K terms in Equation (2.9) and rewrite it

$$\max_{C} [U(C) - \lambda_1(V(C) - V(Y))] + \max_{K} [\lambda_1 V(K) - \lambda_2 T(K)]. \quad (2.10)$$

Let $\lambda_3 = \lambda_2/\lambda_1$. Then we can further reexpress Equation (2.10) as

$$\max_{C} [U(C) - \lambda_1(V(C) - V(Y))] + \lambda_1 \max_{K} (V(K) - \lambda_3 T(K))$$

$$= \max_{C} \{U(C) - \lambda_1(V(C) - V(Y) - \max_{K} (V(K) - \lambda_3 T(K)))\}.$$

$$(2.11)$$

Thus, because Equation (2.11) is merely a rearrangement of Equation (2.9), we have two completely equivalent ways of finding the (constrained) maximum of the owner's utility: either (1) a one-pass solution of the full system (2.6) to (2.8) by way of (2.9), as was done in Section I.D, or (2) a two-pass procedure in which we first solve the subsidiary maximum problem

$$\max_{K} [V(K) - \lambda_3 T(K)],$$

which is to say, maximize the value of the owner's interest in the firm, and then complete the solution by solving

$$\max_{C} \{U(C) - \lambda_1(V(C) - V(Y) - V^*(K))\},$$

where $V^*(K)$ is the maximum value of the owner's interest obtained in the first pass.

Generalizing to the case of a multiowner firm simply involves a reinterpretation of the preceding analysis. Now we let $V(K)$ be the share of an individual owner in the firm's total current market value, and likewise the constraint $T(K) = 0$ represents his implicit share of the firm's production possibilities. From the preceding arguments we then conclude immediately that for any one, and thus each, of the owner's, optimal production decisions by the firm involve maximizing the current market value of withdrawals.

II.D. The Market Value Criterion: Some Problems and Limitations

With the market value criterion in hand, we now have the essential starting point for a systematic attack on the problems of corporation, as opposed to individual, finance. Before moving in this direction, however, we pause very briefly to take a closer look at some of the implications and limitations of the market value criterion.

II.D.1. The market value rule and profit maximization

The market value rule and the separation that it implies between management decisions and owners' tastes is by no means peculiar to the field of finance. On the contrary, it is merely the application to investment and financing decisions of the general principle of "decentralizing" decisions by exploiting markets and market prices—a principle running through all the standard economic theory of value. In the ordinary theory of production, for example, a firm considering whether to produce oranges or bananas is not presumed to base this decision on which of the two the owners happen to prefer for breakfast. The decision problem is resolved, rather, on the basis of the market prices for the alternative outputs, on the costs of the various factor inputs, and the technological possibilities of production. Once a production plan has been determined so as to maximize the net return to owners, they can spend their shares of the proceeds on whatever pattern of fruit or breakfasts appeals to them the most. The situation is exactly analogous in finance where the "commodities" being produced are generalized consumption possibilities at various points in time.

For some students of finance, coming fresh from an introductory course in price theory, this essential similarity is often missed at first, because of a difference in the terminology used in the two courses. The market value of the owner's equity in the firm, in particular, is rarely, if ever, mentioned in the ordinary theory of the firm, most of which is expounded in terms of flow concepts, such as profits and profit maximization.[5] It is important to emphasize, therefore, that properly interpreted, there is no conflict between the stock and the flow form of the criterion. When we speak of maximizing profits in ordinary static price theory, we really mean profits in every unit of time; and clearly if we increase profits in every unit of time, we raise the value of the firm, which is essentially just a weighted sum of the returns per period. Lack of exact correspondence between the two criteria arises only when we deal with particular problems in which increases in returns for some periods involve reductions in other periods; and when this is so, the correct solution requires falling back on the more cumbersome, but universally applicable, market value criterion. Failure to realize that the simple flow criterion is not adequate in problems in which the timing of the returns is of the essence has been responsible for much unnecessary confusion, such as the frequently heard argument that the profit maximization criterion, and

---

[5] Here and throughout we use the term "profits" in its loose conventional sense of net returns, and not in its Knightian sense of an unanticipated windfall.

hence most of economic theory, does not apply to the business world as we know it, because most large firms could certainly raise prices and profits in the short run.

II.D.2. The market value rule and management motivation

On the other hand, there are some genuine and more serious difficulties that have to be considered before attempting to apply the market value criterion. In particular, the reader may have sensed a subtle inconsistency between the criterion of individual choice as developed in Chapter 1 and that of managerial choice as presented here. Originally, we assumed that the individual decision maker was maximizing his own utility function. Because managers are also individuals, what right have we now to assume that they will put aside their own utility functions and maximize instead the market value of the owners' equity in the firm?

This is a good question and one for which economists have not yet been able to supply a completely satisfactory answer. Instead it is usually assumed that there are sufficient additional processes of "control" or motivation to remove any conflicts between the individual and the corporate criterion functions of the managers. Examples of such processes would be incentive schemes, such as bonuses and stock options, that make management's compensation a direct function of stockholders' compensation, or at the other extreme, sanctions, such as stockholder revolts or outside takeover bids, that could be invoked, or threatened, to remove a management failing to act in the best interests of the owners. Still other examples could be derived from elsewhere in the literature of accounting and management control, because the stockholder-management confrontation is merely one special case of the general problem of administration and delegation between levels in the hierarchy that exists throughout the whole firm.

Throughout the book we, too, shall assume in dealing with management decisions both that the stockholders have found a way to impose the market value rule on top management and that they in turn have been able to impose subcriteria to be applied farther down the line that are completely consistent with and equivalent to the master criterion. No alternative approach has yet achieved sufficient coherence or sufficient acceptance in the profession to merit extensive discussion in an introductory book of this kind. Nor despite many years of controversy, has it yet been demonstrated that the market value rule leads to predictions that are so widely at variance with observed management behavior as to rule it out, even as a first approximation, for the class of decision problems to which we shall here be applying it.[6]

---

[6] A recent survey of the issues and the evidence is that of Robert J. Larner, *Management Control and the Large Corporation*. New York: Dunellen Publishing Co., 1970.

II.D.3. The criterion problem under imperfect capital markets

At this point, some readers may well be prepared to accept our working criterion of value maximization under conditions of perfect capital markets but are also impatiently waiting for guidance as to how to extend this criterion to the case of imperfect capital markets. If so, we are sorry to have to inform them that once the assumption of perfect capital markets is abandoned, so, in general, is the "separation" or "decentralization" principle that permits the present or market value of the firm, or, for that matter, any other "objective" magnitude, to serve as a proxy for the utility of the owners. We are back once again with the problems discussed in Section II.A.

Some further insight into the nature of these problems can be obtained from Figure 2.6, which has been designed to illustrate a case in which

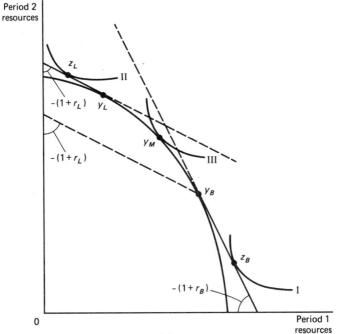

Figure 2.6   Consumption and Production Possibilities When Borrowing and Lending Rates Differ

transaction costs or some other imperfection in the capital markets has led to a situation in which the borrowing rate r_B is considerably higher than the lending rate r_L.[7] For borrowers the optimal production or investment

[7] For example, the stated market interest rate $_1r_2$ might be the same for both borrowers and lenders, but because of brokerage fees the borrower does not realize the full amount of a loan and the lender must pay the broker a fee in addition to the face value of the loan. In this case the effective borrowing and lending rates are such that $r_L < {_1r_2} < r_B$.

decision in Figure 2.6 is the point y_B, where the slope of the transformation curve is $-(1 + r_B)$; for lenders the optimal production decision is the point y_L, where the slope of the transformation curve is $-(1 + r_L)$.

Note that because r_B is a borrowing rate, one can move only down along the line from y_B with slope $-(1 + r_B)$; the (dashed) extension of the line upward from y_B does not represent feasible points. If one wished to use the capital market to move up, the (dashed) line from y_B with slope $-(1 + r_L)$ is relevant; but points along this line are clearly inefficient. On the other hand, because r_L is a lending rate, one can move only up from y_L along the line with slope $-(1 + r_L)$; the dashed extension of this line downward from y_L does not represent feasible points.

Thus when borrowing and lending rates differ, there is no longer a unique production decision that would be made by any current stockholder regardless of his tastes. Stockholders with preferences such as those indicated by the indifference curve I would choose the point y_B and borrow down to z_B. Those with preferences II would choose y_L and lend additional amounts up to z_L. Nor is it simply a matter of replacing one point by two. Stockholders with tastes such as III would choose neither of these points but rather an intermediate point, such as y_M. Hence, without some further assumptions as to stockholders' tastes and how they are compromised, all that we can make is the relatively weak statement that the preferred position lies somewhere on the frontier between the points y_B and y_L.[8]

---

[8] Because no market can ever be literally perfect, we must, of course, always imagine ourselves as having to face some indeterminacy of this form in discussing real-world markets. The perfect market assumption, then, should be interpreted as saying merely that this indeterminacy is small enough to be neglected for the problem under discussion. When imperfections are so large or pervasive as to rule out the perfect market model even as an approximation, one simply tries to approach the problem in some other way, usually very much tailored to the specific circumstances of the case. The hope is that the special formulation adopted, although it may not be strictly optimal, does at least capture the essence of the problem sufficiently well to yield insights that carry beyond the immediate and literal context. And in principle, this is all that we can really hope to do even in the perfect market case—a case that would surely not be worth studying if the "optimal" solutions so derived applied only to situations in which the markets were literally perfect.

But although there is thus certainly nothing impossible or illegitimate in analyzing problems of imperfect as opposed to perfect capital markets, there are important qualitative differences in the kind of theory that emerges in the two cases. Because a perfect market is a single and well-defined concept, we get a body of theory that can subsume a wide variety of seemingly very different problems in a single, unified framework. We merely change the labels on the axes, so to speak. Imperfect markets, by contrast, can be of many different kinds, and for each a very different kind of approach is likely to be appropriate. Hence we have not an organized or unified body of results that can be called a theory of decision under imperfect capital markets but rather a series of separate special cases with very little carry-over of concepts or methods among them.

III. MARKET VALUE, DIVIDENDS, AND STOCKHOLDER RETURNS

Up to this point we have been referring to the market or present value of the equity in a firm without any distinction between the value of the stream of earnings as generated within the firm and the value of the stream of payments actually flowing to the owners. But the multiowner corporation is in law and in fact an entity separate from the owners with entirely separate financial accounts. And more to the point, the owners have access only to that part of the firm's earnings which the directors of the firm choose to declare as dividends. How then does the dividend policy of the directors affect the value of the equity? What would constitute an optimal dividend policy from the standpoint of the current owners? What relations must hold between the stream of corporate earnings and the stream of stockholder returns? It is to these and related questions, which lie at the heart of the field of corporation finance, that we address ourselves in the remainder of the present chapter before going on, in Chapter 3, to consider some of the standard applications of the market value criterion to specific management decisions.[9]

III.A. The Effect of Dividend Policy

III.A.1. Assumptions, notation, and timing conventions

To isolate the dividend decision from all the other managerial decisions impinging on the value of the firm, we assume provisionally that the managers have somehow programmed all the future production, marketing, and investment decisions for the firm and have disclosed this information to the investing public. The question then is, given some such set of future production, marketing, and investment decisions, what effect do the firm's current and future dividend decisions have on the market value of current shareholder equity?

To help remind readers which magnitudes are on a per share basis and which are totals for the firm as a whole we use lowercase letters for the former and capital letters for the latter. As for timing, we continue the convention in Chapter 1 that all payments are made as of the beginning of the period and accrue to the owner of the asset as of the start of the previous period. In particular, $d_i(t)$ designates the dividend per share paid at the start of period t to holders of record as of the start of period $t - 1$. $R_i(t)$ designates the firm's receipts from operations at t, $W_i(t)$ are wages and similar outlays for the services of factors of production not owned by the firm, $I_i(t)$ are outlays on capital account, that is, gross investment, at t, and $R_i(t) - W_i(t) - I_i(t)$ is "net cash flow" at t.

[9] We have, of course, already said a great deal about dividend policy both directly and by implication. Basically, we shall here be merely restating previous results in more general, algebraic form.

III.A.2. *The equal rate of return principle once again*

Turning first to the stream as it appears in the market, we showed in Chapter 1 that in equilibrium, under perfect capital markets, the one-period returns on all securities must be the same in any given period. Otherwise, investors would hold only the securities with the highest return, which is of course inconsistent with equilibrium in the sense of market clearing. Thus, although the stream of cash dividends on a share may stretch on indefinitely, we must have for any period t

$$_t\rho_{i,t+1} \equiv \frac{d_i(t+1) + v_i(t+1) - v_i(t)}{v_i(t)} = {}_t r_{t+1}, \quad \text{for all } i. \quad (2.12)$$

Or equivalently, in present value form,

$$v_i(t) = \frac{1}{1 + {}_t r_{t+1}} [d_i(t+1) + v_i(t+1)], \quad (2.13)$$

where $v_i(t)$ is the price, quoted without or "ex" any dividend at t, of a share in firm i at the start of period t. (Note that because it leads to no ambiguity, we hereafter drop the firm subscript i.)

The same principle extends, of course, to the value of all the shares, that is, to the current owners' total equity in the firm. Thus if there are $n(t)$ shares at the start of period t and if we define $D(t+1) = n(t)d(t+1)$ as total dividends paid by the firm at $t+1$ and $V(t) = n(t)v(t)$ as the total value of all shares outstanding at the start of t, we can reexpress Equation (2.13) in terms of these total values as

$$V(t) = \frac{1}{1 + {}_t r_{t+1}} [D(t+1) + n(t)v(t+1)]. \quad (2.14)$$

Note, however, that we cannot simply write $V(t+1)$ for $n(t)v(t+1)$ in the expression in brackets. The reason is, of course, that $V(t+1)$ is equal to the product of $v(t+1)$ and $n(t+1)$ and the latter does not equal $n(t)$ if new shares are issued at $t+1$. To allow for the possibility of such outside financing, let $m(t+1)$ be the number of new shares, if any, issued at the beginning of period $t+1$ at the then ruling price $v(t+1)$.[10] Then

$$V(t+1) = n(t+1)v(t+1) = n(t)v(t+1) + m(t+1)v(t+1),$$

[10] Here and throughout the rest of this chapter we assume that all outside financing takes the form of new issues of shares rather than of "borrowing." Nothing essential is involved in this assumption, because there is, effectively, only one class of securities possible under conditions of certainty and it matters little what name we give it. Only in Part II, after we have developed a framework for dealing with uncertainty, will we be able to consider problems encompassing both debt and equity securities. Note also that no restriction is placed on the sign of $m(t+1)$. A negative value would mean simply that the firm is buying back its own shares.

and on substituting for $n(t)v(t + 1)$ in Equation (2.14), we obtain

$$V(t) = \frac{1}{1 + {}_t r_{t+1}} [D(t+1) + V(t+1) - m(t+1)v(t+1)]. \quad (2.15)$$

III. B. The Effects of Dividend Policy on the Market Value of the Shares

To complete the conversion to per firm totals, still one further simplifying substitution is possible. Because sources of funds must equal uses of funds, we know that

$$R(t+1) + m(t+1)v(t+1) = D(t+1) + W(t+1) + I(t+1).$$
$$(2.16)$$

If then we substitute $R(t + 1) - D(t + 1) - W(t + 1) - I(t + 1)$ for $-m(t + 1)v(t + 1)$ in Equation (2.15), the $D(t + 1)$ cancels, and we are left with

$$V(t) = \frac{1}{1 + {}_t r_{t+1}} [R(t+1) - W(t+1) - I(t+1) + V(t+1)].$$
$$(2.17)$$

In words, the total market value of the shares outstanding at the start of period t is completely independent of the dividend to be declared by the directors at period $t + 1$. It depends only on (1) the rate of interest for the period, which is a given, market-determined parameter completely external to any single firm under the assumption of perfect capital markets, on (2) the firm's operating earnings and investment outlays, both assumed to have been determined before any dividend declaration for the period, and finally, on (3) the market value of the shares at the start of $t + 1$, which, like any other market value, depends only on events subsequent to the date of the valuation.

Actually, we can make an even stronger statement about dividends and valuation. By repeating the reasoning above, we can show that $V(t + 1)$, and hence $V(t)$, does not depend on $D(t + 2)$, that $V(t + 2)$, and hence $V(t)$ and $V(t + 1)$, does not depend on $D(t + 3)$, and so on, as far into the future as we care to look. Thus we may conclude that given a firm's operating policies, the particular dividend policy that the directors adopt has no effect whatever on the current market value of the shares or the current wealth of the shareholders.

The first time encountered, this proposition on the irrelevance of dividend policy often has an air of paradox about it. This feeling undoubtedly arises in many cases because the qualification "given a firm's operating policies" tends to be overlooked. An additional cash receipt, after all, would always seem to be welcome to the shareholder, or at least to his wife. But if the firm's production and investment plans for the period have really been firmly and finally determined, the only way for the firm to finance this additional dividend distribution would be to obtain the funds from external sources by selling off rights to part of the future dividends to be paid by the firm. Hence although the shareholder would indeed have received a larger dividend check, he would also find that each of his shares was worth less, ex the dividend, than if the additional dividend had not been paid. Under perfect capital markets, the equal returns principle in Equation (2.12) requires these opposing effects to cancel, the higher dividend being exactly offset by the lower capital gain.

More formally, because the receipts of the firm $R(t+1)$ and the disbursements $W(t+1)$ and $I(t+1)$ are assumed to be given, we see from Equation (2.16) that any change in total dividends $D(t+1)$ implies an equal change in $m(t+1)v(t+1)$, the market value of new securities that must be issued. But the effects of these changes on Equation (2.15) are precisely offsetting: Every increase in $D(t+1)$ implies an equal decrease in $V(t+1) - m(t+1)v(t+1)$, which, it will be recalled, is $n(t)v(t+1)$, the part of the total value of the firm at $t+1$ that accrues, or belongs, to the shares outstanding from t. Or in more familiar terms, changes in the dividends to these shareholders at $t+1$ are matched by equal but offsetting changes in their capital gains at $t+1$, so that the total market value of their holdings, and of the firm, at t is completely unaffected by the dividend decision at $t+1$. The same analysis applies to the receipts, disbursements, and market values of each future period, so that in fact $V(t)$ is independent of the dividend decisions for all future periods.

This result is of critical importance. If current shareholder wealth is independent of dividend decisions for any given set of operating decisions, it follows that the firm's operating decisions can be made in accordance with the market value rule and without concern for its financing decisions. Thus, the assumption of perfect capital markets has led to another fundamental independence proposition or separation principle. Earlier we saw that as long as shareholder tastes conform to the nonsatiation axiom, maximizing shareholder wealth is equivalent to maximizing shareholder utility, so that operating decisions by the firm can be made independently of the details of shareholder tastes. Now we have seen that for a given set of production-investment decisions, the market value of the firm and thus of shareholder wealth is independent of the firm's dividend-financing decisions, so that operating and financing decisions can be made independently of each other and of shareholders' tastes.

III.C. A Graphical Illustration

A graphical illustration of the irrelevance of dividend policy is provided in Figure 2.7.[11] The curve X_1Z, as before, represents the two-period trans-

---

[11] An extensive numerical illustration is provided in the appendix to the present chapter.

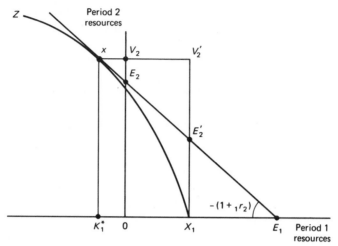

Figure 2.7 Effects of Dividend Policy on Value of Owners' Equity

formation possibilities, with the distance OX_1 representing the resources available in the firm in the first period.[12] Suppose that at the indicated market rate of interest $_1r_2$, the point x represents the set of operating policies chosen by the management. As drawn, this happens to be a tangency point and also to involve a total investment at period 1 of $K_1^* X_1$ that is greater than the OX_1 of resources available from "internal" sources. Some outside financing is thus essential, but management still has considerable choice as to precisely how much.

At one extreme, for example, the management might decide to pay no dividends whatever from current resources and to plow the entire amount OX_1 back into the firm.[13] This would leave the amount $K_1^* O$ to be raised by the sale of shares to outsiders. To see the implications of this decision for shareholders, recall that the current market value of the equity in the firm is completely specified once we know the precise pattern of payments that

[12] Starting the curve at X_1 and allowing it to continue into the negative quadrant provides a "corporate" interpretation to the graph, but in fact the analysis is essentially the same as that in Fig. 2.5.

[13] Note that in referring to this withdrawal as a dividend paid to the period 1 owners, we are using a different timing convention for dividends from that in the algebraic treatments in Sections III.A.2 and III.B. There, it will be recalled, we assumed that dividends would be paid to holders of record as of the previous period, which in this case would be period 0 and which hence would require adding another axis to the graph.

Although the use of different timing conventions at various points throughout the text may require some abrupt adjustments on the part of the reader from time to time, these shifts at least serve to emphasize that the various timing rules are indeed nothing but conventions and that none of the substantive propositions under discussion is in any way dependent on the particular one being used.

will accrue to the current owners in the two periods. Whatever this pattern may be, we can always convert it to a current period 1 value by passing a present value line through the point and recording the intercept on the period 1 axis.

In the present instance, the first coordinate of the payment pattern is clearly zero by virtue of the no-dividend decision. As for the second co-ordinate, note that the distance OV_2 represents the value of the entire firm as of period 2. The present owners, however, are not entitled to all this; they issued K_1^*O of additional shares to finance the firm's operations. Because the new shareholders must receive the market rate of interest on their investment, the value of their holdings at period 2 must be $E_2V_2 = K_1^*O(1 + {}_1r_2)$, leaving OE_2 for the present owners. (In essence, the firm, on behalf of its current shareholders, has borrowed down the present value line from point x to point E_2.) The current market value of the payment pattern to the original owners provided by point E_2 is indicated by point E_1—the same point, of course, as obtained by passing a present value line through the management decision point x.

Suppose now that instead of paying no dividends during period 1, the management had decided to go the other extreme and to pay out to the current shareholders the entire amount of currently available resources OX_1. Then to achieve the required level of investment $K_1^*X_1$, it would be necessary to float exactly this much in a new issue of shares. But this would imply, in turn, that the claim of the new shareholders next period will be $K_1^*X_1(1 + {}_1r_2) = E_2'V_2'$. (In essence, the firm, on behalf of its current share-holders, has borrowed down the present value line from point x to point E_2'.) In this other extreme case as well, the payment pattern to the current shareholders lies on the present value line through the decision point x and hence represents exactly the same value OE_1 for the equity of the current shareholders. For this case, the market value OE_1 is made up of a dividend OX_1 plus the capital value X_1E_1, whereas in the other case there was no current dividend, and OE_1 was simply the value of the shares.

Clearly the same reasoning would apply to any dividend policy between these two extremes; and clearly also the fact that all dividend policies lead to the same present value OE_1 for the equity of the original owners depends only on the assumption that the investment decision indicated by point x be taken as given.[14]

---

[14] Note that the market value of the firm at period 1 implied by the investment decision x is $V_1 = V_2/(1 + {}_1r_2)$, which could be obtained geometrically by drawing a present value line from point V_2 in Fig. 2.7 to the horizontal axis. (Alternatively, V_1 is the value of the equity of the original owners OE_1, plus the minimum quantity K_1^*O that must be raised to finance the decision implied by x.) The decision x maximizes the value of the equity of the original shareholders at period 1 but does not maximize the value of the firm at period 1. The latter maximum would be obtained by pushing investment

III.D. The Independence Proposition Further Considered

III.D.1. The bird-in-the-hand argument

If despite these explanations, a feeling of paradox still remains, it may be due to the seeming conflict between the independence proposition and the very sensible proverb that a bird in the hand is worth two in the bush. Any part of the current period earnings not paid out as dividends is presumably being invested by the management in assets that will yield, hopefully, a further stream of future earnings. Under real-world conditions, however, there is always considerable uncertainty attached to this future stream, and it thus seems natural to suppose that there may well be cases in which, given the investments that management has in mind, the stockholders would prefer the certainty of an immediate cash payment to the problematical future gains that might be obtained from entrusting these funds to the management.

Because all formal consideration of uncertainty has been assigned to Part II, we must, of course, defer until then the presentation of a constructive proof that the value of the shares remains independent of its dividend policy, given the firm's operating policies, even outside the framework of perfect certainty.[15] Actually, however, the full apparatus should not be necessary for readers to see why the bird-in-the-hand analogy breaks down. A review of the assumptions and the key steps in the proof should make clear that the independence proposition does not require stockholders to be indifferent as between a present dividend and a future dividend or capital gain. It says, rather, that once management is committed to undertake and finance a given investment program, an increase in the dividends in any period will simply lead to a corresponding reduction in the ex-dividend value of the shares in the same period. It may be, for example, that even with the

---

to the point where the marginal return, that is, the slope of the transformation function, was zero. Thus the market value rule for current decisions within a firm applies to the market value of the equity of the current owners and not to the total market value of the firm.

[15] To anticipate a bit, the proof depends critically on precisely the same two assumptions as in the certainty case. The first is nonsatiation of wants, that is, the assumption that more wealth is preferred to less, regardless of the form in which it accrues. (In some of the literature on valuation for which this book is intended to serve as an introduction, this assumption is referred to as "rational behavior," but we have here tried to avoid such emotion-laden terms.) The second is the assumption of perfect capital markets, in the broad sense of the term in which tax differentials on different sources of income are also ruled out. In practice, of course, many countries, including the United States, place substantially lower taxes on capital gains than on dividends. Where this is true, the value of the shares is not independent of the dividend policy, but it is still true at least that if the other assumptions continue to hold, paying or raising a dividend cannot increase the value of the shares, given the firm's investment policy.

old dividend, the stockholders were destined to suffer capital losses for the period. If so, raising the dividend would make these losses larger than they would otherwise have been by the exact amount of the dividend increase (or equivalently, by the value of the additional shares that would have to be sold to raise the funds to pay the additional dividends).[16]

III.D.2. Dividend policy and the internal rate of return

Still another reason for the seemingly paradoxical flavor of the independence proposition is its denial of the existence of a unique "optimal" dividend policy for the firm. This denial seems to fly in the face of the commonsensical notion that, although the directors might well be justified in withholding funds when the firm had higher-yielding investment alternatives than the shareholders, they could hardly be acting optimally in withholding funds when the owners actually had, or even only thought that they had, the better opportunities. The point having been made, it is often then illustrated by reference to the celebrated case of a well-known, autocratically managed mail-order house in the years immediately following the Second World War. This company is supposed to have plowed back its earnings into low-yield liquid assets in anticipation of an imminent major depression and to have persisted in this policy long after its competitors and the investing public generally had come to regard such an event as improbable in the extreme. Eventually, however, a palace revolution occurred in which the old management was toppled. The new management promised to end the hoarding and to follow a more generous dividend policy whereupon, at least according to legend, the price of the shares rose from its depressed and discouraged level to a glorious new high.

Quite apart from any questions of fact, and from the always treacherous business of *post hoc, ergo propter hoc* reasoning about stock prices, it should be amply clear by now that tales of this kind, even if true, would in no way conflict with the irrelevance proposition. There is only an appearance of conflict because of the failure once again to distinguish adequately between an optimal dividend policy and an optimal production and investment policy. For if the stock of the mail-order company was indeed depressed by the policies of the management, it was surely the policy of investing in unproductive liquid hoards that should bear the onus. The unwarrantedly

---

[16] If the ex-dividend value of the shares did not drop off *pari passu* with the increase in the dividends, given the firm's investment policy, then Ponzi schemes could be successful. For the benefit of readers under fifty, the notorious Charles Ponzi was a "performance-minded" money manager of the 1920s, who promised and, for a time, apparently delivered very high cash returns to investors in his company. He did it, until the bubble burst, by using the proceeds of sales of new securities to pay the interest and dividends on the old.

low price, in other words, cannot be blamed on a nonoptimal, overconservative dividend policy unless, of course, one is also prepared to argue that the shares would have been less depressed if management had chosen to finance the same level of hoards from new stock issues rather than from retained earnings.

III.E. Some Equivalent Alternative Valuation Formulas

The analysis in the previous sections can also serve to make clear the essential emptiness of the long-standing controversy in the finance literature over whether the market "really" capitalizes the dividends received by the shareholder or the earnings generated by the firm. For the two approaches, provided only that they are consistently carried through, are easily seen to be entirely equivalent.

III.E.1. The stream of dividends approach

If, for example, we wish to focus on the stream of dividend payments, we can use Equation (2.13) as the basis of the valuation formula. Because this equation holds for all t, setting $t = 0$ permits us to express $v(0)$ in terms of $d(1)$ and $v(1)$, which in turn can be expressed in terms of $d(2)$ and $v(2)$, and so on, up to any arbitrary terminal period T.[17] Carrying out these substitutions, and assuming, for simplicity only, that the one-period market rate of interest has the same value r in all periods, we obtain

$$v(0) = \sum_{t=1}^{T} \frac{d(t)}{(1 + r)^t} + \frac{v(T)}{(1 + r)^T} \tag{2.18}$$

as an expression for the present or market value of a share. Equilibrium of the capital markets requires, of course, that $v(0)$ converge to a finite limit as T approaches infinity. But this requires that the remainder term $v(T)/(1 + r)^T$ converge to zero, which is to say nothing more than that beyond some point in time $v(T)$, if it continues to grow at all, it does so at a rate less than r per period.[18] With these additional restrictions, the

---

[17] Note that for the remainder of the present chapter we follow the practice of most of the literature on valuation and take the "present" as being period 0 rather than period 1 as in Chapter 1.

[18] Suppose, on the contrary, that $v(T)$ grows at a rate $q > r$. Then

$$\frac{v(T)}{(1 + r)^T} = \frac{v(0)(1 + q)^T}{(1 + r)^T} = v(0) \left(\frac{1 + q}{1 + r}\right)^T,$$

which approaches infinity as $T \to \infty$, and the price of a share is infinite. The economic implications of the statement that in equilibrium q must be less than r, that is, the price of a share must be finite, are considered in more detail later.

expression for the present value of a share simplifies to

$$v(0) = \sum_{t=1}^{\infty} \frac{d(t)}{(1+r)^t}. \tag{2.19a}$$

We earlier showed that the market value of the firm and that of a share at the beginning of any period are independent of the dividend decisions of all subsequent periods. In terms of Equation (2.13), a change in $d(t+1)$ is matched by an equal but offsetting change in $v(t+1)$. In terms of the dividend approach to valuation, this translates into the statement that a change in $d(t+1)$ is accompanied by an equal but offsetting change in the present value of dividends subsequent to $t+1$, because $v(t+1)$ is, after all, just the present value of these subsequent dividends. Or in other words, dividend policy affects the "time shape" of the dividend stream but not its present value.

Note also that the total value of the firm $V(0)$ is

$$V(0) = n(0)v(0) = \sum_{t=1}^{\infty} \frac{n(0)d(t)}{(1+r)^t}, \tag{2.19b}$$

the present value of the total dividends to be paid in future periods to the shares outstanding at period 0, and not to total dividends paid in all future periods.

III.E.2. Cash flow and earnings approaches

Alternatively, if we wish to focus attention on the stream of earnings generated in the firm, we can start from Equation (2.17). Making the corresponding successive substitutions for the $V(t)$ and adopting the same convention with respect to the vanishing of the remainder, we obtain

$$V(0) = \sum_{t=1}^{\infty} \frac{R(t) - W(t) - I(t)}{(1+r)^t} \tag{2.20}$$

as an expression for the present, or market, value of the shares currently outstanding in terms of the stream of "net cash flows" generated in the firm.[19] For further compactness of notation, as well as to facilitate comparison with some of the analogous treatments in the standard literature,

---

[19] The substitutions involved in obtaining Equation (2.20) from Equation (2.17) are precisely those presented verbally on pp. 80–81 following Equation (2.17), where they were used to derive the conclusion that, given the firm's production-investment decisions, its current market value is independent of all future dividend decisions. This conclusion is, perhaps, now easier to grasp directly from Equation (2.20), which includes only the variables $R(t)$, $W(t)$, and $I(t)$ generated by the firm's production-investment decisions, and the market interest rate r, which, in a perfect capital market, is unaffected by any actions of the firm.

we define $X(t) \equiv R(t) - W(t)$ as the "net operating cash flow" at period t. Substituting, we then have the familiar

$$V(0) = \sum_{t=1}^{\infty} \frac{X(t) - I(t)}{(1 + r)^t} \qquad (2.21)$$

as the basic formula for the current market value of a firm.

To summarize, the dividend valuation formula (2.19) is derived from the market equilibrium condition (2.13); the net cash flow valuation formula (2.21) is derived from Equation (2.17), which is in turn derived from Equation (2.13). Thus the dividend and net cash flow approaches must lead to equivalent expressions for the market value of the firm.

Note, however, that Equation (2.21) does not say that the value of the firm can be expressed simply as the sum of discounted "cash" earnings $X(t)$. The reason for the failure of the latter approach is not, as sometimes asserted, the fact that the corporation is an entity entirely separate from the owners and whose earnings cannot be withdrawn at will by the owners. Nor does the difficulty arise from the fact that the earnings in Equation (2.21) are the cash earnings $X(t) = R(t) - W(t)$, rather than the accounting earnings. Because the latter concept would differ from the former in the present context only by the amount of the depreciation and similar arbitrary accounting adjustments, we can easily convert Equation (2.21) to run explicitly in terms of accounting rather than cash earnings. In particular, if we let $Z(t)$ = the depreciation estimate of the firm's accountants at period t, $A(t) = R(t) - W(t) - Z(t)$ = accounting earnings, and $N(t) = I(t) - Z(t)$ = net investment in the sense of the net change in the accounting book value of assets, we can reexpress Equation (2.21) as

$$V(0) = \sum_{t=1}^{\infty} \frac{A(t) - N(t)}{(1 + r)^t}. \qquad (2.22)$$

Rather, the difficulty with an earnings approach arises from the fact that in order to obtain the indicated future earnings stream, by either definition, additional resources must be committed over time to the production process. If these resources are obtained from the sale of shares to outsiders, the current owners obviously have to compensate the newcomers for their capital contributions by turning over to them a part of the future earnings stream. And if, on the other hand, the existing shareholders supply the funds themselves by way of reduced dividends or fully subscribed preemptive issues, they must offset against the future earnings the opportunity cost in the form of the interest income that might otherwise have been earned on the funds committed. Under perfect certainty and perfect capital markets the value to the owners of the sacrifice required to obtain the additional capital resources in any period t is precisely equal to the value of these resources $I(t)$, regardless of how they may happen to have been obtained. Thus the relevant quantity to discount in obtaining the market value of the firm is the net cash flow $X(t) - I(t)$.[20]

III.E.3. Investment opportunities, growth, and valuation

Some important additional insights into the valuation process and especially the relation between corporate earnings and investor returns can be obtained by considering certain simplified special cases of the valuation formula (2.21). In particular, suppose that the total investment $I(t)$ made by the management of a firm at the beginning of any period t generated a uniform stream of earnings in perpetuity thereafter at the rate of $100r^*(t)$ percent per period.[21] In terms of previous notation and timing conventions this would mean that we could express the elements of the stream $X(t)$ successively as

$$X(2) = X(1) + r^*(1)I(1),$$

$$X(3) = X(2) + r^*(2)I(2) = X(1) + r^*(1)I(1) + r^*(2)I(2),$$

and so on, or more compactly in general form as

$$X(t) = X(1) + \sum_{\tau=1}^{t-1} r^*(\tau)I(\tau), \qquad t = 2, 3, \ldots \infty. \qquad (2.23)$$

Substituting this expression for $X(t)$ in Equation (2.21) and regrouping

---

[20] Once again, we leave the formal proof as an exercise for readers who feel that they could benefit from some additional practice in manipulating present value expressions. *Hint*: Consider first the case in which the currently existing owners plan to supply all the investment funds themselves. Then the opportunity cost to them of the $I(t)$ that they supply at period t is the loss of earnings of $rI(t)$ per period thereafter, starting, by our conventions, in period $t + 1$. But what will be the present value as of the start of t of the perpetual annuity $rI(t)$ at an interest rate of r per period?

[21] We refer to $r^*(t)$ hereafter as the "rate of return on investment" without pausing at this point to explain its relation to the various other possible senses of this term. These subjects come up in due course in Chap. 3. It may be useful, however, at least to reassure readers that no necessary conflict exists between the market value rule for management decisions and our use of examples in which $r^*(t)$ is not equal to r. Our $r^*(t)$ should be thought of as the average rate of return on the total investment budget $I(t)$, which budget a management following the market value rule would push to the point where the rate of return on the last dollar just equaled the market rate of interest.

Note also that by virtue of the assumption that real assets generate uniform perpetual returns no "depreciation" adjustment is required. Hence, net cash flow from operations and accounting earnings are the same, and we use the terms interchangeably. This perpetuity assumption is, of course, much less restrictive in this context than it may seem. Under certainty and perfect capital markets, it is always possible to find an equivalent perpetuity, that is, one with the same present value, for the firm's earnings no matter what the actual pattern of the cash flow or the age composition of the assets.

the terms yield

$$V(0) = \sum_{t=1}^{\infty} \frac{X(1)}{(1+r)^t} + \sum_{t=1}^{\infty} I(t) \left(\sum_{\tau=t+1}^{\infty} \frac{r^*(t)}{(1+r)^\tau} - \frac{1}{(1+r)^t} \right). \quad (2.24)$$

The first term is nothing more than the present value of a uniform perpetuity of $X(1)$ and is immediately evaluated as $X(1)/r$. As for the second term, consider first the inner summation

$$\sum_{\tau=t+1}^{\infty} \frac{r^*(t)}{(1+r)^\tau}.$$

This, too, is a perpetual uniform annuity but one whose start is deferred to the beginning of period $t+1$, which is to say that we can reduce it to standard form as follows:

$$\sum_{\tau=t+1}^{\infty} \frac{r^*(t)}{(1+r)^\tau} = \frac{1}{(1+r)^t} \sum_{\tau=1}^{\infty} \frac{r^*(t)}{(1+r)^\tau} = \left(\frac{r^*(t)}{r} \right) \frac{1}{(1+r)^t}.$$

The second summation in Equation (2.24) thus becomes

$$\sum_{t=1}^{\infty} I(t) \left[\left(\frac{r^*(t)}{r} \right) \frac{1}{(1+r)^t} - \frac{1}{(1+r)^t} \right] = \sum_{t=1}^{\infty} I(t) \left[\frac{r^*(t) - r}{r} \right] \frac{1}{(1+r)^t},$$

and the complete present value expression can then be written as simply

$$V(0) = \frac{X(1)}{r} + \sum_{t=1}^{\infty} I(t) \left(\frac{r^*(t) - r}{r} \right) \frac{1}{(1+r)^t}. \quad (2.25)$$

   In words, the market value of any firm, under our simplifying specifications, has been expressed as the sum of two components. The first is the capitalized value of the earnings stream produced by the assets that the firm currently holds. We now show that the second is the market value of any opportunities that the firm may have to make additional investments in real assets in the future at terms more favorable than those available to investors in the capital markets.[22] There are many kinds of circumstances that might produce such opportunities to earn "economic rents."[23] Our

---

[22] We always speak here of the internal opportunities as being as or more favorable than the external, simply because this is normally the more relevant circumstance from the economic point of view. Formally, however, an expression such as Equation (2.25) would remain valid even for the case of $r^* < r$, a case that would imply an inefficient, nonoptimal investment policy by the management, as shown in Chap. 3.

[23] Students are often bothered by the assumption of an r^* different from r on the grounds that this conflicts with the equal rate of return principle on which the analysis of valuation under certainty is based. Remember, however, that the assumption of perfect markets, from which the equal rate of return principle was derived, applies to the

concern here, however, is not with their origins but their implications for valuation.

By assumption, any such opportunities in period t generate earnings thereafter of $r^*(t)I(t)$ in perpetuity, a stream whose present value as of period t is $I(t)[r^*(t)]/r$. Subtracting out the cost of the resources necessary to produce this stream of earnings, we have as the net present value or "good will" of these opportunities as of the start of period t the quantity

$$I(t)\left(\frac{r^*(t)}{r}\right) - I(t) = I(t)\left(\frac{r^*(t) - r}{r}\right).$$

The value now (period 0) of these eventual opportunities in period t is thus

$$I(t)\left(\frac{r^*(t) - r}{r}\right)\frac{1}{(1 + r)^t},$$

and the value of all such opportunities in all future periods is the expression given by the summation term in Equation (2.25).

Expression (2.25) might thus be viewed as representing the result of an "investment opportunities" approach to the valuation of the firm. But note that it was initially derived from Equation (2.21), which might be called the net cash flow approach, and Equation (2.21) in turn was shown to be equivalent to the discounted dividend formula (2.19). By now it should be clear that the equivalence of these various valuation formulas is due to the fact that all are ultimately direct implications of the equal rate of return principle expressed by Equation (2.12), which in turn is a direct implication of the assumption of perfect certainty and especially perfect capital markets.[24]

---

capital market and requires only that returns on all securities for any period are equal. It does not necessarily imply the absence of imperfections in the markets for goods or for other resources of a kind that would permit rates of return on investment opportunities within the firm to be greater than the market interest rates on securities. In fact, a major purpose of the analysis here is to show that the market value of a firm's securities always fully reflects the market value of any extraordinary production-investment opportunities, with the result that returns on these securities are always in conformance with the equal rate of return principle.

[24] For those already somewhat familiar with the terminology of the capital budgeting literature, note that for the case $_tr_{t+1} = $ a constant r for all t, expression (2.25) also demonstrates why the "cost of capital," in the sense of the minimum rate of return for acceptable investment projects, is always equal to r. From (2.25) it is easy to see that projects with rates of return greater than r increase the current market value of the firm and that projects with rates of return less than r reduce the current value of the firm, because in this case the second term in (2.25) is negative. We emphasize, however, that the notion of a cost of capital as a cutoff rate for investment is only meaningful when one-period interest rates are constant over time. Otherwise there is no single rate with which the firm can compare the rates of return on its investment opportunities, so that in making its investment decisions, the firm must rely directly on the market value rule.

In thus relating future investment opportunities to current valuations, formula (2.25) should help, among other things, to clarify the essential meaning of those much abused terms in the valuation literature, "growth company" and "growth stocks." If a growth company is defined as one on which the market places a high value in relation to current earnings, that is, one for which $V(0)/X(1) > 1/r$, what puts it in this category cannot be simply the fact that its assets and earnings are expected to grow in the future. It is also necessary that the returns on the additional assets to be acquired by the firm be greater than those obtainable by purchasing outstanding shares in the market. For if the yield r^* on the additional investment is no greater than r, the second term in (2.25) is zero, and the firm's price/earnings ratio remains an unglamorous $1/r$ no matter how rapid the expansion in the size of the company.

Note also that in defining a growth company as one with substantial opportunities to earn above-normal returns, the returns being spoken of are those at the level of the firm, not of the investor. For no matter how profitable the future investment opportunities of the firm may be, the equal return principle in Equation (2.12) continues to hold in the capital market. The full value of the special opportunities is reflected in the current price of the shares, and investors buying into these growth companies earn no more, and no less, than if they had bought into less fortunately situated firms.[25]

III.F. Growth Potential and Stockholder Returns

It should, we hope, be easy enough by now to accept the seemingly paradoxical conclusion that stockholder returns will be the same regardless of the firm's growth potential or actual earnings stream, provided only that all the relevant facts about the stream are fully known to the investing public. Nevertheless, it may be useful at this point to take a further and more detailed look at the connections between the streams of returns at the two levels. In doing so, it is convenient to make use of a simple and popular, but also very treacherous, specialization of Equation (2.21) that may be called the constant growth model.

III.F.1. The constant growth model

Specifically, we assume that in every period t the firm's investment $I(t)$ bears some given proportion k to its earnings $X(t)$ for the period and that

---

[25] On the other hand, somebody at some point in time must have received a windfall gain, presumably the promoters when the firm was organized or at least first went public. There is, however, no real inconsistency with the equal rate of return principle as long as we continue to treat such windfalls as unique events which have already occurred in the past and which will not occur again during the time span to be covered by our analysis.

the yield of every period's investment is a constant $100r^*$ percent per period in every period thereafter. These definitions imply in turn that we may express the earnings in any period t as

$$
\begin{aligned}
X(t) &= X(t-1) + r^*I(t-1) \\
&= X(t-1)(1+kr^*) \\
&= X(1)(1+kr^*)^{t-1},
\end{aligned}
\tag{2.26}
$$

where kr^* is the (constant) rate of growth of total firm earnings per period. Substituting $kX(t)$ for the $I(t)$ of the valuation equation (2.25), we have

$$
\begin{aligned}
V(0) &= \frac{X(1)}{r} + \sum_{t=1}^{\infty} kX(t) \left(\frac{r^*-r}{r}\right)\frac{1}{(1+r)^t} \\
&= \frac{X(1)}{r} + kX(1)\left(\frac{r^*-r}{r}\right)\sum_{t=1}^{\infty}\frac{(1+kr^*)^{t-1}}{(1+r)^t} \\
&= \frac{X(1)}{r}\left[1 + \frac{k(r^*-r)}{1+kr^*}\sum_{t=1}^{\infty}\left(\frac{1+kr^*}{1+r}\right)^t\right].
\end{aligned}
\tag{2.27}
$$

As long as the growth rate kr^* is less than the rate of interest r—and recall in this connection the discussion in Section II.E.1 of the vanishing remainder term—the infinite summation in the brackets converges to a finite limit that can easily be shown to be $(1+kr^*)/(r-kr^*)$.[26] Making this substitution and simplifying, we thus obtain

$$
\begin{aligned}
V(0) &= \frac{X(1)}{r}\left[1 + \frac{k(r^*-r)}{r-kr^*}\right] \\
&= \frac{X(1)(1-k)}{r-kr^*}
\end{aligned}
\tag{2.28}
$$

as an expression for the value of the currently outstanding shares in terms of the rate of growth of the firm's earnings.[27]

---

[26] Readers who wish additional practice in working with present value and related formulas will again find it a useful exercise to derive this expression. By way of a hint note that if we define a new variable $\beta = (1+kr^*)/(1+r)$, it is easy to see that the summation in question is nothing more than the sum of a simple geometric progression. Those who have forgotten the formula should be able to reconstruct it after rereading Section II.B.2 in Chap. 1.

[27] Note that, because the value of the firm must be finite, in the constant growth model the condition $kr^* < r$ is a necessary condition of market equilibrium. It simply says that in equilibrium the market rate of interest must be such that no firm has opportunities into the indefinite future to invest the proportion k of each period's earnings at a rate r^* so that $kr^* > r$. Alternatively, because Equation (2.28) applies to the market value

Note that Equation (2.28), perhaps even more dramatically than its more general counterpart (2.25), makes clear the fundamental distinction between mere expansion ($k > 0$) and true "growth potential" ($r^* > r$). For when $r^* = r$, the denominator of Equation (2.28) is $r(1 - k)$; the $(1 - k)$ thus cancels in the numerator and denominator, leaving only $V(1) = X(1)/r$, although the rate of expansion kr of the firm's earnings, and of its total value, may be quite substantial.

III.F.2. The growth of total earnings and the growth of dividends and price per share

Up to this point, the valuation formulas involving growth have focused on events at the level of the firm. It is a relatively straightforward matter, however, to develop the corresponding formulas running in terms of the growth of dividends and the price of individual shares. In particular, consider a share of stock of the constant growth firm whose dividend payment at period 1 is $d(1)$ and whose dividend grows thereafter at a constant rate of g per period. Substituting $d(1)(1 + g)^{t-1}$ for each $d(t)$ in the stream of dividends valuation formula (2.19a), we obtain

$$v(0) = \sum_{t=1}^{\infty} \frac{d(1)(1 + g)^{t-1}}{(1 + r)^t} = \frac{d(1)}{1 + g} \sum_{t=1}^{\infty} \left(\frac{1 + g}{1 + r}\right)^t$$

$$= \frac{d(1)}{r - g} \tag{2.29}$$

as an expression for the value of a share in terms of the current dividend and its rate of growth, assuming, of course $g < r$, so that the summation is finite.

Because an expression of the form (2.29) holds for the price of the share in every time period and because the dividend term in the numerator grows over time at the rate of g per period, it follows that the price per share also grows at the rate of g per period. To say that the dividend and the price per share grow at the same rate is not to suggest, of course, that dividends and capital gains contribute equally to investor returns. On the contrary, as can readily be seen by rewriting Equation (2.29) in the form

$$r = \frac{d(1)}{v(0)} + g, \tag{2.30}$$

---

of each period, in general

$$V(t) = \frac{X(t + 1)(1 - k)}{r - kr^*} = \frac{X(1)(1 + kr^*)^t(1 - k)}{r - kr^*} = V(0)(1 + kr^*)^t,$$

so that the condition $kr^* < r$ says that in equilibrium the rate of interest must be such that the market value of any constant growth firm increases at a rate $kr^* < r$.

the relative contribution of dividends and capital gains to investor returns depends on the relation between g and r. When g is large relative to r, the current price is large relative to the current dividend, and the relative contribution of the immediate cash payment to the total yield is correspondingly small. As g gets smaller in relation to r, the cash component looms larger; and in the special case of $g = 0$, the yield per period would consist entirely of the cash return. But all this is, of course, just the equal rate of return principle again.

As for what determines the value of g in relation to r, we know in a general way from the previous discussion that the key factors are the growth potential of the firm and the financial, that is, dividend, policy that the firm chooses to follow. More precisely, let $k_r =$ the proportion of total earnings retained by the firm in each period. Hence, for dividends we have $D(t) = X(t)(1 - k_r)$, where $(1 - k_r)$ is the so-called "dividend payout ratio." And let $k_e = k - k_r =$ the amount of external capital raised per period by the flotation of new shares, expressed as a proportion of total earnings. If we let $n(0)$, as before, represent the number of shares outstanding at the start of period 0, then by multiplying both sides of Equation (2.29) by $n(0)$, we obtain as one expression for the value of all the currently outstanding shares

$$V(0) = n(0)v(0) = \frac{n(0)d(1)}{r - g} = \frac{D(1)}{r - g} = \frac{X(1)(1 - k_r)}{r - g}.$$

But from Equation (2.28) we also have

$$V(0) = \frac{X(1)(1 - k)}{r - kr^*} = \frac{X(1)(1 - (k_e + k_r))}{r - kr^*}.$$

Equating the two expressions for $V(0)$ and solving for g yields

$$g = kr^* \frac{1 - k_r}{1 - k} - k_e r \frac{1}{1 - k} \tag{2.31}$$

as an explicit expression for the growth rate of dividends, and also the capital gain yield on the shares per period, in terms of the firm's growth rate and its dividend policy.

Note that in the extreme case in which all financing is internal ($k_e = 0$ and $k_r = k$), we have simply $g = kr^*$; that is, the growth rate of dividends per share is exactly the same as the growth rate of the firm itself. In all other cases, however, the growth rate of dividends is less than that of the firm. The reason, of course, is that if new shares are to be issued each period to finance the growth of the firm, the current stockholders must give up part of their claim to the future stream of earnings that the investment generates. They get a higher initial dividend than if the directors had elected to finance all the firm's growth from retained earnings, but their dividend income grows more slowly as the future pie of total dividends gets shared among a larger and larger group of stockholders. The minimum value for g is reached at the other extreme, where all financing is external and where Equation (2.31) thus reduces to

$$g = \frac{k}{1-k}\,[r^* - r].\qquad(2.32)$$

Note that for a true growth company, that is, one for which $r^* > r$, g is positive, and the stream of dividends per share grows over time, although the firm is paying out all its earnings in dividends.

III.F.3. Corporate earnings and investor returns

A further question of some interest is that of the relation between the total earnings of the firm in any period and the total return, dividends plus capital gains, to the shareholders. If we let $G(t + 1)$ be the total capital gains during period t to stockholders of record as of the start of t, we know that

$$_t p_{t+1} V(t) \equiv D(t + 1) + G(t + 1) = X(t + 1)(1 - k_r) + gV(t).\qquad(2.33)$$

Substituting the expression for g in Equation (2.31) and the expression for $V(t)$ implied by Equation (2.28) into the expression above and simplifying yields

$$D(t + 1) + G(t + 1) = X(t + 1)\left[\frac{r(1 - k)}{r - kr^*}\right].\qquad(2.34)$$

Stockholder returns in the market, in other words, are not in general the same as the returns $X(t + 1)$ generated within the firm. Equality between $X(t + 1)$ and $D(t + 1) + G(t + 1)$ occurs only in the case in which the firm has no special growth opportunities in our sense. Where such growth opportunities do exist, however, the expression in brackets on the right-hand side of Equation (2.34) is greater than unity, and total stockholder returns are greater than the earnings of the corporation.

Further insight into this seemingly paradoxical conclusion can be obtained by focusing on the relation between the earnings retained at the corporate level and the capital gains accruing at the shareholder level. Subtracting $D(t + 1)$ from the left-hand side of Equation (2.34) and $(1 - k_r)X(t + 1)$ from the right, we obtain

$$G(t + 1) = k_r X(t + 1) + kX(t + 1)\left[\frac{r^* - r}{r - kr^*}\right].\qquad(2.35)$$

The first term $k_r X(t + 1)$ is just retained earnings at $t + 1$. But total shareholder capital gains are equal to retained earnings only when the firm has no growth opportunities $(r^* = r)$. Otherwise, when $r^* > r$, total shareholder capital gains are in excess of retained earnings by the quantity $kX(t + 1)(r^* - r)/(r - kr^*)$, which, interestingly and perhaps not unexpectedly, is the interest on the total market value at t of the firm's future investment opportunities.[28] Finally, note that if there is growth, capital gains are still earned even in the event that all the firm's earnings are declared in dividends, that is, $k_r = 0$.

IV. SUMMARY

In this chapter, we have sought to extend the simple wealth allocation model in Chapter 1 to allow for the carry-over of resources by way of commodities as well as by securities, and, in particular, by the investment of resources in firms. The extension would have been relatively straight-forward if all firms were simple, owner-managed enterprises. But difficulties arose as soon as we turned to questions of decision making in corporations in which the decision-making power had been delegated to managers and in which there were typically many different owners with very different tastes and resources.

We saw, however, that in at least one special set of circumstances it was possible to surmount these difficulties and develop an "objective" decision-making criterion for a management presumed to be acting on behalf of and in the best interests of the owners. In particular, we showed that under perfect capital markets, a policy of maximizing the current market value of the shares held by the present owners would lead to the same set of operating and investment decisions that each owner would have adopted if he had taken responsibility for the decisions himself.

After discussing briefly some of the implications and limitations of this solution to the criterion problem for management decisions, we turned our attention to the market value itself and the factors that determine it. Special emphasis was given to the role of dividend policy as the nexus between the firm and its owners, and we derived and discussed at some

---

[28] To see this result note that, from Equation (2.28), in the constant growth model the value of the firm at the beginning of t can be written

$$V(t) = \frac{X(t + 1)}{r} + \frac{X(t + 1)}{r}\left[\frac{k(r^* - r)}{r - kr^*}\right].$$

The first term is the market value at t of earnings produced by investments made at t and earlier periods; the second term is the market value of investments in later periods. Multiplying the second term by the rate of interest r gives $kX(t + 1)(r^* - r)/(r - kr)^*$ as the interest on the market value of future investment opportunities.

length the fundamental, but somewhat paradoxical, proposition that dividend policy per se is irrelevant to the current market value of the shares.

We then went on to discuss what does count in valuation and to develop a variety of useful alternative approaches to valuation and valuation formulas. With these results on valuation in hand, on the theoretical level there remains only to illustrate how the market value criterion can be applied to specific problems of managerial decision making. It is to this task that we turn in Chapter 3 and with it conclude the discussion of certainty models and their applications in finance. First, however, we present in the appendix two numerical examples that should provide additional experience and insights into the preceding theoretical analyses.

REFERENCES

The fundamental double-tangency solution in Section I for an individual with both capital market and productive opportunities is due to

Fisher, Irving, *The Theory of Investment.* New York: Augustus M. Kelley, Publishers, 1965. Reprinted from the original 1930 edition.

Some of the problems discussed in Section II involving the extension of the basic model to corporations in which decision-making powers have been delegated to managers were first raised by

Berle, A. A., and Gardiner C. Means, *The Modern Corporation and Private Property.* New York: The Macmillan Company, 1932.

Among the leading recent critics of the market value rule as descriptive of actual management behavior have been

Baumol, William J., *Business Behavior, Value and Growth.* New York: The Macmillan Company, 1959.

Marris, Robin, *The Economic Theory of "Managerial" Capitalism.* London: Macmillan & Co., Ltd., 1964.

and

Williamson, Oliver E., "Managerial Discretion and Business Behavior," *American Economic Review,* vol. 53 (December 1963), pp. 1032–1057.

A recent survey of the issues and the evidence on the descriptive validity of the market value rule is that of

Larner, Robert J., *Management Control and the Large Corporation.* New York: Dunellen Publishing Co., 1970.

The treatment of market valuation and dividend policy in Section III is based on that in

Miller, Merton H., and Franco Modigliani, "Dividend Policy, Growth and the Valuation of Shares," *Journal of Business,* vol. 34, no. 4 (October 1961), pp. 411–432.

The leading academic critique of the dividend independence proposition in Section III.A is that of

Gordon, Myron J., *The Investment, Financing and Valuation of the Corporation.* Homewood, Ill.: Richard D. Irwin, Inc., 1962.

A briefer and more sharply focused presentation of his bird-in-the-hand argument is given in

Gordon, Myron J., "Optimal Investment and Financing Policy," *Journal of Finance,* vol. 18 (May 1963), pp. 264–272.

There have been innumerable empirical studies of the effects of dividend policy on the value of shares. A survey stressing some of the pitfalls is that of

Friend, Irwin, and Marshall Puckett, "Dividends and Stock Prices," *American Economic Review,* vol. 44, no. 3 (September 1964), pp. 656–682.

The literature on growth and valuation is also extensive. A typical practitioner-oriented treatment with an extensive further bibliography is that of

Wendt, Paul F., "Current Growth Stock Valuation Methods," *Financial Analysts Journal,* vol. 21, no. 2 (March–April 1965), pp. 91–103.

APPENDIX

Valuation Formulas:
Some Numerical Illustrations

I. FINANCIAL POLICY, RETURNS, AND VALUATION

Consider a firm with initial, and perpetual, earnings $X(1)$ =\$100 per period and suppose, further, that its investment policy involves investing \$100 at the beginning of each of periods 1, 2, and 3. Each year's investment produces perpetual annual cash earnings of \$20 per period, with the earnings commencing at the beginning of the period following the investment. Thus the cash earnings of the firm will be \$120 at period 2, \$140 at period 3, and \$160 in all subsequent periods. The one-period market interest rates for periods 0 to 2 are, respectively, 1 percent, 5 percent, and 10 percent; for all subsequent periods the rate is 20 percent.

Because for $t > 3$, $_t r_{t+1} = 0.2$, and $X(t+1) - I(t+1) = X(t+1) = 160, the market value of the firm at the beginning of period 3, and all subsequent periods, can easily be computed from Equation (2.21) as[1]

$$V(3) = \sum_{\tau=1}^{\infty} \frac{[X(3+\tau) - I(3+\tau)]}{(1.2)^\tau} = \sum_{\tau=1}^{\infty} \frac{160}{(1.2)^\tau} = \frac{160}{0.2} = \$800.$$

[1] Recall that

$$\sum_{\tau=1}^{\infty} \frac{1}{(1+r)^\tau} = \frac{1}{r}.$$

From Equation (2.17) the value of the firm at the beginning of period 2 can then be computed as

$$V(2) = \frac{1}{1 + {_2r_3}} [X(3) - I(3) + V(3)]$$

$$= \frac{1}{1.1} [140 - 100 + 800] = \$763.63,$$

and, of course, Equation (2.17) can also be used to compute $V(1)$ and $V(0)$.

We now examine the return each period to a share of stock in the firm under two extreme assumptions concerning financial or dividend policy. The relevant numbers are presented in Table 1. Table 1a shows the values each period of variables that are not affected by financial policy. At some point the reader should indeed convince himself that the values of $V(t)$, $t = 0, 1, 2, \ldots$, are the same when computed by means of Equation (2.19) as when computed by Equation (2.21). Table 1b presents the values of the variables needed to compute the return each period on a share under the assumption that all investment is financed internally, that is, with retained earnings; Table 1c presents the values of the same variables under the assumption that all earnings are paid out as dividends, so that new investments are financed entirely externally, that is, by new shares.

When investments are financed entirely with retained earnings, the computation of the return on a share each period is simple. Total dividends $D(t)$ are just earnings minus investment, $X(t) - I(t)$. Because no new shares are issued, $m(t) = 0$ and $n(t) = 1000$ for all t. Thus for each period the price per share $v(t) = V(t)/1000$ and dividends per share $d(t) = D(t)/1000$.

The arithmetic becomes more involved, however, when investments are financed entirely with new shares. Total dividends $D(t)$ are then just total earnings $X(t)$. The price of a share at the beginning of any period can be obtained by noting that

$$v(0) = \frac{V(0)}{n(0)} = \frac{738.92}{1000} = \$0.7389,$$

$$m(t) \cdot v(t) = I(t),$$

and

$$v(t + 1) = \frac{V(t + 1) - m(t + 1)v(t + 1)}{n(t)}.$$

The number of new shares issued at the beginning of period $t + 1$ can then be computed as

$$m(t + 1) = \frac{m(t + 1)v(t + 1)}{v(t + 1)} = \frac{I(t + 1)}{v(t + 1)}.$$

The first important point to note is that for both financial policies considered in Table 1 the price per share at the beginning of period 0, $v(0)$, is $0.7389, although the time shape of the stream of dividends per share is much different for the two policies. Indeed when investments are financed with retained earnings, the undiscounted sum of dividends per share for a long period of time greatly exceeds the dividends paid on a share when investments are financed with new shares. With internal (retained earnings)

TABLE 1a

The Initial Data

$t =$	0	1	2	3	≥ 4
$I(t)$		100	100	100	0
$X(t)$		100	120 ·	140	160
$r^t{}_{t+1}$	0.01	0.05	0.10	0.20	0.20
$V(t)$	738.92	746.31	763.63	800	800

TABLE 1b

Results When Investments Are Financed through Retained Earnings

$D(t)$		0	20	40	160
$v(t)$	0.7389	0.7463	0.7636	0.80	0.80
$m(t)v(t)$		0	0	0	0
$n(t)$	1000	1000	1000	1000	1000
$m(t)$		0	0	0	0
$d(t)$		0	0.0200	0.0400	0.1600
$v(t+1) - v(t)$	0.0074	0.0173	0.0364	0	0

TABLE 1c

Results When Investments Are Financed Entirely through New Shares

$D(t)$		100	120	140	160
$v(t)$	0.7389	0.6463	0.5747	0.5268	0.5268
$m(t)v(t)$		100	100	100	0
$n(t)$	1000	1154.7	1328.7	1518.5	1518.5
$m(t)$		154.7	174.0	189.8	0
$d(t)$		0.1000	0.1039	0.1054	0.1054
$v(t+1) - v(t)$	-0.0926	-0.0716	-0.0479	0	0

financing, however, dividends per share in the early periods are much lower than with external (new share) financing, so that at the beginning of time period 0 the present values, that is, market prices $v(0)$, of the dividend streams obtained under the two financing alternatives are equal.

In addition, it is important to note, and the reader should check, that under both financial policies the one-period return on a share during any given period is equal to the market rate of interest $_t r_{t+1}$ for the period; that is,

$$\frac{d(t+1) + v(t+1) - v(t)}{v(t)} = {}_t r_{t+1}.$$

Thus the returns under both financial policies are 0.01 in period 0, 0.05 in period 1, 0.1 in period 2, and 0.2 thereafter. Moreover, the returns on the shares are equal to the market interest rates in spite of the fact that the firm has opportunities to invest, at least for three periods, at rates of return greater than market interest rates. With perfect capital markets, the market prices at all times take account of future investment opportunities. As a result, the returns on the shares are just equal to the market interest rates.

Although the rates of return period by period are the same with the two financial policies, in the early periods the distribution of returns between dividends and capital gains is different. In fact, for the particular example being considered, with external financing there are only capital losses and never gains. Because the initial price per share $v(0)$ is the same under both financial policies, this implies that, for $t > 0$, $v(t)$ is lower when investments are financed externally than when financed internally. This results, of course, from the fact that when new shares are issued, the part of the total value of the firm in future periods that accrues to the current shareholders is lower than when investments are financed with retained earnings.

The reader can convince himself, however, that by relending the difference between dividends per share in each of the first three periods under the two financial policies, the stream of dividends and capital gains obtained when investments are financed internally can be transformed into the stream obtained when investments are financed with new shares. Or, vice versa, by selling part of his holdings at the end of each of the first three periods, the stream of dividends and capital gains obtained when investments are financed internally can be transformed into the stream of dividends and capital losses obtained when investments are financed externally. But these opportunities are, of course, just implications of the fact that with perfect certainty and perfect capital markets, any stream of net cash flows with present value $0.7389 at the beginning of period 0 can, by borrowing or lending in the market, be transformed into any other stream with present value $0.7389.

II. AN EXAMPLE USING THE CONSTANT GROWTH MODEL

We now consider a numerical example based on the constant growth model. The example involves three different firms, all with the same level of current earnings $X(1) = 100$, the same proportion of income invested each period, $k = 0.4$, the same return on investment opportunities, $r^* = 0.2$, but different financial policies. The purpose of the example is to examine the effects of financial policy on dividends, stock prices, and returns to shareholders. The relevant information is summarized in Table 2.

Expression (2.28) can be used to compute the market value of each of the three firms at the beginning of any time period. Because (2.28) does not contain variables that depend on financial policy, the market values of the three firms are equal at any point in time. For example, at the beginning of time period $t = 0$,

$$V(0) = \frac{X(1)(1-k)}{r - kr^*} = \frac{100(0.6)}{0.10 - (0.4)(0.2)} = \frac{60}{0.02} = \$3000$$

for all three firms.

We now examine the returns per share provided by each firm. Firm I follows the policy of financing all investment with retained earnings; that is, $k_r = k = 0.4$ and $k_e = 0$. Investment at the beginning of period 1 is

$$I(1) = kX(1) = 0.40(100) = \$40.$$

Because firm I finances all its investment with retained earnings, total dividends and dividends per share are respectively

$$D(1) = X(1) - I(1) = 100 - 40 = \$60,$$

and

$$d(1) = \frac{D(1)}{n(0)} = \frac{60}{1000} = \$0.06.$$

TABLE 2

Firm	I	II	III
X(1)	100	100	100
r	0.10	0.10	0.10
r*	0.20	0.20	0.20
k	0.40	0.40	0.40
k_r	0.40	0	0.20
k_e	0	0.40	0.20
V(0)	$3000	$3000	3000
I(1)	$ 40	$ 40	$ 40
n(0)	1000	1000	1000
v(0)	$ 3.00	$ 3.00	$ 3.00

For all three firms total earnings at the beginning of period 2 are

$$X(2) = X(1) + kr^*X(1) = 100 + 8 = \$108,$$

so that $$V(1) = \frac{X(2)(1 - k)}{r - kr^*} = \frac{108(0.6)}{0.10 - 0.4(0.2)} = \frac{64.8}{0.02} = \$3240.$$

Thus for firm I the price of a share of stock at the beginning of $t = 1$ is

$$v(1) = \frac{V(1)}{n(1)} = \frac{3240}{1000} = \$3.24,$$

and the one-period return from holding the stock during time period 0 is

$$\frac{d(1) + v(1) - v(0)}{v(0)} = \frac{0.06 + 3.24 - 3.00}{3.00} = 0.10 = r.$$

Thus when the firm finances its investment opportunities with retained earnings, the shareholder does indeed earn the market rate of interest on his investment. Moreover, the shareholder earns only r, although the return on the firm's investment is $r^* > r$. The reason, of course, is that with perfect certainty and perfect capital markets the price of a share at every point in time fully reflects the market value of current and future investment opportunities, so that from period to period the shareholder earns only his opportunity costs, the market rate of interest r.

The rate of growth of share prices and dividends is given by Equation (2.31). In this case, however, because $k_e = 0$, g is the same as the rate of growth of the firm, $kr^* = 0.4(0.2) = 0.08$.

Firm II is just the opposite of firm I. It pays out all its earnings as dividends and finances new investment entirely by issuing new shares; that is, $k_r = 0$, but $k = k_e = 0.40$. Thus dividends per share at the beginning of time $t = 1$ are $X(1)/n(0) = \$0.10$. The price of a share in firm II at the beginning of time period $t = 1$ can be computed as follows. The value of the firm at the beginning of $t = 1$ is, from Equation (2.25), $V(1) = \$3240$, the same as for firm I, because Equation (2.25) does not contain variables dependent on financial policy. However, $V(1)$ does not accrue in full to the shares outstanding at the beginning of time $t = 0$. At period 1 new shares were issued that had total value

$$m(1)v(1) = I(1) = \$40.$$

The price of a share of stock at the beginning of time period 1 is then

$$v(1) = \frac{V(1) - m(1)v(1)}{n(0)} = \frac{\$3240 - 40}{1000} = \$3.20,$$

and the return on a share held during $t = 0$ is

$$\frac{d(1) + v(1) - v(0)}{v(0)} = \frac{0.10 + 3.20 - 3.00}{3.00} = 0.10 = r,$$

which is, of course, the market rate of return. The larger dividends per share of firm II relative to firm I are exactly balanced by the smaller capital gains of firm II.

The value of $v(1)$ computed above can be obtained by a different approach. We saw earlier that in the constant growth model

$$v(t) = v(0)[1 + g]^t,$$

where g is the rate of growth of price per share. For firm II, according to Equation (2.31),

$$g = 0.4(0.2)\,\frac{1}{0.6} - 0.4(0.1)\,\frac{1}{0.6}$$

$$= \frac{0.04}{0.6} = 0.0667,$$

so that $v(1) = 3.00[1 + 0.0667] = \$3.00 + 0.20 = \$3.20,$

which is exactly the price as previously computed. Because g is also the rate of growth of dividends per share, we see that, although the dividends per share of firm II are initially higher than those of firm I, their rate of growth is lower (0.0667 as compared with 0.08).

Unlike firms I and II, firm III uses both external and internal sources, in equal parts, to finance its investment projects; that is, $k = 0.40$, as before, but $k_r = k_e = 0.20$. By reasoning similar to case II we find that

$$v(1) = \frac{V(1) - m(1)v(1)}{n(0)},$$

$$m(1)v(1) = I(1) - [X(1) - D(1)] = 40 - [100 - 80] = \$20,$$

$$v(1) = \frac{3240 - 20}{1000} = \$3.22,$$

and $\dfrac{d(1) + v(1) - v(0)}{v(0)} = \dfrac{0.08 + 3.22 - 3.00}{3.00} = 0.10 = r.$

Again the return is r, the market rate of interest.

For firm III the rate of growth of price and dividends per share is

$$g = 0.08 \frac{0.80}{0.60} - 0.2(0.1) \frac{1}{0.60}$$

$$= 0.10667 - 0.0333 = 0.07334.$$

Thus $v(1) = v(0)[1 + g] = 3.00 + 3.00(0.7334) = \$3.22$, just as we saw by another route above.

Thus for all three firms the rate of return from holding a share of stock during $t = 0$ is precisely equal to the market interest rate $r = 0.10$. The rates of return are the same for all firms in spite of the fact that widely different policies are followed in financing new investment and in spite of the fact that the new investment has an average rate of return $r^* > r$.

Finally the market values of the three firms at any point in time can be computed from Equation (2.29), the formula for the dividend approach to valuation when applied to the constant growth model. The results are the same as those obtained earlier in the present section with Equation (2.28). Thus for firm I with Equation (2.29) we get

$$V(0) = \frac{D(1)}{r - g}$$

$$V(0) = \frac{60}{0.10 - 0.08} = \frac{60}{0.02} = \$3000;$$

for firm II,

$$V(0) = \frac{100}{0.10 - 0.0667} = \frac{100}{0.0333} = \$3000;$$

and for firm III,

$$V(0) = \frac{80}{0.10 - 0.07334} = \frac{80}{0.02666} = \$3000.$$

The reader should now be in a position to carry on the numerical example on his own. In particular, he should be able to show that, although dividends per share grow at different rates for the three firms, total dividends paid per period grow at the same rate for all firms. To test his understanding, the reader will also find it a useful exercise to carry out the computations for an additional time period and to convince himself that by borrowing or lending in the market, the dividends and capital gains obtained from any one of the firms can be transformed into the dividends and capital gains obtained from either of the others.

3

CRITERIA FOR OPTIMAL INVESTMENT DECISIONS

In this chapter we consider the investment decisions of firms whose shares are traded in perfect capital markets and whose managements are following the market value criterion, that is, maximize the market value of the shares outstanding before the investment decision is made. Strictly speaking, such decisions are technological rather than "financial" problems and so belong to the field of "production." For a variety of reasons, however, the general subject of "capital budgeting" has come to be taught in finance courses, and a considerable part of the literature in finance is focused on this class of problems.

One reason is that the criteria for optimal investment, as we shall see, are closely bound up with the present value apparatus developed in Chapters 1 and 2, and, in fact, capital budgeting is often introduced in finance courses as essentially merely one important application of this apparatus. Perhaps even more decisive in associating capital budgeting with finance is the fact that under uncertainty, one of the key, and most controversial, questions that immediately arise is whether and to what extent the firm's choice of financing method—bonds versus stock issues versus retained earnings, and so on—does or should influence investment decisions. This class of questions, often referred to as the "cost of capital problem," has been a major preoccupation in the field of corporation finance. Some aspects of this problem, notably, the issue of internal versus external financing, have already been treated in the previous chapter, but we postpone most of the discussion of this problem to Part II of the book in the context of models allowing for uncertainty.

Because our concern is mainly with the literature on capital budgeting, we restrict our attention here fairly narrowly to the central issue of the appropriate criterion—actually, appropriate equivalent alternative criteria—for investment decisions. We shall have little to say, and certainly little encouraging to say, about computational problems, nor except incidentally and in passing, shall we discuss how the model can be specialized and adapted to deal with different kinds of technological and market settings. Issues of the latter kind, along with the related ones of the construction of macroinvestment functions, are best left to standard economics courses.

The chapter itself is divided into two main sections. The first is concerned mainly with the formal derivation and representation of the criteria for optimality consistent with the market value rule. Much of the discussion here is also concerned with showing how the apparatus for optimal investment decisions, as presented in the theory of finance, is related to the apparatus used to represent optimal output decisions in the standard microeconomic theory of the firm. The second section of the chapter then attempts to show how the criteria for optimal investment decisions can be used as a critical guide in surveying the literature of applied capital budgeting. The two sections of the chapter, however, can be read independently.

I. THE REPRESENTATION OF OPTIMAL INVESTMENT DECISIONS[1]

I.A. The Case of a Single Capital Good and Two Time Periods

As usual, we find it helpful to begin, not by considering the problem in all its complexity, but by focusing on a simple special case and then adding

[1] To simplify and shorten the presentation of the optimality conditions in Section I of this chapter, we make extensive use of the fact that any constrained maximization problem of the form max $F(\bullet)$ subject to $G(\bullet) = 0$ can be restated as an equivalent unconstrained maximization problem of the form max $F(\bullet) - \lambda G(\bullet)$, where λ is a so-called "lagrangian multiplier." Readers for whom the lagrangian technique is unfamiliar should simply skim over the equations in which it is used—or if they are more venturesome, translate them back into the more familiar constrained form—and move on to the graphical and verbal discussions.

complications one by one. In particular we start by assuming the existence of a firm that meets the following conditions:

1. The firm produces a single, homogeneous, nonstorable commodity in each time period t and sells it in a perfect market at known prices. In the language of the ordinary theory of the firm, the firm is a pure competitor or price taker or quantity adjuster. Extension to the case of monopoly, in which price as well as quantity must be determined, is relatively straightforward, but for our purposes the additional insights of such an extension are not worth the cost of carrying along the additional decision variable.

2. The production can be accomplished by the services of a stock of a single, homogeneous capital good or machine, owned by the firm, in conjunction with a single, homogeneous type of cooperating labor not owned by the firm. Both machines and man-hours of labor are purchased in perfect markets at known prices and wages, respectively, and there are no internal costs or lags involved in adjusting either factor to its desired level. For both productive factors, the volume of services rendered is taken as strictly proportional to the number of units employed.[2]

3. The technological production possibilities in any period can be described by a "production function" of the form

$$q_t = F_t(l_t, k_t),$$

where q_t represents the number of units of the commodity to be produced, l_t the number of units of labor services used, and k_t the number of machines, with the function F_t assumed to be everywhere concave. In the language of the theory of the firm it is characterized by "diminishing returns to factor proportions" and "decreasing returns to scale."[3] The assumption that returns to scale are decreasing everywhere is much stronger than needed and is introduced solely to simplify the presentation.

4. The firm has a finite planning horizon of two periods. At the end of the second period, production ceases, and all machines held are sold.

5. The shares of the firm are traded in a perfect capital market, and the firm's management follows the market value criterion. Our conventions as to timing are that sales of product produced during t and payments to labor

---

[2] This means among other things that the only way the firm can alter the capital intensity of its production process is by varying the number of machines that it holds. In practice, of course, a firm typically has many other ways to vary its effective stock of capital goods—for example, by using equipment that is more durable. For simplicity of presentation, however, and especially with a view to making the optimality conditions stand out as sharply as possible, all consideration of these additional dimensions to the capital stock are deferred until Sec. II.

[3] Mathematically, these assumptions imply that (1) F'_{t,l_t}, $F'_{t,k_t} > 0$, (2) F''_{t,l_t}, $F''_{t,k_t} \leq 0$, and (3) $F_t(\lambda l_t, \lambda k_t) \leq \lambda F_t(l_t, k_t)$.

employed in this production take place at the start of period $t + 1$ but the purchase of machines takes place at the beginning of the production period. The sale of any machines remaining at the end of a period takes place at the price as of the start of the next period.[4]

Given these conditions, the decisions of the management with respect to output, employment, and the purchase, and sale, of machines in each of the two periods can be represented formally as the solution to the problem

$$\max V_1 = K_1 + \frac{K_2}{1 + {}_1r_2} = -I_1 + \frac{X_2 + V_2}{1 + {}_1r_2}$$

$$= -\pi_1(k_1 - k_0) + \frac{p_2q_1 - w_2l_1 + \pi_2k_1}{1 + {}_1r_2} \quad (3.1)$$

subject to

$$q_1 = F_1(l_1,k_1), \quad (3.2)$$

where p_2 is the unit price of output at period 2, w_2 the wage rate per unit of labor, π_1 and π_2 the purchase and sale prices, respectively, of a unit of machinery, and the K's, V's, X's, and I's have the same meanings as in Chapter 2. Expressions (3.1) and (3.2) can be reformulated as the unconstrained problem

$$\max_{q_1, l_1, k_1, \lambda_1} V_1 = \pi_1(k_1 - k_0) + \frac{p_2q_1 - w_2l_1 + \pi_2k_1}{1 + {}_1r_2} - \lambda_1(q_1 - F_1(l_1,k_1)),$$

$$(3.1')$$

where λ_1 is the lagrangian multiplier for the production function constraint.[5]

I.B. Graphical Representation of the Complete Solution

Because there are so many distinct decision variables, no very simple representation of the optimal decisions is possible in a single, all-inclusive graph. We can, however, regroup the component terms in the maximand so as to present the full, simultaneous solution as if it were actually being

---

These conventions are the same as those in Chap. 2. It is important to emphasize that they are mere conventions and the reader who prefers different ones can readily adjust all our results to suit his own tastes without affecting anything of substance. For example, if one wants to regard the wages as being paid in advance rather than at the end of the period, one merely redefines the wage rate as $w_1' = w_2/(1 + {}_1r_2)$, and so on.

[5] In principle, there are also nonnegativity constraints for q, l, and k, but as has been our practice throughout, we assume that these are always satisfied. We also continue to omit the second-order or sufficiency conditions for optimality, beyond noting here that the assumptions in Sec. I.A. do guarantee that they will indeed be met.

reached in a sequence of separate steps. In fact, there are several ways in which this can be accomplished, depending on which particular decisions happen to be of most interest.

For example, given a firm that sells its product in a perfect market, the main interest in the ordinary theory of the firm usually attaches to the output decision. If so, and assuming, for simplicity, that $k_0 = 0$, the problem can be restated as

$$\max_{q_1, l_1, k_1} V_1 = \frac{p_2 q_1 - w_2 l_1}{1 + {}_1 r_2} - k_1 \left(\pi_1 - \frac{\pi_2}{1 + {}_1 r_2} \right) - \lambda_1 (q_1 - F_1(l_1, k_1))$$

$$= \max_{q_1} \left[\frac{p_2 q_1}{1 + {}_1 r_2} + \max_{l_1, k_1} \left[-\frac{w_2 l_1}{1 + {}_1 r_2} - k_1 \left(\pi_1 - \frac{\pi_2}{1 + {}_1 r_2} \right) - \lambda_1 (q_1 - F_1(l_1, k_1)) \right] \right]$$

$$= \max_{q_1} \left[\frac{p_2 q_1}{1 + {}_1 r_2} - \min_{l_1, k_1} \left[\frac{w_2 l_1}{1 + {}_1 r_2} + k_1 \left(\pi_1 - \frac{\pi_2}{1 + {}_1 r_2} \right) + \lambda_1 (q_1 - F_1(l_1, k_1)) \right] \right].$$

(3.3)

In words, the "scenario" visualized in this regrouping would be as follows: First, pick some arbitrary value for q_1, and solve the minimum problem in the inner brackets; that is, find the minimum total discounted costs, say, C, of producing this particular level of output. Once the minimum cost has

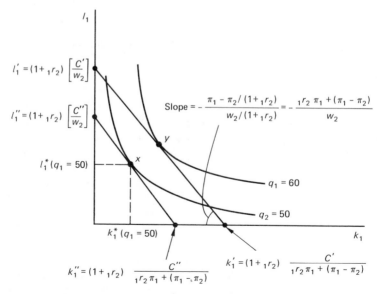

Figure 3.1   Optimal Combinations of Labor and Machines for Specified Levels of Output

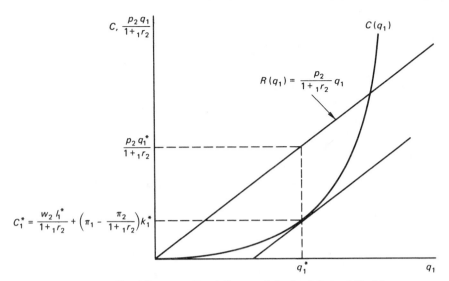

Figure 3.2   Total Revenue, Total Cost, and Optimal Output Decision

been found for every value of q_1, select the one that maximizes the "profit" for the period, that is, the difference between total (discounted) revenue obtained from the sale of the output and the minimum cost of producing it.

This scenario is shown graphically in Figures 3.1 and 3.2. In Figure 3.1, the indifference curves, usually referred to as "isoquants" in this application, show the various combinations of labor units and machine units that can be used to produce a given level of output. Each of the parallel straight lines shows a different level of total discounted costs C, and the points along the line represent the quantities of labor services and machine services that could be purchased with this level of total expenditure at the given prices of $w_2/(1 + {}_1r_2)$ per unit of labor and $\pi_1 - \pi_2/(1 + {}_1r_2)$ per machine. Note that the economic "cost" of the capital services provided by a machine is not simply the initial outlay π_1 but the initial outlay minus the resale value after the period's use (discounted back to the present). Or to approach it another way, because

$$\pi_1 - \frac{\pi_2}{1 + {}_1r_2} = \frac{{}_1r_2\pi_1 + (\pi_1 - \pi_2)}{1 + {}_1r_2} = \pi_1 \left[{}_1r_2 + \left(\frac{\pi_1 - \pi_2}{\pi_1} \right) \right] \frac{1}{1 + {}_1r_2},$$

the (discounted) cost of capital services can be seen to be the interest foregone on the initial purchase price plus the rate of depreciation (or minus the rate of appreciation if $\pi_2 > \pi_1$).[6]

---

[6] The term $[{}_1r_2\pi_1 + (\pi_1 - \pi_2)]/(1 + {}_1r_2)$ is often referred to in the literature as the "rental value" of the machine.

Each of the tangency points, such as x or y, represents the minimum cost combination of productive services for the indicated quantity of output, and the actual value of total cost C that this combination represents is easily determined from the value of either intercept.[7]

Having found the minimum cost combinations, we can plot the minimum value of total cost for each value of q_1 as in the curve $C(q_1)$ in Figure 3.2. The remaining term in the maximand (3.3), $p_2 q_1/(1 + {}_1 r_2)$, represents the sales proceeds or total (discounted) revenue as a function of q_1 and is graphed in Figure 3.2 as the straight line with slope $p_2/(1 + {}_1 r_2)$. The optimal q_1^* is found at that value of q_1 for which the distance between the $R(q_1)$ and $C(q_1)$ curves is a maximum, which can easily be shown to be the point at which the slopes of the two functions are identical. Alternatively and equivalently, as in Figure 3.3, we could directly graph the slopes of the

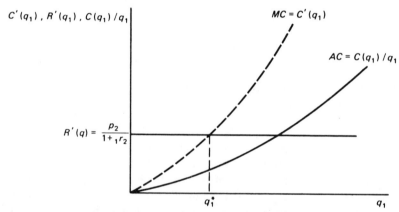

Figure 3.3   Marginal Conditions and Optimal Output

$R(q_1)$ and $C(q_1)$ functions, obtaining the optimal q_1^* at the intersection of the marginal revenue and marginal cost curves in the manner standard in the elementary theory of the firm.

[7] The first-order conditions for minimum total cost for a given output are

$$\frac{\partial C}{\partial l_1} = 0 = \frac{w_2}{1 + {}_1 r_2} - \lambda_1 F'_{1l},$$

$$\frac{\partial C}{\partial k_1} = 0 = \pi_1 - \frac{\pi_2}{1 + {}_1 r_2} - \lambda_1 F'_{1k},$$

which together imply

$$F'_{1k}/F'_{1l} = [\pi_1 - \pi_2/(1 + {}_1 r_2)]/w_2/(1 + {}_1 r_2) = [{}_1 r_2 \pi_1 + (\pi_1 - \pi_2)]/w_2;$$

that is, the ratio of the marginal physical product of capital to the marginal physical product of labor—the slope of the isoquant at the given value of q_1—equals the ratio of the cost of a unit of capital services to the cost of a unit of labor services—the slope of the "price line" in Fig. 3.1.

I.C. An Alternative Representation Highlighting the Investment Decision

But in contrast with the elementary theory of the firm the main concern of the theory of finance is the investment decision rather than the output decision. Once again, however, we can obtain a highlighting of the variable of interest k_1 by a regrouping and reinterpretation of the maximand (3.1'). In particular, we can rewrite it as

$$\max_{q_1, l_1, k_1} V_1 = \max_{k_1} \left[\max_{q_1, l_1} \left[\frac{p_2 q_1 - w_2 l_1}{1 + {}_1r_2} - \lambda_1(q_1 - F_1(l_1, k_1)) \right] - k_1 \left(\pi_1 - \frac{\pi_2}{1 + {}_1r_2} \right) \right]. \quad (3.4)$$

In words, Equation (3.4) tells us to pick some value for k_1 and then determine values of q_1 and l_1 that yield the maximum possible discounted "quasirent" or discounted "cash flow"

$$\frac{X_2}{1 + {}_1r_2} = \max_{q_1, l_1} \left[\frac{p_2 q_1 - w_2 l_1}{1 + {}_1r_2} - \lambda_1(q_1 - F_1(l_1, k_1)) \right]$$

that could be attained with this amount of k_1. This maximum is, of course, a constrained maximum, the constraint being the production function $q_1 = F_1(l_1, k_1)$. Attainment of the maximum discounted cash flow implies that we keep adding labor to the given stock of machines until the sales value of the additional output so obtained no longer exceeds the cost of the added labor, that is, until the value of the marginal product of labor equals the wage rate.[8]

Having found the maximum return for any given number of machines, call it $X_2(k_1)/(1 + {}_1r_2)$, we can plot these maxima for all values of k_1 as in Figure 3.4. The function $C(k_1) = k_1[\pi_1 - \pi_2/(1 + {}_1r_2)]$ in this figure is the cost of the capital services of k_1 machines, and the optimum number of machines k_1^* is found at the point of maximum distance between the two curves.[9]

---

[8] Because maximizing $X_2/(1 + {}_1r_2)$ is equivalent to maximizing X_2, the first-order conditions for maximum discounted cash flow for a given stock of capital are

$$\frac{\partial X_2}{\partial l_1} = 0 = \frac{-w_2}{1 + {}_1r_2} + \lambda_1 F'_{1l},$$

$$\frac{\partial X_2}{\partial q_1} = 0 = \frac{p_2}{1 + {}_1r_2} - \lambda_1,$$

which together imply $w_2 = p_2 F'_{1l}$.

[9] The values of q_1, and l_1, corresponding to this solution are, of course, precisely the same as illustrated in Fig. 3.2, because Eqs. (3.3) and (3.4) are mathematically equivalent.

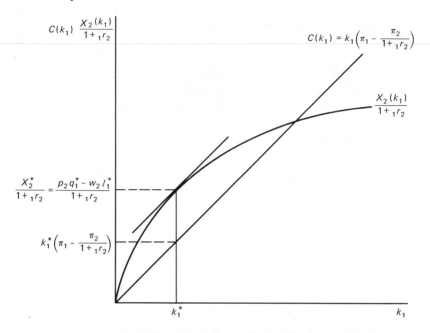

Figure 3.4   Total Cash Flow, Total Cost of Capital Services, and Optimal Stock of Machines

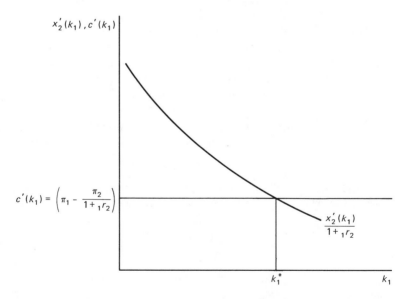

Figure 3.5   Marginal Cash Flow, Marginal Cost of Capital Services, and Optimal Stock of Machines

As before, we can also express this solution in terms of the marginal rather than the total conditions. In Figure 3.5, for example, the function $x_2'(k_1)/(1 + {}_1r_2)$ represents the marginal discounted cash flow from investment in machines, assuming optimal output and manning, and is, of course, simply the slope of the total cash flow function in Figure 3.4. The optimum stock of capital k_1^* is then found at the point at which the marginal cash flow is equal to the marginal cost of capital services per unit, that is, at the point satisfying the condition

$$\frac{x_2'(k_1)}{1 + {}_1r_2} = \pi_1 - \frac{\pi_2}{1 + {}_1r_2} \equiv c'(k_1) \tag{3.5a}$$

or more compactly

$$x_2'(k_1) = {}_1r_2\pi_1 + (\pi_1 - \pi_2).^{10} \tag{3.5b}$$

I.C.1. Alternative forms for the optimizing conditions

There are, of course, still other ways in which this fundamental criterion $(3.5b)$ can be expressed. A popular one, which we make great use of in subsequent sections, is the "present value" form:

$$\pi_1 = \frac{x_2'(k_1)}{1 + {}_1r_2} + \frac{\pi_2}{1 + {}_1r_2}. \tag{3.6}$$

In words, add to the capital stock until the present value of the marginal cash flow plus the resale value of the last unit exactly equals the initial purchase price per unit. An equally if not more popular alternative is the internal yield or rate of return form. In particular, if we define the marginal (one-period) internal yield as

$${}_1r_2^*(k_1) \equiv \frac{x_2'(k_1)}{\pi_1} + \frac{\pi_2 - \pi_1}{\pi_1}, \tag{3.7}$$

---

[10] Note that the marginal cash flow $x_2'(k_1)$, which is the total differential $dx_2(k_1)/dk_1$, is not the same as the marginal product of capital F'_{1k}, because the function $x_2'(k_1)$ does not keep the quantity of labor constant as k_1 varies but allows it to be adjusted optimally to the particular value of k_1. In equilibrium, of course, but only there, the two are the same, as is easily seen by noting that the first-order conditions for a maximum of (3.3) include

$$\frac{\partial V_1}{\partial k_1} = 0 = -\pi_1 + \frac{\pi_2}{1 + {}_1r_2} + \lambda_1 F'_{1k},$$

$$\frac{\partial V_1}{\partial q_1} = 0 = \frac{p_2}{1 + {}_1r_2} - \lambda_1,$$

which together imply

$$p_2 F'_{1k} = {}_1r_2\pi_1 + (\pi_1 - \pi_2).$$

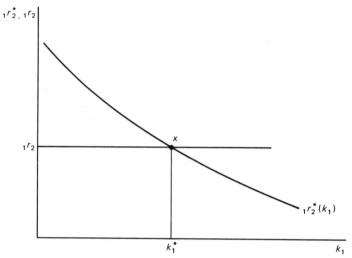

Figure 3.6   Marginal Conditions in Rate of Return Form

the criterion becomes simply

$$_1r_2^*(k_1) = {}_1r_2. \tag{3.8}$$

In words, add to the capital stock until the marginal internal yield on the capital stock, optimally utilized, exactly equals the market rate of interest. The condition is shown graphically in Figure 3.6.[11]

I.C.2. Optimal capital stock and optimal investment

The optimality conditions have so far been stated in terms of the physical stock variable k_1, but in the field of finance and in applied capital budgeting the variable more directly of interest is "total net investment," which is the value in money units of the net change in the stock of capital. In the present context, however, going from one variable to the other really involves nothing more than a relabeling of the abscissa in graphs, such as Figure 3.6, to obtain one like Figure 3.7a. Under our assumptions, the initial capital stock k_0 is a known constant—for simplicity, we set its value at zero—so that the value of the investment I_1 at the beginning of the period is simply $I_1 = \pi_1 \Delta k = \pi_1 k_1 - \pi_1 k$, which is just a scale-changing, linear transformation of the variable k_1, that is, a transformation of the form $y =$

---

[11] Still another way of saying the same thing would be that the market rate of interest is the "cutoff" rate for capital budgeting or the "cost of capital" in the sense of the minimum yield that an addition to the capital stock must offer to be just worth undertaking from the standpoint of the owners.

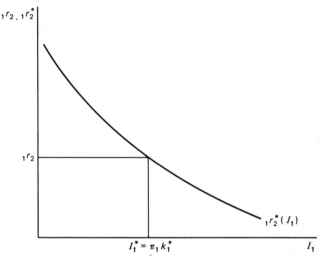

Figure 3.7a   Optimal Level of Investment

$a + bx$. In what follows we make use of both variables in discussing the optimality conditions, depending on the context.

I.D. Extension to the Case of Many Different Machines

We can also extend the analysis in fairly straightforward if tedious fashion to allow for the existence of many different types of machines, including of course, the same machine at different ages and hence different efficiencies. Suppose, to be concrete, that there are two machines, type i and type j. Then the full problem corresponding to Equation (3.1) would be, assuming $k_{i0} = k_{j0} = 0$,

$$\max_{q_1, l_1, k_{i1}, k_{j1}} V_1 = -\pi_{i1}k_{i1} - \pi_{j1}k_{j1} + \frac{p_2q_1 - w_2l_1 + \pi_{i2}k_{i1} + \pi_{j2}k_{j1}}{1 + {}_1r_2} \quad (3.9)$$

subject to

$$q_1 = F_1(l_1, k_{i1}, k_{j1}). \quad (3.10)$$

Once again, we can highlight the decision for either machine, say, type i, by regrouping and treating type j as merely another cooperating factor along with l_1. In particular, corresponding to Equation (3.4), we should have

$$\max_{q_1, l_1, k_{i1}, k_{j1}} V_1 = \max_{k_{j1}} \left[\max_{q_1, l_1, k_{i1}} \left[\frac{p_2q_1 - w_2l_1 - k_{j1}[{}_1r_2\pi_{j1} + \pi_{j1} - \pi_{j2}]}{1 + {}_1r_2} \right.\right.$$

$$\left.\left. - \lambda_1(q_1 - F_1(l_1, k_{i1}, k_{j1})) \right] - k_{il}\left[\frac{{}_1r_2\pi_{i1} + \pi_{i1} - \pi_{i2}}{1 + {}_1r_2} \right] \right]. \quad (3.11)$$

Despite the added complexity, the only substantive change, insofar as graphical representations, such as Figures 3.4 to 3.6, are concerned, is that the net cash flow X_{i2} of the machine i, and the measures derived from it, such as $x_2'(k_{i1})$ or $_1r_{i2}^*$, must be taken as net not only of wages but also of the net costs of the services of machine j, adjusted optimally to the specified value of k_{i1}. The last phrase is particularly important; in representing the decision problem for a single machine in graphical form, we must not forget that the optimum investment decision for the machine is embedded in a much larger optimizing problem.

When the concern is not with a single machine in isolation but with total investment in all machines, that is, with the total capital budget and its allocation, the desired representation can be obtained by simple aggregation of relations like those in Figure 3.7a, as shown for a two-machine example in Figure 3.7b. The scenario amounts to first specifying a value for the total investment budget I_1 and then solving the complete production and investment problem (3.9) and (3.10) subject to an additional provisional constraint of the form

$$\pi_{i1}k_{i1} + \pi_{j1}k_{j1} = I_1. \tag{3.12}$$

The optimality conditions require that the total budget of I_1 dollars be allocated between the two machines so that the marginal one-period yields are the same for each machine. Otherwise it would clearly pay to transfer funds from one machine to the other. This common value for the marginal internal yields at any level of total investment $_1r_2^*$, which, of course, is not the same as $_1r_2$ except at the optimum value of I_1, gives the required values for the vertical axes for each of the machines. And the combined investment

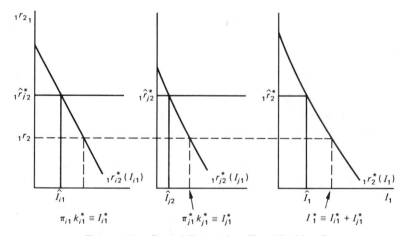

Figure 3.7b Capital Budget in a Two-Machine Case

function for the firm is obtained simply by adding the two curves together
horizontally, as shown in the third panel of the figure.

I.E. The Investment Decision and the Transformation Curve

The preceding analysis permits us at long last to justify the use of
transformation functions $T(K_1,K_2) = 0$ in contexts other than those of the
"seed corn" variety. In Chapter 2, it will be recalled, the transformation
function was defined as an implicit function showing the maximum consumption possibilities, or "withdrawals," in period 2, K_2, that could be
obtained for any given level of consumption withdrawals in period 1, K_1.
Thus, to go back to a single-machine context, points on the transformation
function are really nothing more than solutions, for different values of K_1,
to a series of problems of the type

$$\max K_2 = \max_{q_1,l_1} \left[p_2 q_1 - w_2 l_1 \right] + \pi_2 k_1$$

subject to the constraints

$$K_1 = K_1' - I_1 = K_1' - \pi_1 k_1,$$

$$q_1 = F_1(k_1,l_1),$$

where K_1' represents the resources withdrawable at the start of period 1.

In Figure 3.7c, for example, we start by picking a trial value for K_1, such
as $\hat{K}_1$. As drawn, the firm is assumed to have no withdrawable resources in
the first period, so that the "consumption possibility" would actually be
negative, that is, $\hat{K}_1 = -\hat{I}_1$. At the ruling price for machines, π_1, the

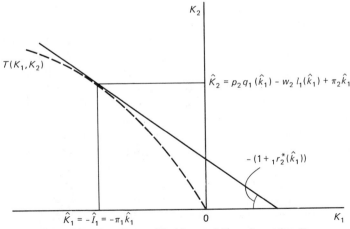

Figure 3.7c   Investment Decision and Transformation Curve

investment of $\hat{I}_1$ dollars translates into $\hat{I}_1/\pi_1 = \hat{k}_1$ units of physical capital service to which are then added cooperating labor services $l_1(\hat{k}_i)$ until the value of the marginal product of labor equals the wage rate. The sales proceeds from the output $q_1(\hat{k}_1)$ so determined plus the resale value of the $\hat{k}_1$ machines minus the wage bill then constitutes the consumption possibility $\hat{K}_2$ for the next period; that is, $\hat{K}_2 = p_2 q_1(\hat{k}_1) - w_2 l_1(\hat{k}_1) + \pi_2 \hat{k}_1 = X_2(\hat{k}_1) + \pi_2 \hat{k}_1$, and so on, for every other value of K_1 until the whole function is traced out.

It should also be easy to see that the slope of the transformation function at any point such as $\hat{K}_1$, $\hat{K}_2$ is indeed really nothing more than $-[1 + {}_1 r_2^*(\hat{k}_1)]$, where ${}_1 r_2^*(\hat{k}_1)$ is the one-period internal yield for a capital stock of size $\hat{k}_1$. We leave the derivation as an exercise for the reader.

I.F. Extension to More than Two Time Periods

I.F.1. The case of perfect markets for capital goods

The extension of the model to allow for many periods is a simple matter as long as we maintain the assumption that capital goods can be bought or sold in a perfect market; that is, at the beginning of any period t the firm can buy or sell as many units as it likes of the capital good at a known fixed price π_t. In such a case, the selection of the optimal capital stock in each period, in the many-machine as well as the single-machine case, turns out to be merely a sequence of independent, two-period decisions of exactly the kind that we have been discussing; that is, just as the optimal k_1^* in the one-machine case was specified in terms of π_1, π_2, p_2, w_2, and ${}_1 r_2$, so the optimal k_t^* depends solely on π_t, π_{t+1}, p_{t+1}, w_{t+1}, and ${}_t r_{t+1}$ independently of all prices and decisions of all other periods. And similarly for the many-machine version.

This one-period horizon or "myopic" property of the model may seem somewhat paradoxical at first glance, because the machines are durable after all and must in general be considered as producing net returns for the firm over many more than a single period. Remember, however, that as long as the markets for machines are perfect, the firm can adjust its capital at will. Hence, no matter what stock it may happen to have acquired in any period t, it can sell out the whole lot at the start of $t + 1$ and then buy back at the same price whatever quantity that it deems appropriate to carry through $t + 1$. Because no costs are incurred in such a rollover, the firm can clearly never be worse off as a result of proceeding in this one step at a time manner.

Another way of making the same point is to note that, for the purposes of the investment at t, the assumption that the market for capital goods is perfect implies that the value to the firm at $t + 1$ of any unit of capital equipment is precisely π_{t+1}, its resale price at this time. For if the value of any unit to the firm were less than its resale price, the firm could and would sell it at $t + 1$. On the other hand, if the value to the firm at $t + 1$ of any unit of capital were more than the then ruling market price, precisely this excess of value over cost could be obtained by purchasing the unit at $t + 1$. Thus to justify purchasing the unit at t, the present value at t of (1) the cash flows that it generates at $t + 1$ plus (2) the resale price at $t + 1$ must be at least as great as π_t, the price of the unit at period t.

More formally, let

$$\frac{X_{t+1}(k_t)}{1 + {}_t r_{t+1}} = \max_{q_t, l_t} \left[\frac{p_{t+1} q_t - w_{t+1} l_t}{1 + {}_t r_{t+1}} - \lambda_t (q_t - F_t(l_t, k_t)) \right];$$

that is, $X_{t+1}(k_t)$ is the maximum of revenues minus labor costs, that is, net cash flow, at $t + 1$ consistent with k_t units of capital goods held at t. And let $x'_{t+1}(k_t)$, as before, be the corresponding marginal net cash flow. Then the preceding argument indicates that the decision criterion for t, expressed in present value form, involves pushing the stock of capital goods to the point at which

$$\pi_t = \frac{x'_{t+1}(k_t) + \pi_{t+1}}{1 + {}_t r_{t+1}},$$

which is the exact counterpart of the two-period rule (3.6).

I.F.2. The case of fixed capital

We have postponed until this late point any consideration of cases in which capital goods could not be freely bought and sold at fixed prices in a perfect market. This delay is not to suggest, of course, that such cases are of less importance empirically. Quite the contrary—although situations involving active secondhand markets are much more frequent than the distribution of emphasis in the standard capital budgeting literature would lead one to suspect. Our strategy rather reflects the fact that the representation of the optimality conditions is inevitably a good deal more complex without the perfect market assumption and the exposition can be at least somewhat facilitated by using the results in the simpler case for comparison and contrast.

To see the nature of the difficulties, consider the case of a firm using a single "fixed" capital good that cannot be resold at any time once installed, and for further simplicity suppose that the installation must take place at the start of the first period. Then the firm's decision problem for a three-period case can be stated as

$$\max_{q_1, q_2; l_1, l_2; k_1} V_1 = -\pi_1 k_1 + \frac{p_2 q_1 - w_2 l_1}{1 + {}_1 r_2} + \frac{p_3 q_2 - w_3 l_2}{(1 + {}_1 r_2)(1 + {}_2 r_3)}$$

subject to

$$q_1 = F_1(l_1, k_1),$$

$$q_2 = F_2(l_2, k_1).$$

The major and decisive point of contrast between this problem and the corresponding one in Section I.A. lies in the second of the two production function constraints. The production possibilities in the second period now depend on the capital installation decisions made during the previous period. We can, in other words, no longer break the decision into a series of independent, one-period problems but must consider simultaneously the decisions in all periods.

Fortunately, however, our concern is with the representation rather than the computation of the optimality conditions, and much of the earlier graphical representation can in fact be salvaged with only minor reinterpretations, at least as long as we continue to assume the existence of a finite planning horizon.[12] Consider first the decision problem as it appears to the firm at the start of the second period. The stock of capital having been determined in the previous period, call it $\hat{k}_1$, the firm's problem is then simply that of determining the optimal amounts of cooperating labor to employ and total output to produce during the second period. Formally,

$$V_2(\hat{k}_1) = \max_{q_2, l_2} \left[\frac{p_3 q_2 - w_3 l_2}{1 + {}_2 r_3} - \lambda(q_2 - F_2(l_2, \hat{k}_1)) \right],$$

where $V_2(\hat{k}_1)$ is the maximum market value of the firm at period 2 consistent with holding k_1 units of the capital good at period 1. This will be recognized, of course, as exactly the kind of one-period problem that we have already considered, and the optimizing condition is the by now familiar equality between the value of the marginal product of labor and the wage rate. By repeating this calculation for every possible value of the initial capital stock, we can obtain the function $V_2(k_1)$, which shows the value as of the start of period 2 of any amount of capital carried over and optimally employed during this period. In terms of the earlier representation, this function is essentially the same as the function $X_2(k_1)/(1 + {}_1 r_2)$ in Figure 3.4, and the curve marginal to $V_2(k_1)$, to be denoted by $v_2'(k_1)$, corresponds to the function $x'(k_1)/(1 + {}_1 r_2)$ in Figure 3.5.

To complete the solution, and in particular to obtain the optimal value of k_1, we take one step backward in time to the start of the first period. The

---

[12] An infinite horizon would impose no insuperable mathematical difficulties, but it would unduly complicate the exposition at this stage of the proceedings. We shall consider some (small-scale) problems involving infinite horizons later in the applications discussion in Section II.

problem can then be stated formally as

$$
\max_{q_1, l_1, k_1} V_1 = \max_{k_1} \left[\max_{q_1, l_1} \left[\frac{p_2 q_1 - w_2 l_1}{1 + {}_1 r_2} - \lambda(q_1 - F_1(l_1, k_1)) \right] \right.
$$

$$
\left. - k_1 \left(\pi_1 - \frac{V_2(k_1)/k_1}{1 + {}_1 r_2} \right) \right]. \qquad (3.13)
$$

Note that Equation (3.13) is a one-period problem exactly the same as that defined earlier in Equation (3.4) except that the terminal value of the stock of capital is given by the function $V_2(k_1)$ rather than $\pi_2 k_1$. Or to put it another way, Equation (3.4) is merely that special case of Equation (3.13) for which, by virtue of the perfect market assumption, $V_2(k_1)/k_1$, the average terminal value per unit, is exactly equal to the market price per unit of capital, π_2, for all values of k_1.

Once this relation between the two problems is understood, it is easy to see how the optimality conditions must be restated in the fixed capital case.[13] In particular, the optimum stock of capital k_1 is found at the point at which the present value of the marginal cash flow, with other factors and total output optimally adjusted, plus the marginal terminal value of the stock, assuming an optimally adjusted cash flow to this stock in period 3, is exactly equal to the initial purchase price per unit, that is, the point for which

$$
\pi_1 = \frac{x_2'(k_1) + v_2'(k_1)}{1 + {}_1 r_2}. \qquad (3.14)
$$

In equivalent one-period rate of return form the criterion is thus

$$
{}_1 r_2 = \frac{x_2'(k_1)}{\pi_1} + \frac{v_2'(k_1) - \pi_1}{\pi_1} \equiv {}_1 r_2^*(k_1); \qquad (3.15)
$$

that is, the capital stock is increased until the optimal marginal cash flow yield plus the optimal marginal rate of appreciation, or minus the marginal rate of depreciation of the stock, exactly equals the first-period rate of interest. And in cost of capital services form, it is

$$
x_2'(k_1) = {}_1 r_2 \pi_1 + (\pi_1 - v_2'(k_1)); \qquad (3.16)
$$

that is, expand the stock until the marginal cash flow in the coming period exactly equals the interest on the capital invested in the marginal unit plus the marginal appreciation or depreciation.

---

[13] It is also easy to see how the model can be generalized to the case of many machines along the lines of Section I.D.

Note finally that we can, if we choose, string together present value conditions, such as Equation (3.14), and obtain an exactly similar criterion running in terms of the cash flows and interest rates over the entire life span of the equipment. In particular, for the example we have

$$v_2'(k_1) = \frac{x_3'(k_1)}{1 + {}_2r_3}.$$

Substituting this expression into Equation (3.14), we obtain as our criterion

$$\pi_1 = \frac{x_2'(k_1)}{1 + {}_1r_2} + \frac{x_3'(k_1)}{(1 + {}_1r_2)(1 + {}_2r_3)}. \tag{3.17}$$

Or in words, expand the stock of capital until the present value of the marginal cash flows, with all other cooperating factors and total output optimally adjusted in each period, exactly equals the initial purchase price per unit of capital. And the extension of the criterion to the general n-period case is rather obvious.

With the development of this generalized present value rule, we have completed the derivation of the optimality conditions for investment decisions by the firm. We may turn now to consider some of the problems involved in the application of such rules to capital budgeting.

II. INVESTMENT DECISIONS AND CAPITAL BUDGETING

II.A. Problems in the Application of the Present Value Criterion

The generalized present or market value rule with which we concluded the previous section may seem so simple and familiar that no further discussion is required. Actually, however, it is by no means always immediately clear how it is to be implemented in specific concrete applications even quite apart from the (serious) problems of determining the values of the optimally adjusted marginal cash flows or allowing for the inevitable uncertainties.[14]

II.A.1. Marginal versus average present values

To see the nature of one of the difficulties, consider the following typical problem in capital budgeting: A firm is considering building a large cen-

---

[14] We remind readers that we are not here attempting to provide a comprehensive or well-rounded survey of the field but merely focusing on a limited number of topics illustrating some of the important concepts and results that we have worked with up to this point. Students not previously exposed to the literature on capital budgeting will find a good introductory survey in the first part of the text by Harold Bierman, Jr., and Seymour Smidt, *The Capital Budgeting Decision*, 2d ed. New York: The Macmillan Co., 1966. An extensive bibliography is also provided.

tralized warehouse to facilitate the distribution of its finished products. Research studies of the savings permitted by the new facility have produced reliable or at least accepted figures for the projected cash flow in each year of the life of the facility. The present value of these flows at the accepted interest rate, or rates if they differ over time, is, say, $4 million. The construction cost of the facility is $3 million. Should the firm undertake the project?

At first glance, the answer would seem to be yes, obviously. But a closer look at our criterion shows that on the basis only of the evidence presented, the most we can really say is maybe, for our decision rule was not stated in terms of "projects" but of units of capital, or, equivalently, units of investment in the capital good.[15] There may, perhaps, be cases in which a choice really is of the all or nothing, single-project variety. But such would surely not be the case in general for a warehouse that could be built in many different sizes and with varying degrees of durability. Clearly, then, we cannot make our final decision until all these opportunities have been taken into account.

A more appropriate way of structuring the decision in such cases is given in Table 1. (For simplicity, we assume that the rate of interest is a constant 5 percent per period, and we bypass the question of durability for the moment by assuming that the facilities have infinite life). Column 1 is some physical measure of warehouse size, such as millions of cubic feet of usable storage space. Column 2 is an estimate of the total cost of constructing a facility of this size, and column 3 is the estimate of the corresponding total annual cash flow. Column 4 is the present value of these cash flows. As can readily be seen, the present value exceeds the construction cost for all the listed warehouse sizes.

TABLE 1

(Columns 2 to 7 are in units of millions of dollars)

(1) Size, Millions of Cu Ft	(2) Cost of Construction	(3) Total Annual Cash Flow	(4) Present Value of Cash Flow at 5 Percent	(5) Marginal Construction Cost	(6) Marginal Present Value of Cash Flow	(7) Net Present Value, Column 4 − Column 2
1	1	0.100	2.0	1	2.0	1.0
2	2.1	0.185	3.7	1.1	1.7	1.6
3	3.3	0.240	4.8	1.2	1.1	1.5
4	4.6	0.290	5.8	1.3	1	1.2
5	6.1	0.315	6.3	1.5	0.5	0.2

[15] See footnote 2, page 110.

Given the data in Table 1, we have two entirely equivalent ways of determining the optimal size. On the one hand, we can compute the series marginal to those in columns 2 and 4, as in the representation of the optimality conditions shown in Figure 3.5. In the present case, for example, we can then see immediately from columns 5 and 6 that a warehouse of a capacity of 1 million cu ft would not be an optimal decision, for if we increased the design by 1 million cu ft, we should increase the value of the facility by $1.7 million at an added cost of only $1.1 million. By the same token, sizes of 4 and 5 million cu ft are also not optimal, because the cost of added capacity exceeds its present value at both levels. As for the size that should be chosen, we can say that the optimal size under the circumstances is greater than 1 million and less than 3 million cu ft, and if necessary, we could narrow this range further by using a less coarse grid. (Note that without looking at warehouse sizes between 1 and 2 million cu ft, we cannot conclude that the optimal size is 2 million cu ft or greater, although the change from 1 to 2 million increases net present value.)

We could also have arrived at the identical conclusion, not by looking for the marginal equality, but simply by searching directly for the maximum difference between the value of the cash flow and the cost of acquiring it (in the spirit of the representation in Figure 3.4). These differences, essentially what we have earlier called the "net present value" or "goodwill" of an investment, are listed in column 7.[16]

II.A.2. Comparing investments with different lives

The previous example focused on differences in capacity or scale at different levels of investment. There are, however, other ways in which the capital intensity of a project can be varied, such as by changing its dura-

[16] Note that the criterion of choice is that of the maximum absolute difference between columns 4 and 2 and not the maximum relative difference or the maximum ratio of value to cost. This ratio, which has come to be called the "present value index," would clearly give the wrong decision in the present case, because its maximum value is for a warehouse of size 1 (or perhaps even smaller).

It may strike some readers as paradoxical that a warehouse of size 2, which has a cost of $2.1 million, a present value of $3.7 million, and a net present value index of 1.8 (or equivalently, a net "rate of return" of about 80 percent) could ever be preferable to a warehouse of size 1, which not only has a higher present value index (and rate of return) but requires a much smaller initial outlay on the part of the firm. Remember, however, that under the assumption of perfect capital markets the firm faces no limitations on obtaining funds to finance profitable projects, so that the absolute size of investments, whether mutually exclusive or not, is completely irrelevant. It is true, of course, that not all firms are in so fortunate a position and may well face, or feel that they face, limits on their total investment budgets. But if so, there would still be no reason to believe that the present value index would be a reliable guide to decision making or even that such an index has any particular economic meaning. We return to a variant of this "rationing" problem in another context below.

bility. Suppose, for example, that we can provide 2 million cu ft of storage space either by a very solidly built structure with a life of 40 years, a gross present value over this period of $2 million, and costing $1.5 million or by a much lighter structure with a life of only 30 years, a gross present value of $1.5 million, and costing $1.2 million. Despite the fact that the more durable structure has the larger net present value, we cannot conclude that it is the preferable choice in this case. We first must make some allowance for the cash flows that would be earned during the years between 30 and 40 if the firm adopted the less durable alternative.

Precisely how to make this allowance is a problem to which our theory, as such, can make no contribution. In practice and in standard textbook discussions the assumption most typically made about the cash flow in the overlap intervals is that a facility, at the end of its economic life, is replaced by one of exactly the same kind. In the present case, the 30-year warehouse would thus be presumed to be replaced by another of 30 years' life, which would in turn open a gap of 20 years as compared with the single, 40-year warehouse. But this too is presumed to be replaced by a similar unit, and by repeating this process, we eventually match exactly the lengths of the two chains at 120 years, the lowest common multiple of 30 and 40. Applying the net present value rule over this interval, entering the cost of the future replacements as negative cash flows in the appropriate years, then in principle yields the correct choice as to durability.

Fortunately, however, there is a much simpler way to perform the calculation, and this, curiously enough, is to assume that the chain of like replacements actually extends all the way to infinity. Although this greatly increases the presumed time span, it also permits the use of the simple and compact perpetuity results noted earlier in Chapter 1. In particular, and assuming, of course, a given constant rate of interest in all periods, we first compute the net present value of any one link in either of the two chains, call them $V(30)$ and $V(40)$, respectively. The net present value to infinity of a warehouse replaced every 30 years is then[17]

$$V(30, \infty) = V(30) \left(1 + \frac{1}{(1+r)^{30}} + \frac{1}{((1+r)^{30})^2} + \cdots\right)$$

$$= V(30) \frac{1}{1 - 1/(1+r)^{30}} = V(30) \left[\frac{(1+r)^{30}}{(1+r)^{30} - 1}\right] \quad (3.18)$$

and similarly for the other chain.

The same result can also be expressed in another way, particularly popular among engineers. Instead of working with the stock values $V(30, \infty)$

[17] Note again that for $0 < x < 1$

$$(1 + x + x^2 + x^3 + \cdots + \cdots) = \frac{1}{1 - x}.$$

and $V(40, \infty)$, we can, if we choose, work with their flow equivalents, that is, with the flows, in perpetuity, that have the same present values as the stocks. These flows, which we denote by $\bar{X}(30)$ and $\bar{X}(40)$ and which are typically referred to in the engineering literature as "time-adjusted average cash flows," can be obtained simply by multiplying the present value of each infinite chain by the rate of interest, so that we have

$$\bar{X}(30) = rV(30, \infty) = V(30) \left[\frac{r(1 + r)^{30}}{(1 + r)^{30} - 1} \right] \qquad (3.19)$$

and similarly for $\bar{X}(40)$. The basic decision rule restated in terms of these (time-adjusted) average cash flows is to pick the higher of the two, which will always and necessarily be the one with the higher net present value.

Note that the term in brackets in the expression for the time-adjusted average cash flow is the so-called "capital recovery factor," which was derived and discussed in a somewhat different connection in Chapter 1. Thus, for example, $\bar{X}(30)$ is the uniform cash flow per year for 30 years that has a present value of $V(30)$. When it is assumed that the 30-year warehouse is always replaced by one of exactly the same type, $\bar{X}(30)$ is also the cash flow per period in perpetuity that has a present value of $V(30, \infty)$.[18]

II.B. Replacement Policies and the Optimal Economic Life of Equipment

In the previous illustrations, we took the length of life of our various alternative warehouses as fixed. But the life of any given capital good is rarely, if ever, determined solely by purely physical or technological considerations. The decision to terminate the life of a machine, by sale or scrapping, and to replace it with a different and presumably younger one is an economic choice. In principle, therefore, our criterion should apply in this case as well. But, once again, a certain amount of care has to be exercised to establish a meaningful comparison of the alternatives.

In particular, consider the following hypothetical problem. A firm now has an old warehouse that it proposes to demolish and replace with a new one of identical capacity whose economic life, for the moment, is assumed to be 30 years. (We later consider how this economic life itself is determined.) For simplicity, it is assumed that the gross cash flow before expenses of the two warehouses would be exactly the same. But of course the operating expenses of a new building—repairs, maintenance, heating, and so on— would be less than those of an old one. The decision would then seem to hinge on whether the present value of the "savings" from the new ware-

---

[18] Like most of the other present value concepts the time-adjusted cash flow has its counterpart in rate of return form. In particular if I is the amount of initial investment, then $rV(n, \infty)/I$ is the time-adjusted perpetual rate of return on the investment. The concept has found its main usefulness in valuation theory (see the $r^*(t)$ in Chap. 2, Sec. III.E.3).

house, that is, the difference between the operating costs of the old and the new buildings, is larger than the cost of construction of the new building plus the net cost of demolition.

The question remains, however, over precisely what time period these savings are to be computed. The previous discussion of the matching of streams for present value calculations might seem to suggest that the appropriate time span was 30 years, that is, the given full life of the new building. But it would be madness to project operating costs for the old warehouse over the next 30 years, for the firm would surely not keep the old building for so long. Hence, most of the savings being discounted would be purely "phantom savings" that would never in fact be realized.[19]

To obtain a proper comparison, we must allow somehow for the fact that the old warehouse will eventually be replaced, which may seem to involve us in a circularity, because this is the decision that we are currently trying to make. The paradox is resolved, however, as soon as we rephrase our initial question so that the decision problem is stated, not as whether to replace the old warehouse, but when to do so.

In particular, proceeding systematically, let us first compare replacing the warehouse at the beginning of this year (say, year $t - 1$ in the life of the warehouse) versus next year (year t in its life). If we replace it immediately, the present value of all future costs of warehousing—operating costs, construction costs and demolition costs—can be expressed as $V(30, \infty)$, assuming, as in the previous section, that the new warehouse, in its turn, will be replaced by an identical one with identical costs after 30 years and similarly thereafter. If, on the other hand, we delay the replacement until next year, the present value of our costs to infinity will be $W(t)/(1 + r) + V(30, \infty)/(1 + r)$, where $W(t)$ represents the costs of operating the old warehouse during the current year, assumed to be paid at the beginning of year t. Our decision rule can then be stated simply as follows: Replace now in preference to next year if

$$\frac{W(t)}{1 + r} + \frac{V(30, \infty)}{1 + r} \geq V(30, \infty).^{20} \qquad (3.20)$$

---

[19] We owe the expressive term "phantom savings" as well as many others that have become standard in replacement theory to George Terborgh whose book *Dynamic Equipment Policy*, New York: McGraw-Hill Book Company, 1949, still remains among the best available treatments of the practical as well as theoretical sides of replacement decisions.

[20] Stating the criterion in terms of the conditions for minimum cost rather than maximum net present value is permissible mathematically under our assumption that the gross revenue of the warehouses is the same; that is, if R stands for gross revenue, W for operating cost, and Z for the set of decision variables, then

$$\max_{z}(R - W) = \max_{z} R + \max_{z}(-W) = \max_{z} R - \min_{z} W = k - \min_{z} W$$

Note that our calculations could end at this point, although we have explicitly compared only two of the many possible replacement strategies. For example, suppose that Equation (3.20) holds, so that costs of an immediate replacement are less than those of a delay until next year. Then as long as the costs of operating the old warehouse increase with time, we know that it is actually optimal to replace now; that is, if Equation (3.20) holds and $W(t + 1) > W(t)$, it is easy to show that

$$\frac{W(t+1)}{(1+r)^2} + \frac{V(30,\infty)}{(1+r)^2} + \frac{W(t)}{1+r} > \frac{W(t)}{1+r} + \frac{V(30,\infty)}{(1+r)^2} \geq V(30,\infty),$$

so that replacement now is more profitable than replacement next year, which is in turn more profitable than replacement in 2 years. Applying this reasoning period by period leads to the conclusion that as long as Equation (3.20) holds, the optimal decision is to replace now.

If, on the other hand, the costs of immediate replacement are greater than the cost of another year's operation, our one-period calculation would certainly not tell us when the replacement will occur. But, in this problem, this is something that we do not really need to know. The calculation has solved the immediate action question, and we can safely postpone any further calculation until the future, when we shall in due course face the problem again.

Note, finally, that as in so many cases before, we can express our decision criterion in other entirely equivalent forms that may provide additional insights into the nature of the problem. In particular, a simple rearrangement of the inequality in Equation (3.20) yields the following rule: Replace now if

$$W(t) \geq rV(30,\infty). \tag{3.21}$$

In words, and recalling our discussion in the previous section, replace if the marginal cost of extending the life of the "defender" for one more year is greater than the (time-adjusted) average cost of the "challenger."[21]

---

in any case in which R is a given constant k. From the economic point of view, however, we must regard this as, strictly speaking, a suboptimal solution, because the difference in cost should in general lead to differences in output, prices, and their product, gross revenue. In practical applications, however, including also most inventory and related operations research models, the gain in simplicity by way of the minimum cost formulation more than compensates for the (normally) minor error of approximation involved.

[21] The rule in this form can easily be extended to allow for any salvage values connected with the defender. If S_1 is the current salvage value and S_2 the salvage value next period, the marginal cost of extending the life of the defender is $W_1 + rS_1 + (S_1 - S_2)$, that is, the sum of the operating cost, the interest that could otherwise have been earned on the salvage value plus the change, presumably decline, in salvage value. The criterion in this form should have a thoroughly familiar look to it.

Stating the criterion in this form helps to show, among other things, how we can complete the analysis by dropping our provisional assumption that we already know in advance the life span of the best challenger, for the replacement time for any challenger itself must be determined by the criterion (3.21). The details of the calculation for a given challenger are shown in Figure 3.8. The broken line $W(t)$ represents the actual operating costs that would be incurred each period, costs that are assumed to rise steadily as the warehouse ages. The curve $\bar{W}(t)$, lying below it, shows the time-adjusted average annual operating costs. As in Equation (3.19) the time-adjusted average annual operating cost is the present value of the operating costs per period up to period t converted to a uniform flow equivalent by way of the appropriate capital recovery factor. These costs too rise with time but less rapidly than $W(t)$ because of both the "discounting" built into the time adjustment and the fact that $\bar{W}(t)$ is a composite of the operating costs for all periods up to t. The curve $\bar{K}(t)$ represents the time-adjusted average annual "capital cost," that is, the construction cost for the warehouse converted to a flow equivalent by the capital recovery factor. This component of total cost falls steadily with age, as in any other case in which a "fixed" cost is spread over a larger number of time units. The curve $\overline{TC}(t)$, which is just the sum of $\bar{K}(t)$ and $\bar{W}(t)$, is the time-adjusted average combined cost, or average total cost, for short, and it will clearly be U-shaped, given the assumed behavior of $\bar{W}(t)$ and

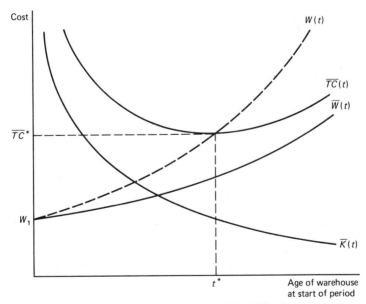

Figure 3.8   Optimal Length of Life of Warehouse

$\bar{K}(t)$. The optimum economic length of life is then found at that age t^* for which the average total cost is a minimum. And at this age the $W(t)$ curve intersects $\overline{TC}(t)$, because, from Equation (3.21), the fact of replacement at t^* must imply that at this point in time the marginal cost of extending the life is equal to the average cost of replacement with an identical warehouse, and this average cost is just

$$\overline{TC}(t^*) = rV(t^*,\infty).^{22}$$

To determine the optimal type of warehouse, that is, the best challenger, an analysis like that in Figure 3.8 would have to be carried out for each type to determine its optimal economic life and minimum average time-adjusted annual cost. The best challenger would then be the one with the overall minimum average annual cost.

II.C. Maximizing Present Value Subject to Constraints

Still another area in which the application of the present value criterion raises some questions and difficulties is the problem of capital budgeting subject to financial constraints. Several reasonably sophisticated formulations of this problem can now be found in the literature, all bringing to bear on the question some of the tools and concepts of mathematical programming.[23] One such formulation, which we can regard as typical for our purposes, visualizes a set of projects x_j, $j = 1, 2, \ldots, n$, that the firm may undertake in any period from now (period 1) up to some finite horizon period T. With each such project, there is associated in each period a cash flow c_{jt} that may be negative, as, for example, in the period during which it is purchased; or positive, as during its normal earning life; or zero, implying either that it has not started yet or that its life is already over. Given these cash flows, we can compute a net present value b_j, $j = 1, 2, \ldots, n$, for each project by applying the given market rates of interest to the flows in exactly the manner considered in previous sections.

[22] From Fig. 3.8 we can also see how the analysis can readily be extended to allow for at least some fairly simple and regular kinds of technological improvement, and hence, by implication, of technological obsolescence. The curve $W(t)$ can be considered the absolute value of the operating cost per year, or we could shift our origin to the point W_1, the operating costs of the first year, and interpret $W(t)$ as the excess cost above that incurred with a new machine. To the extent that each vintage of new machines incorporates improvements that result in lower operating costs in the first year, and all subsequent years, we can treat this improvement as an additional "obsolescence cost" to be added to $W(t)$ to obtain the complete excess cost of operating with an old rather than the best new machine then available. The rest of the calculation then proceeds as before. For an extensive discussion and illustration see Terborgh, *op. cit.*
[23] One of the best examples, and the one that is serving as the model for our discussion here, is that of H. M. Weingartner, *Mathematical Programming and the Analysis of Capital Budgeting Decisions.* Englewood Cliffs, N.J.: Prentice-Hall, Inc., 1963.

If there were no financial constraints, our problem would then be simply

$$\max \sum_{j=1}^{n} b_j x_j$$

subject to $$0 \le x_j \le 1, \qquad j = 1, 2, \ldots, n,$$

$$x_j \text{ integer}$$

which is just another minor variant of our standard "maximize present value" format, the special wrinkle here being the added integer constraint whose function, of course, is to ensure that any project is either rejected completely ($x_j = 0$) or accepted in toto ($x_j = 1$).[24]

Suppose, however, that we imposed the further restriction that the amount invested in projects in any period could not exceed the available cash throw-off during the period from previously undertaken projects plus a specified amount of outside borrowing B_t, which might be zero. This would constitute an additional set of constraints of the form

$$\sum_{j=1}^{n} c_{jt} x_j \ge -B_t, \qquad t = 1, 2, \ldots, T.$$

The optimal x_j for this more tightly constrained problem are clearly different from those of the original problem whenever one or more of the financial constraints is binding. For when such constraints are present, every project now contributes to the total present value in two ways: directly, by way of its b_j term in the maximand, and indirectly, by way of its cash flow terms c_{jt}, which loosen or tighten the financial constraint in a bottleneck period and thus permit or rule out other profitable projects.

But although this procedure certainly yields a solution to the problem of capital budgeting subject to such financial constraints, there are certain reservations that must also be entered about its use in any practical setting, quite apart from such matters as where the numbers are supposed to come from or how to deal with the severe computational difficulties involved in large-integer programming problems. For the problem, as formulated, really involves a conceptual inconsistency between the maximand and the constraints. The maximum present value criterion is invoked in investment and other corporate decisions, not as an end itself, but because it can serve

---

[24] The integer constraint also makes it possible to allow for many kinds of dependencies between projects without overly complicating the statement of the problem. For example, to indicate that projects m and n are mutually exclusive, we need add only a constraint of the form $x_m + x_n \le 1$. To make project r conditional on the undertaking of project s, we impose the restriction $x_r \le x_s$.

as a surrogate for the best interests of the owners of the firm in certain circumstances. These circumstances, as we have seen, include the existence of a perfect capital market in which firms and individuals can borrow and lend indefinite quantities at the going rate of interest.

Given this rationale for the maximand, what sense can we make of the constraints? If the firm really does face approximately perfect markets, the financial constraints are arbitrary impositions of the management contrary to the best interests of the owners. The solution from their point of view would not be optimal, although it had been formally derived by a "maximization" process. On the other hand, if the constraints were genuine and the firm really faced limitations on outside funds, it is the maximand that would be purely arbitrary. For what point is there in discounting a stream with market interest rates that do not represent actual opportunities for the firm in question? The firm might just as well use the rates of a foreign country or any other set of numbers plucked out of the air.[25]

To say that programming models of this kind suffer from logical difficulties is not to suggest, of course, that such mathematical programming approaches have no value in capital budgeting problems. Setting aside the obvious problems of data collection, allowance for uncertainty, and so on, the programming models may well have an important role to play when the relevant constraints are not financial. For rapidly expanding firms the key limitations are often those of certain specialized kinds of manpower, and the programming approach, which would represent, in effect, an attempt to provide a computationally feasible simplification of one of the fixed capital models considered in Section I, would aim at an optimal allocation of this resource over projects and time periods.

Moreover, even models with financial constraints might have valid uses, provided that these constraints were treated as provisional planning estimates rather than as inviolable policies or even desirable targets; that is, an initial trial run-through of the model with an internal funds restriction could be used to highlight which future periods would be tight and thus provide a basis for an appropriate program of external financing to overcome

---

[25] From an esthetic point of view, "rationing" models, in which the objective is to maximize the terminal value of the firm as of some horizon date rather than its supposed present value, offer some advantages. This formulation does at least maintain consistency between the interest rates in the functional and in the constraints, which can be set up to take account of whatever borrowing and lending opportunities are actually available. Moreover, it is at least possible to imagine special utility functions for the owners for which the resultant policies would be optimal. Examples of this type of formulation can be found in Weingartner, *op. cit.*, and in Charnes, Cooper, and Miller, "An Application of Linear Programming to Financial Budgeting and the Costing of Funds," *Journal of Business*, vol. 32, no. 1 (January 1959).

the binds. In sum, there are more uses for mathematical models in the applied areas of finance than just that of literal, direct, on-line, real-time decision making, and, in the present state of the art, these planning uses, in which a simplified formal model serves mainly to organize and explore some of the grosser implications of policy decisions, are likely to be more important.

II.D. The Rate of Return Criterion: Uses and Abuses

As noted at several points in Section I of this chapter and in Chapter 2, the criterion for optimal investment decisions may be stated either in present value form or in rate of return form. Once again, however, a certain amount of care has to be taken to avoid meaningless comparisons, and this is particularly true when the rate of return computed happens to be that variant known as the "discounted cash flow internal rate of return"— the variant most widely used at least in the standard popular treatments of capital budgeting.

II.D.1. The discounted cash flow rate of return

The discounted cash flow internal rate of return on an investment is defined as that rate of discount for which the net present value of the investment would be exactly zero. Algebraically, this means finding a root ρ^* of the nth-order polynomial

$$v(\rho^*) = \frac{x_1}{(1 + \rho^*)} + \frac{x_2}{(1 + \rho^*)^2} + \cdots + \frac{x_n}{(1 + \rho^*)^n} - I_0 = 0, \quad (3.22)$$

where the x_t are the net cash flows per period and I_0 is the amount of any initial outlay. The logic of the calculation is shown in Figure 3.9. First set the discount rate equal to zero and solve Equation (3.22) for $v(0)$, in this case, merely by summing the x_t and subtracting I_0. Next set the discount rate equal to some small positive amount and again solve Equation (3.22). Assuming the x_t all positive, the net present value so obtained must be lower than $v(0)$, because each x_t element in the summation is multiplied by a number $1/(1 + \rho)^t < 1$. Repeat the process for successively higher values of the discount rate, tracing out the entire curve $v(\rho)$, as in Figure 3.9. The value of the discount rate at which this curve cuts the horizontal axis is the DCF internal rate of return ρ^*.

A glance at Figure 3.9 also helps to make clear the sense in which this rate of return can provide a criterion equivalent to the present value rule. For whenever the actual market rate of interest is less than ρ^*, the net present value of the investment is necessarily positive under our assumptions, and the investment is worth considering. Conversely, if $r > \rho^*$, the

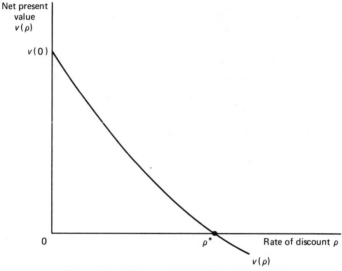

Figure 3.9   Discounted Cash Flow Rate of Return

net present value is negative, and the investment would not meet the present value test.[26]

In using the DCF rate of return as an alternative to a present value calculation, it should be kept in mind that the equivalence of the two procedures holds only if the rate of interest is assumed to be the same in all periods. If not, there is no single rate of interest to be compared with ρ^*, and the DCF rate of return cannot be used as the basis of an investment decision criterion.[27]

[26] Note that there is no need to refine the calculation further by allowing for the fact that the cash throw-off from the project may have to be reinvested at rates lower than ρ^*. Because the lowest such reinvestment opportunity is always at least r, taking it into account could never reverse the direction of the inequality.

[27] This limitation on the use of the DCF rate of return is perhaps not of great practical consequence, because it is rare in actual capital budgeting to use anything but an assumed constant rate of interest or cost of capital. Nevertheless as a reminder of the shortcomings of the DCF rate of return as an investment criterion, consider the following example, involving two infinite streams of cash flows:

$t =$	1	2	3	≥ 3
$_{t-1}r_t$	0.01	0.05	0.10	0.20
Stream 1	0	2.00	4.00	16.00
Stream 2	10.00	10.39	10.54	10.54

When discounted at the market interest rates, both streams have present ($=$market)

II.D.2. Mutually exclusive investments and multiple rates of return

Although the DCF rate of return thus has its perfectly legitimate and consistent uses as an alternative form of the present value criterion, at least when interest rates are constant in time, there are some types of decisions even then in which its application runs into difficulties. One of the most important of these arises when a choice must be made between mutually exclusive investment opportunities. The nature of the difficulty is shown in Figure 3.10, which shows the $v(\rho)$ curves for two different machines A and B being considered as alternatives for the same task.[28] Both machines require an initial outlay of $25. Machine A has a net revenue stream of $5 per year at the beginning of each of the following 10 years, but B produces

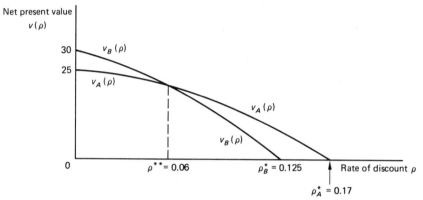

Figure 3.10   Rates of Return for Mutually Exclusive Investment Opportunities

$1, $2, $3, and so on, up to $10. The DCF internal rate of return on A, ρ_A^*, is about 17 percent, but ρ_B^* is about 12.5 percent.

As for the criterion of choice in such a comparison, it might seem that the rule should be to select the one with the higher rate of return, just as, under the present value criterion, we select the alternative with the higher net present value. In the case pictured, the higher rate of return rule would

---

value of $73.89. An investor who bought stream 1 at this price, however, would obtain a DCF rate of return of 15.1 percent; stream 2 would yield only 14.1 percent. The difference in rates of return has absolutely no economic significance, however, because in a perfect capital market a stream of cash flows with a given market value can always be exchanged for any other stream with the same market value.

[28] In an important sense, of course, the mutually exclusive case is the standard one, because, as we have emphasized earlier, any project is really a whole set of investments of different capital intensity in many different dimensions.

The specific example in the text is taken from A. Alchian, "The Rate of Interest, Fisher's Rate of Return over Cost, and Keynes' Internal Rate of Return," *American Economic Review* (December 1955).

lead to the selection of machine A. But, as can readily be seen from the graph, this choice might conflict with that signaled by the present value criterion. For whenever the actual rate of interest is less than ρ^{**}, the net present value of machine B is higher than that of machine A. Which rule should be followed?

The answer is the present value criterion, of course. The reader for whom this conclusion is not obvious by now may perhaps be able to convince himself by asking why the crossover of the two $v(\rho)$ functions occurs at all. He will soon realize that the key to the different rates of decline of the two functions lies in differences in the timing of cash flows for the two projects. Project B has increasing cash flows across its lifetime. Thus at low market interest rates the higher cash flows at the end of its life contribute heavily to its present ($\equiv$market) value. Project A, on the other hand, has a constant cash inflow throughout its life. It produces larger cash inflows than B in the early years but smaller flows in the later years. When the market interest rate is high, later cash flows have low current market value, so that machine A then has a higher present value than B because of the larger early cash inflows of A.[29]

II.D.3. A modified rate of return rule for the mutually exclusive case

For the example given, it is relatively easy to define a somewhat more elaborate rate of return criterion that would overcome the difficulties discussed above and guarantee reaching the correct decision with a rate of return rule. In particular, first select the machine with the larger rate of return, in this case, machine A, and compare this rate with the market rate of interest r. If the rate of return is less than r, reject both alternatives; if it is greater than r, accept the machine provisionally as the defender. Then compute the rate of return of the challenger, in this case, machine B, over the defender, that is, compute the rate of return on the differences in the cash flow and outlay streams period by period. The reader should convince himself that, in Figure 3.10, this would be the rate ρ^{**}. The last step in the rule would then be to compare ρ^{**} with the rate of interest; if $\rho^{**} > r$, accept the challenger, and if $\rho^{**} < r$, accept the defender.[30]

---

[29] Any reader still unconvinced that the present value criterion is always the correct one should turn back to Chap. 2, Sec. II, in which the maximize present value rule was shown to be an implication of maximum utility for the firm's owners under the perfect capital market assumption.

[30] It is important not to neglect the first step, because ρ^{**}, which is often called the "relative" rate of return, may be positive and greater than r, although the values of ρ^*, or "absolute" rate of return, may be negative. In such a case, ρ^{**} would merely serve to indicate which of the two alternatives would produce the smaller loss.

To see that ρ^{**} is indeed the rate of return of the challenger over the defender, note

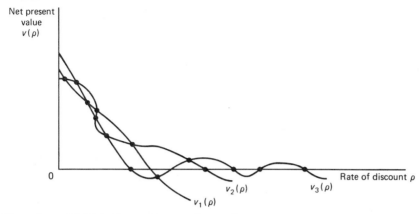

Figure 3.11   Multiple Rates of Return in the Case of Many Alternative Opportunities

Although a simple rule could easily be stated for this special case, the difficulties of statement mount rapidly when we consider more alternatives and alternatives whose $v(\rho)$ curves are less nicely behaved. Consider, for example, the mess shown in Figure 3.11. Note first that machine 3, the one with the highest absolute rate of return, actually has, not one, but five distinct rates of return or crossings of the $v_3(\rho)$ curve with the horizontal axis. There is nothing really remarkable in this, because the basic defining equation (3.21) is, after all, an nth-order polynomial, and from Descartes's rule of signs we can say only that there can be no more such distinct positive roots, in this case, DCF rates of return, than there are changes of sign of the coefficients, that is, the x_t. As a practical matter, moreover, net negative cash flows in some periods are perfectly sensible, the classical illustration being that of periodic pumpings of water or gas into oil wells to restore the pressure and increase the rate of oil flow.[31] A less exotic case would be that of periodic major overhauls of equipment or major replacements, for remember, in making the comparison between alternatives, we must match the length of the streams.

---

that the present value at the discount rate ρ of the differences between the cash flow and outlay streams for the two machines is just the difference between their total net present values at the rate ρ, that is, the difference between the two present value curves in Fig. 3.10. The rate of return of the challenger over the defender is the rate of discount for which the present value of the differences between the cash flow and initial outlay stream is 0. But this is just the rate of discount for which $v_B(\rho) - v_A(\rho) = 0$, that is, the rate ρ^{**}.

[31] A simple example is provided by Ezra Solomon, "The Arithmetic of Capital Budgeting Decisions," *Journal of Business* (April 1956). Suppose that a project has an immediate cash outflow of $1600, a net inflow next period of $10,000, and a final net outflow two periods from now of $10,000. As the reader can check, the project has two DCF rates of return, 25 and 400 percent.

As for the crossings between the curves, we have no less than nine of which one has been drawn to occur below the horizontal axis. Clearly, however, with a little patience, one could devise a routine to search through the maze and present a conditional "decision tree" running solely in terms of rates of return for matching challengers against defenders so as to determine the true champion. In this sense, then, it would still be true that the rate of return is equivalent to the present value criterion. But the rule would be so long and complex as to destroy the rationale for having used a rate of return calculation in the first place.

The popularity of the rate of return in applied capital budgeting is, after all, at least in part a reflection of its simplicity. Many people, apparently, find it more intuitively appealing to compare two rates than two present values. Much more important in its popularity, however, has been the fact that the rate of return approach seems to permit a convenient administrative separation of the decision process. The technicians or engineers are supposed to estimate the cash flows and compute rates of return on the various investment projects that they send upstairs for approval. The finance staff in the treasurer's office then independently computes the appropriate rate of interest or cost of capital for the firm. And top management maintains control over capital spending by putting the two sets of estimates together and selecting the specific projects to be implemented.[32] But the previous example makes clear that this neat separation runs into difficulties when many mutually exclusive alternative possibilities for accomplishing a given task are available, as they normally are.

II.E. The Rate of Return, Rankings of Projects, and Financial Constraints

The seeming ability to define a DCF rate of return independently of the rate of interest or cost of capital has given the DCF ρ^* tremendous appeal for those concerned with investment planning for firms, particularly small ones, who face or feel they face limits on the funds available for investment.[33] Some treatises recommend, for example, that the firm compute the DCF ρ^* for each proposed investment project and rank all the projects in decreasing order of rate of return. The optimal "cutoff point" is then supposed to be found simply by marching down this schedule, accepting lower and lower rated projects until the allotted total investment budget has been exhausted.

---

[32] This description, of course, is a statement of the ideal and not of how the system actually works in practice.

[33] For simplicity, we speak here only of a presumed absolute limitation on the funds to be employed. The same strictures apply with equal force, however, to analyses in which the firm is pictured as facing a cost of capital function that rises with the amount invested in any period.

Despite the fact that this procedure may bear some superficial resemblance to the process shown in Figure 3.7, it should be amply clear by now that it is really only a caricature of the underlying theory of investment. For one thing, we have seen that the calculations of investment productivity cannot proceed in any meaningful way without some prior assumptions as to the relevant market rate of interest. Before one could even assemble the list of projects to be ranked, the rate of interest would have had to be invoked in choosing between mutually exclusive alternatives. Moreover, even if it were somehow possible to find a list of independent, all or nothing projects whose DCF rates could be computed without reference to an interest rate, the very notion of a ranking of such projects by rate of return runs counter to the basic rationale of the procedure. The DCF rate of return is an interesting number for such projects only because a rate higher than the market rate of interest signals that the project is worth doing. It provides, as it were, a simple go versus no-go criterion and says nothing about the relative desirability of projects to the firm.[34] If the objective is to maximize the net wealth of the owners, all such projects that flash the go signal must be undertaken regardless of how strong the flash.[35]

These objections to rate of return ranking are perhaps obvious enough in the case of perfect capital markets, in which the simple accept or reject decision is all that we need; but the idea of ranking by rate of return becomes doubly nonsensical in the presence of financial constraints. It is more than just a matter of an inconsistency between the maximand and the constraints of the kind discussed earlier in connection with the con- strained version of the present value rule. In this case, it was at least clear what was being maximized, if not why, and the indirect contributions of the projects by way of their effects on the constraints were also taken into account. If, however, we merely march down a rate of return ranking until we run out of money without taking into account the indirect effects on later constraints, we have something like the disembodied smile of the Cheshire cat—a maximizing condition, but one not derived from or even related to any known maximand.

II.F. Conclusion

In this chapter we began by deriving the criteria for optimal investment decisions by the firm under certainty and relating these criteria both to the standard theory of the firm and to our earlier treatment of wealth allocation

---

[34] For example, the reader should find it easy to construct examples where the rankings of projects according to their DCF rates of return is not the same as the rankings provided by their net present values. (See Fig. 3.10 when $r < 0.06$.)
[35] Recall the similar remarks with respect to the "present value index" in Sec. II.A.1.

and security valuation in perfect capital markets. We then went on not so much to consider how these criteria could or should be applied in practice—real-world decision problems normally involving uncertainty in crucial ways that our simple apparatus cannot encompass—but rather to call attention to some of the pitfalls and inconsistencies to which mechanical application of standard capital budgeting procedures can all too easily lead. With this, the task begun in Chapter 1—the analysis of the role of capital markets in the allocation of wealth with respect to time—has been completed, and we now turn to the task of extending the analysis to allow for uncertainty.

REFERENCES

The great burst of interest in recent years in both the theoretical and applied aspects of capital budgeting was triggered off by a number of books that appeared in the late 1940s and early 1950s, of which the most influential have been

Dean, Joel, *Capital Budgeting*. New York: Columbia University Press, 1951.

Lutz, Frederick, and Vera Lutz, *The Theory of Investment of the Firm*. Princeton, N.J.: Princeton University Press, 1951.

Terborgh, George, *Dynamic Equipment Policy*. New York: McGraw-Hill Book Company, 1949.

Also extremely important in making capital budgeting one of the main themes in the field of finance was the collection of readings that appeared a decade or so later under the editorship of Ezra Solomon:

Solomon, Ezra (ed.), *The Management of Corporate Capital*. New York: The Free Press, 1959.

Most of the articles cited in Section II can be found in this collection.

A good introductory survey of capital budgeting along standard lines with many drill problems can be found in the first section of

Bierman, Harold, Jr., and Seymour Smidt, *The Capital Budgeting Decision*, 2d ed. New York: The Macmillan Company, 1966.

One of the best treatments of the capital rationing problem remains that of

Weingartner, H. Martin, *Mathematical Programming and the Analysis of Capital Budgeting Problems*. Englewood Cliffs, N.J.: Prentice-Hall, Inc., 1963.

UNCERTAINTY MODELS

The second part of the book is concerned with the same general
topics as the first; that is, we discuss models for decision making
by individuals and firms and the way these decisions at the micro
level interact to determine the nature of equilibrium in the capital
market. Moreover, as in the first part of the book, almost all our
work is carried out in the context of a perfect capital market.
Simply stated, our goal now is to study how the analyses and
conclusions of the preceding chapters can be adjusted to allow for
the effects of uncertainty.

Thus the major results with respect to the nature of optimal
production-financing decisions by firms obtained for a certainty
world are the two separation principles in Chapter 2. Specifically,
(1) given its production decisions, a firm's financing decisions are
a matter of indifference to its security holders, so that production
and financing decisions are separable; and (2) optimal production
decisions for a firm simply involve adherence to the market value
rule, so that such decisions are independent of the details of owner
tastes. In Chapter 4, we see that these separation or independence
principles hold also in a world of uncertainty, and in fact their
validity requires only the assumed existence of a perfect capital
market.

In a certainty world, and given a perfect capital market,
implementation of the market value rule is a simple matter, because
market values are always determined by applying known interest
rates to cash flows whose values are also known for certain. In a
world of uncertainty, however, a perfect capital market is not in
itself a sufficient basis for a model of price determination. To
derive meaningful, that is, testable, statements about how the
current price of a probability distribution of future payoff is
determined in the market, we first need a more detailed specification
of investor tastes. Thus, in Chapter 5, we present such a theory of
choice under uncertainty: the expected utility model.

But we find that the expected utility model does not carry us all
the way to the goal. The model simply says that investors rank
probability distributions on the basis of the expected or average
value of utility for each distribution. To develop first a testable

theory of investor decision making and then one of market equilibrium, the dimensionality of the investor's decision problem must somehow be reduced; that is, we must somehow determine either additional restrictions on investor tastes—for example, some assumption about the form of utility functions—or assumptions about common properties of probability distributions of returns—for example, all are normal—that allow us to describe the different alternatives available to an investor in terms of a finite number of parameters—for example, means and variances of return distributions—that are common to all alternatives.

Thus Chapter 6 is concerned with two-parameter models of investor decision making under uncertainty. In brief, these models assume that investors are risk-averse, a term whose precise meaning is obtained from the expected utility model, and that they find it possible to summarize any probability distribution of return in terms of two parameters, the mean of the distribution, and some measure of the dispersion of possible return values like the variance or standard deviation.

Chapter 7 is then concerned with the implications of the two-parameter model for the characteristics of capital market equilibrium; that is, given a market in which investors make decisions according to a two-parameter model, what can we say about the determination of the market values of securities and firms? Specifically, what is the appropriate way to measure the risk of an asset, and what kind of relationships might be expected between risk and return?

Finally, Chapters 6 and 7 concentrate entirely on two-period models. In Chapter 8 the analysis is extended to the multiperiod case. As we shall see, this is in keeping with our practice of proceeding from the simple to the more difficult.

4

FINANCING DECISIONS, INVESTMENT DECISIONS, AND THE COST OF CAPITAL

I. INTRODUCTION

In Chapter 2 we considered the problems of optimal operating-financing decisions by firms in a world of perfect certainty and perfect capital markets. Two fundamental "separation principles" were established. First, it was shown that given its operating, that is, production-investment, decisions, the market value of a firm at any point in time is independent of its financing decisions; thus operating decisions need not be affected by financing decisions.[1] Second, in making its operating decisions, an optimal policy for the firm is to maximize the market value of the holdings of its current owners, irrespective of the details of owner tastes. Finally, in Chapter 3 it was then shown that with perfect certainty and perfect capital

[1] As in preceding chapters, the terms "production," "investment," and "operating decisions" are used interchangeably. Likewise we feel free to refer to an individual as a "consumer," an "investor," or a "consumer-investor."

markets, observed market interest rates provide the appropriate cutoff rates or "costs of capital" for the firm's production-investment decisions.

In this chapter we show that the two separation principles continue to hold when the perfect certainty assumption is dropped. The goal is to demonstrate that the validity of these propositions is a direct implication of the assumed existence of a perfect capital market. We find, however, that in a world of uncertainty the perfect capital market assumption is not sufficient to give real meaning to the notion of a cutoff rate or cost of capital for a firm's investment decisions.

The first separation principle is considered in Section III. We initially take a "market equilibrium" approach in which the effects of the capital structure or financing decisions of firms on the market values of their securities is discussed in the context of the entire process by which the equilibrium holdings and prices of holdings by all investors in all firms are determined in the market. Although most general and in fact quite simple, this market equilibrium approach may seem, at least to the beginning reader, a little overly abstract. Thus for purposes of illustration two other somewhat more concrete, but correspondingly more restrictive, approaches are also used to present the major propositions concerning the effects of financing decisions on market values. In these the method of analysis is to derive the market value of a firm's securities from the market values of other securities that provide identical investment positions.

In Section IV we consider the problem of determining criteria for optimal operating decisions by firms. We find that, as in a world of perfect certainty, the "market value rule," that is, maximize the market values of currently outstanding securities, is a criterion for investment decisions that is optimal in a perfect capital market. In a world of uncertainty, however, implementation of this criterion runs into difficulties, because firms can have more than one type of security outstanding—for example, bonds and common stock—and an investment decision that maximizes market value for one group of security holders need not do so for others.

Finally, neither the analysis of the effects of capital structure on market values nor the discussion of criteria for optimal investment decisions make use of the concept of a cost of capital. The chapter concludes by considering the somewhat limited role of this concept in a world of uncertainty.

The immediate order of business, however, is a description of the market setting—a discrete-time, two-period model—within which most of the analysis takes place.

II. MARKET SETTING

For convenience, the economic agents that carry on production activities are called firms. At the beginning of period 1 firms purchase the services of inputs—labor, machinery, and so on—and use these to produce goods and services to be sold at the beginning of period 2, at which time all firms are disbanded. A firm finances its outlays for production in period 1 by issuing financial assets or securities that are claims against its total market value at period 2. In a discrete-time, two-period world the market value of a firm at period 2 is just the difference between cash revenues and costs at period 2, and this total market value is paid in full to the investors holding the firm's securities from period 1.

At the beginning of period 1, investors are assumed to have given quantities of resources—labor, which will be sold to some firm, and portfolio assets, which are the securities of firms carried forward from previous periods—that must be allocated to consumption for period 1 and a portfolio investment whose market value at period 2 determines the investor's period 2 consumption. For simplicity, we assume that the investor will be paid for his labor at period 1.[2]

A given set of production decisions by firms at period 1 determines the number of firms actually producing as well as the set of probability distributions on market values of firms at period 2 that will be available in the capital market at period 1.[3] These distributions are the basic objects that must be priced and cleared from the capital market at the beginning of period 1.

But the capital market also includes financial opportunities through which probability distributions on market value at period 2 can be fragmented into new distributions in different ways. We can distinguish two major types of fragmentations of the probability distribution on a firm's market value: (1) a division into different types of securities or claims—for example, bonds and common stock—and (2) a division of a particular financial asset into equivalent units—for example, the common stock of a firm is subdivided into individual shares.

Some fragmentations of the distribution of a firm's period 2 market value will be provided by the firm itself when it issues securities. Additional fragmentations may be carried out by investors by issuing claims against securities or portfolios of securities purchased from firms.

Equilibrium at the beginning of period 1 is assumed to be reached through a process of tâtonnement with recontracting; that is, investors come to market with their resources, tastes, and expectations on market values for period 2, and firms bring their production opportunity sets. Firms announce tentative production and financing decisions, investors offer their labor to

---

[2] As in earlier chapters, for brevity we commonly use the phrase "at period t" when we have in mind the longer phrase "at the beginning of period t."

[3] A brief review of the elementary statistical concepts that are required background for the uncertainty section of this book is provided in the Appendix to Chap. 5.

firms and begin bidding for consumption goods and securities, and a tentative set of prices for consumption goods, labor, and securities is established. Prices and decisions are tentative, because it is agreed that no decisions will be executed until an equilibrium set of prices, that is, a set of prices at which all markets can clear at period 1, has been determined. Our treatment of this model, however, concentrates on the nature of equilibrium in the capital market.

III. CAPITAL STRUCTURE AND MARKET VALUES

The effects of the financing decisions of firms on the market values of their securities is analyzed first in the context of the entire process by which the equilibrium holdings and prices of holdings by all investors in all firms are simultaneously determined in the capital market. The advantage of this market equilibrium approach is its generality; major propositions about the effects of capital structure can be presented without specifying much about the details of either investor tastes or the types of claims against firms that can and will be held when equilibrium is reached. By way of contrast, and for purposes of illustration, we later discuss two common and much more highly specified approaches, the "states of the world" model of Arrow [6], Debreu [7], Hirschleifer [5], and others and the original "risk class" model of Modigliani and Miller [1], in which the effects of financing decisions on market values was first given rigorous treatment. Most of the discussion in this section concentrates on the two-period case. We later show that the major results are easily generalized to a multiperiod context.

III.A. Two-Period Market Equilibrium Model

Suppose that the capital market and the tastes of individual investors are characterized by the following general conditions, which we say define a perfect capital market in the context of the two-period model:

1. The capital market is frictionless in the sense that all securities are infinitely divisible, information is costless and available to everybody, and there are no transactions costs or taxes.

2. Any financial arrangements available to firms are equally available to individuals; that is, any claims that a firm can issue at period 1 against its probability distribution of market value at period 2 can also be issued by any investor who holds an equivalent distribution. Thus, for example, it is assumed that, although his portfolio may include other probability distributions, an investor can issue claims against a given distribution with his liability limited only to the period 2 market value obtained from this distribution. In short, the limited liability of shareholders in firms applies

also to investors who issue securities on personal account. More generally, the possible ways in which a given probability distribution of period 2 market value can be fragmented and sold in the market at period 1 are independent of whether the distribution is presented to the market by an individual or a firm.

3. In choosing among available probability distributions on market value at period 2, investors are not concerned with who happens to issue a distribution; in particular, investors are not concerned with whether a distribution is issued by an individual or a firm.

4. Investors perceive that there are always perfect substitutes for any securities issued by an individual investor or firm, and individual investors and firms are "atomistic competitors" in the sense that their activities in the capital market have no effect on the prices of securities issued by other investors and firms. In short, as usual, we assume that investors and firms are price takers in the capital market.[4]

5. Finally, as in any perfect market, a certain amount of maximizing behavior on the part of investors is presumed. Specifically, investors are assumed to protect themselves against any sort of "financing decisions" by individuals or firms that have the effect of expropriating their positions without appropriate compensation. For example, suppose that at period 1 a firm initially has one bond outstanding, issued in some earlier period, which at this point is simply a promise to pay $R(2)$ at period 2. If the firm issues no new bonds at period 1, the outstanding bond is in effect a promise to pay the lesser of $R(2)$ or the market value of the firm $V(2)$ at period 2. But suppose that the firm issues one additional bond, which is again simply a promise to pay $R(2)$ at period 2. If there are no further priority arrangements, each bond now represents a claim to the lesser of $R(2)$ or $\frac{1}{2}V(2)$. If $V(2)$ turns out to be equal to or greater than $2R(2)$, the old bond receives $R(2)$, just as it would if no new bond were issued. But when $V(2)$ turns out less than $2R(2)$, the payoff on the old bond is strictly less than if no new bond were issued. In effect, by issuing a new bond with no priority arrangements, the firm has expropriated without compensation part of the distribution of $V(2)$ that would belong to the old bond if no

---

[4] A note for the more sophisticated: Because we have not presented a complete theory of market value determination under uncertainty, at this point we cannot really say exactly what constitutes a perfect substitute for a given security; that is, a model of market value determination would tell us what characteristics of a security's probability distribution of period 2 market value are looked at by the market when it prices the security at period 1. A perfect substitute for the security would then be defined in terms of these characteristics of return distributions that are relevant in the pricing process. Thus what we are saying is that, whatever the relevant theory of market value determination, there always are perfect substitutes for the securities issued by any investor or firm.

new bond were issued. But the old bond could easily have been protected against such infringements by a "me first" rule; that is, the contract on the old bond explicitly states that any new bonds issued can only have claim to observed market values greater than $R(2)$. Our concept of a perfect market assumes that bondholders protect themselves with such "me first" rules, and in fact, such priority arrangements are common practice.

Likewise, we also assume that a firm's common stockholders do not allow it to engage in capital structure changes that result in uncompensated shifts of holdings from them to the bondholders. For example, suppose that at period 1 the firm initially has two bonds of equal priority outstanding, each of which is a fixed claim to $R(2)$ at period 2. If $V(2) \geq 2R(2)$, the bondholders receive full payment at period 2, but if $V(2) < 2R(2)$, each bondholder receives only $\frac{1}{2}V(2)$. Now suppose that the firm uses retained earnings, which would otherwise be paid to the stockholders, or issues additional common stock at period 1 and uses the proceeds to "retire" one of the bonds. For any realized market value $V(2) < 2R(2)$ at period 2 the remaining bond receives a higher payoff than it would if the other were not retired. Thus, the claims of the remaining bond against the firm have implicitly been increased without compensation to the shareholders. The moral is clear: To avoid uncompensated shifts of holdings from shareholders to bondholders, the firm should either retire an entire bond issue, or in repurchasing part of an issue, it should allow the claims represented by the repurchased bonds technically to remain outstanding either by paying the bonds themselves as dividends to its stockholders or, equivalently, by holding the repurchased bonds as assets. Moreover, it is also easy to show that the firm should retire lower priority bonds before higher priority bonds; that is, the second mortgage should be retired before the first, because the reverse would lead to an uncompensated increase in the holdings of the second mortgagors.[5]

The major result of capital structure theory is then the "first separation principle": For any given set of operating decisions by firms at period 1, when the capital market is perfect, the equilibrium total market value of any firm at period 1 is unaffected by its financing decisions. Moreover, the firm's financing decisions have no effects on either the wealths or the capital market opportunities of its security holders, so that these decisions are a matter of indifference to the security holders. It follows that optimal

---

[5] It is clear, however, that stockholders and bondholders need only worry about protecting themselves from one another when the bonds of the firm are risky, that is, there is some chance that the market value of the firm at period 2 will be insufficient to cover the total promised payments to all bondholders. When all bonds are riskless, protective arrangements are unnecessary.

operating decisions for the firm do not depend on its financing decisions; that is, operating and financing decisions are separable.[6]

In essence, establishing these propositions involves showing that, given its operating decisions, the financial decisions of firms have no effect either on (1) the set of probability distributions on market value at period 2 that investors can bid for before equilibrium is established in the capital market at period 1 or on (2) the distributions that can be offered for sale by investors who come to market at period 1 with the securities of firms as part of their resources carried forward from period 0. In short, the financing decisions of firms have no effect on the opportunities facing investors. It then follows that the financing decisions of firms cannot affect either the ultimate equilibrium holdings of an individual investor in a given firm—that is, the fragmentation of the distribution of the firm's total market value at period 2 held by the investor at period 1—or the prices of these holdings. Thus the financing decisions of firms are a matter of indifference to investors. And because the sum of the period 1 market values of all holdings by all investors in any given firm is the firm's total market value, this also is unaffected by its financing decisions.

Let us expand. In a perfect market any types of claims that a firm can issue against its probability distribution of market value at period 2 can be issued by any investor who holds an equivalent distribution. It follows that a firm's financial decisions cannot affect the set of fragmentations of the distribution of its period 2 market value that could possibly be bid for when investors come to market at period 1.[7]

It is somewhat more tedious to show that the probability distributions that can be offered for sale in the market at period 1 by investors who hold the securities of a firm as part of their resources carried forward from period 0 are also unaffected by the firm's financing decisions. It is convenient to consider separately two reasons that a firm might want to issue new securities at period 1. First, the firm may have to cover outlays for production. If the firm's bondholders always use "me first" rules to protect

[6] In discussing these propositions in this section, we limit attention, for simplicity, and without departing too much from reality, to a world in which firms issue only the usual types of bonds, which provide for a stated maximum payoff at period 2, and common stock. Eventually the reader should be able to convince himself, however, that the analysis is not dependent on the types of securities that exist in the market and would, for example, also apply to the states of the world model, to be considered later, in which there are fixed payoff securities in the form of "contingent claims" that pay fixed sums but only if given states of the world are realized at period 2.

[7] Note that the analysis never requires that investors have the same view of the probability distribution on a firm's period 2 market value. Investors must simply be able to recognize when claims against a given distribution that are issued by investors are equivalent to claims against the same distribution that are issued by firms.

themselves against uncompensated expropriations of their holdings, any new securities issued to finance production have no effect on the distributions that can be offered to the market at period 1 by the holders of bonds outstanding from period 0. Thus any effects of the financing decision must fall on the shareholders. But in a perfect capital market the firm and its shareholders are atomistic competitors with respect to all types of securities. Thus if the firm chooses one configuration of new securities[8] and its shareholders, individually or as a group, would prefer some other configuration, the shareholders can achieve their desired positions by repurchasing the securities issued by the firm—with the shareholder who owns the proportion α of the firm's common stock purchasing the proportion α of the new securities—and issuing their desired configurations of securities on personal account. The probability distributions on market value at period 2 presented to the market are then exactly as if the firm itself had chosen to issue the configurations of new securities preferred by its shareholders. Moreover, in a perfect capital market the firm cannot provide any configuration of new securities that could not be offered by its shareholders on personal account. Thus new issues of securities by the firm to finance production have no effect on the distributions of period 2 market value that can be offered for sale at period 1 by investors who hold the firm's common stock outstanding from period 0.

The second reason that the firm may issue new securities at period 1 is that it may simply wish to bring about some change in its capital structure. In this case it issues new claims—bonds, common stock, or retained earnings—and either pays the proceeds directly to the stockholders or uses them to repurchase old claims. But in a perfect capital market such shifts in capital structure amount to refragmentations of the distribution of the firm's period 2 market value in which in any market equilibrium the firm's security holders acquire holdings with a given market value in exchange for other holdings with exactly the same market value. Thus, given atomistic competition, any security holder can always reacquire his former position by simply reversing the exchange on personal account, using his new holdings to reacquire his old holdings. Moreover, in a perfect capital market the firm cannot carry out any refragmentation of security holder positions that could not be obtained by the security holder on personal account. Thus, like financing decisions made to finance production, simple changes of capital structure also have no effect on the distributions of period 2 market value

[8] The term "securities" includes cash earnings obtained at period 1 from the production of period 0 that are retained to finance the production of period 1. In terms of their effects on the distributions of period 2 market values accruing to the old shareholders, such retained earnings are formally equivalent to a preemptive issue of new common stock, with each shareholder using dividends paid by the firm to purchase the new issue in proportion to his holdings of the shares outstanding from period 0.

that can be offered for sale at period 1 by investors who hold the firm's securities.[9]

In sum, because in a perfect market investors can issue the same sorts of claims as firms, the financial decisions of firms have no effect on the fragmentations of distributions on total market values of firms at period 2 that could be bid for by investors at period 1. Moreover, the distributions that can be offered to the market by investors who come to market at period 1 with the securities of a given firm as part of their resources are also unaffected by the financial decisions of the firm. Thus, a given set of financial decisions by firms neither provides investors with opportunities to trade probability distributions on market value at period 2 that are not available with any other set of financing decisions nor precludes opportunities that would be available with other financing decisions.[10] Moreover, in a perfect market, investors are not concerned with whether a given distribution of period 2 market value is offered by an individual or a firm. It then follows that the financial decisions of firms cannot affect the ultimate equilibrium holdings of individual investors in firms, that is, the fragmentations of distributions of period 2 market values held by investors, or the equilibrium prices of these holdings. More formally, any equilibrium sets of holdings and prices of holdings that can be reached with one set of financing decisions

[9] To give some concreteness to this analysis, consider a firm that has had no debt in its capital structure prior to period 1 and at period 1 simply wishes to bring about some change in its capital structure, with any proceeds from issuing debt going directly to the shareholders. In this case, all investors realize that regardless of what the equilibrium price of the firm's debt turns out to be, the firm's shareholders are always compensated precisely the amount needed by them to reacquire an unlevered position, that is, repurchase the bonds, if they so desire. Thus, before equilibrium is reached, the shareholders can proceed to undertake tentative trades exactly as if the firm will not lever their shares. And, of course, if the firm did not lever their shares, the shareholders could still offer to provide the levered positions to other investors by creating debt claims against the shares, exactly as would the firm, and then offering to sell the debt and the resulting levered shares separately.

[10] These conclusions are, however, critically dependent on the assumption that bondholders and shareholders protect themselves against uncompensated expropriations of their positions. For example, we saw earlier that if the bondholders do not insist on "me first" rules, their holdings in the distribution of the firm's period 2 market value can be reduced if the firm issues new bonds with no priority arrangements; thus the distributions of period 2 market value that can be offered for sale at period 1 by the holders of the old bonds can be affected by the firm's financing decisions. Moreover, in this case the firm's shareholders cannot similarly "dilute" the positions of its bondholders by issuing additional debt on personal account, so that their trading positions can also be affected by the firm's financing decisions. On the other hand, we also saw earlier that if the firm retires part of a debt issue, it implicitly increases the claims against the firm of the remaining bonds in the issue, so that again the firm's financing decisions can affect the distributions of period 2 market value that can be offered for sale at period 1 by its different security holders.

by firms can equally well be reached with any other set of financing decisions. Because a firm's total market value at period 1 is just the sum of the market values of all holdings by all investors, it follows that the total market values of firms are unaffected by their financial decisions. And because these results hold for any set of operating (production-investment) decisions by firms—that is, for any set of operating decisions by firms, the financing decisions of firms are a matter of indifference to their security holders—it follows that operating and financing decisions are separable.

III.B. Multiperiod Model

In the two-period model to establish the proposition that the total market value of a firm at period 1 is unaffected by the firm's financing decisions, it is fairly clear and unobjectionable to specify that the objects of concern to investors in their portfolio decisions at period 1 are probability distributions on market value at period 2. Because the proposition is not concerned with what does determine market values, for its purposes we need not specify the nature of investor tastes or the process generating period 2 market values in more detail. The proposition is a consequence of a perfect market and in particular of the perfect market assumptions that (1) any claims that firms can issue against the future realizations of production decisions can also be issued by the firm's security holders against their holdings in these same realizations; (2) investors are concerned only with the "real characteristics" of a claim and not with who happens to issue it; and (3) there are always perfect substitutes for the securities issued by any investor or firm, and investors and firms are atomistic competitors in the capital market.

But the logic of the two-period model applies equally well to corresponding multiperiod models. In a multiperiod world, specifying the characteristics of an uncertain payoff stream that are relevant to investors is generally much more difficult than in a similar two-period model. The market value of a firm at any point in time depends in some way on the current and future production-investment opportunities of this firm and other firms, all of which are uncertain and must be specified in different ways, depending on the model in hand. Nevertheless, although it may be difficult to develop in detail models that tell what does determine the market value of a firm at any point in time, if investors and firms are atomistic competitors in the capital market, if investors are concerned only with the real characteristics of securities, somehow defined, and if any claims that firms can issue against the future realizations of production and investment decisions can also be issued by the firm's security holders against their shares in these realizations—in short, if the capital market is perfect—

then exactly the reasoning of the preceding section applies; that is, a firm's financing decisions at any point in time are a matter of indifference to its security holders, so that operating and financing decisions are separable.

III.C. Two Partial Equilibrium Treatments

The preceding discussions analyze the effects of the capital structure or financing decisions of firms on their total market values in the context of the process by which the equilibrium holdings and prices of holdings by all investors in all firms are simultaneᴖusly determined in the market. The advantage of this market equilibrium approach is its generality; the important capital structure propositions were established without specifying much about the details of either investor tastes or the types of claims against firms that would be held when a market equilibrium is reached.

The two approaches to be discussed now are much more concrete but correspondingly less general. They can be characterized as partial equilibrium models in the sense that they take the financing decisions and prices of securities of all firms but one as given and then examine the effects of this firm's financing decisions on its total market value. The mode of analysis is to derive the market value of the firm and its securities from the known market values of equivalent positions in other firms, that is, positions that provide payoff streams identical with those of the securities of the firm.

Two partial equilibrium models are discussed: (1) a two-period states of the world model very similar to that of Hirshleifer [5] and (2) a model based on the existence of risk classes more or less in the sense defined by Modigliani and Miller [1]. The primary purpose is to provide some contrast with and insight into the reasoning of the market equilibrium approach presented above.

III.C.1. Two-period states of the world model

In the two-period model the basic objects that must be priced in the capital market at period 1 are the probability distributions on the total market values of individual firms at period 2. The fragmentations of these distributions made possible by financial opportunities represent ways of subdividing the risks of any given distribution among investors. The types of fragmentations that are carried out by investors depend in part on their tastes and in part on the characteristics of the process generating distributions of period 2 market values. One especially simple specification of tastes and opportunities is the states of the world model of Arrow [6], Debreu [7], Hirshleifer [5], and others.

At period 1 suppose that investors agree that there are a finite number S of mutually exclusive possible states of the world[11] at period 2 and that for a given set of production decisions by firms at period 1 the market value for certain of firm j if state s occurs is $V_j(2,s)$. All uncertainty attaches to the states of the world at period 2, and investors need not assign the same probabilities to states. Finally, in their portfolio decisions investors are assumed to be concerned only with the total number of dollars obtained in each state at period 2, and, other things equal, they always prefer more dollars in any given state to less.[12]

A simple way in which such a market might be organized at period 1 would be to have S separate contingent claims, where a given contingent claim is a promise to pay dollars at period 2 only if a given state of the world occurs. Firms might then fragment their distributions of total market value at period 2 into the values that occur in each state and then sell these separately in the market. The total dollars in each state made available by firms and the tastes of investors then determine S prices for contingent claims $p(1)$, $p(2)$, ..., $p(S)$, where $p(s)$ is the price at period 1 of a dollar to be delivered at period 2 only if state s occurs.

But suppose that firms do not issue contingent claims but rather issue only the more conventional bonds and common stock. If investors are still free to trade contingent claims among themselves, and if $v_k(2,s)$ is the market value of an arbitrary security k in state s at period 2, and if there are not to be arbitrage opportunities, the price $v_k(1)$ of security k at period 1 must be

$$v_k(1) = \sum_{s=1}^{S} p(s)v_k(2,s).$$

That is, investors can always replicate the payoffs across states provided by any security by purchasing the appropriate numbers of contingent claims to dollars to be delivered in each possible future state. Thus, assuming that investors can both issue and purchase contingent claims, if there are not to be arbitrage opportunities, the market value of any security at period 1 must be just the sum of the market values of the contingent

[11] The complex problem of defining what is meant by a state has not been adequately treated in the literature, and fortunately it is not necessary to do so here.

[12] This is not inconsistent with the analyses in the preceding sections in which investors were viewed as choosing among probability distributions on market value at period 2. Given an assignment of probabilities to states, in choosing among possible arrays of total dollars to be received in each state, the investor is choosing among probability distributions on market value at period 2. The distributions are determined by the dollars to be received in each state and the distribution of probabilities across states. Of course no such specifications of either tastes or opportunities were required in the market equilibrium approach.

claims (the dollars to be delivered in each possible future state) that
it implies.

It follows directly that, regardless of its financing decisions, the total
market value at period 1 of any firm, that is, the market value of bonds plus
common stock, is just

$$V_j(1) = \sum_{s=1}^{s} p(s) V_j(2,s),$$

where $V_j(2,s)$ is the market value of the firm in state s at period 2; that is,
given the firm's production decisions at period 1, its period 1 total market
value is independent of its financing decisions and is always just the sum
of period 1 market values, computed by means of the prices of contingent
claims, of the total dollars to be delivered in each possible future state.

For example, suppose that there are two possible states of the world at
period 2, and that if state 1 occurs the value of firm j is 10, and that if
state 2 occurs the value of firm j is 15. Suppose first that the firm has only
common stock in its capital structure. Then the market value of the firm,
and its stock, at period 1 is

$$V_j(1) = p(1)10 + p(2)15.$$

Alternatively, suppose that the firm issues both debt and common stock,
and the debt is in the form of a promise to pay 5 whichever state occurs at
period 2. Then the period 1 market value $B_j(1)$ of the firm's debt must be

$$B_j(1) = p(1)5 + p(2)5.$$

The stockholders, as the residual claimants, get 5 if state 1 occurs and 10 if
state 2 occurs. The total value of the stock is thus

$$S_j(1) = p(1)5 + p(2)10,$$

so that $\quad V_j(1) \equiv S_j(1) + B_j(1) = p(1)10 + p(2)15.$

Finally, the firm might issue both debt and common stock, with the debt
now being a promise to pay 12 in either state at period 2. But because the
firm's value in state 1 is only 10, full payment on the debt occurs only in
state 2, so that

$$B_j(1) = p(1)10 + p(2)12,$$

$$S_j(1) = p(1)0 + p(2)3,$$

$$V_j(1) = B_j(1) + S_j(1) = p(1)10 + p(2)15.$$

Thus the period 1 market value of the firm is the same under all three
different assumptions about financing decisions and in fact is always just

equal to the sum of the period 1 values of the total resources generated by the firm in each possible future state.[13]

To show that, given its operating decisions, a firm's financing decisions have no effect on its total market value is not to show, however, that operating and financing decisions are separable. The separation principle requires that the firm's financing decisions do not affect the wealths, which in this model determine the trading opportunities, of any of its security holders. But at this point it is easy to see that in the states of the world model a firm's financing decisions are indeed a matter of indifference to its security holders. If, in accordance with the perfect market assumption, security holders always protect themselves from one another, shifts in capital structure by a firm always result in exchanges of positions among security holders in which any security holder always receives a position with market value identical with any position he gives up. Because the market value of any security is just the sum of the market values of the contingent claims that it implies, the security holder can always recover his initial position, or any other position consistent with the total market value of his resources, in the market for contingent claims.

Thus, for example, if, given its operating decisions, a firm shifts its capital structure by issuing additional bonds, the shareholders lose claim to some period 2 resources, but the market value of their losses is precisely equal to the receipts that they obtain from issuing the bonds. On the other hand, if a firm uses retained earnings to retire debt, the bondholders receive the current market value of the claims to future resources that they give up, so that they can purchase contingent claims in the open market and regain precisely the positions that they give up. The shareholders, in turn, give up current resources with market value identical with the claims to future resources that they receive, so that their trading opportunities are also unaffected by the firm's financing decision. Hence, given its operating decisions, the firm's financing decisions are a matter of indifference to its security holders, so that operating and financing decisions are separable.

The separation principle is also easily established in a multiperiod states of the world model, and we leave this as an exercise for the reader. The reader may also find it useful to illustrate the preceding discussion of the irrelevance of capital structure decisions to a firm's security holders with a numerical example similar to the one presented earlier in this section.

III.C.2. The market value of a firm in the two-period risk class model

In the states of the world model the market prices of a firm's securities are derived by comparing them with the prices of perfect substitutes that

---

[13] The reader may find it helpful to show what would happen in this example if this result did not hold. By this time the required arbitrage arguments should be so familiar that this is an easy task.

are themselves just combinations of contingent claims. In the original treatment of capital structure problems by Modigliani and Miller [1] a different approach is taken. The market prices of a firm's securities are derived by comparing them with prices of identical positions in other firms from the same risk class.

We say that two firms i and j are in the same risk class if for all t,

$$X_i(t) = \lambda_i X_j(t) \qquad \text{and} \qquad I_i(t) = \lambda_i I_j(t), \qquad (4.1)$$

where $X_i(t)$ and $X_j(t)$ are the net cash earnings, before interest, of the firms at t, $I_i(t)$ and $I_j(t)$ are cash outlays at t for investment, and λ_i is a proportionality factor, which, it should be noted, is the same for all t for both earnings and investment. In periods before t, earnings and investments at t are uncertain; but for the two firms to be in the same risk class, investors must agree that whatever values earnings and investment outlays take in any period, for these two firms they are always proportional by the factor λ_i and hence perfectly correlated.[14]

In our initial discussions of the effects of financing decisions in the context of the risk class model, we concentrate as in preceding sections, on the two-period case. The results are then generalized to the multiperiod case.

In the two-period model we presume as always that firms make production decisions at period 1 and that these production decisions yield probability distributions on net cash earnings to be received at period 2. Each firm is presumed to pay out its earnings in full to those who hold its securities from period 1, and these earnings are the only source of returns on these securities at period 2. The role of the capital market at period 1 is to establish market prices for the securities. Our goal initially is to use the risk class model to establish the by now familiar proposition that, given its production decision at period 1, or equivalently, the probability distribution of its total earnings at period 2, the total market value of a firm is inde-

---

[14] This is not the definition of a risk class used by Modigliani and Miller in their initial paper [1], in which condition (4.1) is imposed only on the average earnings of firms in the same risk class. Thus, in their original definition only the average earnings, assumed to be uncertain, of firms in the same risk are assumed to be perfectly correlated, whereas in our definition this assumption is applied to the perceptions of investors concerning realized values of earnings. Their definition imposes fewer restrictions on the characteristics of the earnings streams of firms in the same risk class, but implicitly imposes more restrictions on the tastes of investors, because investors must be assumed to be concerned only with the average earnings of firms over time.

In their later empirical work, Modigliani and Miller apply (4.1) to realized earnings in defining a risk class [4, fn. 3], but (4.1) is not imposed on investment outlays. Some such condition on investment outlays is usually necessary, however, if the securities of firms in the same risk class are to be perfect substitutes. Intuitively, even if their earnings are proportional, the securities of the two firms need not be perfect substitutes if the earnings streams are obtained with nonproportional and uncertain investment outlays.

pendent of its financing decisions, that is, the way the distribution of period 2 earnings is fragmented and sold at period 1 to the different classes of security holders. Later we complete the proof of the separation principle by showing that a firm's financing decisions are a matter of indifference for any of its security holders, so that operating and financing decisions are separable.

For simplicity, the argument centers on an example involving two firms from the same risk class, one of which, firm L, is levered, that is, it has bonds as well as common stock in its capital structure at period 1, and the other, firm u, is unlevered, that is, its capital structure is composed entirely of common stock. It is assumed that the two firms not only are in the same risk class but also are anticipated to have the same total net cash earnings at period 2; that is, whatever period 2 earnings turn out to be, investors anticipate at period 1 that they will be identical for the two firms:

$$X_L(2) = X_u(2) = X(2).$$

Consider first an investor who holds the fraction α of the shares of the unlevered firm u. The market value of his investment at period 1 is thus

$$\alpha V_u(1) = \alpha S_u(1),$$

and his return at period 2 is

$$\alpha X_u(2) = \alpha X(2).$$

The investor could obtain this same return, however, by buying the proportion α of both the bonds and the common stock of the levered firm; that is, he could invest $\alpha B_L(1)$ in the debt of the levered firm, which debt has total market value $B_L(1)$, and invest $\alpha S_L(1)$ in the firm's shares, which have total market value $S_L(1)$. If $R_L(2)$ is the total payment to the firm's debtholders at period 2, his investment in the firm's debt yields $\alpha R_L(2)$, and his shares in the firm yield $\alpha(X(2) - R_L(2))$.[15] Thus his total return is

$$\alpha[X(2) - R_L(2)] + \alpha R_L(2) = \alpha X(2),$$

which is indeed identical with the return that he gets from holding the proportion α of the shares of the unlevered firm. His total investment in the levered firm is

$$\alpha[V_L(1) - B_L(1)] + \alpha B_L(1) = \alpha V_L(1).$$

Thus if $V_L(1)$ were less than $V_u(1)$, our investor, or any other investor, would not hold the shares of the unlevered firm, because the returns provided by these shares can be obtained at lower cost by buying both the

---

[15] Previously we used $R(2)$ to denote the promised payments to bondholders at period 2. In this section $R(2)$ represent actual payments, which may, of course be uncertain at period 1.

bonds and the shares of the levered firm. It follows that the total value of the unlevered firm must be equal to or less than that of the levered firm.

In holding the shares of the unlevered firm u, the investor has claim to an unlevered equity return from the particular risk class under consideration. When he buys equal proportions of the bonds and shares of the levered firm, he also has claim to an unlevered equity return from this class. In effect, by buying both the bonds and shares of the levered firm, he has unlevered the firm's capital structure, at least as far as his own portfolio is concerned. We now see that likewise an investor can use a combination of personal debt and the shares of the unlevered firm to obtain returns identical with those provided by the shares of the levered firm. In this case the investor levers the shares of the unlevered firm, at least as far as his own portfolio is concerned. And the availability of these types of transactions in a perfect market is shown to imply that the period 1 market values of the two firms must be identical.

Thus consider now an investor who owns the fraction α of the shares of the levered firm L. The market value of his shares at period 1 is

$$\alpha S_L(1) = \alpha[V_L(1) - B_L(1)],$$

and his return at period 2 is

$$\alpha[X(2) - R_L(2)].$$

Exactly the same return could be obtained by purchasing the fraction α of the shares of the unlevered firm, financing the purchase in part by issuing $\alpha B_L(1)$ of personal debt, using the shares of the unlevered firm as collateral. In a perfect capital market, if the debt of the levered firm, issued against its period 2 earnings $X(2)$, has market value $B_L(1)$ at period 1, the investor, borrowing against his ownership of $\alpha X(2)$ of the period 2 earnings of the unlevered firm, must be able to obtain $\alpha B_L(1)$ of personal debt at period 1 by promising to pay lenders α times whatever turn out to be the bond payments of the levered firm at period 2. Thus the net period 1 cost of the position involving "homemade" leverage is

$$\alpha V_u(1) - \alpha B_L(1) = \alpha[V_u(1) - B_L(1)],$$

and the return at period 2 from this combination of personal debt and shares in the unlevered firm is

$$\alpha X(2) - \alpha R_L(2) = \alpha[X(2) - R_L(2)],$$

which is indeed identical with the return obtained by holding the fraction α of the shares of the levered firm.

But the investment cost at period 1 of holding the shares of the levered firm is greater than the cost of the combination of personal debt and shares of firm 2 if $V_L(1) > V_u(1)$. It follows that if the shares of the levered firm are to be held, $V_L(1)$ must be equal to or less than $V_u(1)$. Our first example established, however, that $V_u(1) \leq V_L(1)$. Thus we can conclude that in equilibrium the total period 1 market values of the two firms must be equal. In short, given their production decisions, or equivalently given the probability distributions of their period 2 earnings, the period 1 market values of the firms are unaffected by the differences in their capital structures.

III.C.3. The market value of a firm in a multiperiod risk class model

Extension of this result to a multiperiod risk class model is conceptually straightforward, although notationally the model becomes rather cumbersome. Thus let $V_i(t)$ and $V_j(t)$ be the market values at period t of firms i and j. The two firms are assumed to be in the same risk class, so that

$$X_i(t) = \lambda_i X_j(t) \qquad \text{and} \qquad I_i(t) = \lambda_i I_j(t). \qquad (4.1)$$

We want to establish the following proposition: If there is some t such that $V_i(t) = \lambda_i V_j(t)$, then for all $\hat{t} \leq t$, $V_i(\hat{t}) = \lambda_i V_j(\hat{t})$, regardless of the financial decisions of the firms.[16]

The total value at period t of the shares and bonds of firm j that were outstanding from $t - 1$ is

$$[D_j(t) + S_{j,t-1}(t)] + [R_j(t) + B_{j,t-1}(t)], \qquad (4.2)$$

where $S_{j,t-1}(t)$ and $B_{j,t-1}(t)$ are respectively the market values at t of the common stocks and bonds outstanding from $t - 1$; $D_j(t)$ are total dividends paid at t, and it is assumed that any new stock issued at t does not share in these dividends; and $R_j(t)$ are actual payments[17] at t on bonds outstanding from $t - 1$. At period $t - 1$ the values of most period t variables are uncertain. Nevertheless, because cash inflows at t must equal outflows, we must have

$$X_j(t) + b_j(t) + s_j(t) = I_j(t) + R_j(t) + D_j(t), \qquad (4.3)$$

where $s_j(t)$ and $b_j(t)$ are respectively the market values of the new stocks and bonds issued at t. Thus first solving Equation (4.3) for $D_j(t)$ and then noting that

$$S_{j,t-1}(t) = V_j(t) - B_{j,t-1}(t) - s_j(t) - b_j(t),$$

for the total wealth expression (4.2), we can obtain

$$[D_j(t) + S_{j,t-1}(t)] + [R_j(t) + B_{j,t-1}(t)] = X_j(t) - I_j(t) + V_j(t). \qquad (4.4)$$

---

[16] The assumed condition $V_i(t) = \lambda_i V_j(t)$ is met, for example, if the life of the risk class is finite and terminates at period t. Then $V_j(t) = X_j(t)$ and $V_i(t) = X_i(t) = \lambda_i X_j(t) = \lambda_i V_j(t)$.

[17] Which are, of course, equal to or less than promised payments.

Similarly, the total value at t of the securities of firm i outstanding from $t - 1$ is

$$[D_i(t) + S_{i,t-1}(t)] + [R_i(t) + B_{i,t-1}(t)] = X_i(t) - I_i(t) + V_i(t).$$

$$(4.5)$$

Arguments similar to those advanced with the two-period model could be used now to show that equilibrium in the capital market implies $V_i(t - 1) = \lambda_i V_j(t - 1)$. For example, an unlevered position in firm j, that is, a direct ownership in the total return $X_j(t) - I_j(t) + V_j(t)$, could be obtained at $t - 1$ by purchasing the proportion α of both the bonds and shares of the firm. But precisely the same return at period 2 could be obtained by purchasing the proportion α/λ_i of both the bonds and shares of firm i, because

$$X_i(t) - I_i(t) + V_i(t) = \lambda_i[X_j(t) - I_j(t) + V_j(t)],$$

so that $\dfrac{\alpha}{\lambda_i} [X_i(t) - I_i(t) + V_i(t)] = \alpha[X_j(t) - I_j(t) + V_j(t)].$

The costs of unlevered investments in the two firms are equal, however, only if $V_i(t - 1) = \lambda_i V_j(t - 1)$.

Alternatively, using this type of argument, one could show that if $V_i(t - 1) < \lambda_i V_j(t - 1)$, a return identical with that provided by the shares of firm j can be obtained from a combination of the securities of firm i with personal borrowing or lending, and the investment cost at $t - 1$ of this combination is less than the cost of the shares of firm j. It follows that with $V_i(t - 1) < \lambda_i V_j(t - 1)$, no investor is willing to hold the shares of firm j. Likewise if $V_i(t - 1) > \lambda_i V_j(t - 1)$, an investor could combine the securities of firm j with personal borrowing or lending at period $t - 1$ and obtain a return at t identical with that provided by the shares of firm i but at a cost lower than the cost of the shares of firm i. It would then follow that if $V_i(t - 1) > \lambda_i V_j(t - 1)$, no investors would hold the shares of firm i at $t - 1$. We could thus conclude that if the shares of both firms are to be held, that is, if we are to have a market equilibrium, it must be the case that $V_i(t - 1) = \lambda_i V_j(t - 1)$. And the same arguments could then be applied to the values at $t - 2$, $t - 3$, and so on.

But because the approach is so similar to that of the preceding section, we leave its detailed development as an exercise for the reader[18] and consider instead a different route to establishing the proposition, stated at the

---

[18] *Hint*: A simple way to go about this is as follows: First suppose that $V_i(t - 1) \neq \lambda_i V_j(t - 1)$. Then show that the capital structure of the "undervalued" firm can be unlevered by the investor on personal account, and then personal debt can be introduced to obtain a return at period t identical with that to be obtained from the shares of the "overvalued" firm but at a cost less than the cost of the shares of the overvalued firm.

beginning of this section, about the market values of firms in the same risk class. This alternative proof centers on showing that if firms i and j are in the same risk class and if $V_i(t) = \lambda_i V_j(t)$ but $V_i(t-1) \neq \lambda_i V_j(t-1)$, there are arbitrage opportunities, that is, opportunities for investors to earn sure profits without expending any of their own resources.[19] Because this is inconsistent with market equilibrium, we must have $V_i(t-1) = \lambda_i V_j(t-1)$.

Suppose that $V_i(t-1) > \lambda_i V_j(t-1)$. Our hypothesis is that this would imply that firm i is "overpriced" relative to firm j. We show that an investor could take advantage of this by issuing two claims at $t-1$ whose payoffs at t are tied directly to those of the stocks and bonds of firm i and then using the proceeds from his private issues to purchase an equivalent position in the securities of firm j. Specifically, on one of his private issues he promises to pay $[D_i(t) + S_{i,t-1}(t)]/V_i(t-1)$, whatever the (as of $t-1$) uncertain values of $D_i(t)$ and $S_{i,t-1}(t)$ turn out to be; and on the other he promises to pay $[R_i(t) + B_{i,t-1}(t)]/V_i(t-1)$. As long as he can deliver on these promises, and we see later that this is true as long as $V_i(t-1) \geq \lambda_i V_j(t-1)$, in a perfect capital market their market values at $t-1$ must be $S_i(t-1)/V_i(t-1)$ and $B_i(t-1)/V_i(t-1)$; that is, in a perfect market if the common stock of firm i has market value $S_i(t-1)$ at $t-1$, the investor's promise to pay $[D_i(t) + S_{i,t-1}(t)]/V_i(t-1)$ at t must have market value $S_i(t-1)/V_i(t-1)$, and his promise to pay $[R_i(t) + B_{i,t-1}(t)]/V_i(t-1)$ must have market value $B_i(t-1)/V_i(t-1)$ at $t-1$. Thus the total proceeds from his two private issues are exactly \$1, and, making use of Equations (4.1) and (4.5) and the assumption that $V_i(t) = \lambda_i V_j(t)$, at period t he pays[20]

$$\frac{[D_i(t) + S_{i,t-1}(t)] + [R_i(t) + B_{i,t-1}(t)]}{V_i(t-1)}$$

$$= \frac{X_i(t) - I_i(t) + V_i(t)}{V_i(t-1)} = \frac{\lambda_i[X_j(t) - I_j(t) + V_j(t)]}{V_i(t-1)}. \quad (4.6)$$

Just as he issues common stock and debt in exactly the proportions in which they are outstanding in the capital structure of firm i at period $t-1$, the investor takes the \$1 proceeds from his private issues and invests

---

[19] Cf. Chap. 1, Sec. II.B.1.

[20] Equivalently, at $t-1$ the investor "short-sells" the stocks and bonds of firm i in the amounts $S_i(t-1)/V_i(t-1)$ and $B_i(t-1)/V_i(t-1)$; that is, he borrows these amounts of the stocks and bonds of firm i from investors who hold them at $t-1$ and promises to return them at t and to pay any dividends and interest declared by the firm at t. After borrowing the securities at $t-1$, he immediately sells them in the market and then proceeds to purchase the securities of firm j in the manner to be described in the text.

$S_j(t-1)/V_j(t-1)$ in the common stock of firm j at $t-1$ and $B_j(t-1)/V_j(t-1)$ in its bonds. From Equation (4.4) the dollar return at t from these investments is

$$\frac{[D_j(t) + S_{j,t-1}(t)] + [R_j(t) + B_{j,t-1}(t)]}{V_j(t-1)} = \frac{X_j(t) - I_j(t) + V_j(t)}{V_j(t-1)}.$$

(4.7)

Comparing Equations (4.6) and (4.7), if $V_i(t-1) > \lambda_i V_j(t-1)$, the investor's dollar returns at t are greater than the claims he must pay, and this is true regardless of the realized values of $V(t)$, $X(t)$, and $I(t)$ for the two firms.[21] (Thus $V_i(t-1) > \lambda_i V_j(t-1)$ does indeed imply that the investor can always deliver on his promises at t.)

But remember that the investor realizes this sure profit at t without any expenditure of this own resources. Thus any investor could take advantage of such opportunities, and there is no reason for anyone to limit the extent to which he does so. In short, as long as $V_i(t-1) > \lambda_i V_j(t-1)$, the existence of arbitrage opportunities implies that the market cannot clear.[22] On the other hand, if $V_i(t-1) < \lambda_i V_j(t-1)$, there are likewise arbitrage (sure profit at no cost) opportunities in which investors issue claims equivalent to those of firm j and use the proceeds to purchase the securities of firm i. And such opportunities are also inconsistent with equilibrium. Thus market equilibrium at $t-1$ requires $V_i(t-1) = \lambda_i V_j(t-1)$. But the same reasoning then applies to the market values of $t-2$ and then to those of $t-3$, and so on, so that the proposition stated at the beginning of this section is established by induction.

III.C.4. The effects of financing decisions on the firm's bondholders and shareholders

The preceding discussion of the risk class model has been concerned with showing that, given a firm's operating (production-investment) decisions, its total market value at any point in time is independent of its financing

---

[21] But this statement is true only if $X_j(t) - I_j(t) + V_j(t) \geq 0$. In fact this must always be the case. Making use of Equation (4.3),

$$X_j(t) - I_j(t) + V_j(t) = R_j(t) + D_j(t) - [b_j(t) + s_j(t)] + V_j(t).$$

Thus $X_j(t) - I_j(t) + V_j(t) < 0$ implies $b_j(t) + s_j(t) > V_j(t) + D_j(t) + R_j(t)$. But because $D_j(t)$ and $R_j(t)$ must be nonnegative, this last condition implies $b_j(t) + s_j(t) > V_j(t)$; that is, the firm raises new capital in excess of its total market value. This is, of course, inconsistent with a perfect capital market, because it means that the new security holders suffer an immediate loss. Thus, necessarily, $X_j(t) - I_j(t) + V_j(t) \geq 0$.

[22] Alternatively, if we think of investors as exercising the arbitrage opportunity by short-selling the securities of firm i and using the proceeds from sale of these securities at $t-1$ to purchase the securities of firm j, no investors will want to hold the securities of i and the market cannot clear.

decisions. It is well to reemphasize, however, that the firm's security holders are indifferent to its financing decisions, so that operating and financing decisions are separable, only if the financing decisions have no effect on their separate market values or trading positions. Thus to complete the treatment of the risk class model, we now show that this indifference proposition always holds. The analysis, however, is valid outside the context of the risk class model, and indeed one of its major advantages is in more closely relating the results of this chapter to those obtained with the perfect certainty model in Chapter 2.

Given that a firm is going to make an operating decision that requires outlays of $I(t)$ at period t,[23] we now examine the effects, if any, of different financing arrangements on the wealth at t

$$W_{S,t-1}(t) = D(t) + S_{t-1}(t) \qquad (4.8a)$$

of the common stock that is outstanding from $t - 1$ and on the wealth at t

$$W_{B,t-1}(t) = R(t) + B_{t-1}(t) \qquad (4.8b)$$

of the bonds outstanding from $t - 1$.

If the firm finances the outlay $I(t)$ with retained earnings, total dividends paid at t are

$$D(t) = X(t) - I(t) - R(t); \qquad (4.9)$$

that is, the dividend is just net cash earnings $X(t)$ less the outlay $I(t)$, less the interest payments $R(t)$.[24] Likewise

$$S_{t-1}(t) = V(t) - B_{t-1}(t); \qquad (4.10)$$

that is, because no new securities are issued, the market value at t of the shares outstanding from $t - 1$ is just the total market value of the firm less the market value at t of the bonds outstanding from $t - 1$. Thus

$$W_{S,t-1}(t) = D(t) + S_{t-1}(t) = X(t) - I(t) + V(t) - [R(t) + B_{t-1}(t)].$$
$$(4.11)$$

Suppose now that the firm finances all or part of the outlay $I(t)$ with new shares. If, as always, we assume that the new shares do not participate in dividends paid at t and if the market value of the new shares is $s(t)$, we have

$$D(t) = X(t) - I(t) - R(t) + s(t), \qquad (4.12)$$

$$S_{t-1}(t) = V(t) - B_{t-1}(t) - s(t), \qquad (4.13)$$

so that $\quad W_{S,t-1}(t) = X(t) - I(t) + V(t) - [R(t) + B_{t-1}(t)]. \qquad (4.14)$

---

[23] Except that we now drop the subscript identifying the firm, the notation is the same as that for the multiperiod risk class model.

[24] Equivalently, Equation (4.9) is obtained directly from Equation (4.3) by setting the value of new security issues, $b(t) + s(t)$, equal to zero.

In previous sections it has already been established that, given the firm's operating decisions, the value of the firm $V(t)$ is independent of its financing decisions. Moreover, as long as the firm's bondholders and stockholders protect themselves from one another in the manner described in Section III.A,[25] the wealth $[R(t) + B_{t-1}(t)]$ of the firm's bondholders depends only on the terms of the debt, that is, the payments promised, and on the firm's operating decisions, which are the sole determinant of the firm's future earnings prospects and thus of its "ability to pay." Thus because $I(t)$ is taken as given and $X(t)$ is the result of previous operating decisions, and is thus independent of current financing decisions, a comparison of Equations (4.14) and (4.11) shows that the wealth of the old shares at t is the same whether the outlay $I(t)$ is financed with retained earnings or new shares.

And if we compare Equations (4.9) and (4.10) with (4.12) and (4.13), we find the reason, already familiar from Chapter 2, for this result. With new share financing the dividend $D(t)$ is higher by the amount of the new issue $s(t)$, but the old shareholders' part of the value of the firm is also lower by the same amount. In more familiar terms, new share financing allows the firm to pay a higher current dividend than when retained earnings financing is used, but there is an immediate equal and offsetting reduction in capital gains, so that the old shareholders are no better off with one form of financing than with another.

Finally consider now the case in which the firm perhaps issues both bonds, in the amount $b(t)$, and shares, $s(t)$, to over all or part of its investment $I(t)$. Then

$$D(t) = X(t) - I(t) - R(t) + b(t) + s(t), \qquad (4.15)$$

$$S_{t-1}(t) = V(t) - B_{t-1}(t) - b(t) - s(t), \qquad (4.16)$$

so that, as in the two previous cases,

$$W_{s,t-1}(t) = X(t) - I(t) + V(t) - [R(t) + B_{t-1}(t)]. \qquad (4.17)$$

This result is again easily explained when we compare Equations (4.15) and (4.16) with (4.9) and (4.10) and with (4.12) and (4.13). Like share financing, new bonds allow the firm to pay higher current dividends than when retained earnings are used, but the new bonds lead to an immediate equal and offsetting reduction in the old stockholders' share of $V(t)$, the market value of the firm. The net result is that the wealth of the current shareholders is the same under all three methods of financing, as is the wealth of the current bondholders.

---

[25] That is, the bondholders protect themselves with "me first" rules, and the stockholders require the firm to avoid the types of financing decisions, that is, retiring the first mortgage before the second, that lead to increase in the positions of the bondholders at the expense of those of the shareholders.

Thus given the firm's operating decisions, its financing decisions are a matter of indifference to its security holders. It follows that operating and financing decisions are separable; that is, they can be made independently.

III.C.5. Summary

The partial equilibrium approaches to examining the effects of financing decisions are obviously quite restrictive. For example, the states of the world model requires that investors agree on the relevant states of the world at period 1; the risk class model requires the existence of meaningful risk classes, that is, containing more than one firm. But concentrating on the restrictiveness of any particular model obscures the important fact that the propositions concerning the "irrelevance of financing decisions" are direct consequences of a perfect capital market and not of restrictions imposed by more detailed specifications of the market context. This fundamental point comes through clearly in the market equilibrium approach, which is free of the restrictions of the partial equilibrium models.

III.D. Market Imperfections: The Effects of Tax Laws

In this section we consider briefly the effects of certain market imperfections on the propositions derived in previous sections concerning the irrelevance of financing decisions. Our attention concentrates on the effects of tax laws, and our goal is simply to show that the class of market imperfections that arise from existing provisions of tax laws can be treated with the same analytical apparatus used in the perfect market model.

III.D.1. The tax deductibility of corporate interest payments

We give most attention to those United States corporate tax laws by which a firm can deduct interest payments on its debt in computing its income for tax purposes, but other payments, that is, dividends, to security holders are not tax-deductible in this way. We find that this type of law should lead to higher market values for levered firms than for equivalent unlevered firms.

The analysis is carried out primarily in the context of the two-period risk class model. We assume again the existence of two firms identical in all respects except capital structure: one firm L is levered; the other firm u is not. The market anticipates that at period 2 earnings before interest and taxes are the same for the two firms,

$$X_u(2) = X_L(2) = X(2),$$

and the firms pay out all their period 2 posttax earning to their security holders.

Because interest payments are deductible in computing corporate taxes, however, the posttax earnings available to security holders are not the same for the two firms. In particular, if τ is the tax rate, the posttax earnings of the unlevered firm are

$$X(2) - \tau X(2) = X(2)(1 - \tau),$$

and the posttax earnings available to the security holders of the levered firm are

$$X(2) - \tau[X(2) - R_L(2)] = X(2)(1 - \tau) + \tau R_L(2).$$

The expression on the left of the equality reflects the fact that the levered firm pays taxes only on earnings net of interest payments. In terms of the expression on the right of the equality, we see that this means that the posttax earnings available to the security holders of the levered firm are greater than those available to the security holders of the unlevered firm by the quantity $\tau R_L(2)$, which represents the tax saving of the levered firm that arises from having debt in its capital structure. It is as if the government paid a subsidy of $\tau R_L(2)$ to the levered firm for having debt in its capital structure.

We now show that, just as the posttax earnings of the levered firm at period 2 are greater than those of the unlevered firm by the amount of the tax saving $\tau R_L(2)$, the market value of the levered firm at period 1, $V_L(1)$, must be greater than the market value of the unlevered firm $V_u(1)$ by the amount of the market value at period 1 of the period 2 tax saving. As in earlier sections, the method of proof is to compare investment positions in the two firms that yield identical returns to the investor at period 2 and then to show the relationship between the period 1 market values of the two firms that must hold if, as must be the case in a market equilibrium, the equivalent positions are to sell at the same investment cost.

First, consider a position in which at period 1 the investor holds the proportion α of the common stocks of the levered firm. The return at period 2 on his holdings is

$$\alpha\{X(2) - \tau[X(2) - R_L(2)] - [R_L(2) + B_L(2)]\}$$
$$= \alpha X(2)(1 - \tau) - \alpha[R_L(2) + B_L(2)] + \alpha\tau R_L(2)$$
$$= \alpha X(2)(1 - \tau) - \alpha(1 - \tau)R_L(2) - \alpha B_L(2);$$

that is, the period 2 returns to the common stock of the levered firm are less than total pretax cash earnings $X(2)$ by the sum of (1) total tax payments $\tau[X(2) - R_L(2)]$ and (2) payments to bondholders of interest $R_L(2)$ and principal $B_L(2)$.[26]

---

[26] In our previous treatment of a world with no taxes we used $R_L(2)$ to represent total payments—interest and principal—to bondholders at period 2. Now, however, the differential tax treatment makes it necessary to distinguish between interest and principal.

As usual, however, it is possible to replicate the cash resources at period 2 to be provided by the shares of the levered firm with a combination of personal debt and the shares of the unlevered firm. In particular, the investor purchases $\alpha V_u(1) = \alpha S_u(1)$ of the shares of the unlevered firm and finances the purchase in part by issuing personal debt in the form of a promise to pay $\alpha(1 - \tau)R_L(2)$ and $\alpha B_L(2)$ at period 2. Thus the investor's cash return at period 2 is

$$\alpha X(2)(1 - \tau) - \alpha(1 - \tau)R_L(2) - \alpha B_L(2),$$

which is indeed identical with what he would get from simply holding the proportion α of the shares of the levered firm.

Note that to get a cash return from the shares of the unlevered firm that is the same as that obtained from those of the levered firm, the investor does not simply replicate the debt of the levered firm on personal account; that is, rather than issuing a promise to pay $\alpha[R_L(2) + B_L(2)]$, he promises to pay only $\alpha[R_L(2)(1 - \tau) + B_L(2)]$. This reflects the fact that $\tau R_L(2)$ of the levered firm's total debt payments are in effect "paid" by the government in terms of the tax saving, or government subsidy, on interest payments. Thus in issuing debt to finance a position in the unlevered firm, the investor replicates on personal account that part of the levered firm's total debt payments which is "paid" by the levered firm itself.

Now the total investment cost at period 1 of the combination of personal debt and the shares of the unlevered firm is

$$\alpha V_u(1) - \alpha[B_L(1) - \tau v_{R_L(2)}(1)];$$

that is, in a perfect market if the period 2 debt payments $R_L(2) + B_L(2)$ of the levered firm have market value $\alpha B_L(1)$ at period 1, the investor's promise to pay $\alpha(1 - \tau)R_L(2)$ and $B_L(2)$ at period 2, or equivalently, his promise to pay $\alpha[R_L(2) + B_L(2) - \tau R_L(2)]$, must have period 1 market value $\alpha B_L(1)$ less $\alpha \tau v_{R_L(2)}(1)$, where $v_{R_L(2)}(1)$ is the period 1 market value of the interest payment $R_L(2)$. On the other hand, the period 1 investment cost that would be incurred by simply holding the proportion α of the shares of the levered firm is

$$\alpha S_L(1) = \alpha[V_L(1) - B_L(1)].$$

Because the cash returns at period 2 from these shares of the levered firm are identical with those obtained from the combination of personal debt with the shares of the unlevered firm, in a market equilibrium the period 1 investment costs of the two positions must be equal; that is, we must have

$$\alpha[V_L(1) - B_L(1)] = \alpha V_u(1) - \alpha[B_L(1) - \tau v_{R_L(2)}(1)],$$

which implies

$$V_L(1) = V_u(1) + \tau v_{R_L(2)}(1); \tag{4.18}$$

that is, just as the posttax earnings available at period 2 to the security holders of the levered firm exceed those available to the security holders of the unlevered firm by the amount of the tax saving $\tau R_L(2)$, the market value of the levered firm at period 1 exceeds that of the unlevered firm by the amount of the period 1 market value of the tax saving.[27]

Of course when the market values of the two firms are in the equilibrium given by Equation (4.18), there are no advantages or disadvantages to the investor who purchases the shares of the levered firm rather than the equivalent position involving personal debt and the shares of the unlevered firm. Likewise the reader should convince himself that there are no advantages or disadvantages in holding the shares of the unlevered firm rather than the equivalent unlevered position involving the bonds and shares of the levered firm.

But the shareholders of any firm are better off whenever the firm increases the amount of debt in its capital structure. Indeed the ideal situation would be to have a capital structure that is all debt. This would of course be a ruse, and one that almost surely would not fool the tax collector, because the debt in this case is common stock. And we must admit that at this point there is little in the way of convincing research, either theoretical or empirical, that explains the amounts of debt that firms do decide to have in their capital structure.

Finally, the result given by Equation (4.18) is easily generalized to the multiperiod case. Without going into details, which, at this point, the interested reader could surely provide, we simply state that in a market equilibrium the market value of a levered firm must be equal to the value of an equivalent unlevered firm from the same risk class plus the current market value of all anticipated future corporate tax savings, including those on debt to be issued in the future as well as those on currently outstanding debt, that result from the tax deductibility of corporate interest payments.[28]

---

[27] More rigorously, we could obtain Equation (4.18) by first noting that if $V_L(1) > V_u(1) + \tau v_{RL(2)}(1)$, no investors would hold the shares of the levered firm, because an equivalent period 2 cash return could be obtained with lower period 1 investment cost from a combination of personal debt with the shares of the unlevered firm. On the other hand, and we leave it to the reader to show that, if $V_L(1) < V_u(1) + \tau v_{RL(2)}(1)$, then no investors would hold the shares of the unlevered firm, because the cash return that they provide at period 2 can be obtained with lower investment cost at period 1 by buying a combination of the debt and shares of the levered firm.

[28] For the more sophisticated, we note that our analysis and conclusions with respect to the effects of corporate tax laws differ somewhat from those of Modigliani and Miller in Ref. 1 or 4. In particular, they argue that the market value of the tax saving of the levered firm is just τ times the market value of its debt; that is,

$$V_L(1) = V_u(1) + \tau B_L(1).$$

This result holds under several special cases: (1) in the two-period model when all the

III.D.2. The tax deductibility of personal interest payments

But we have concentrated so far on the effects of corporate tax laws. Suppose now that, in computing personal income taxes, investors have the same tax privileges as corporations; that is, as is the case with United States tax laws, interest payments on personal debt are deductible in computing taxable personal income just as interest payments on corporate debt are deductible in computing corporate taxable income. Does this reverse our preceding conclusions concerning the effects of corporate tax laws on market values; that is, can the individual investor replicate the tax advantages of corporate debt on personal account, so that in equilibrium the market value of a levered firm is once again equal to the market value of an equivalent unlevered firm from the same risk class?

These questions are easily answered, and in the usual way. Reverting again to the two-period model, we need only compare the cash returns at period 2 on the shares of a levered firm with those of an equivalent combination of personal debt with the shares of the unlevered firm. Now, however, the relevant comparison is in terms of cash returns net of both corporate and personal taxes.

Thus let τ_c represent the corporate tax rate and τ_p the personal tax rate, which for simplicity is assumed to be the same for all investors. Suppose now that the shareholders of the unlevered firm issue debt on personal account equivalent to the total debt of the levered firm; that is, at period 1 the share holders of the unlevered firm issue a promise to pay a total of $R_L(2)$ at period 2. (For simplicity we assume that the total debt payment $R_L(2)$ is interest.) Hence their net cash returns, after both corporate and personal income taxes, are

$$[X(2)(1 - \tau_c) - R_L(2)](1 - \tau_p)$$
$$= X(2)(1 - \tau_c)(1 - \tau_p) - R_L(2) + \tau_p R_L(2). \quad (4.19)$$

The first term, $X(2)(1 - \tau_c)(1 - \tau_p)$, represents the net posttax earnings of the unlevered firm; the second term, $R_L(2)$, is the payment by the shareholders on their personal debt; and the last term, $\tau_p R_L(2)$, is the savings in personal taxes that result from the tax-deductible debt payment $R_L(2)$.

On the other hand, at period 2 the shareholders of the levered firm obtain

$$\{X(2) - \tau_c[X(2) - R_L(2)] - R_L(2)\}(1 - \tau_p)$$
$$= X(2)(1 - \tau_c)(1 - \tau_p) - R_L(2) + \tau_p R_L(2) + \tau_c R_L(2)(1 - \tau_p). \quad (4.20)$$

---

firm's debt payments at period 2 are tax-deductible and (2) in the multiperiod model when all the firm's debt is in the form of a perpetuity and no additional debt is ever issued nor is any existing debt ever repurchased or, equivalently, when all debt is immediately replaced when it matures and there are never net new additions to or reductions from the amount of outstanding debt.

Thus comparing Equations (4.19) and (4.20), we see that by introducing personal debt identical with that of the levered firm, the shareholders of the unlevered firm were nevertheless unsuccessful in replicating the period 2 posttax cash return of the shareholders of the levered firm. The return to the shares of the levered firm is greater by the quantity $\tau_c R_L(2)(1 - \tau_p)$, and this simply represents the fact that investors cannot reproduce on personal account the tax savings that arise at the level of the firm from having debt in its capital structure. We leave it to the reader to show that in fact the presence of personal taxes does not affect the relationship between the market values of the levered and unlevered firms as given by Equation (4.18).

III.D.3. Some closing comments on market imperfections

We could extend a little further this analysis of the effects of the market imperfections that arise from tax laws. Rapidly, however, the conclusions that we could obtain would become more and more ambiguous, and the discussion would become more philosophical than analytical.

For example, we could use the techniques of the preceding sections to analyze the effects of those provisions of United States tax laws by which the dividends and interest received by individuals are treated as regular income for tax purposes but the tax rate on capital gains is at most half the rate on regular income. In itself this tax provision would destroy the equivalence of dividends and capital gains as sources of wealth in a perfect market, and it would lead to a preference for wealth received in the form of capital gains. An exact analysis of these effects, however, is complicated by the fact that the tax benefits of capital gains depend somewhat on the tax bracket of the investor, and indeed there are some large investors, primarily nonprofit institutions, that pay no taxes and so have no tax incentives to seek out capital gains rather than dividends.

Thus rather than speculate about the none too clear-cut effects of these and other market imperfections on the relationships between the financing decisions of firms and their market values, we leave the study of these effects to future research, both theoretical and empirical. The rest of this book is concerned with developing further the implications of a perfect capital market in a world of uncertainty. The justification for limiting the analysis in this way is threefold: (1) it is consistent with the goal of this book, which is to present those ideas in finance which have clear-cut rigorous foundations, and models based on a perfect market are the only ones that satisfy this criterion; (2) at the very least such models help us to organize our thinking about the ubiquitous "real world"; and finally (3) hopefully models based on seemingly unrealistic assumptions yield insights and hypotheses that help to explain real market data. And we argue in Chapter 8 that this is in fact the case.

IV. THE FIRM'S OBJECTIVE FUNCTION: THE MARKET VALUE RULE

Given perfect capital markets, the major result that we have derived so far for a world of uncertainty is what we call the first separation principle; that is, for given operating (production-investment) decisions, the financing decisions of a firm are a matter of indifference to its security holders, so that production and financing decisions are separable. This result, however, just tells us that operating decisions can be made independently of financing decisions; it does not provide a criterion, or decision rule, for optimal operating decisions. The goal of this section is to establish such a decision rule. In particular, we show that, given perfect capital markets, optimal operating decisions for a firm at any point in time involve maximizing the market value of those securities outstanding before the operating decision is made; that is, optimal operating decisions are independent of, or separable from, the details of security holder tastes and can be made according to the market value rule.

Having obtained this "second separation principle," we will have generalized to a world of uncertainty most of the major results concerning investment-financing decisions by firms obtained in the first part of this book under the assumption of perfect certainty. And this should suffice to show that the necessary ingredient for these results is the assumption of a perfect capital market.

We shall find, however, that implementation of the market value rule for a firm's operating decisions is much less straightforward in a world of uncertainty than in a world of certainty. First of all, a firm may have more than one type of security outstanding, and operating decisions that maximize the market value of one type of security need not do so for others.[29] Second, the assumption of perfect capital markets does not in itself lead to a theory of how market values are determined. The assumption allows us to make the negative statement that financing decisions do not affect market values, but positive statements regarding how market values are determined require a more detailed specification of the market context. Thus to say that a firm should follow the market value rule in operating decisions is to say very little until a theory of how market values are determined has been presented.

IV.A. The Market Value Rule: Derivation

Because the arguments here are very similar, it is well to review the basis of the market value rule in a world of perfect certainty. With perfect certainty, the assumption of perfect capital markets is taken to mean (1) no transactions costs or other frictions in making portfolio adjustments, (2) equal access to capital markets by individuals and firms, and (3) firms and individuals are atomistic competitors in the capital market; that is, their individual actions in the market have no effect on the ruling one-

---

[29] The problems that arise on this score, however, were not inconceivable in a world of certainty. See, for example, Chap. 2, p. 71, footnote 4.

period market interest rates. It follows from this definition that an individual's consumption-investment opportunities can be determined from knowledge of his wealth—the current market value of all the resources he has or will obtain in time—and the sequence of one-period interest rates. Because it is assumed that the activities of any individual firm do not affect market interest rates, the only way that the firm can maximize its security holders' consumption-investment opportunities is by maximizing their wealths.

Given a similar specification of the capital market, precisely the same line of reasoning applies to a world of uncertainty. And we have in fact already assumed that the capital market is perfect in the sense that (1) there are no transactions costs, (2) there is equal access to financial opportunities by all individuals and firms, and (3) investors perceive that there are always close substitutes for any securities of a firm and the firm's decisions have no effect on the prices of the securities issued by other investors and firms.

What constitutes a close substitute for the securities of a firm is a simple matter in a world of perfect certainty. There it is always possible to replicate the (sure) payoffs through time to be provided by a firm's securities in terms of simple claims to resources to be obtained in future periods. (See, for example, Chapter 1, especially Section II.A.) Things are not so simple in a world of uncertainty, however, in which the future returns to be received on a firm's securities are now subject to probability distributions, and the notion of what constitutes a perfect substitute for a security depends both on investor tastes, that is, the characteristics of return distributions that are important to investors, and on the nature of the distributions, that is, the ways in which the distributions can be summarized.[30]

---

[30] Much of the rest of this book is concerned with developing such detailed specifications of investor tastes and the nature of distributions of investment returns and then with how these combine to produce a theory of market equilibrium, that is, a theory that says what is of positive importance in determining the market values of securities.

We might note, however, that one quite simple model of this sort has already been presented—the states of the world model in Section III.C.1. In the two-period version of this model, there are perfect substitutes for any probability distributions on period 2 market value generated by a firm as long as its production decisions do not affect prices of contingent claims for any state and the firm is an atomistic competitor in the capital market. In this model the payoffs in different states provided by any of a firm's securities can be replicated simply by purchasing the equivalent numbers of contingent claims to dollars to be delivered in each state.

On the other hand, the risk class model gave us a way of obtaining perfect substitutes for the securities of a firm that did not require a complete theory of how market values are determined; that is, when Equation (4.1) holds between two firms, the securities of one firm can be used to obtain perfect substitutes for the securities of the other, regardless of the model determining the market values of the two firms. But the conditions of Equation (4.1) are obviously quite strong, and in the model of later chapters we shall see that less stringent conditions are sufficient for firms to be in the same risk class.

Nevertheless, whatever model is used to obtain the definition of a perfect substitute, given a perfect capital market, including the assumed existence of perfect substitutes, the reasoning underlying the market value rule for a firm's operating decisions is precisely the same in a world of uncertainty as in a world of perfect certainty; that is, given a security holder's wealth, the firm's operating decisions do not affect the consumption-investment opportunities that are available to the security holder in the market. Thus all that the firm can affect with its operating decisions is the wealth of its security holders, and here the optimal path is clear: more wealth is preferred to less.

IV.B. The Market Value Rule: Implementation

Translating the conclusion that in a perfect capital market the firm should maximize the wealths of its security holders into a concrete criterion for optimal production decisions is straightforward if there is a production-investment plan that maximizes the wealths of all security holders. Potential problems arise only when maximum wealth for one group does not imply maximum wealth for others.

Thus suppose that firms issue only the usual types of bonds and common stock. From Equation (4.5) we know that for a given firm the sum of $W_{B,t-1}(t)$, the wealth at period t of the bonds outstanding from $t - 1$, and $W_{S,t-1}(t)$, the wealth at period t of the stock outstanding from $t - 1$, is

$$W_{B,t-1}(t) + W_{S,t-1}(t) = [R(t) + B_{t-1}(t)] + [D(t) + S_{t-1}(t)]$$
$$= V(t) - I(t) + X(t), \qquad (4.21)$$

where $B_{t-1}(t)$ and $S_{t-1}(t)$ are the market values at t of the bonds and stocks outstanding from $t - 1$, $R(t)$ and $D(t)$ are interest and dividend payments on these bonds and stocks, and, as always, $V(t)$, $I(t)$, and $X(t)$ are, respectively, the market value of the firm, outlays for operating (production-investment) decisions made at period t, and net cash earnings.

In these discrete-time models $X(t)$ is assumed to be a result of production-investment decisions of previous periods and thus to be unaffected by the decisions taken at period t. It is therefore clear from Equation (4.21) that a production-investment decision at t that maximizes $V(t) - I(t)$ also maximizes the combined wealths of the bonds and shares outstanding from $t - 1$.[31]

[31] But why do we talk only about the bonds and shares outstanding from $t - 1$? The reason is that there is nothing the firm can do to help, or hurt, those who buy any new securities issued at t to finance the operating decisions made at t. In a perfect capital market these new securities are always sold at prices that "fully reflect" the operating decisions to be made at t, and these new securities do not provide investors with any new types of investment opportunities that would not be available, and at the same prices, if the firm made some other operating decision at t.

The situation here is the same as that obtained in a world of perfect certainty in which

There are some important circumstances in which the production-investment rule, maximize $V(t) - I(t)$, maximizes the separate as well as the combined wealths of the firm's security holders. This is the case, in order of decreasing obviousness:

1. By chance, or perhaps as a general rule.
2. When the firm has only one type of security, common stock, in its capital structure.
3. When the firm has debt as well as common stock in its capital structure but the debt is riskless; that is, the firm is always able to make full payment on its debt promises, regardless of the operating decisions that it makes, so that its operating decision at t does not affect the wealth of its debtholders.
4. The firm's bondholders and stockholders are free to compensate one another for the effects of operating decisions that increase the wealth of one group but not the other. In this case, because maximizing $V(t) - I(t)$ maximizes the combined wealths of bondholders and shareholders, there may be some way, and indeed there may be many ways, that side payments between the bondholders and shareholders can be arranged, so that with the operating decision that maximizes $V(t) - I(t)$, every security holder's wealth is at least as great as it would be with any other operating decision.

The rule of maximize $V(t) - I(t)$ for the firm's operating decisions can fail to maximize the separate as well as the combined wealth of its bondholders and stockholders in the case in which the firm's debt is risky and side payments between the firm's bondholders and stockholders are ruled out. Then it is easy to construct examples in which a production plan that maximizes shareholder wealth does not maximize bondholder wealth, or vice versa.

Thus in the two-period states of the world model, consider a firm that has two mutually exclusive production decisions a and b available at period 1, and either can be carried out without additional expenditures of resources at period 1; that is, for both decisions $I(1) = 0$. There are also assumed to be two possible states of the world at period 2. The price $p(1)$ at period 1

---

any excess of value over cost generated by the firm's operating decision made at period t goes to shares outstanding from previous periods. New shares issued to finance the operating decision of period t are issued at a price that "fully reflects" the effects of the operating decision on cash flows. The difference between the certainty and uncertainty results, of course, is that under certainty the term "fully reflects" simply implies pricing of known cash flows at known market interest rates, whereas under uncertainty the pricing model must be somewhat more complicated.

TABLE 1

Production Plan	Payoff at Period 2		Market Values at Period 1		
	State 1	State 2	$V(1)$	$B(1)$	$S(1)$
a	7	7	7	5	2
b	1	10	5.5	3	2.5

NOTE: $p(1) = p(2) = 0.5$. Promised payment on debt is $5 at period 2.

of a contingent claim to $1 to be received only if state 1 occurs at period 2 is $0.5; and likewise the price $p(2)$ at period 1 of $1 to be received at period 2 if state 2 occurs is $0.5. At period 1, the firm is assumed to have bonds in its capital structure in the form of a promise to pay $5 at period 2, whichever state occurs.

For each of the production decisions, Table 1 shows the payoffs in the two states at period 2, along with the period 1 market values of the firm, its bonds, and its common stock. Thus if production plan a is chosen, the period 1 market value of the firm's bonds is $B(1) = 5(0.5) + 5(0.5) = 5$, and the value of the shares is $S(1) = 2(0.5) + 2(0.5) = 2$. On the other hand, if plan b is chosen, the firm is not able to deliver in full on its debt promise if state 1 occurs. Hence with this production plan the period 1 market value of the bonds is $B(1) = 1(0.5) + 5(0.5) = 3$, and the value of the shares is 2.5.

Thus the market value of the shares is higher with plan b, but the market value of the bonds is higher with plan a. If side payments between the bondholders and shareholders were possible, the bondholders could give the shareholders a subsidy of $0.5 to induce them to choose plan a; then the shareholders would have as much wealth as if plan b were chosen, and the bondholders would have more.[32] But if side payments are ruled out and the shareholders control the firm, plan b is chosen. And it is well to note that, although this decision maximizes shareholder wealth, it does not maximize $V(1) - I(1)$, which in this case is just $V(1)$.

From a practical viewpoint, however, situations of potential conflict between bondholders and shareholders in the application of the market value rule are probably unimportant. In general, investment opportunities that increase a firm's market value by more than their cost both increase the value of the firm's shares and strengthen the firm's future ability to meet its current bond commitments. A much more important impediment to the application of the market value rule is the fact that we have not yet

---

[32] Indeed the bondholders would be willing to make side payments up to $2 to induce the adoption of plan a rather than b.

developed a theory of how market values are determined,[33] and until we do, in later chapters, the market value rule remains somewhat empty as a criterion for optimal operating decisions.

But this leads us naturally to the last topic of this chapter.

V. THE COST OF CAPITAL AND THE RETURN ON A FIRM'S SHARES

Our analysis so far in this chapter has made no use of terms like "cost of capital," "discount rate," and "present value." And indeed such concepts are unnecessary, and would be somewhat distracting, in the development of capital structure theory. This theory does not propose to say exactly how the market value of a firm and its securities is determined but only that market values, however determined, are unaffected by financing decisions, so that operating and financing decisions are separable.

But discount rates and costs of capital, interpreted as prices that determine current values for future payoffs, imply more positive statements about the determination of market values. Interpreting discount rates and costs of capital in this way requires a detailed theory of investor, firm, and market equilibrium that would specify, among other things, the characteristics of probability distributions on future payoffs that are important to investors and the way in which optimal consumption-investment decisions by all individuals and operating decisions by all firms combine to produce a market equilibrium in which discount rates are appropriately interpreted as prices that determine market values. The capital structure model of this chapter does not, of course, provide this much detail.

V.A. Discount Rates and the Cost of Capital

If one is willing to assign them a much less positive role, however, discount rates and cost of capital can be introduced into, or perhaps more accurately, imposed on, the model, and more or less in the way described by Modigliani and Miller [1]. Concentrating again on the two-period model, for any firm j we can always define a proportionality factor $1/(1 + \rho_j)$ relating $V_j(1)$, the market value of the firm at period 1, to $E[X_j(2)]$, its expected net cash earnings at period 2, as

$$V_j(1) \equiv \frac{1}{1 + \rho_j} E[X_j(2)]. \qquad (4.22)$$

It is then natural to think of ρ_j as the one-period rate of discount of the

---

[33] Although the states of the world model is such a theory of market value determination, in our view its usefulness at this time is mainly pedagogical, that is, in providing a concrete framework for illustrating basic notions in finance and other areas of economics. Because as yet the model has yielded little in the way of testable implications, we are reluctant to use it as the cornerstone in our treatment of uncertainty.

expected period 2 earnings. But we could just as well have defined a proportionality factor $1/(1 + \delta_j)$ relating $V_j(1)$ to, say, the 0.95 fractile of the distribution of $X_j(2)$, and then δ_j could be thought of as the rate of discount for the 0.95 fractile. The important point is that in the primitive models of this chapter, an expression like Equation (4.22) is just a definition; it does not imply that $V_j(1)$ was determined in the market by applying a proportionality factor or a discount rate to the period 2 expected earnings.[34]

If we restrict attention to the risk class model, a similarly limited concept of the cost of capital can be introduced and again more or less in the way described by Modigliani and Miller. To accomplish this, we must further assume that all production plans available to a firm at period 1 are associated with probability distributions on earnings at period 2 from the same risk class; that is, in the manner of Equation (4.1), the period 2 earnings provided by any given production plan would always be proportional to those of any other production plan available to the firm. Thus if $X_j(2)$ and $X_j(2)'$ are the earnings at period 2 for two such production plans, we have

$$X_j(2)' = \lambda' X_j(2); \qquad (4.23)$$

that is, regardless of what the value of $X_j(2)$ turned out to be at period 2, $X_j(2)'$ would always be proportional to it by the factor λ'.

Thus the different production plans available to a firm can be viewed as potentially generating different firms in the same risk class. And from our earlier analysis of the risk class model, we know that when Equation (4.23) holds and the capital market is perfect, we must have

$$V_j(1)' = \lambda' V_j(1); \qquad (4.24)$$

that is, the current market values implied by the two production plans must be proportional by the same factor that relates their future earnings. Moreover, because Equation (4.23) holds for all possible values of future earnings for the two plans, it must also hold between their expected values; that is,

$$E[X_j(2)'] = \lambda' E[X_j(2)]. \qquad (4.25)$$

Suppose now that we define the proportionality factor $1/(1 + \rho_j)$ such that

$$V_j(1) \equiv \frac{1}{1 + \rho_j} E[X_j(2)], \qquad (4.26)$$

---

[34] Modigliani and Miller state this point rather clearly in sec. I.A. of Ref. 1. But their subsequent analysis makes such heavy use of terms like "capitalization rate" and "cost of capital" that the important qualifications provided in their initial discussion are sometimes overlooked.

or equivalently

$$1 + \rho_j = \frac{E[X_j(2)]}{V_j(1)} .$$

But from Equations (4.24) and (4.25) we know that

$$\frac{E[X_j(2)']}{V_j(1)'} = \frac{E[X_j(2)]}{V_j(1)} .$$

Thus we must have

$$V_j(1)' = \frac{1}{1 + \rho_j} E[X_j(2)'], \qquad (4.27)$$

so that, comparing Equations (4.26) and (4.27), the proportionality factor, $1/(1 + \rho_j)$, relating the period 1 market value of the firm to its expected period 2 earnings, is the same for the two production plans in the same risk class.

Suppose now that in its production decisions the firm abides by the rule, maximize $V_j(1) - I_j(1)$. Thus in comparing two production plans, one of which requires an incremental outlay of $dI_j(1) = I_j(1)' - I_j(1)$ more than the other, the plan with the higher outlay provides a larger excess of value over cost if $dV_j(1) - dI_j(1) > 0$, where $dV_j(1) = V_j(1)' - V_j(1)$. But, letting $dE[X_j(2)] = E[X_j(2)'] - E[X_2(2)]$, from Equations (4.26) and (4.27),

$$dV_j(1) = \frac{1}{1 + \rho_j} dE(X_j(2)),$$

so that

$$dV_j(1) - dI_j(1) > 0$$

implies

$$dE(X_j(2)) > dI_j(1)(1 + \rho_j).$$

In other words, the one-period expected return on the incremental outlay $dI_j(1)$ must be greater than ρ_j. Thus we can interpret ρ_j as a cost of capital in the sense that it is the minimum required expected rate of return on incremental outlays for production activities of the particular risk class available to the firm. And using the same line of reasoning, it is easy to show that the same cost of capital applies to all firms in the same risk class.

It is evident, however, that we have more or less forced this concept of a cost of capital on the model by restricting attention to production activities that generate probability distributions of earnings from the same risk class. Even with this restrictive specification, however, we cannot interpret ρ_j as a meaningful economic price that determines current values; that is, our primitive models do not imply that investors are concerned with expected values or any other specific characteristics of probability distributions. Nor do they imply, or rule out, any sort of discounting mechanism operating in the market to determine market values.[35] As noted throughout, such implications could only be derived from a model that specified in detail the characteristics of probability distributions that are relevant to investors and the way in which optimal decisions by investors and firms combine to determine the structure of equilibrium market prices.

It is important to emphasize, however, that we are not suggesting that the market does not use discounting to determine market prices. Our only goal here is to show that without a formal model that shows how the interactions of individual economic units lead to the determination of discount rates that in turn are used in determining market values, an investment criterion based on a discounting procedure is not on a rigorous theoretical footing. Although the importance of discount rates in the perfect certainty model may lead us to suspect that they should also play a fundamental role in any uncertainty model, this is nothing more than a hunch until such an uncertainty model is actually available.

In short, the Modigliani-Miller capital structure propositions are much more generally valid than the concepts of capitalization rates and cost of capital. In essence, their important conclusion that production and financing decisions are separable depends only on the assumption of a perfect capital market, but a meaningful cost of capital requires a much more detailed specification of the market context.

V.B. The Expected Return on Common Stock

It is possible, however, to get a little more mileage, in the form of additional insights concerning the major capital structure propositions, from an extension of the preceding discussion of the interpretation of expected

---

[35] To make these comments more concrete, suppose that the market setting is as described by the two-period states of the world model; that is, there are S possible states of the world at period 2, and $p(s)$ is the price at period 1 of a dollar delivered at period 2 if state s occurs. If $X_j(2,s)$ is the earnings of firm j at period 2 if state s occurs, the market value of the firm at period 1 is

$$V_j(1) = \sum_{s=1}^{S} p(s) X_j(2,s).$$

In this model the prices for contingent claims $p(s)$ provide direct period 1 valuations of the market values in each period 2 state generated by a production activity, and the notion of a cost of capital relating current market values to the expectation of the distribution of future market values is somewhat out of place. Nevertheless, such a cost of capital can be forced on the model in exactly the manner described above if one is willing to assume that for any state s the relative payoff $X_j(2,s)/X_j(2,1)$ is the same for all production plans. And this is precisely the assumption necessary to ensure that all distributions of period 2 earnings that the firm can generate are from the same risk class.

rates of return in the context of the two-period risk class model. Rearranging expression (4.26), we can get

$$\rho_j \equiv \frac{E[X_j(2)] - V_j(1)}{V_j(1)} \; ; \tag{4.28}$$

that is, the cost of capital ρ_j is just the expected one-period, or percentage, return that the firm earns on its period 1 market value $V_j(1)$. We can likewise define the expected one-period returns on the firm's bonds and on its common stock as

$$r_j \equiv \frac{E[R_j(2)] - B_j(1)}{B_j(1)} , \tag{4.29}$$

$$i_j \equiv \frac{E[X_j(2)] - E[R_j(2)] - S_j(1)}{S_j(1)} , \tag{4.30}$$

where $E[R_j(2)]$ is the expected, or mean, value of all payments to all bondholders at period 2 and $B_j(1)$ and $S_j(1)$ are the total period 1 market values of all the firm's debt and common stock.

The analysis in the preceding section established, in effect, that in a given risk class the period 1 market values of firms must be such that ρ_j, the expected one-period return on the total market value of firm j, is the same for all firms in the class. Moreover, the earlier analyses also established that, given its operating decisions, the firm's financing decision at period 1 does not affect the period 1 wealths of those who hold its bonds and shares outstanding from period 0. This does not mean, however, that the expected one-period returns on the firm's common stock and on all the bonds, new and old, in its capital structure at period 1 are independent of the period 1 financing decision. In particular, the risk of the firm's shares as well as the risk of any new debt issued at period 1 certainly depends on the firm's financing decisions, and this might affect the expected returns on the bonds and the shares. Let us now see if we can give these rather vague suspicions some formal content.

From Equations (4.28) and (4.29) we can obtain

$$E[X_j(2)] = (1 + \rho_j) V_j(1) \quad \text{and} \quad E[R_j(2)] = (1 + r_j) B_j(1).$$

Thus Equation (4.30) for the expected one-period return on the shares of firm j can be rewritten as

$$i_j = \frac{(1 + \rho_j) V_j(1) - (1 + r_j) B_j(1) - S_j(1)}{S_j(1)} ,$$

or because $S_j(1) = V_j(1) - B_j(1)$ and $V_j(1) = S_j(1) + B_j(1)$,

$$i_j = \frac{\rho_j[S_j(1) + B_j(1)] - r_j B_j(1)}{S_j(1)} = \rho_j + (\rho_j - r_j)\frac{B_j(1)}{S_j(1)}. \quad (4.31)$$

Because the total debt of the firm can never be more "risky" than the shares of an equivalent unlevered firm from the same risk class,[36] in general we would expect that in a market dominated by risk averters $\rho_j > r_j$. Thus Equation (4.31) says that the expected one-period, or percentage, return on a levered share in firm j is just ρ_j, the percentage yield on the expected income from a share in an equivalent unlevered firm in the same risk class, plus a risk premium that depends on the debt/equity ratio of firm j.

The discussion can be summarized as follows. The probability distribution and thus the risk of the period 2 earnings before interest of the firm depends on the operating decision that the firm makes at period 1. The risk implied by the operating decision is not affected by the way that it is financed; that is, the risk implied by the probability distribution on the total earnings of the firm depends on the nature of the operating decision, which alone generates the probability distribution of earnings. This probability distribution cannot be changed by different ways of financing the operating decision. The effect of the financing decision is merely to package the given total risk of the firm into different bundles; that is, for given assets the more bond financing used, the riskier the earnings that accrue to the common shareholders and to the bondholder. Specifically the more bond financing used, the higher the chance of default on at least part of the firm's debt and the higher the chance that the stockholders receive nothing. To reflect this risk, the shares and bonds of highly levered firms sell to yield higher expected returns than those of less highly levered firms.

At this point, however, it should be clear that the fact that the firm can affect the risks of its securities through its financing decisions does not imply that its security holders are concerned with these decisions. The important fact is that in a perfect capital market the firm's financing decisions do not affect the wealths of its security holders, nor do they provide or preclude any investment opportunities, that is, levels of risk, that its security holders could not obtain either from other firms or on personal account. Thus given its operating decisions, the firms financing decisions are a matter of indifference to its shareholders, so that the operating and financing decisions are separable.

---

[36] Note that when a firm's capital structure is 100 percent debt, this debt is identical with the common stock of an equivalent unlevered firm from the same risk class. Thus the total risk of the firm is the upper limit on the risk of the firm's debt.

VI. SUMMARY AND CONCLUSIONS

But the discussion of risk and risk aversion in the preceding section is a little vague, as indeed it must be at this stage of the game. A rigorous treatment of risk requires a definition of risk, which in turn requires a more detailed specification of investor tastes than has been made in this chapter; that is, in order to define the risk of an investment instrument, we have to say something about the characteristics of investor tastes, which then allow us to specify the characteristics of the investment instrument that determine its risk.

All that we have assumed about investor tastes in this chapter is the nonsatiation axiom in Chapter 1; that is, other things equal, the investor always prefers more consumption to less. In combination with a perfect capital market, this simple assumption about tastes has allowed us to establish two important separation principles analogous to those obtained for the perfect certainty model in Chapter 2; that is, (1) given its operating (production-investment) decisions, the firm's financing decisions are a matter of indifference to its security holders, so that operating and financing decisions are separable, and (2) the operating decisions of the firm can be made according to the market value rule and without regard to the details of security holder tastes.

In the absence of a theory that tells us how market values are determined, however, to say that operating decisions should be made according to the market value rule is to say very little. The goal of the next three chapters is to develop such a theory of market value determination. In line with the development of the perfect certainty model in the first part of this book, we first present a more detailed theory of consumer choice under uncertainty (Chapter 5). This is then combined with a detailed treatment of market opportunities into a theory of investor decision making (Chapter 6). And finally (Chapter 7) the theory of investor equilibrium is used to develop a model of market value determination and a theory of optional operating decisions by firms.

REFERENCES

The first rigorous treatment of the capital structure propositions presented in this chapter is in
1. Modigliani, Franco, and Merton H. Miller, "The Cost of Capital, Corporation Finance, and the Theory of Investment," *American Economic Review*, vol. 48 (June 1958), pp. 261–297.

Their other important works in this area include
2. Modigliani, Franco, and Merton H. Miller, "Corporation Income Taxes and the Cost of Capital: A Correction," *American Economic Review*, vol. 53 (June 1963), pp. 433–443.

3. Miller, Merton H., and F. Modigliani, "Dividend Policy, Growth and the Valuation of Shares," *Journal of Business*, vol. 34 (October 1961), pp. 411–433.
4. Miller, Merton H., and F. Modigliani, "Some Estimates of the Cost of Capital to the Electric Utility Industry," *American Economic Review*, vol. 56 (June 1966), pp. 334–391.

The Modigliani–Miller work is within the context of the risk class model. Their capital structure propositions were derived from the states of the world model in

5. Hirshleifer, J., "Investment Decision under Uncertainty: Choice Theoretic Approaches," *Quarterly Journal of Economics*, vol. 79 (November 1965), pp. 509–536.

General, and the original, discussions of the states of the world model are in

6. Arrow, K. J., "The Role of Securities in the Optimal Allocation of Risk Bearing," *Review of Economic Studies*, vol. 31 (April 1964), pp. 91–96.
7. Debreu, G., *The Theory of Value*. New York: John Wiley & Sons, Inc., 1959.

Analyses of the idiosyncrasies of United States tax laws and their effects on the perfect markets capital structure propositions can be found in

8. Farrar, Donald E., and Lee L. Selwyn, "Taxes, Corporate Financial Policy and Return to Investors," *National Tax Journal*, vol. 20 (1967), pp. 444–454.
9. Myers, Stewart C., "Taxes, Corporate Financial Policy and the Return to Investors: Comment," *National Tax Journal*, vol. 20 (1967), pp. 455–462.

For a discussion of more traditional, that is, pre-Modigliani-Miller, views on the effects of financing decisions on market values see

10. Solomon, Ezra (ed.), *The Management of Corporate Capital*. New York: The Free Press, 1959.

Of special interest in this book are the two papers by David Durand, "Costs of Debt and Equity Funds: Trends and Problems of Measurement" and "The Cost of Capital in an Imperfect Market: A Reply to Modigliani and Miller." The latter first appeared in the *American Economic Review* of June 1959, along with a rejoinder by Modigliani and Miller; the former first appeared as a 1952 publication of the *National Bureau of Economic Research*.

5

THE EXPECTED UTILITY APPROACH TO THE PROBLEM OF CHOICE UNDER UNCERTAINTY[1]

I. INTRODUCTION

In this chapter we begin to develop a model for consumption-investment decisions by individuals under conditions of uncertainty. The general problem can be described as follows: Consider an individual who must make a consumption-investment decision at each of τ discrete points in his lifetime. At the first decision point he has a quantity of wealth w_1 that represents the maximum possible level of consumption during time period 1. At the beginning of period 1, w_1 must be split between current consumption c_1 and investment $h_1 = w_1 - c_1$. At the beginning of period 2, the individual's wealth level is

$$\tilde{w}_2 = h_1(1 + \tilde{R}_2) = (w_1 - c_1)(1 + \tilde{R}_2),$$

[1] It is assumed here that the reader is familiar with elementary statistical concepts, such as expected value, probability distribution, and variance. A brief review of these concepts is provided in the Appendix to this chapter.

where $\tilde{R}_2$ is the one-period or percentage return at the beginning of period 2 per dollar of investment at the beginning of period 1.[2] The return $\tilde{R}_2$ is assumed to be a random variable, that is, the observed value of $\tilde{R}_2$ is drawn from some probability distribution. Thus the wealth level $\tilde{w}_2$ is also a random variable.[3]

At the beginning of period 2, $\tilde{w}_2$ must in turn be allocated to consumption and investment, and the consumption-investment decision problem is faced at the beginning of each subsequent period until period τ, the last period of the individual's life, at which time the entire available wealth $\tilde{w}_\tau$ is consumed and a bequest is considered consumption. The individual is assumed to derive satisfaction only from consumption, and his problem is to map out a consumption-investment strategy that maximizes the level of satisfaction provided by anticipated consumption over his lifetime.

Under uncertainty the decision problem is of course complicated by the fact that the actual lifetime consumption sequence is to some extent unpredictable, because, as indicated above, the wealth levels produced through time by any given investment strategy are usually random variables. Thus in order to solve the individual's sequential consumption-investment problem, we need a theory of choice under uncertainty that defines the criteria that the individual uses in choosing among different probability distributions of lifetime consumption. Developing such a theory of choice is the purpose of this chapter.

II. THE EXPECTED UTILITY MODEL: GENERAL AXIOMATIC TREATMENT

The theory of choice under uncertainty that we apply to the consumption-investment problem is the "expected utility hypothesis." In general terms, the expected utility hypothesis states that when faced with a set of mutually exclusive actions, each involving its own probability distribution of "outcomes," the individual behaves as if he attaches numbers called, purely for convenience, utilities to each outcome and then chooses that action whose associated probability distribution of outcomes provides maximum expected utility.[4]

[2] In general, the one-period or percentage return at $t+1$ on the investment h_t undertaken at t is

$$\tilde{R}_{t+1} = \frac{\tilde{w}_{t+1} - h_t}{h_t}.$$

[3] Tildes ($\sim$) are used throughout this and following chapters to denote random variables. When we talk about a specific observed value of such a variable, however, the tilde is dropped.

[4] The expected or average value of utility of any probability distribution of outcomes is computed like any other expected value; that is, the utility of each possible outcome

In the τ period consumption-investment problem, an outcome is a complete sequence of lifetime consumptions $C_\tau = (c_1, c_2, \ldots, c_\tau)$, and an action is a τ period consumption-investment strategy that produces a probability distribution for different possible lifetime consumption sequences. But because the consumption-investment problem is just one possible application of the expected utility model, we initially present the model in the most general terms and then turn to its applications that are of major interest in finance.[5]

Thus we envisage a decision maker faced with a set S of prospects, whose characteristics are at this point purposely left unspecified, from which a choice must be made. S includes all the prospects that are relevant for the decision at hand. Moreover, S can include both "elementary prospects," for each of which there is only one possible outcome, and "random prospects," which are probability distributions of mutually exclusive elementary prospects.

At this point we could simply assume that the decision maker's behavior conforms to the expected utility model; that is, he behaves as if he assigned utilities to elementary prospects and then ranked random prospects on the basis of expected utility. Alternatively, we can show that behavior in conformity with the expected utility model is implied by a more basic set of axioms concerning how the individual ranks outcomes and probability distributions of outcomes, just as behavior in conformity with the ordinary utility model in Chapter 1 can be shown to follow from a more basic set of axioms concerning consumer choice under conditions of certainty. Because an axiomatic treatment can help to produce a better understanding of the model, this approach is taken here.

---

is weighted (multiplied) by the probability of the outcome, and the sum of these products over all possible outcomes is the expected or average value of utility for this probability distribution of outcomes.

Note that we say that the individual behaves as if he were an expected utility maximizer. As always, we do not presume that he formally goes through the optimization process prescribed by the theory. Rather his observable behavior is assumed to be as if his decision process conformed to the model (compare Chap. 1, Sec. I). As usual, however, we use words a little loosely and talk about an individual maximizing his utility. But such statements are always meant to be interpreted in an "as if" sense.

[5] The reader who finds the general treatment in this section overly abstract is nevertheless encouraged to continue. Later sections provide concrete applications of the expected utility model, and these give some perspective on the initial development of the model presented here. (Indeed the reader may find it helpful to reconsider the material in this section after reading through the chapter.) Our mode of presentation is designed to provide a more general understanding of the expected utility model than would be obtained only from its specific application to the consumption-investment problem.

II.A. The Axiom System

The set of axioms we use is as follows:

Axiom 1 (Comparability). The individual can define a complete preference ordering over the set of prospects in S; that is, for any two prospects x and y in S, he can say that $x > y$ or $y > x$ or $x \sim y$.[6]

Axiom 2 (Transitivity). The ordering of prospects assumed in Axiom 1 is also completely transitive. For example, $x > y$ and $y > z$ imply $x > z$; or $x \sim y$ and $y \sim z$ imply $x \sim z$; or $x \sim y$ and $y > z$ imply $x > z$; and so on.

Axiom 3 (Strong Independence). If $x \sim y$, then for any third prospect z in S, $G(x,z:\alpha) \sim G(y,z:\alpha)$. Here $G(x,z:\alpha)$ represents a gamble, that is, a random prospect, in which the individual gets either x, with probability α, or z, with probability $1 - \alpha$, and $G(y,z:\alpha)$ likewise represents a gamble that produces either y or z, with probabilities α and $1 - \alpha$. We also assume that if $x > y$, then $G(x,z:\alpha) > G(y,z:\alpha)$; or if $x \geq y$, then $G(x,z:\alpha) \geq G(y,z:\alpha)$. In short, the rankings of two prospects are not changed when each is combined in the same way into a gamble or probability distribution involving a common third prospect.

Axiom 4. If the prospects x, y, and z are such that either $x > y \geq z$ or $x \geq y > z$, there is a unique α such that

$$y \sim G(x,z:\alpha).$$

Axiom 5. If $x \geq y \geq z$ and $x \geq u \geq z$, and $y \sim G(x,z:\alpha_1)$ and $u \sim G(x,z:\alpha_2)$, then $\alpha_1 > \alpha_2$ implies $y > u$ and $\alpha_1 = \alpha_2$ implies $y \sim u$.

Axioms 1 and 2 are analogous to the axioms of comparability and transitivity assumed in the theory of choice under certainty in Chapter 1. And as in the certainty model, these two axioms are sufficient to define a consistent preference ordering for all prospects in S. But if in addition we wish to say that the ordering of random prospects in S is according to expected utility, additional behavioral postulates are required. Axioms 3 to 5 provide one possible set of such additional behavioral restrictions.

---

[6] The notation $x > y$ is read "x is strictly preferred to y," and $x \sim y$ is read "x and y are regarded as equivalent." Likewise $x \geq y$ is read "x is at least equivalent to y."

Note that in the statements of the axioms there is no restriction on whether the prospects are elementary or random. For example, in Axiom 1, x and y can be elementary or random prospects.

Axiom 3 is the "strong independence" axiom. Intuitively, the importance of the axiom to the expected utility model is easy to see. If the expected utility rule is to be applicable—that is, if the utility of a random prospect is to be just the weighted sum of the utilities of its component elementary prospects, with weights equal to the probabilities of obtaining each of the elementary prospects—then necessarily the decision maker's attitudes toward particular (mutually exclusive) prospects cannot be affected when these are combined in various ways into random prospects. And this is the direct assumption of Axiom 3.

In judging the reasonableness of the strong independence axiom as a description of behavior, one must keep in mind that a random prospect is a probability distribution of mutually exclusive elementary prospects; ultimately one obtains only one of the elementary prospects in the probability mixture. Thus although in general one may not be willing to say that an ordering of objects is unchanged when the objects are combined into some mixture, in the case of a probability mixture of mutually exclusive outcomes this assumption may seem more reasonable.

For example, the elementary prospects under consideration may be bundles of consumption goods with all the goods in a given bundle to be consumed by the decision maker. The decision maker's rankings of different elementary prospects (bundles) is usually affected by the degrees of complementarity and substitutability among the goods in a particular bundle, so that the separate ranks of each good may not be a good indication of the rank of the bundle. (Or in utility terms, it is not usually possible to rank a consumption bundle by assigning utilities to each good, without regard to the quantities of other goods in the bundle, and then obtain the utility of the bundle as the sum of the separate utilities of each good.) But in ranking probability distributions of such bundles, because a particular distribution ultimately yields only one of its component bundles, one may well find it reasonable to assume the strong independence axiom for such probability mixtures. Thus, for example, one may be willing to say that if x and y are two commodity bundles such that $x \sim y$, then for any third bundle z, the individual is indifferent between (1) a gamble in which either x is obtained with probability α or z with probability $1 - \alpha$ and (2) the corresponding gamble in which either y is obtained with probability α or z with probability $1 - \alpha$.

Intuitively it is clear that ranking random prospects, which are just probability distributions of elementary prospects, according to expected utility requires a utility function in which the differences between the utility levels assigned to different elementary prospects have some meaning; that is, if the utility of a random prospect is to be just the expected or average value of the separate utilities of each of its component elementary prospects, differences in utility levels must have some meaning.[7] In later discussions we shall see that Axioms 4 and 5 play a critical role in defining utility functions for which this is the case.

Before moving on, however, we should note that the axiom system that we have chosen is far from the least restrictive set of behavioral postulates that could be shown to lead to the expected utility rule. We chose this particular set of axioms to simplify the derivation of the expected utility rule and to make this derivation contribute as much as possible to a fuller understanding of the model. The reader who is interested in a derivation from less restrictive assumptions is encouraged to seek out the references at the end of the chapter, especially Herstein and Milnor [2].

II.B. Derivation of the Expected Utility Rule

To show that the expected utility rule follows from the axioms, we must show that the axioms imply two things:

1. There exists an order-preserving utility function; that is, if $U(\cdot)$ is the function, $U(x) > U(y)$ implies $x > y$ and $U(x) = U(y)$ implies $x \sim y$.[8]
2. The ordering of random prospects given by the function is according to expected utility; that is, $U(G(x,y:\alpha)) = \alpha U(x) + (1 - \alpha)U(y)$.

For simplicity let us suppose that the set S of prospects is bounded by two extreme prospects a and b, such that $a > b$ and for any prospect x in S either

$$a > x \geq b$$

or

$$a \geq x > b.$$

Axioms 4 and 5 can then be used to rank all prospects in S in terms of the two extreme prospects a and b. Thus let us define the function $\alpha(x)$ as the probability such that

$$x \sim G(a,b: \alpha(x));$$

that is, $\alpha(x)$ is the probability value for which the individual is indifferent between (1) obtaining the prospect x for certain and (2) engaging in a gamble, or equivalently, obtaining a probability distribution, that yields

[7] This is of course in contrast with a purely ordinal function, such as those in Chap. 1, or those which would be implied by the first two axioms of the expected utility model, in which only the ordering of prospects provided by the function is meaningful and, except for sign, differences in assigned levels of utility are completely arbitrary.
[8] We use the notation $U(\cdot)$ when we talk about the function in general terms, that is, without reference to any specific value of its argument.

either prospect a with probability $\alpha(x)$ or prospect b with probability $1 - \alpha(x)$. The existence and uniqueness of $\alpha(x)$ for any x in S is guaranteed by Axiom 4, and existence and uniqueness mean that $\alpha(x)$ is a function defined for all prospects in S. Thus for the prospect y, $\alpha(y)$ is the probability value such that

$$y \sim G(a,b:\alpha(y)).$$

Indeed from Axiom 5 we can see immediately that $\alpha(x)$ is an order-preserving utility function; that is, $\alpha(x) > \alpha(y)$ implies $x \succ y$, and $\alpha(x) = \alpha(y)$ implies $x \sim y$. Thus to show that the expected utility rule follows from the axioms, it remains only to show that the function $\alpha(x)$ ranks random prospects according to expected utility; that is, consider a random prospect $G(x,y:\beta)$ in which the individual obtains either x, with probability β, or y, with probability $1 - \beta$. From Axiom 4 we know that there is always a unique probability $\alpha(G(x,y:\beta))$ such that

$$G(x,y:\beta) \sim G(a,b:\alpha(G(x,y:\beta)));$$

that is, there is always a probability $\alpha(G(x,y:\beta))$ such that the individual is indifferent between (1) engaging in the gamble $G(x,y:\beta)$ and (2) engaging in the gamble $G(a,b:\alpha(G(x,y:\beta)))$ in which he obtains either a, with probability $\alpha(G(x,y:\beta))$, or b, with probability $1 - \alpha(G(x,y:\beta))$. We already know that $\alpha(G(x,y:\beta))$ ranks $G(x,y:\beta)$ relative to other prospects in S. It remains only to show that

$$\alpha(G(x,y:\beta)) = \beta\alpha(x) + (1 - \beta)\alpha(y);$$

that is, the ranking is according to expected utility, where $\alpha(\cdot)$ is the utility function. And we see that at this stage in the analysis, Axiom 3 (strong independence) begins to play a critical role.

Because

$$x \sim G(a,b:\alpha(x)),$$

from Axiom 3 we can conclude that

$$G(x,y:\beta) \sim G(G(a,b:\alpha(x)),y:\beta). \tag{5.1}$$

Here $G(G(a,b:\alpha(x)),y:\beta)$ represents a gamble in which (1) with probability β the individual obtains the prospect $G(a,b:\alpha(x))$, which is of course itself a random prospect, or (2) with probability $1 - \beta$ he obtains the prospect y. Likewise, because

$$y \sim G(a,b:\alpha(y)),$$

from Axiom 3 we can again conclude that

$$G(G(a,b:\alpha(x)),y:\beta) \sim G(G(a,b:\alpha(x)),G(a,b:\alpha(y)):\beta). \tag{5.2}$$

Applying Axiom 2 (transitivity) to expressions (5.1) and (5.2), we obtain

$$G(x,y:\beta) \sim G(G(a,b:\alpha(x))),G(a,b:\alpha(y)):\beta). \qquad (5.3)$$

Now $G(G(a,b:\alpha(x)),G(a,b:\alpha(y)):\beta)$ is a double gamble in which either (1) with probability β the individual engages in the gamble $G(a,b:\alpha(x))$ or (2) with probability $1 - \beta$ he engages in the gamble $G(a,b:\alpha(y))$. But both of these component gambles involve only the extreme prospects a and b. Indeed the reader can easily determine that $G(G(a,b:\alpha(x)),$ $G(a,b:\alpha(y)):\beta)$ is identical with $G(a,b:\beta\alpha(x) + (1 - \beta)\alpha(y))$, a gamble in which the individual obtains either the prospect a, with probability $\beta\alpha(x) + (1 - \beta)\alpha(y)$, or the prospect b, with probability $1 - [\beta\alpha(x) + (1 - \beta)\alpha(y)]$. Thus from Equation (5.3) and Axiom 2

$$G(x,y:\beta) \sim G(a,b:\beta\alpha(x) + (1 - \beta)\alpha(y)).$$

But from Axiom 4

$$G(x,y:\beta) \sim G(a,b:\alpha(G(x,y:\beta))).$$

And because Axiom 4 also tells us that $\alpha(G(x,y:\beta))$ is unique, we must have

$$\alpha(G(x,y:\beta)) = \beta\alpha(x) + (1 - \beta)\alpha(y).$$

Thus the ranking of random prospects provided by the function $\alpha(\cdot)$ is indeed according to expected utility.

To review, Axioms 4 and 5 allowed us to define a utility function that ranked prospects in S in terms of the two extreme prospects a and b. The strong independence axiom then played a critical role in showing that this utility function $\alpha(\cdot)$ ranks random prospects according to expected utility.

II.C. Some Properties of the Utility Functions Implied by the Expected Utility Model

It is useful to examine the utility function $\alpha(\cdot)$ in a little more detail. Note first that we must have

$$a \sim G(a,b:1) \qquad \text{and} \qquad b \sim G(a,b:0),$$

so that $\alpha(a) = 1$ and $\alpha(b) = 0$. Thus the function ranges from 0 to 1, and the utility value assigned to any particular prospect depends, from Axiom 4, on how the probabilities of obtaining a gamble involving a and b must be balanced to make the individual indifferent between the prospect and the gamble.

We must emphasize, though, that $\alpha(\cdot)$ is not the only utility function consistent with the expected utility rule. Once we have shown that the axioms imply the expected utility rule, any function that provides the same rankings of prospect as $\alpha(\cdot)$ and also ranks random prospects according to expected utility is equivalent to $\alpha(\cdot)$ as a representation of the individual's tastes. In fact, we now see that any positive linear transformation of $\alpha(\cdot)$ is equivalent to $\alpha(\cdot)$.

Thus consider the function

$$U(\cdot) = \gamma_1 + \gamma_2 \alpha(\cdot), \qquad \gamma_2 > 0.$$

We want to examine the rankings of two arbitrary gambles, $G(x,y:\beta)$ and $G(u,z:\phi)$, provided by the functions $\alpha(\cdot)$ and $U(\cdot)$. We know that the rankings provided by $\alpha(\cdot)$ are according to expected utility; that is,

$$\alpha(G(x,y:\beta)) = \beta\alpha(x) + (1 - \beta)\alpha(y), \tag{5.4}$$

$$\alpha(G(u,z:\phi)) = \phi\alpha(u) + (1 - \phi)\alpha(z). \tag{5.5}$$

On the other hand, if we use the function $U(\cdot)$ to compute the expected utilities $E(\tilde{U})$ of the two gambles, we get[9]

For $G(x,y:\beta) : E(\tilde{U}) = \beta U(x) + (1 - \beta) U(y)$

$$= \beta[\gamma_1 + \gamma_2\alpha(x)] + (1 - \beta)[\gamma_1 + \gamma_2\alpha(y)]$$

$$= \gamma_1 + \gamma_2[\beta\alpha(x) + (1 - \beta)\alpha(y)]; \tag{5.6}$$

For $G(u,z:\phi) : E(\tilde{U}) = \gamma_1 + \gamma_2[\phi\alpha(u) + (1 - \phi)\alpha(z)]. \tag{5.7}$

Comparing Equations (5.6) and (5.7) with Equations (5.4) and (5.5), we see that the expected utility rankings of the two gambles given by the function $U(\cdot)$ is the same as that given by the function $\alpha(\cdot)$.

This result is easy to explain. An expected utility is just a linear combination of the utilities of elementary prospects, that is, the expected utility of a given probability distribution of elementary prospects is obtained by first multiplying the probability of each elementary prospect by the utility of the prospect and then summing the resulting products. Thus when we take a positive linear transformation of the function $\alpha(\cdot)$, the result is the same positive linear transformation of the expected utilities of all random prospects, that is, utilities and expected utilities are all first multiplied by a positive constant γ_2, and then another constant γ_1 is added to each. But these operations leave the rankings of the prospects completely unchanged. And the same kind of reasoning can be used to conclude that in general a nonlinear transformation of the utility function $\alpha(\cdot)$ does not provide the same expected utility rankings of random prospects as the function $\alpha(\cdot)$. We summarize these results with the statement that the utility functions implied by the expected utility hypothesis are unique up to positive linear transformations.

[9] Note that the level of utility to be obtained from a gamble is indeed a random variable: thus the tilde over the U in $E(\tilde{U})$.

In sum, Axioms 1 and 2 would provide an ordinal utility function, say, $V(\cdot)$, for prospects in the set S. As always, the function would be ordinal in the sense that it would provide only an ordering of prospects in S; any transformation of $V(\cdot)$, say, $Z(V(\cdot))$, that is an increasing function of values of V would provide a representation of the individual's tastes that is equivalent to $V(\cdot)$. Adding Axioms 3 to 5, however, has allowed us to imply a finer or more exact calibration of utilities: finer in the sense that random prospects can be ranked on the basis of expected utilities. But the utility functions implied by the expanded axiom set are themselves unique only up to positive linear transformations, and so in a mathematical sense they are not strictly cardinal, that is, unique. Following the common usage of the utility literature, however, we henceforth refer to these utility functions as cardinal.

It is clear that with utility functions that are unique only up to positive linear transformations, levels of utility do not have hedonic meaning, so that, for example, interpersonal comparisons of utility are not possible. The latter require utility functions that are strictly cardinal, that is, unique.

But with the utility functions of the expected utility model, the change in the level of utility from one prospect to another is unique up to a proportionality factor; that is, if $U(\cdot)$ and $\alpha(\cdot)$ are two utility functions that provide the same expected utility rankings of all prospects, there must be a positive constant γ such that for any two prospects x and y in S, $U(x) - U(y) = \gamma[\alpha(x) - \alpha(y)]$. This means that with the utility functions implied by the expected utility rule, one can sensibly talk about increasing and decreasing marginal utility, which, as we soon see, is important in developing meaningful notions of risk aversion and risk preference. By way of contrast, recall that with a purely ordinal utility function only the signs of marginal utilities have meaning.

III. THE TIMELESS EXPECTED UTILITY OF WEALTH MODEL

The initial application of the expected utility model is to the problem of choice from among various available "timeless" gambles. Specifically, we assume that at the beginning of period 1 the individual has the opportunity to use his initial wealth w to engage in gambles whose outcomes, in this case, levels of wealth, are known before the consumption-investment decision for period 1 is made. The gambles are timeless in the sense that no consumption takes place between the time when a gamble is undertaken and the time when its outcome is realized. We assume that the individual's behavior in this decision is in conformity with the axioms of the expected utility model, so that he chooses the gamble or the "portfolio" of gambles that maximizes his expected utility. We want to show first how a utility of wealth function can be obtained from the axioms and then introduce the notions of risk aversion, risk preference, and risk neutrality.

III.A. Obtaining the Utility of Wealth Function from Axiom 4

In the timeless expected utility of wealth model, elementary prospects are just levels of wealth; random prospects are probability distributions of wealth levels. Moreover, a nonsatiation axiom is usually added to the five axioms presented in the preceding section;[10] that is, it is assumed that more wealth for certain is preferred to less.

To say that the utility of wealth functions implied by the axioms of the expected utility model are unique only up to positive linear transformations is equivalent to saying that two points on a utility function can be assigned arbitrarily, as long as they are assigned in accordance with the nonsatiation axiom. Then, as we now see, the remaining points on the utility function can be determined from Axiom 4.

Thus suppose that we assign

$$U(\$0) = 0 \qquad \text{and} \qquad U(\$100) = 100.$$

According to Axiom 4, for any specific wealth level w between \$0 and \$100, there is a unique probability α such that

$$w \sim G(100,0:\alpha).$$

Thus, given that we now know that the axiom system implies ranking of random prospects according to expected utility, the utility of w is just the expected utility of the gamble

$$U(w) = \alpha U(100) + (1 - \alpha) U(0) = 100\alpha.$$

Thus one can determine $U(w)$ for a particular individual by asking the following question: What is the probability α that would make you indifferent between w dollars of wealth for certain and a gamble that could result in \$100 of wealth with probability α and \$0 with probability $(1 - \alpha)$? Because we know $U(0)$ and $U(100)$, the answer to this question defines $U(w)$.

The utility of a wealth level w greater than \$100 can be determined by noting that according to Axiom 4 the individual can always define a probability α such that

$$100 \sim G(w,0:\alpha),$$

from which, applying the expected utility rule to G, we can infer that

$$U(100) = \alpha U(w) + (1 - \alpha) U(0), \qquad \text{for a specific } w > \$100.$$

---

[10] And the reader may well find it useful to restate these five axioms in terms of the current problem.

Thus one asks the individual the following question: What is the probability α that would make you indifferent between a wealth level of $100 for certain and a gamble involving a probability α that wealth will be w and $(1 - \alpha)$ that it will be $0? The answer to this question defines $U(w)$ as

$$U(w) = \frac{U(100) - (1 - \alpha) U(0)}{\alpha}$$

$$= \frac{100}{\alpha}.$$

Thus once two points on an individual's utility of wealth function have been assigned arbitrarily, the remaining points on the function can, in principle, be determined by a series of questions of the type presented above.

III.B. Usual Types of Utility of Wealth Functions: Risk Aversion, Risk Preference, and Risk Neutrality

The nonsatiation axiom says that all utility functions must be monotone-increasing functions of wealth. Thus to indicate that marginal utility is always positive, a graph of utility against wealth must have a positive slope at all levels of wealth. Given this basic restriction, there are three general types of utility functions: (1) linear, (2) concave, and (3) convex, which apply respectively to individuals who (1) have neither risk aversion nor risk preference, (2) have risk aversion, and (3) have risk preference.

We can best elaborate on the implications of the individual's attitudes toward risk for the shape of his utility of wealth function by reference to Figure 5.1, which shows the three general types. Let us begin by noting some of the general properties of the three types of functions. A linear utility function (Figure 5.1a) implies constant marginal utility of wealth at all levels of wealth. Mathematically, the first derivative of the function is a constant. A loss in wealth of ϵ decreases utility by exactly the same amount that an equivalent gain of ϵ would increase it. On the other hand, if the individual's utility function is strictly concave (Figure 5.1b), marginal utility is a decreasing function of wealth. The graph of utility against wealth is monotone-increasing, but utility increases with wealth at a slower and slower rate. Mathematically, the first derivative of utility with respect to wealth is positive, but the second derivative is negative. A loss in wealth of ϵ decreases the individual's level of utility more than an equivalent gain of ϵ would increase it. Finally, if the individual's utility of wealth function is strictly convex (Figure 5.1c), marginal utility is an increasing function of wealth; utility increases with wealth at a faster and faster rate. Mathematically, the second derivative of utility with respect to wealth is positive, so that the first derivative is an increasing function of wealth. An increase

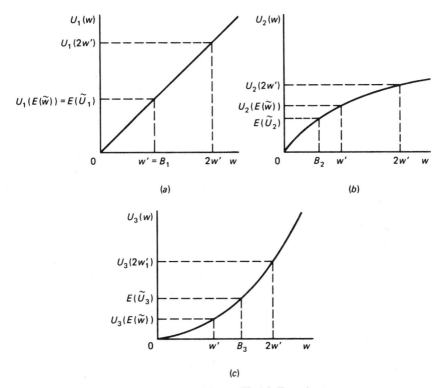

Figure 5.1   Utility of Wealth Functions

in wealth of ϵ increases the individual's level of utility more than an equivalent loss of ϵ would decrease it.[11]

Suppose now that at the beginning of period 1 the individual's wealth
level is w'. Suppose that if gamble A is chosen, his wealth w is $2w'$ with
probability 0.5 and 0 with probability 0.5. The expected utility of A·is

$$E(\tilde{U}) = 0.5U(0) + 0.5U(2w'),$$

which is just halfway between 0 and $U(2w')$ along the vertical axes of
each of the three graphs in Figure 5.1.

If we assume that the three graphs in Figure 5.1 represent the utility
of wealth functions of three different individuals, what can we say about

[11] The statements concerning first and second derivatives hold only if these derivatives
exist. It is easy to show that the axioms of the expected utility hypothesis imply the
existence of a continuous utility of wealth function, but the function need not be
differentiable.

the attitudes of these three individuals toward A? For individual i, $i = 1, 2, 3$, define the certainty equivalent level of wealth corresponding to the probability distribution of wealth provided by the gamble A as the level of wealth B_i, $i = 1, 2, 3$, such that

$$U_i(B_i) = E(\tilde{U}_i);$$

that is, as far as individual i with utility function U_i is concerned, a probability distribution of wealth with expected utility $E(\tilde{U}_i)$ is exactly equivalent to B_i of wealth obtained for certain. The individual would be indifferent in a choice between B_i for certain and the probability distribution of wealth associated with action A.

The relationship between the expected value of wealth provided by a given probability distribution and the certainty equivalent level of wealth for this distribution gives us a way of defining whether the individual is a risk averter, has risk preference, or is risk-neutral. For example, for the individual in Figure 5.1b, the certainty equivalent level of wealth B_2 for the probability distribution of A is less than $w' = E(\tilde{w})$, the expected value of wealth provided by A. Or in other words, for this individual the money value of A is less than the expected wealth provided by A. (Or reading along the vertical axis of the figure, the expected utility of A is less than the utility of the expected wealth provided by A.) The individual regards any level of wealth obtained for certain that is greater than B_2 as superior to the probability distribution of wealth provided by the gamble A. Thus if A were the only gamble available, he would be willing to pay an insurance premium of $w' - K$, $(K \geq B_2)$, in order to avoid A and obtain a level of wealth of K for certain.[12]

In general, for an individual with a strictly concave utility of wealth function, the certainty equivalent level of wealth associated with a given probability distribution is always less than the expected value of wealth associated with the distribution. Or in other words, the money value of the distribution to the individual is less than the expected value of its payoff. Thus it is convenient to classify such a person as a risk averter.

By contrast, for the individual in Figure 5.1c, whose utility of wealth function is strictly convex, the certainty equivalent level of wealth B_3 for the probability distribution of the gamble A is greater than $w' = E(\tilde{w})$, the expected level of wealth provided by A. For this individual the money value of A is greater than the expected payoff from A. In essence for him the chance of a large gain is more than sufficient to compensate for an equal chance of an equivalent large loss. Moreover, given a strictly convex

---

[12] Thus this analysis explains in part why people buy insurance, although insurance is in general an unfair gamble; that is, the expected value of the payoff is less than the premium that must be paid. In essence they are willing to pay to avoid the probability distributions of losses that must be faced in the absence of insurance.

utility function, these results hold with respect to all probability distributions of terminal wealth; the individual would always prefer to have the distribution rather than its expected value for certain. Thus it is meaningful to classify such a person as having risk preference.

For the individual in Figure 5.1a, whose utility of wealth function is linear, the certainty equivalent level of wealth B_1 for the probability distribution of A is exactly equal to $w' = E(\tilde{w})$; the money value of the distribution is exactly equal to its expected money payoff. Or in other words, the expected utility of the distribution and the utility of its expected value are equal. Moreover, these results hold with respect to all probability distributions of wealth; if his utility function is linear, the individual chooses among probability distributions of wealth solely in terms of their expected values, always choosing the distribution with maximum expected value. The "dispersion" or "riskiness" of the distributions has no effect on his choice. Thus such a person is neutral with respect to risk; he has neither risk aversion nor risk preference.

Finally, for convenience of exposition we have assumed that an individual is a consistent risk averter, risk preferrer, or neutral with respect to risk at all levels of wealth. This is, of course, not necessarily the case, and mixtures of the three types of utility functions are possible. The only real restrictions on the shape of the function are that it must be continuous and its slope must be positive at all levels of wealth. Given these conditions, there is no reason why the function cannot be concave over some regions of wealth, convex over others, and linear over still others.

IV. EXPECTED UTILITY AND THE THEORY OF FINANCE

IV.A. The Multiperiod Expected Utility of Consumption Model

The timeless expected utility of wealth model is useful for introducing important concepts like risk aversion and risk preference. But the basic problem in finance is the allocation of resources through time. Thus in the τ period consumption-investment problem, the individual is concerned with his lifetime consumption sequence

$$C_\tau = (c_1, c_2, \ldots, c_\tau).$$

In this model the elementary prospects are the different possible lifetime consumption sequences, that is, the different possible values of C_τ, and random prospects are probability distributions of lifetime consumption sequences, that is, probability distributions of C_τ. If we assume that the individual's behavior in solving this problem conforms to the axioms of the expected utility model, when these axioms are, of course, restated in terms of C_τ, then we can infer that the individual's tastes can be represented by a utility function

$$U(C_\tau) = U(c_1,c_2,\ldots,c_\tau),$$

and the rankings of random prospects are according to expected utility.

If we assume the nonsatiation axiom—that is, holding consumption in other periods constant, more consumption in any given period is preferred to less—then the marginal utility of consumption in any period is positive. Moreover, as in the timeless expected utility of wealth model, concavity, convexity, and linearity of the utility function $U(C_\tau)$ respectively imply risk aversion, risk preference, and risk neutrality.

Thus, by definition, strict concavity of the function $U(C_\tau)$ says that for any two consumption sequences $C_\tau = (c_1,c_2,\ldots,c_\tau)$ and $\hat{C}_\tau = (\hat{c}_1,\hat{c}_2,\ldots,\hat{c}_\tau)$, and any α such that $0 < \alpha < 1$,

$$U(\alpha c_1 + (1-\alpha)\hat{c}_1, \alpha c_2 + (1-\alpha)\hat{c}_2, \ldots, \alpha c_\tau + (1-\alpha)\hat{c}_\tau)$$
$$> \alpha U(c_1,c_2,\ldots,c_\tau) + (1-\alpha)U(\hat{c}_1,\hat{c}_2,\ldots,\hat{c}_\tau); \quad (5.8)$$

or equivalently

$$U(\alpha C_\tau + (1-\alpha)\hat{C}_\tau) > \alpha U(C_\tau) + (1-\alpha)U(\hat{C}_\tau), \qquad 0 < \alpha < 1.\text{[13]}$$
$$(5.9)$$

In words, strict concavity of the function U implies that the utility of a weighted average of two consumption sequences is greater than the weighted average of the utilities of the two sequences. Geometrically, a straight line between any two points on U lies below the function.

But suppose now that we consider a gamble in which the individual obtains the consumption sequence C_τ with probability α or the sequence $\hat{C}_\tau$ with probability $1 - \alpha$. Thus the expected payoff from the gamble is $\alpha C_\tau + (1-\alpha)\hat{C}_\tau$; its expected utility is $\alpha U(C_\tau) + (1-\alpha)U(\hat{C}_\tau)$. Then expression (5.9) tells us that when the individual's utility function is concave, the expected utility of the gamble is less than the utility of its expected payoff: the individual is risk-averse in the sense that if given the choice, he would prefer to have the expected payoff for certain rather than engage in the gamble.

---

[13] The notation $\alpha C_\tau + (1-\alpha)\hat{C}_\tau$ is just a convenient way of summarizing the operations involved in obtaining a weighted average of the two consumption sequences, as written out explicitly in Equation (5.8); that is, for $t = 1, 2, \ldots, \tau$ we simply compute $\alpha c_t + (1-\alpha)\hat{c}_t$. These are, of course, just the usual conventions for multiplication of a vector by a scalar and for addition of vectors.

On the other hand, when the individual's utility function is strictly convex,

$$U(\alpha C_\tau + (1 - \alpha)\hat{C}_\tau) < \alpha U(C_\tau) + (1 - \alpha)U(\hat{C}_\tau), \qquad 0 < \alpha < 1.$$

Thus the expected utility of a gamble that pays C_τ with probability α and $\hat{C}_\tau$ with probability $1 - \alpha$ is greater than the utility of the expected payoff: the individual has risk preference in the sense that he would prefer to engage in the gamble rather than obtain its expected payoff for certain.

Finally, when the individual's utility function is linear,

$$U(\alpha C_\tau + (1 - \alpha)\hat{C}_\tau) = \alpha U(C_\tau) + (1 - \alpha)U(\hat{C}_\tau).$$

The individual is risk-neutral in the sense that he is indifferent between (1) engaging in a gamble that pays C_τ with probability α or $\hat{C}_\tau$ with probability $1 - \alpha$ or (2) receiving for certain the expected payoff $\alpha C_\tau + (1 - \alpha)\hat{C}_\tau$ from the gamble.

It is well to note that risk aversion (concavity) or risk preference (convexity) in the utility function $U(C_\tau) = U(c_1, c_2, \ldots, c_\tau)$ implies risk aversion or risk preference with respect to consumption in any given period. Thus, for example, if $U(C_\tau)$ is concave in C_τ, it is also concave with respect to any component c_t of C_τ; that is, holding consumption in other periods constant, $U(C_\tau)$ is a concave function of c_t for any $t = 1, 2, \ldots, \tau$. Indeed as a function of c_t, $U(C_\tau)$ looks in this case like the utility of wealth function shown in Figure 5.1b. Likewise if $U(C_\tau)$ is convex, as a function of consumption in any given period $U(C_\tau)$ looks like the utility of wealth function shown in Figure 5.1c.

And these remarks are of more than passing interest. The next two chapters concentrate on two-period consumption-investment models, that is, the case $\tau = 2$. In these two-period models, given some level of consumption at period 1, the individual's period 1 portfolio decision depends on the shape of his utility function $U(c_1, c_2)$ as a function of consumption in period 2. Thus, for example, we know now that if the individual is risk-averse, that is, $U(c_1, c_2)$ is concave in (c_1, c_2), then $U(c_1, c_2)$ is a concave function of c_2, and the individual behaves like a risk averter in choosing among different probability distributions of period 2 consumption associated with different investment decisions at period 1.

Finally, although we say that utility functions that are concave, convex, and linear respectively imply risk aversion, risk preference, and risk neutrality, the direction of causation is, of course, the other way around: The individual's tastes determine the shape of his utility function. Thus, for example, his utility function is concave because he is risk-averse. It is always well to keep in mind that a utility function is just a convenient way of representing tastes. The individual's behavior is guided by his tastes, which we, as outside observers, find convenient to summarize in terms of a utility function.

IV.B. Utilities for Consumption Dollars from Utilities for Consumption Goods

In the problems involving intertemporal allocation of resources that are of most interest in finance it is convenient to deal with utility functions for aggregate consumption, that is, utility functions for dollars of consumption. We must nevertheless recognize, as in Chapter 1, that the individual's tastes for aggregate consumption ultimately derive from his tastes for consumption goods. More specifically, utilities for consumption dollars are just the utilities obtained from optimal allocation of these consumption dollars to goods and services. For example, in the two-period case the utility function $U(c_1,c_2)$ for aggregate consumption is obtained from the utility function $V(Q_1,Q_2)$ for consumption goods as[14]

$$U(c_1,c_2) = \max_{Q_1,Q_2} V(Q_1,Q_2) \qquad (5.10a)$$

subject to the constraints

$$\sum_{k=1}^{K(1)} p_{1k}q_{1k} = c_1 \quad \text{and} \quad \sum_{k=1}^{K(2)} p_{2k}q_{2k} = c_2, \qquad (5.10b)$$

where $K(1)$ and $K(2)$ are the numbers of consumption goods available in periods 1 and 2, q_{1k} and q_{2k} are quantities of good k consumed in periods 1 and 2, p_{1k} and p_{2k} are the per unit prices of these goods, and $Q_1 = (q_{11},q_{12},\ldots,q_{1,K(1)})$, $Q_2 = (q_{21},q_{22},\ldots,q_{2,K(2)})$ are the vectors of quantities of commodities consumed.

Although the subject is briefly considered again in Chapter 8, for our purposes the detailed relationships between utility functions for consumption goods and utility functions for consumption dollars are not a topic of major concern. We wish, however, to make a few points in passing, and without proof.[15]

First, as stated in Equation (5.10), the individual's tastes for aggregate consumption derive from his tastes for consumption goods. Thus if we assume that he can choose among prospects stated in terms of consumption dollars on the basis of expected utility, his tastes with respect to consumption goods must also satisfy the axioms of the expected utility model. In

---

[14] The notation

$$\max_{Q_1,Q_2} V(Q_1,Q_2)$$

is read "choose Q_1 and Q_2 in such a way as to maximize $V(Q_1,Q_2)$."
[15] The reader with a stronger interest in this area is referred to Fama [5].

short, cardinal utilities for aggregate consumption derive from cardinal utilities for consumption goods.

Second, in deriving the utility function $U(c_1,c_2)$ as in Equation (5.10), we have implicitly assumed that the prices of consumption goods in both periods are known; that is, a utility function for consumption dollars is conditional on some set of prices of consumption goods. Thus rather than writing $U(c_1,c_2)$, for completeness, we should write $U(c_1,c_2 \mid P_1,P_2)$, where $P_1 = (p_{11},p_{12},\ldots,p_{1,K(1)})$ and $P_2 = (p_{21},p_{22},\ldots,p_{2,K(2)})$ are the vectors of prices of consumption goods in the two periods. Assuming that tastes with respect to consumption goods conform to the axioms of the expected utility model, the function $U(c_1,c_2 \mid P_1,P_2)$ could then be used to order random prospects involving uncertainty with respect to both dollar levels of consumption and prices of consumption goods on the basis of expected utility. This possibility is only mentioned here, however, because subsequent chapters bypass almost completely questions concerning the effects of uncertainty in the prices of consumption goods on optimal consumption-investment decisions. But this omission is consistent with the current state of the literature: A most pressing field for future research is accounting for the effects of uncertain prices for consumption goods first on the nature of optimal consumption-investment decisions by individuals and then on the process of price formation in the capital market.

V. CONCLUSION

Our discussion of the expected utility model as a way of representing tastes, that is, as a theory of choice, in a world of uncertainty is now completed. We turn in the next chapter to the other side of the consumption-investment problem, representing the market opportunities available to the individual. In the usual manner, tastes and opportunities are then combined into a theory of consumer-investor equilibrium, that is, a theory of optimal consumption-investment decisions by individuals. The model of consumer-investor equilibrium presented in the next chapter is then the basic building block for the model of capital market equilibrium to be developed in Chapter 7.

REFERENCES

Although the expected utility model dates back at least several centuries to the work of Daniel Bernoulli, the first axiomatic development of the model is due to

1. Von Neumann, John, and Oskar Morgenstern, *Theory of Games and Economic Behavior*. Princeton, N.J.: Princeton University Press, 1947.

An elegant derivation of the model from, apparently, the least restrictive set of axioms is in

2. Herstein, I. N., and John Milnor, "An Axiomatic Approach to Expected Utility," *Econometrica*, vol. 21 (April 1953), pp. 291–297.

First recognition of the importance of the strong independence axiom is due to

3. Samuelson, Paul A., "Probability, Utility, and the Independence Axiom," *Econometrica*, vol. 20 (October 1952), pp. 670–678.

An important study of the concept of risk aversion is

4. Pratt, John W., "Risk Aversion in the Small and in the Large," *Econometrica*, vol. 32 (January–April 1964), pp. 122–136.

The relationships between utility functions for money and utility functions for commodities are treated in

5. Fama, Eugene F., "Ordinal and Measurable Utility." To appear in *Studies in the Theory of Capital Markets*, edited by Michael Jensen. New York: Praeger (forthcoming).

A detailed and, more or less, elementary discussion of the expected utility model is in

6. Markowitz, Harry, *Portfolio Selection: Efficient Diversification of Investments*. New York: John Wiley & Sons, Inc., 1959, chaps. 10–13.

APPENDIX

Statistical Review

I. INTRODUCTION

The purpose of this appendix is to present a brief review of some of the statistical concepts that are used in the analysis of uncertainty.

II. EXPECTED VALUES OF WEIGHTED SUMS OF RANDOM VARIABLES

A "random variable" is simply a variable that is subject to a probability distribution; that is, an observed value of the variable represents a drawing from some probability distribution.

The "expected value" of a random variable is just the mean of its probability distribution. For example, consider a bounded and discrete random variable $\tilde{W}$, where boundedness plus discreteness implies that the variable can only take on a finite number N of values W_i, $i = 1, 2, \ldots, N$, with associated probabilities $p(W_i)$, $i = 1, 2, \ldots, N$. The expected value of $\tilde{W}$ is then just

$$E(\tilde{W}) = \sum_{i=1}^{N} W_i p(W_i),$$

where $p(W_i)$ is the probability that the random variable takes the value W_i. Thus the expected value is just the weighted average of the different possible values of W, where the probabilities are used as weights. Another way of writing $E(\tilde{W})$ is

$$E(\tilde{W}) = \sum_W Wp(W),$$

where $\sum_W$ is read the sum over all possible values of W.[1]

Consider now two different random variables $\tilde{W}_1$ and $\tilde{W}_2$. The expected value of the sum $(\tilde{W}_1 + \tilde{W}_2)$ is just

$$E(\tilde{W}_1 + \tilde{W}_2) = \sum_{W_1} \sum_{W_2} (W_1 + W_2)p(W_1,W_2),$$

where $p(W_1,W_2)$ is the joint probability of W_1 and W_2; that is, it provides the probability that a joint drawing from the W_1 and W_2 distributions results in a particular pair (W_1,W_2).

Now the joint probability can always be expressed as the product of an unconditional and a conditional probability in either of two ways:

$$p(W_1,W_2) = p(W_1)p(W_2 \mid W_1) = p(W_2)p(W_1 \mid W_2),$$

where $p(W_2 \mid W_1)$ is the conditional probability of W_2 given W_1; that is, it is the probability that a particular W_2 is observed in the drawing from the W_2 distribution, given that a particular W_1 is observed in the drawing from the W_1 distribution. Similarly, $p(W_1 \mid W_2)$ is the conditional probability distribution of W_1 given that a particular W_2 is observed in the drawing from the distribution of W_2. Conditional probability distributions have the usual properties of probability distributions; that is, $p(W_1 \mid W_2) \geq 0$ and $\sum_{W_1} p(W_1 \mid W_2) = 1$.

---

[1] If the random variable W is continuous and unbounded, its expected value is defined as

$$E(\tilde{W}) = \int_{-\infty}^{\infty} Wf(W) \, dW,$$

where $f(W)$ is the density function of W.

In general the reader should note that all the concepts presented in this appendix apply equally well to both discrete and continuous random variables. The change from discrete to continuous variables simply involves replacing summations with the appropriate integrals.

Thus the expected value of the sum $(\tilde{W}_1 + \tilde{W}_2)$ can always be written as

$$E(\tilde{W}_1 + \tilde{W}_2) = \sum_{W_1} \sum_{W_2} (W_1 + W_2) p(W_1, W_2)$$

$$= \sum_{W_1} \sum_{W_2} W_1 p(W_1) p(W_2 \mid W_1) + \sum_{W_1} \sum_{W_2} W_2 p(W_2) p(W_1 \mid W_2)$$

$$= \sum_{W_1} W_1 p(W_1) \sum_{W_2} p(W_2 \mid W_1) + \sum_{W_2} W_2 p(W_2) \sum_{W_1} p(W_1 \mid W_2)$$

$$= \sum_{W_1} W_1 p(W_1) + \sum_{W_2} W_2 p(W_2)$$

$$= E(\tilde{W}_1) + E(\tilde{W}_2).$$

Thus the expectation of a sum is just the sum of the expectations. And it is important to note that this result holds regardless of the degree of dependence between the two variables.

Using similar arguments, it can also be shown that the expectation of a sum of any number of random variables is just the sum of the individual expectations; that is,

$$E(\tilde{W}_1 + \tilde{W}_2 + \cdots + \tilde{W}_m) = E(\tilde{W}_1) + E(\tilde{W}_2) + \cdots + E(\tilde{W}_m).$$

Suppose now that the variable $\tilde{W}_1$ is weighted by the constant A and $\tilde{W}_2$ is weighted by the constant B. The expected value of the weighted sum is then

$$E(A\tilde{W}_1 + B\tilde{W}_2) = \sum_{W_1} \sum_{W_2} (AW_1 + BW_2) p(W_1, W_2)$$

$$= AE(\tilde{W}_1) + BE(\tilde{W}_2),$$

where the reader can fill in the missing steps from the derivation above. Thus the expectation of a weighted sum is the weighted sum of the expectations of the individual variables.

III. THE VARIANCE OF A WEIGHTED SUM OF RANDOM VARIABLES

The variance of a random variable is just the expectation of the squared deviation of the variable from its mean or expected value. Thus

$$\sigma^2(\tilde{W}) = \text{var} (\tilde{W}) = E\{[\tilde{W} - E(\tilde{W})]^2\} = \sum_{W} [W - E(\tilde{W})]^2 p(W).$$

The variance provides a measure of the degree of dispersion in the probability distribution of a random variable. The more common measure of variability, however, is the standard deviation σ, which is just the square root of the variance

$$\sigma(\tilde{W}) = \sqrt{\sigma^2(\tilde{W})}.$$

It is interesting to examine the relationship between the variance and another measure of dispersion, the second moment. Expanding the expression for the variance, we get

$$\sigma^2(\tilde{W}) = E\{[\tilde{W} - E(\tilde{W})]^2\} = E[\tilde{W}^2 - 2\tilde{W}E(\tilde{W}) + E(\tilde{W})^2]$$
$$= E(\tilde{W}^2) - E(\tilde{W})^2.$$

$E(\tilde{W}^2)$ is called the second moment of the random variable $\tilde{W}$. Thus the variance is just the second moment minus the square of the mean.[2]

If the variable $\tilde{W}$ is weighted by the constant A, the variance of the weighted variable $A\tilde{W}$ is just

$$\sigma^2(A\tilde{W}) = E\{[A\tilde{W} - E(A\tilde{W})]^2\}$$
$$= \sum_W A^2[\tilde{W} - E(\tilde{W})]^2 p(W)$$
$$= A^2\sigma^2(\tilde{W}).$$

Thus the variance of a weighted random variable is just the weight squared times the variance of the unweighted random variable.

We now consider the variance of a sum of many random variables; that is, we want

$$\sigma^2(\tilde{W}_1 + \tilde{W}_2 + \cdots + \tilde{W}_N)$$
$$= E\{[(\tilde{W}_1 + \tilde{W}_2 + \cdots + \tilde{W}_N) - E(\tilde{W}_1 + \tilde{W}_2 + \cdots + \tilde{W}_N)]^2\}$$
$$= E\{([\tilde{W}_1 - E(\tilde{W}_1)] + [\tilde{W}_2 - E(\tilde{W}_2)] + \cdots + [\tilde{W}_N - E(\tilde{W}_N)])^2\}$$
$$= E\{[\tilde{w}_1 + \tilde{w}_2 + \cdots + \tilde{w}_N]^2\},$$

where $\tilde{w}_i \equiv \tilde{W}_i - E(\tilde{W}_i)$. Expanding the squared sum, we get

$$\sigma^2(\tilde{W}_1 + \tilde{W}_2 + \cdots + \tilde{W}_N) = E \begin{bmatrix} \tilde{w}_1{}^2 + \tilde{w}_1\tilde{w}_2 + \tilde{w}_1\tilde{w}_3 + \cdots + \tilde{w}_1\tilde{w}_N \\[2mm] + \tilde{w}_2\tilde{w}_1 + \tilde{w}_2{}^2 + \tilde{w}_2\tilde{w}_3 + \cdots + \tilde{w}_2\tilde{w}_N \\[2mm] + \tilde{w}_3\tilde{w}_1 + \tilde{w}_3\tilde{w}_2 + \tilde{w}_3{}^2 + \cdots + \tilde{w}_3\tilde{w}_N \\[2mm] + \cdots \cdots \cdots \cdots \cdots \cdots \cdots \cdots \cdots \cdots \cdots \\[2mm] + \cdots \cdots \cdots \cdots \cdots \cdots \cdots \cdots \cdots \cdots \cdots \\[2mm] + \tilde{w}_N\tilde{w}_1 + \tilde{w}_N\tilde{w}_2 + \tilde{w}_N\tilde{w}_3 + \cdots + \tilde{w}_N{}^2 \end{bmatrix}$$

[2] In general the kth moment of $\tilde{W}$ is $E(\tilde{W}^k)$. Thus the mean is the first moment, and the variance is the second moment minus the square of the first.

This, however, is just the expectation of a sum, which is just the sum of the expectations, so that

$$\sigma^2(\tilde{W}_1 + \tilde{W}_2 + \cdots + \tilde{W}_N) = \sum_{k=1}^{N} E(\tilde{w}_k{}^2) + \sum_{k=1}^{N} \sum_{\substack{j=1 \\ j \neq k}}^{N} E(\tilde{w}_k \tilde{w}_j).$$

The first term on the right of the equality is just the sum of the individual variances of the $\tilde{W}$'s. The second term is a sum of terms of the form

$$E(\tilde{w}_k \tilde{w}_j) = E\{[\tilde{W}_k - E(\tilde{W}_k)][\tilde{W}_j - E(\tilde{W}_j)]\}, \qquad j \neq k.$$

This expression is called the "covariance" between $\tilde{W}_k$ and $\tilde{W}_j$ for which we henceforth use the notation σ_{kj} or cov $(\tilde{W}_k, \tilde{W}_j)$. The covariance is a measure of the relationship between the variables $\tilde{W}_k$ and $\tilde{W}_j$. For example, if values of $\tilde{W}_k$ above $E(\tilde{W}_k)$ tend to be associated with values of $\tilde{W}_j$ above $E(\tilde{W}_j)$ and values of $\tilde{W}_k$ below $E(\tilde{W}_k)$ tend to be associated with values of $\tilde{W}_j$ below $E(\tilde{W}_j)$, then cov $(\tilde{W}_k, \tilde{W}_j)$ is positive. In this case we say that there is "positive dependence" in the relationship between the two variables. Similarly a negative covariance implies "negative dependence"; that is, on the average the deviations of $\tilde{W}_k$ and $\tilde{W}_j$ from their respective means tend to have opposite signs.[3]

It is also interesting to note that the order in which the terms in the covariance are written is irrelevant; that is,

$$E(\tilde{w}_k \tilde{w}_j) = E(\tilde{w}_j \tilde{w}_k) = \text{cov}\ (\tilde{W}_j, \tilde{W}_k) = \text{cov}\ (\tilde{W}_k, \tilde{W}_j) = \sigma_{kj} = \sigma_{jk}.$$

Finally, the variance of a random variable can also be regarded as a covariance; it is the covariance of the variable with itself:

$$\sigma^2(\tilde{W}_j) = E(\tilde{w}_j \tilde{w}_j) = \sigma_{jj}.$$

With these comments in mind, it is easy to see that the variance of a sum can be written in many equivalent ways. In particular,

$$\sigma^2\left(\sum_{i=1}^{N} \tilde{W}_i\right) = \sum_{k=1}^{N} \sigma^2(\tilde{W}_k) + \sum_{k=1}^{N} \sum_{\substack{j=1 \\ j \neq k}}^{N} \sigma_{kj}$$

$$= \sum_{k=1}^{N} \sigma^2(\tilde{W}_k) + 2 \sum_{k=1}^{N} \sum_{j=k+1}^{N} \sigma_{kj}$$

$$= \sum_{k=1}^{N} \sum_{j=1}^{N} \sigma_{kj}.$$

[3] The covariance is closely related to a more familiar measure of association, the correlation coefficient. The correlation coefficient is just

$$\text{corr}\ (\tilde{W}_k, \tilde{W}_j) = \frac{\text{cov}\ (\tilde{W}_k, \tilde{W}_j)}{\sqrt{\sigma^2(\tilde{W}_k)\sigma^2(\tilde{W}_j)}}.$$

It is also easy to show, and the reader should convince himself, that if each variable $\tilde{W}_k$ is weighted by the constant A_k, the variance of the weighted sum is

$$\sigma^2 \left(\sum_{k=1}^{N} A_k \tilde{W}_k \right) = \sum_{k=1}^{N} A_k{}^2 \sigma^2 (\tilde{W}_k) + \sum_{k=1}^{N} \sum_{\substack{j=1 \\ j \neq k}}^{N} A_k A_j \sigma_{kj}$$

$$= \sum_{k=1}^{N} A_k{}^2 \sigma^2 (\tilde{W}_k) + 2 \sum_{k=1}^{N} \sum_{j=k+1}^{N} A_k A_j \sigma_{kj}$$

$$= \sum_{k=1}^{N} \sum_{j=1}^{N} A_k A_j \sigma_{kj}.$$

Means and variances of weighted sums appear repeatedly in the models in following chapters. The reader should be sure to have a thorough familiarity with these concepts before moving on from here.

6

THE TWO-PERIOD CONSUMPTION–INVESTMENT MODEL

A. INTRODUCTION

In the previous chapter the expected utility model was presented, in somewhat general terms, as a model of choice under uncertainty. In this chapter the model is applied to the consumption-investment problem of an individual consumer. Throughout this chapter we are concerned with a simplified two-period case in which the individual must divide a given amount of wealth w_1 between consumption c_1 for the current period (period 1) and a portfolio investment $h_1 = w_1 - c_1$ that will provide a level of terminal wealth $\tilde{w}_2$ to be completely consumed during period 2, that is, $\tilde{c}_2 = \tilde{w}_2$.[1]

As always, w_1 is just the market value at period 1 of the consumer's resources. Thus it includes the market value of portfolio assets carried forward from previous periods plus the market value of any occupational income to be

---

[1] As in Chap. 5, tildes ($\sim$) are used throughout to denote random variables.

earned. To keep things simple, we assume that the consumer only sells labor at period 1; in period 2 he only consumes. And he receives payment at the beginning of period 1 for any labor services to be rendered during the period. Alternative approaches to the occupational decision are, however, considered briefly in a later section.

Finally, we assume throughout that the consumer is faced with a perfect capital market in the sense that he can buy as much as he wants of any investment asset without affecting its price; all investment assets are infinitely divisible; and there are no transactions costs or taxes.

At first glance the two-period model would seem to be a rather special case and of little general interest. In fact, however, we show in Chapter 8 that the results for the two-period model provide the core of the analysis for the general multiperiod problem. Thus at this point we bypass detailed justification and turn directly to the two-period model.

As in previous chapters, we proceed from simpler to more complex cases. For example, initially we treat a situation in which the individual's investment opportunities at period 1 are limited to two assets, one of which is riskless. Later in the chapter, however, this restriction is dropped, and the general N-asset problem is considered. In addition, as in previous chapters, the analysis is presented verbally, geometrically, and algebraically whenever possible. Indeed, the formal analysis may seem to become quickly rather complicated; thus we begin here with an intuitive discussion of the major results to be obtained in more rigorous manner later.

I.A. The Mean–Standard Deviation Model: An Overview

In principle the expected utility hypothesis itself is a complete theory of choice under uncertainty; that is, the individual just examines the expected utility associated with every possible consumption-investment decision and then chooses the one that maximizes expected utility. But this prescription is empty. From a normative or decision-making viewpoint, the individual faces the impossible task of examining in complete detail the probability distribution on period 2 consumption associated with each possible consumption-investment choice—of which there are also in principle an infinite number. And, from a substantive viewpoint, the expected utility model per se provides no observable or testable propositions about consumer behavior. In order to make the model practicable and to give it economic substance, we must impose more structure on the problem.

In the present chapter the consumption-investment problem is simplified by considering only situations in which the individual finds it possible to summarize his investment opportunities solely in terms of means and some measure of dispersion, usually standard deviations, of the distributions of the one-period percentage returns on different portfolios; that is, we are concerned with situations in which, given the total amount of funds to be invested, the individual can rank a portfolio relative to other portfolios by looking only at two parameters of the distribution of the return on the portfolio, and thus ignoring other aspects of the distribution.

One special case in which such an approach is legitimate is when distributions of returns on all portfolios are normal. A normal distribution can be fully described once its mean (expected value) and standard deviation are known. Thus all the differences between any number of normal distributions can be determined from their means and standard deviations. In the consumption-investment model this implies that all portfolios can be ranked by the individual on the basis of these two parameters of their return distributions.

But the assumption that return distributions are normal is just one way to obtain a two-parameter portfolio model. We show later that there are other two-parameter distributions that can serve the same role in our analysis, and we even argue that these alternative distributions seem to fit the available return data better than the normal. The properties of normal distributions are probably more familiar to most readers than those of the alternatives, however, and for this reason most of this chapter deals with a consumption-investment model based on the assumption of normally distributed portfolio returns. But little is lost in this approach; we show later that the major results of the normal model are easily obtained from corresponding models based on other two-parameter distributions. In short, on the side of the opportunity set, the critical ingredient of the model is that return distributions can be fully described in terms of two parameters, means and some measure of dispersion like the standard deviation, with the specific distribution assumed having little effect on the analysis.

The one-period two-parameter consumption-investment model also requires some specifications of the individual's tastes. In particular, he is assumed to behave as if he wished to make a consumption-investment decision that maximized expected utility, computed from the function $U(c_1,c_2)$, which is assumed to be monotone-increasing and strictly concave in (c_1,c_2). We emphasize that the individual's behavior is as if he were an expected utility maximizer; as in all utility theory (see Chapter 1), in making his decisions, he need not have a utility function or expected utility consciously in mind. The assumption is that his observable behavior is indistinguishable from that of an expected utility maximizer.

If, for mathematical simplicity, we assume that the first partial derivatives of the utility function $U(c_1,c_2)$ exist for all values of (c_1,c_2), monotonicity implies

$$\frac{\partial U(c_1,c_2)}{\partial c_1} > 0 \qquad \text{and} \qquad \frac{\partial U(c_1,c_2)}{\partial c_2} > 0. \qquad (6.1)$$

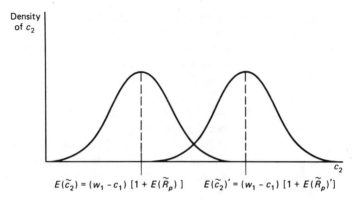

$$E(\tilde{c}_2) = (w_1 - c_1)\,[1 + E(\tilde{R}_p)\,] \qquad E(\tilde{c}_2)' = (w_1 - c_1)\,[1 + E(\tilde{R}_p)'\,]$$

Figure 6.1

On the other hand, strict concavity implies that for any two nonidentical points (c_1,c_2) and (c_1',c_2')

$$U(xc_1 + (1 - x)c_1',\; xc_2 + (1 - x)c_2')$$
$$> xU(c_1,c_2) + (1 - x)U(c_1',c_2'), \qquad 0 < x < 1. \quad (6.2)$$

Geometrically, (6.1) says that U is positively sloping in the direction of both c_1 and c_2, and (6.2) says that a straight line between any two points on the function lies everywhere below the function. Economically, monotonicity implies that the marginal utility of consumption is always positive; concavity implies that the marginal utility decreases as consumption in either period increases. As in the timeless expected utility of wealth model, under uncertainty concavity of the utility function is characteristic of a risk averter, and indeed the theory is directed entirely toward such risk-averse consumer-investors.

Let $\tilde{R}_p$ be the one-period percentage return—alternatively, the one-period return, or more simply just the return—on the portfolio p.[2] Then if $(w_1 - c_1)$ is invested in p at period 1, consumption in period 2 is

$$\tilde{c}_2 = (w_1 - c_1)(1 + \tilde{R}_p).$$

If the distribution of $\tilde{R}_p$ is normal, the distribution of $\tilde{c}_2$ is normal, and the mean $E(\tilde{c}_2)$ and standard deviation $\sigma(\tilde{c}_2)$ of $\tilde{c}_2$ are related to $E(\tilde{R}_p)$ and $\sigma(\tilde{R}_p)$ according to

$$E(\tilde{c}_2) = (w_1 - c_1)[1 + E(\tilde{R}_p)] \qquad \text{and} \qquad \sigma(\tilde{c}_2) = (w_1 - c_1)\sigma(\tilde{R}_p).$$

[2] As always, the one-period percentage return on any investment is just the market value of the investment at period 2 less its market value at period 1, all divided by the market value at period 1.

We now argue, in intuitive terms, that, given initial consumption c_1, total investment $(w_1 - c_1)$, and normally distributed portfolio returns, a risk-averse consumer's expected utility is an increasing function of mean return $E(\tilde{R}_p)$ and a decreasing function of standard deviation or dispersion of return $\sigma(\tilde{R}_p)$.

First, with $(w_1 - c_1)$ and $\sigma(\tilde{R}_p)$ constant, if $E(\tilde{R}_p)$ is increased to, say, $E(\tilde{R}_p)'$, with normally distributed portfolio returns the net effect is a shift in the distribution of $\tilde{c}_2$ toward higher values of c_2; that is, as illustrated in Figure 6.1, a normal distribution of given dispersion is simply moved to the right along the c_2 line: In other words, the probability that $\tilde{c}_2$ exceeds any given value is greater for the distribution with the higher expected return. Thus given positive marginal utility of c_2, it seems that, other things equal, in particular, c_1 and $\sigma(\tilde{R}_p)$, the consumer must prefer more expected return to less; expected utility is an increasing function of expected portfolio return.

On the other hand, other things equal, in this case, c_1 and $E(\tilde{R}_p)$, an increase in standard deviation of return from any $\sigma(\tilde{R}_p)$ to $\sigma(\tilde{R}_p)'$ results in a flattening of the distribution of $\tilde{c}_2$ about a given expected value, as illustrated in Figure 6.2. The chance of extremely high levels of period 2 consumption is increased with the higher $\sigma(\tilde{R}_p)'$, but from the symmetry of the normal distribution there is an equal increase in the chance of extremely low levels of consumption. Given a risk-averse consumer—and thus decreasing marginal utility of period 2 consumption—the better chance of high levels of period 2 consumption does not increase expected utility so much as the better chance of low levels of consumption decreases it. In short, with normally distributed portfolio returns for a risk averter expected utility is a declining function of standard deviation of return $\sigma(\tilde{R}_p)$.

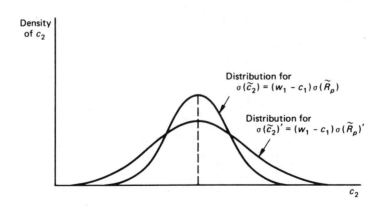

Figure 6.2

These results have an important implication. Consider the set of $E(\tilde{R})$, $\sigma(\tilde{R})$ efficient portfolios, where, by definition, a portfolio is $E(\tilde{R})$, $\sigma(\tilde{R})$ efficient if no portfolio with the same or higher expected return $E(\tilde{R}_p)$ has lower standard deviation $\sigma(\tilde{R}_p)$. Then for any given initial consumption c_1 and thus total investment $w_1 - c_1$, if expected utility is an increasing function of $E(\tilde{R}_p)$ and a decreasing function of $\sigma(\tilde{R}_p)$, the expected utility–maximizing, or optimal, portfolio must be a member of the efficient set. The particular efficient portfolio that is optimal depends on the level of c_1, but whatever the optimal level of c_1, with normally distributed portfolio returns:

Efficient Set Theorem. The optimal portfolio for a risk-averse consumer must be $E(\tilde{R})$, $\sigma(\tilde{R})$ efficient.

In brief, the assumptions of consumer risk aversion and normally distributed portfolio returns narrow down substantially the portfolios that the individual must consider in order to make an expected utility–maximizing consumption-investment decision. The assumption of normally distributed portfolio returns allows him to rank portfolios on the basis of means and standard deviations of returns; the assumption of risk aversion further allows him to restrict attention to $E(\tilde{R})$, $\sigma(\tilde{R})$ efficient portfolios.

I.B. A Familiar Picture

The efficient set theorem is easily given a geometric interpretation. First, for any given level of initial consumption c_1 and thus investment $w_1 - c_1$, an indifference curve of $E(\tilde{R})$ against $\sigma(\tilde{R})$ is defined by the set of com-

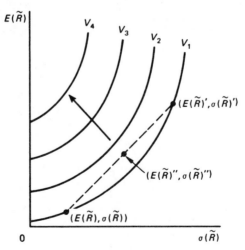

Figure 6.3   Consumer Indifference Curves

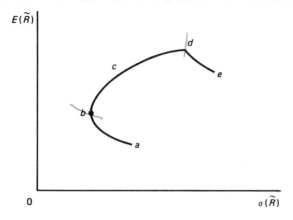

Figure 6.4   Portfolio Opportunities

binations of $E(\tilde{R})$ and $\sigma(\tilde{R})$ that yield some fixed level of expected utility.
The fact that expected utility is an increasing function of expected return
$E(\tilde{R}_p)$ and a decreasing function of standard deviation $\sigma(\tilde{R}_p)$ implies that
any such indifference curve must be positively sloping; to get the consumer
to take on more $\sigma(\tilde{R})$, he must be compensated with greater $E(\tilde{R})$. In
addition, as indicated by the arrow in Figure 6.3, expected utility increases
from lower to higher indifference curves, that is, upward and to the left.
We also show later that consumer risk aversion and normally distributed
portfolio returns imply that indifference curves are convex as shown.

Intuitively, it is clear that $E(\tilde{R})$, $\sigma(\tilde{R})$ efficient portfolios must lie
somewhere along the upper left boundary of the set of all feasible portfolios.
We show later that a reasonable general representation of the left boundary
of the feasible set is the curve $abcde$ in Figure 6.4. Only portfolios along the
positively sloping segment bcd are efficient, however, because, as the reader
can easily check, portfolios along ab and de do not satisfy the efficiency
criterion. We also show later that, like the curve bcd, the efficient boundary
must be concave.

The optimal portfolio for the given period 1 consumption c_1 and investment $w_1 - c_1$ is that which allows the consumer to attain the highest
possible indifference curve. Because the set of efficient portfolios traces a
positively sloping concave curve in the $E(\tilde{R})$, $\sigma(\tilde{R})$ plane and the indifference curves are convex, the optimal portfolio is generally given by a
tangency between an indifference curve and the efficient set curve, as
illustrated, for example, by the point e in Figure 6.5. Except for the new
variables $E(\tilde{R})$ and $\sigma(\tilde{R})$ on the axes, the picture here is similar to many
we have met in previous chapters.

A graph like Figure 6.5 shows the optimal portfolio for a given split of

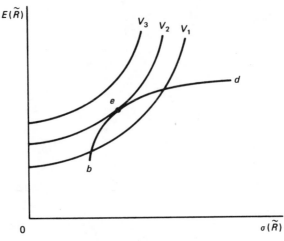

Figure 6.5   Consumer Equilibrium

initial wealth w_1 between consumption c_1 and investment $w_1 - c_1$. Using this geometric procedure, one could in principle determine the optimal portfolio for every possible choice of c_1 and in this way determine the overall consumption-investment decision that maximizes expected utility. Although our analysis continues to concentrate on the characteristics of the optimal portfolio decision, we should always keep in mind that the choice of period 1 consumption c_1 is made simultaneously with the portfolio decision, and the two are of course interrelated.

In fact, we really have nothing of much substance to say about the characteristics of an optimal split of initial wealth between consumption and investment. To say anything specific here would require that we impose additional restrictions on the form of the individual's utility function, and we have chosen not to do so here. Rather, the formal analysis, in this chapter and the next, is primarily concerned with presenting, in more rigorous terms than above, the major implications for optimal portfolio decisions of the two-parameter consumption-investment model. In simplest terms, in this chapter we are concerned primarily with using the assumptions of consumer risk aversion and normally distributed portfolio returns to establish the characteristics of consumer tastes and market opportunities that lead to the efficient set theorem and the view of consumer equilibrium provided by Figure 6.5.

II. THE CONSUMER'S TASTES

In this section we formally derive the properties of the consumer's tastes that follow from the assumptions of risk aversion and normally distributed portfolio returns. The first step is to show that with normally distributed portfolio returns, an optimal consumption-investment decision amounts to optimal choices of c_1 and a feasible combination of $E(\tilde{R}_p)$ and $\sigma(\tilde{R}_p)$. Next we show that with risk aversion and normally distributed portfolio returns, expected utility is an increasing function of expected return $E(\tilde{R}_p)$ and a decreasing function of standard deviation $\sigma(\tilde{R}_p)$, which leads directly to the efficient set theorem; that is, the consumer's optimal portfolio is $E(\tilde{R})$, $\sigma(\tilde{R})$ efficient. Finally, the properties of indifference curves of $E(\tilde{R})$ against $\sigma(\tilde{R})$ are established.[3]

*II.A. Portfolio Decisions Based on $E(\tilde{R})$ and $\sigma(\tilde{R})$

Define the standardized variable

$$\tilde{r} \equiv \frac{\tilde{R}_p - E(\tilde{R}_p)}{\sigma(\tilde{R}_p)}. \tag{6.3}$$

If the distribution of $\tilde{R}_p$ is normal with mean $E(\tilde{R}_p)$ and standard deviation $\sigma(\tilde{R}_p)$, the distribution of $\tilde{r}$ is normal with mean $E(\tilde{r}) = 0$ and standard deviation $\sigma(\tilde{r}) = 1$. In the statistical literature $\tilde{r}$, defined as in Equation (6.3), is usually called the "unit normal variable."

Consumption in period 2 is related to the one-period return $\tilde{R}_p$ on the consumer's portfolio according to

$$\tilde{c}_2 = (w_1 - c_1)(1 + \tilde{R}_p).$$

But because the distribution of $\tilde{R}_p$ is assumed to be normal, making use of Equation (6.3), $\tilde{c}_2$ can be written in terms of $E(\tilde{R}_p)$, $\sigma(\tilde{R}_p)$, and the unit normal variable $\tilde{r}$ as

$$\tilde{c}_2 = (w_1 - c_1)[1 + E(\tilde{R}_p) + \sigma(\tilde{R}_p)\tilde{r}]. \tag{6.4}$$

The expected utility associated with a choice of current consumption c_1 and portfolio p is then

$$E[U(c_1, \tilde{c}_2)] = \int_{-\infty}^{\infty} U(c_1, (w_1 - c_1)[1 + E(\tilde{R}_p) + \sigma(\tilde{R}_p)r])f(r)\, dr, \tag{6.5}$$

where $f(r)$ is the density function of r.

Because the distributions of $\tilde{R}_p$ for all portfolios are normal, in the

---

[3] The remainder of Sec. II relies heavily on concepts from elementary calculus. It is possible for the mathematically wary reader to skip directly to Sec. III. We encourage even the mathematically wary to continue on in this section, however; the verbal arguments presented will probably help in understanding the intuitive analysis presented in Sec. I.

definition of expected utility provided by Equation (6.5), the variable r and the density function $f(r)$ are the same for all portfolios. Differences between the expected utilities for different consumption-investment decisions depend entirely on c_1, $E(\tilde{R}_p)$, and $\sigma(\tilde{R}_p)$, so that consumption-investment alternatives can be ranked on the basis of these three variables. Formally,

$$E[U(c_1,\tilde{c}_2)] = V(c_1,E(\tilde{R}_p),\sigma(\tilde{R}_p)). \qquad (6.6)$$

*II.B. Marginal Expected Utilities and the Efficient Set Theorem

We are interested now in the properties of expected utility as a function of expected return $E(\tilde{R}_p)$ and standard deviation or dispersion $\sigma(\tilde{R}_p)$. First, as long as the consumer invests some of his initial wealth, from Equation (6.5), the marginal expected utility of expected return $E(\tilde{R}_p)$

$$\frac{\partial E[U(c_1,\tilde{c}_2)]}{\partial E(\tilde{R}_p)} = (w_1 - c_1) \int_{-\infty}^{\infty} \frac{\partial U(c_1,c_2)}{\partial c_2} f(r)\, dr > 0, \qquad (6.7)$$

because the marginal utility of c_2 is positive for all values of (c_1,c_2). Thus, other things equal, expected utility is an increasing function of expected return.

On the other hand, the marginal expected utility of return dispersion or standard deviation $\sigma(\tilde{R}_p)$

$$\frac{\partial E[U(c_1,\tilde{c}_2)]}{\partial \sigma(\tilde{R}_p)}$$

$$= (w_1 - c_1) \int_{-\infty}^{\infty} \frac{\partial U(c_1, (w_1 - c_1)[1 + E(\tilde{R}_p) + \sigma(\tilde{R}_p)r])}{\partial c_2} rf(r)\, dr < 0.$$

$$(6.8)$$

Here the inequality is a little more difficult to see. It follows from (1) the fact that $U(c_1,c_2)$ is concave, so that $\partial U(c_1,c_2)/\partial c_2$ is a positive but decreasing function of c_2 and thus of r, and (2) $f(r)$ is symmetric about 0. The result is perhaps best illustrated by reference to Figure 6.6. In the integral of Equation (6.8), for each value of r, the variable over which we are integrating, we have a product of three terms, $\partial U(c_1,c_2)/\partial c_2$, r, and $f(r)$, and this product is negative for $r < 0$ and positive for $r > 0$. But $\partial U(c_1,c_2)/\partial c_2$ is a positive but decreasing function of c_2 and thus of r, and

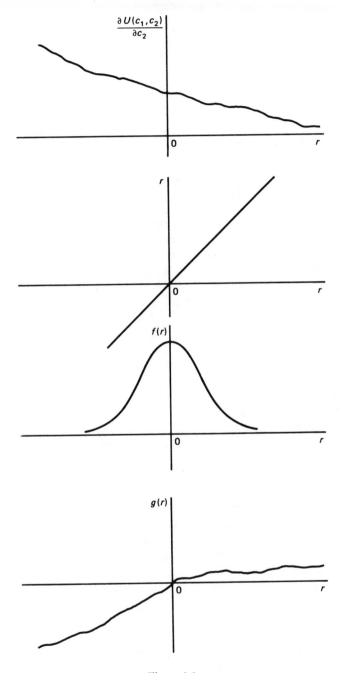

Figure 6.6

$f(r)$ is symmetric about 0, for $r > 0$, so that

$$\left| \frac{\partial U(c_1, (w_1 - c_1)[1 + E(\tilde{R}_p) + \sigma(\tilde{R}_p)(-r)])}{\partial c_2} (-r)f(-r) \right|$$

$$> \frac{\partial U(c_1, (w_1 - c_1)[1 + E(\tilde{R}_p) + \sigma(\tilde{R}_p)r])}{\partial c_2} rf(r).$$

But this implies that, as indicated in the bottom part of Figure 6.6, the product of the three terms, labeled $g(r)$ in the figure, is more negative at any point $-r$ than it is positive at the corresponding point r. Thus the integral in Equation (6.8) is negative; expected utility is a declining function of standard deviation $\sigma(\tilde{R}_p)$.

In short, given a value of initial consumption c_1 and thus investment $w_1 - c_1$, Equation (6.7) says that for any given value of standard deviation $\sigma(\tilde{R}_p)$ the consumer prefers more expected return $E(\tilde{R}_p)$ to less; Equation (6.8) says that for given $E(\tilde{R}_p)$ he prefers less $\sigma(\tilde{R}_p)$ to more. But this implies that the optimal portfolio must be such that no portfolio with the same or higher expected return has lower standard deviation of return; that is, the optimal portfolio for any given split of w_1 between consumption c_1 and investment $w_1 - c_1$ must be $E(\tilde{R})$, $\sigma(\tilde{R})$ efficient. Thus the best portfolio for the optimal split of w_1 between c_1 and investment $w_1 - c_1$ must also be $E(\tilde{R})$, $\sigma(\tilde{R})$ efficient. But this of course is just the efficient set theorem.

*II.C. Properties of Indifference Curves in the Two-Parameter Model

Finally, we now want to show that the properties of the consumer's indifference curves of $E(\tilde{R})$ against $\sigma(\tilde{R})$ are as hypothesized in Figure 6.3. Recall that for any given level of period 1 consumption c_1 and thus investment $w_1 - c_1$, an indifference curve of $E(\tilde{R})$ against $\sigma(\tilde{R})$ is defined by the set of $E(\tilde{R})$, $\sigma(\tilde{R})$ combinations that yields some fixed level of expected utility, say, V. From Equations (6.7) and (6.8) we know already that, as indicated in Figure 6.3, any such indifference curve must be positively sloping and that the direction of increasing levels of expected utility must be upward and to the left, that is, from lower to higher curves. Thus the task of this section is completed if we can show that indifference curves must also be convex.[4]

---

[4] But it is well to note that the conditions on marginal expected utilities given by Equations (6.7) and (6.8) are all we need to establish the important efficient set theorem. The additional convexity property of indifference curves just helps to make geometric analyses a lot neater.

To establish convexity it is sufficient to show that if $(E(\tilde{R}),\sigma(\tilde{R}))$ and $(E(\tilde{R})',\sigma(\tilde{R})')$ are any two points on some arbitrarily chosen indifference curve, say, the curve for expected utility V_1 in Figure 6.3, the expected utility of any point

$$(E(\tilde{R})'',\sigma(\tilde{R})'') = (xE(\tilde{R}) + (1 - x)E(\tilde{R})', x\sigma(\tilde{R}) + (1 - x)\sigma(\tilde{R})'),$$
$$0 < x < 1,$$

is greater than V_1. With expected utility increasing upward and to the left in the $E(\tilde{R})$, $\sigma(\tilde{R})$ plane, this implies that $(E(\tilde{R})'', \sigma(\tilde{R})'')$ is on a higher indifference curve than V_1, which in turn implies convexity.

First let

$$c_2 = (w_1 - c_1)[1 + E(\tilde{R}) + \sigma(\tilde{R})r], \tag{6.9}$$

$$c_2' = (w_1 - c_1)[1 + E(\tilde{R})' + \sigma(\tilde{R})'r], \tag{6.10}$$

$$c_2'' = xc_2 + (1 - x)c_2'.$$

But substituting from Equations (6.9) and (6.10) and simplifying, we obtain

$$c_2'' = (w_1 - c_1)[1 + E(\tilde{R})'' + \sigma(\tilde{R})''r]. \tag{6.11}$$

Because we are concerned with a particular indifference map, the value of c_1 is fixed. The concavity of $U(c_1,c_2)$ then implies

$$U(c_1,c_2'') > xU(c_1,c_2) + (1 - x)U(c_1,c_2'), \qquad 0 < x < 1.$$

Substituting from Equations (6.9) to (6.11) for any given r,

$$U(c_1, (w_1 - c_1)[1 + E(\tilde{R})'' + \sigma(\tilde{R})''r])$$
$$> xU(c_1, (w_1 - c_1)[1 + E(\tilde{R}) + \sigma(\tilde{R})r])$$
$$+ (1 - x)U(c_1, (w_1 - c_1)[1 + E(\tilde{R})' + \sigma(\tilde{R})'r]). \tag{6.12}$$

Because the density function $f(r)$ is nonnegative for all values of r, taking expectations over r in the manner of Equation (6.5) preserves the direction of the inequality in (6.12), so that

$$E\{U(c_1, (w_1 - c_1)[1 + E(\tilde{R})'' + \sigma(\tilde{R})''\tilde{r}])\}$$
$$> xE\{U(c_1, (w_1 - c_1)[1 + E(\tilde{R}) + \sigma(\tilde{R})\tilde{r}])\}$$
$$+ (1 - x)E\{U(c_1, (w_1 - c_1)[1 + E(\tilde{R})' + \sigma(\tilde{R})\tilde{r}])\}, \tag{6.13}$$

which implies

$$E\{U(c_1, (w_1 - c_1)[1 + E(\tilde{R})'' + \sigma(\tilde{R})''\tilde{r}])\} > V_1.$$

Thus we have reached our goal: As indicated in Figure 6.3, $(E(\tilde{R}\ ), \sigma(\tilde{R})'')$ is indeed on a higher indifference curve than $(E(\tilde{R}), \sigma(\tilde{R}))$ and $(E(\tilde{R})', \sigma(\tilde{R})')$, so that the curve on which these points fall must be convex.

Finally, an indifference map like Figure 6.3 provides the indifference curves for a given level of initial consumption c_1. There are, of course, similar indifference maps for other levels of c_1, but all indifference curves and indifference maps have the general properties discussed above. In determining the individual's optimal consumption-investment decision, we do not, of course, consider c_1 fixed, so that it is necessary to examine the indifference maps for all levels of consumption. This is getting a little ahead of ourselves, however; in order to determine the optimal consumption-investment decision, we must first consider the opportunity set facing the individual.

III. THE INVESTMENT OPPORTUNITY SET: TWO-ASSET CASE

For simplicity, in the initial consideration of the opportunity set, we assume that only two investment assets are available to the individual: a riskless asset f that yields the one-period return R_f with perfect certainty[5] and a risky asset a whose one-period return $\tilde{R}_a$ has a normal distribution with mean $E(\tilde{R}_a)$, assumed to be greater than R_f, and standard deviation $\sigma(\tilde{R}_a)$. We do not claim, of course, that such a two-asset opportunity set is at all realistic. The goal here is simply to introduce some elementary tools and concepts that are used throughout our later discussions. We eventually consider more general cases in which there are many types of investment assets.

Although there are only two investment assets available to the individual, the fact that the assets are infinitely divisible gives him an infinite number of portfolio possibilities. Specifically, if his total portfolio investment is $h_1 = w_1 - c_1$ and if h_{1f} and h_{1a} are the funds allocated to the assets f and a, he can invest any fraction $x = h_{1f}/h_1$, $0 \leq x \leq 1$, in the riskless asset f and put the remainder $1 - x = (h_1 - h_{1f})/h_1 = h_{1a}/h_1$ in the risky asset a. The return on such a portfolio is

$$\tilde{R}_p = \frac{\tilde{w}_2 - h_1}{h_1} = \frac{h_{1f}(1 + R_f) + h_{1a}(1 + \tilde{R}_a) - h_1}{h_1}$$

[5] Note that an asset that is riskless for one horizon period need not be riskless for another. A government bill with one year to maturity and no intermediate coupon payments is riskless for an individual with a one-year horizon; at the end of the year he just cashes it in for its face value. The same bill is not riskless for an individual with a shorter horizon, however, because in selling the bill before maturity, he faces a probability distribution on price that results from the fact that short-term interest rates are to some extent random.

or

$$\tilde{R}_p = xR_f + (1 - x)\tilde{R}_a, \qquad 0 \le x \le 1. \qquad (6.14)$$

Because R_f is a constant and the distribution of $\tilde{R}_a$ is normal with mean $E(\tilde{R}_a)$ and standard deviation $\sigma(\tilde{R}_a)$, the one-period portfolio return $\tilde{R}_p$ also has a normal distribution with mean

$$E(\tilde{R}_p) = xR_f + (1 - x)E(\tilde{R}_a), \qquad 0 \le x \le 1, \qquad (6.15a)$$

and standard deviation

$$\sigma(\tilde{R}_p) = (1 - x)\sigma(\tilde{R}_a), \qquad 0 \le x \le 1. \qquad (6.15b)$$

It is easy to see that by varying the value of x in Equations (6.15a) and (6.15b), we can define the trade-off between mean and standard deviation obtained in forming portfolios according to Equation (6.14). An exact description of this trade-off can be obtained as follows: First solve Equations (6.15a) and (6.15b) for x to obtain

$$x = \frac{E(\tilde{R}_p) - E(\tilde{R}_a)}{R_f - E(\tilde{R}_a)}, \qquad (6.16a)$$

$$x = \frac{\sigma(\tilde{R}_a) - \sigma(\tilde{R}_p)}{\sigma(\tilde{R}_a)}. \qquad (6.16b)$$

Equating the right-hand sides of these two expressions and then solving for $E(\tilde{R}_p)$, we get

$$E(\tilde{R}_p) = R_f + \left(\frac{E(\tilde{R}_a) - R_f}{\sigma(\tilde{R}_a)}\right)\sigma(\tilde{R}_p). \qquad (6.17)$$

Thus Equations (6.15a) and (6.15b) imply a linear relationship between $E(\tilde{R}_p)$ and $\sigma(\tilde{R}_p)$ for portfolios defined by Equation (6.14). A plot of Equation (6.17) for some assumed values of the parameters R_f, $E(\tilde{R}_a)$, and $\sigma(\tilde{R}_a)$ would look something like the line $R_f a$ in Figure 6.7. The line terminates on the $E(\tilde{R})$ axis at the point R_f; from Equation (6.15b) we see that the portfolio with $\sigma(\tilde{R}_p) = 0$ corresponds to the value $x = 1$; that is, all portfolio funds are invested in the riskless asset f. On the other hand, at the point a, $x = 0$ and all portfolio funds are invested in the risky asset a; thus the expected return and standard deviation for this portfolio are $E(\tilde{R}_a)$ and $\sigma(\tilde{R}_a)$. By varying x between 1 and 0, which is the same as varying $\sigma(\tilde{R}_p)$ between 0 and $\sigma(\tilde{R}_a)$, we obtain portfolios along the line $R_f a$ in Figure 6.7. From Equation (6.17) the slope of the line is $(E(\tilde{R}_a) - R_f)/\sigma(\tilde{R}_a)$; when portfolios are formed according to Equation

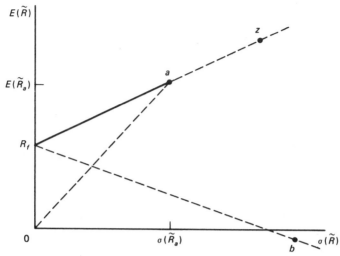

Figure 6.7   Portfolio Opportunities: Two-Asset Case

(6.14), a unit increase in $\sigma(\tilde{R}_p)$ leads to an increase of $(E(\tilde{R}_a) - R_f)/\sigma(\tilde{R}_a)$ units of $E(\tilde{R}_p)$.[6]

By varying our assumptions slightly, we can obtain some useful additional insights into the investment opportunity set. For example, suppose that it is possible to sell-short either or both of the assets f and a. For our purposes a short sale is defined as an exchange in which the individual borrows units of an asset at the beginning of period 1, agreeing to repay the lender the market value of these units at the beginning of period 2.

For the riskless asset f, a short sale is simply borrowing in which the individual agrees to repay $1 + R_f$ dollars at period 2 per dollar borrowed at period 1. To simplify the arguments, suppose that the individual can borrow as much as he likes at the rate R_f[7] and that he uses his borrowings to increase his investment in the risky asset a. In this case Equations (6.14) to (6.17) remain valid, but now x is allowed to take on negative values. In terms of Figure 6.7, negative values of x yield portfolios along the extension of $R_f a$ through the point a, that is, along the line from a through z in the

---

[6] If these statements are not obvious, the reader may find it helpful to illustrate them with a numerical example of his own construction. He will then probably also find it helpful to extend the example to the analyses in subsequent paragraphs.

[7] A note for the more sophisticated: It is interesting to ponder why anyone would lend to our investor at the riskless rate, because there is some chance that he will not be able to repay the debt. But the primary goal here is simply to develop familiarity with the geometric representation of the opportunity set; thus for the moment we bypass this issue.

figure. Because it is assumed that any amount of borrowing is possible, the line can be extended indefinitely.

For a short sale of the risky asset a, if we assume that the investor sells the borrowed units of a in the market and uses the proceeds to increase his investment in the riskless asset f, the one-period portfolio return and its mean are still given by Equations (6.14) and (6.15a), except that x can now take values greater than 1. But the standard deviation of the portfolio return becomes

$$\sigma(\tilde{R}_p) = |\, 1 - x \,|\, \sigma(\tilde{R}_a) = (x - 1)\sigma(\tilde{R}_a), \qquad x \geq 1. \qquad (6.18)$$

The relationship between $E(\tilde{R}_p)$ and $\sigma(\tilde{R}_p)$ for portfolios involving short sales of asset a can be obtained by solving Equation (6.18) for x to get

$$x = \frac{\sigma(\tilde{R}_p) + \sigma(\tilde{R}_a)}{\sigma(\tilde{R}_a)}, \qquad x \geq 1. \qquad (6.19)$$

Equating the right-hand sides of Equations (6.19) and (6.16a) and then solving for $E(\tilde{R}_p)$, we get the linear equation

$$E(\tilde{R}_p) = R_f + \frac{R_f - E(\tilde{R}_a)}{\sigma(\tilde{R}_a)}\, \sigma(\tilde{R}_p). \qquad (6.20)$$

Note that the slope $(R_f - E(\tilde{R}_a))/\sigma(\tilde{R}_a)$ is just the negative of the slope in Equation (6.17). Geometrically, portfolios involving short sales of asset a fall along the line $R_f b$ in Figure 6.7.

Finally, let us admit one more type of investment into the opportunity set. In particular, suppose that the investor has the option of holding some or all of his portfolio funds in money, which is assumed to be riskless; that is, a dollar now is a dollar at the end of the period. To simplify the analysis, assume that if the investor holds some cash, the remainder of his portfolio funds must be put either into the riskless asset f or into the risky asset a, but not both. Portfolios of cash and f with the proportion x of portfolio funds held in cash and $(1 - x)$ in f produce the sure return

$$R_p = (1 - x)R_f, \qquad 0 \leq x \leq 1;$$

portfolios of cash and the risky asset a have return

$$\tilde{R}_p = (1 - x)\tilde{R}_a, \qquad 0 \leq x \leq 1,$$

with mean

$$E(\tilde{R}_p) = (1 - x)E(\tilde{R}_a), \qquad 0 \leq x \leq 1,$$

and standard deviation given by Equation (6.15b). Geometrically, portfolios involving cash and the riskless asset f lie along the $E(\tilde{R})$ axis between 0 and R_f; portfolios involving cash and the risky asset a lie along the line Oa.

The $E(\tilde{R})$, $\sigma(\tilde{R})$ efficient set for the portfolio opportunity set represented in Figure 6.7 can be determined by inspection: All efficient portfolios lie along the line from R_f through a and z; that is, the only efficient portfolios are those involving the riskless asset f, in either positive or negative amounts, and nonnegative amounts of the risky asset a. Portfolios along the line from R_f through b, that is, those involving positive amounts of f and short sales of a, are not efficient, because for any point along $R_f b$ there is a point along $R_f z$ with the same value of $\sigma(\tilde{R})$ but higher $E(\tilde{R})$. For the same reason points along OR_f (portfolios of cash and the riskless asset f) and points along Oa (portfolios of cash and the risky asset a) cannot be efficient.

Thus the only efficient portfolios in our simplified opportunity set are combinations of the riskless asset f and the risky asset a. Less risky efficient portfolios are formed by mixing positive amounts of f and a, obtaining points along the segment $R_f a$; more risky efficient portfolios are formed by borrowing at the rate R_f and then investing both the borrowings and the initial portfolio funds in the risky asset a, obtaining portfolios along the segment from a through z.[8]

Figure 6.8 shows how the optimal portfolio is determined for a given value of initial consumption c_1. The investor wants to reach the highest possible indifference curve, that is, to maximize expected utility conditional on c_1. In general, the optimal portfolio is at the tangency point between an indifference curve and the efficient set, as at the point d in Figure 6.8a. If such a tangency exists, it is unique, because the efficient set is linear and the indifference curves are strictly convex.

But it is also possible that the investor's optimal portfolio for the given level of c_1 is a "corner" portfolio, as illustrated in Figure 6.8b. Here the highest attainable indifference curve is everywhere steeper than the efficient set line; for the given value of c_1, the individual is unwilling to accept any amount of $\sigma(\tilde{R})$ at the rate of exchange of $E(\tilde{R})$ for $\sigma(\tilde{R})$

---

[8] Although it is of no particular consequence in our models, there is an interesting and important result here. In particular, with perfect markets and a riskless, positive return investment asset, money is not part of any efficient portfolio, and there is no reason for a consumer to hold any money from period 1 to period 2. And this is a result that is not at all specific to the two-period two-asset model under consideration here.

In short, with perfect markets and riskless, positive return investment assets, there can be no "wealth demand" for money. Rather, a demand for money arises only in imperfect markets in which there are transactions costs in exchanging investment assets and consumption goods, and carrying out these exchanges in terms of money lowers these costs. And such a demand for money is most appropriately called a "transactions demand."

Thus in the perfect markets models in this book, when we use the terms *money* or *dollars*, we mean to refer to some ordinary consumption good that has been chosen to act as numéraire.

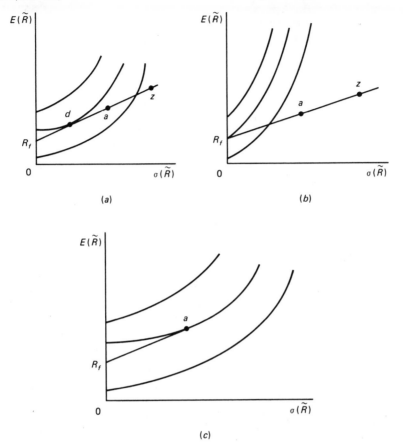

Figure 6.8   Consumer Equilibrium: Two-Asset Case

implied by the efficient set line. Thus he concentrates all his portfolio investment in the riskless asset f.

If borrowing portfolios are prohibited, another type of corner solution is possible. Here the efficient set is just the line segment $R_f a$ in Figure 6.8c. For the indifference curves shown in the figure the optimum portfolio is just the risky asset a. Moreover, the optimum is not a tangency point, because the indifference curve at a is flatter than the efficient set. The individual would be willing to take on more $\sigma(\tilde{R})$ in exchange for $E(\tilde{R})$, but this possibility is not open to him.

IV. THE EFFICIENT SET AND CONSUMER EQUILIBRIUM WITH N ASSETS

The next step in the development of a model for the two-period two-parameter consumption-investment problem is to expand the opportunity set to include an arbitrary number N of investment assets. We maintain the assumption that the distributions of one-period returns on all assets and portfolios are normal, although this assumption is discussed in detail later.

The procedure is to introduce first the definitions and elementary expressions for the N-asset model. Then a geometric representation of the N-asset opportunity set is developed and combined in the usual way with the investor's indifference curves to get a picture of consumer equilibrium. The determination of equilibrium in the N-asset problem is then analyzed algebraically. The section concludes with a discussion of some peripheral issues, for example, what is the meaning of the statement "diversification pays"?

IV.A. Definitions and Elementary Expressions for the N-Asset Model

If $h_1 = w_1 - c_1$ is the initial wealth invested in the portfolio, let h_{1i} be the initial wealth invested in asset i. Then the level of wealth $\tilde{w}_2$, and thus consumption $\tilde{c}_2$, produced by the portfolio at the beginning of period 2 is

$$\tilde{w}_2 = \sum_{i=1}^{N} h_{1i}(1 + \tilde{R}_i) = \tilde{c}_2, \tag{6.21}$$

where $\tilde{R}_i$ is the one-period return on asset i and N is the number of investment assets available to the individual. Thus $\tilde{R}_p$, the one-period return on the individual's portfolio, is

$$\tilde{R}_p = \frac{\tilde{w}_2 - h_1}{h_1} = \frac{\sum_{i=1}^{N} h_{1i}(1 + \tilde{R}_i) - h_1}{h_1}. \tag{6.22}$$

We assume that all h_1 is invested, so that

$$\sum_{i=1}^{N} h_{1i} = h_1. \tag{6.23}$$

Short sales can be introduced, when appropriate, by letting h_{1i} be negative. If

$$x_i \equiv \frac{h_{1i}}{h_1} \tag{6.24}$$

is the proportion of the portfolio investment in asset i, from Equations

(6.22) and (6.23)

$$\tilde{R}_p = \sum_{i=1}^{N} x_i \tilde{R}_i, \qquad (6.25)$$

and

$$\sum_{i=1}^{N} x_i = 1. \qquad (6.26)$$

Thus the one-period return on the portfolio is just the weighted average of the one-period returns on the individual assets in the portfolio, and the weights are the proportions of investment funds in the individual assets. If the one-period returns on the individual assets have normal distributions, the returns on portfolios of these assets also have normal distributions. From Equation (6.25) the expected return on a portfolio is

$$E(\tilde{R}_p) = \sum_{i=1}^{N} x_i E(\tilde{R}_i), \qquad (6.27)$$

where $E(\tilde{R}_i)$ is the expected return on asset i.

Let

$$\sigma_{ij} \equiv \text{cov } (\tilde{R}_i, \tilde{R}_j) \equiv E\{[\tilde{R}_i - E(\tilde{R}_i)][\tilde{R}_j - E(\tilde{R}_j)]\} \qquad (6.28)$$

be the covariance between the one-period returns on assets i and j. Note that the variance of the one-period return on asset i is just

$$\sigma^2(\tilde{R}_i) = E\{[\tilde{R}_i - E(\tilde{R}_i)]^2\} = \sigma_{ii}. \qquad (6.29)$$

Thus the variance can be regarded as the covariance of asset i with itself. From Equations (6.25), (6.28), and (6.29), the variance of the one-period return on the portfolio can be written

$$\sigma^2(\tilde{R}_p) = \sum_{i=1}^{N} x_i^2 \sigma^2(\tilde{R}_i) + \sum_{i=1}^{N} \sum_{\substack{j=1 \\ j \neq i}}^{N} x_i x_j \sigma_{ij} = \sum_{i=1}^{N} \sum_{j=1}^{N} x_i x_j \sigma_{ij}. \qquad (6.30)$$

Thus the expected return on the portfolio is just a weighted average of the expected returns on the individual assets in the portfolio, and the variance of the one-period return on the portfolio is just a weighted average of the variances of the returns on the individual assets and the covariances between the returns on the assets.[9]

---

[9] Note that the covariance terms in Equation (6.30) are far more numerous than the variance terms. There are $N(N-1)$ terms involving the σ_{ij}, $j \neq i$, whereas there are only N terms involving the $\sigma^2(\tilde{R}_i) = \sigma_{ii}$. The implications of this fact are discussed below.

We beg the essentially empirical question of where we obtain the basic inputs, that is, the means, variances, and covariances of the distributions of one-period returns on individual assets, which allow us to define the mean and variance of the distribution of the one-period return provided by a given portfolio. For our purposes, which are completely theoretical, the inputs for the analysis are taken as given.

IV.B. Geometric Representation of Consumer Equilibrium

In the geometric treatment of the N-asset model, the first order of business is to develop a picture of the efficient set.

Consider first two arbitrarily chosen assets or portfolios[10] a and b with expected returns $E(\tilde{R}_a)$ and $E(\tilde{R}_b)$ and standard deviations $\sigma(\tilde{R}_a)$ and $\sigma(\tilde{R}_b)$. We want to examine geometrically the combinations of expected return $E(\tilde{R}_p)$ and standard deviation of return $\sigma(\tilde{R}_p)$ that can be obtained from portfolios formed by investing the proportion x of h_1 in asset a and $(1 - x)$ in b. The one-period return on such portfolios is

$$\tilde{R}_p = x\tilde{R}_a + (1 - x)\tilde{R}_b, \tag{6.31}$$

with mean

$$E(\tilde{R}_p) = xE(\tilde{R}_a) + (1 - x)E(\tilde{R}_b), \tag{6.32}$$

and standard deviation

$$\sigma(\tilde{R}_p) = [x^2\sigma^2(\tilde{R}_a) + (1 - x)^2\sigma^2(\tilde{R}_b) + 2x(1 - x) \text{ cov } (\tilde{R}_a,\tilde{R}_b)]^{1/2}$$

$$= [x^2\sigma^2(\tilde{R}_a) + (1 - x)^2\sigma^2(\tilde{R}_b) + 2x(1 - x)k_{ab}\sigma(\tilde{R}_a)\sigma(\tilde{R}_b)]^{1/2}, \tag{6.33}$$

where we make use of the fact that k_{ab}, the correlation coefficient between $\tilde{R}_a$ and $\tilde{R}_b$, is just

$$k_{ab} = \frac{\text{cov } (\tilde{R}_a,\tilde{R}_b)}{\sigma(\tilde{R}_a)\sigma(\tilde{R}_b)}. \tag{6.34}$$

From the earlier discussion of the two-asset model we know that the relationship between $E(\tilde{R}_p)$ and $\sigma(\tilde{R}_p)$ for portfolios formed according to Equation (6.31) is linear if either a or b is riskless, that is, its standard deviation is 0. We now show that the relationship is also linear when the returns on the assets are perfectly positively correlated, that is, $k_{ab} = 1$.

---

[10] For present purposes the distinction between assets and portfolios is completely irrelevant.

In this case

$$\sigma(\tilde{R}_p) = [x^2\sigma^2(\tilde{R}_a) + (1-x)^2\sigma^2(\tilde{R}_b) + 2x(1-x)\sigma(\tilde{R}_a)\sigma(\tilde{R}_b)]^{1/2}$$

$$= x\sigma(\tilde{R}_a) + (1-x)\sigma(\tilde{R}_b). \tag{6.35}$$

Solving both Equations (6.32) and (6.35) for x and then equating the resulting expressions, we get an expression for $E(\tilde{R}_p)$ that is linear in $\sigma(\tilde{R}_p)$:

$$E(\tilde{R}_p) = E(\tilde{R}_b) + \frac{E(\tilde{R}_a) - E(\tilde{R}_b)}{\sigma(\tilde{R}_a) - \sigma(\tilde{R}_b)}(\sigma(\tilde{R}_p) - \sigma(\tilde{R}_b)). \tag{6.36}$$

For $0 \le x \le 1$ in Equation (6.31), the plot of Equation (6.36) for some assumed values of $E(\tilde{R}_a)$, $E(\tilde{R}_b)$, $\sigma(\tilde{R}_a)$, and $\sigma(\tilde{R}_b)$ is the line ab in Figure 6.9.

The opposite extreme from perfect positive correlation is, of course, perfect negative correlation, that is, $k_{ab} = -1$. In this case the standard deviation of the portfolio return is

$$\sigma(\tilde{R}_p) = [x^2\sigma^2(\tilde{R}_a) + (1-x)^2\sigma^2(\tilde{R}_b) - 2x(1-x)\sigma(\tilde{R}_a)\sigma(\tilde{R}_b)]^{1/2},$$

which has the two roots

$$\sigma(\tilde{R}_p) = x\sigma(\tilde{R}_a) - (1-x)\sigma(\tilde{R}_b) = -\sigma(\tilde{R}_b) + x[\sigma(\tilde{R}_a) + \sigma(\tilde{R}_b)] \tag{6.37}$$

and

$$\sigma(\tilde{R}_p) = (1-x)\sigma(\tilde{R}_b) - x\sigma(\tilde{R}_a) = \sigma(\tilde{R}_b) - x[\sigma(\tilde{R}_a) + \sigma(\tilde{R}_b)].^{11} \tag{6.38}$$

For both Equations (6.37) and (6.38), $\sigma(\tilde{R}_p) = 0$ when x is equal to

$$\frac{\sigma(\tilde{R}_b)}{\sigma(\tilde{R}_a) + \sigma(\tilde{R}_b)}. \tag{6.39}$$

When x is greater than the value implied by (6.39), Equation (6.37) yields positive values of $\sigma(\tilde{R}_p)$, and (6.38) yields negative values; the reverse is true when x is less than (6.39). Because standard deviations must always be nonnegative, Equation (6.37) is relevant when x is greater than the value given by (6.39), and Equation (6.38) is relevant when x is less. Thus solving Equations (6.32) and (6.37) for x and equating the resulting

---

[11] Alternatively, and equivalently,

$$\sigma(\tilde{R}_p) = |x\sigma(\tilde{R}_a) - (1-x)\sigma(\tilde{R}_b)|. \tag{6.38a}$$

expressions gives

$$E(\tilde{R}_p) = E(\tilde{R}_b) + \frac{E(\tilde{R}_a) - E(\tilde{R}_b)}{\sigma(\tilde{R}_a) + \sigma(\tilde{R}_b)} (\sigma(\tilde{R}_p) + \sigma(\tilde{R}_b)), \qquad (6.40)$$

which is relevant for portfolios of a and b with x greater than $\sigma(\tilde{R}_b)/[\sigma(\tilde{R}_a) + \sigma(\tilde{R}_b)]$. On the other hand, solving Equations (6.32) and (6.38) for x and equating the resulting expressions gives

$$E(\tilde{R}_p) = E(\tilde{R}_b) - \frac{E(\tilde{R}_a) - E(\tilde{R}_b)}{\sigma(\tilde{R}_a) + \sigma(\tilde{R}_b)} (\sigma(\tilde{R}_p) - \sigma(\tilde{R}_b)), \qquad (6.41)$$

which is relevant for portfolios of a and b with x less than $\sigma(\tilde{R}_b)/[\sigma(\tilde{R}_a) + \sigma(\tilde{R}_b)]$. In Figure 6.9 the line ca is the plot of Equation (6.40), and cb is the plot of Equation (6.41). Thus acb represents the combinations of $E(\tilde{R}_p)$ and $\sigma(\tilde{R}_p)$ that can be obtained when portfolios are formed according to Equation (6.31) and $k_{ab} = -1$.

In the general case, however, the correlation between the returns on two assets or portfolios is not perfect, either positive or negative. From Equation (6.32) we see that the expected portfolio return is unaffected by the degree of correlation. Inspection of expression (6.33), however, tells us that for any given x $(0 < x < 1)$, the maximum value of the standard deviation of portfolio returns occurs when $k_{ab} = 1$ and that the minimum value occurs when $k_{ab} = -1$. It follows that when $0 < x < 1$ and $-1 < k_{ab} < 1$, portfolios of a and b lie strictly to the left of the line ab in Figure 6.9 and to the right of the lines cb and ca; that is, with $-1 < k_{ab} < 1$, for any given value of $E(\tilde{R}_p)$, the value of $\sigma(\tilde{R}_p)$ must be to the left of the relevant

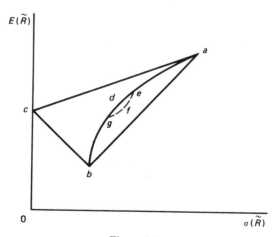

Figure 6.9

point along the perfect positive correlation line ab and to the right of the relevant point along the perfect negative correlation lines cb and ca.[12]

In fact, continuing these arguments, in the case of less than perfect correlation, different combinations of any two assets or portfolios a and b always fall along a curve between the two points in the $E(\tilde{R})$, $\sigma(\tilde{R})$ plane. And any positively sloping segment of this curve must be strictly concave; any negatively sloping segment must be strictly convex. To see this, suppose, on the contrary, that the curve describing combinations of a and b is positively sloping but contains a wiggle, that is, a nonconcave segment, like the curve $aefgb$ in Figure 6.9. Applying the arguments of the previous paragraphs, however, we know that weighted combinations of the portfolios e and g must lie on or to the left of a straight line between e and g in Figure 6.9. Thus the segment efg cannot represent combinations of portfolios e and g. Because e and g are in turn just combinations of a and b, the segment efg cannot represent weighted combinations of a and b. This sort of argument establishes the concavity of any positively sloping segment of the curve representing combinations of assets or portfolios a and b. It also implies convexity for any negatively sloping segment of the curve. Thus, for example, in Figure 6.10 the curve $aefgb$ cannot represent combinations of a and b, because with $-1 < k_{ab} < 1$, combinations of e and g, which are in turn just combinations of a and b, must lie to the left of a straight line between e and g.[13]

These geometric results provide our first important insights into the effects of diversification on the distribution of the one-period return on a portfolio. When we form a portfolio by taking combinations of the assets or portfolios a and b, the expected return on the portfolio is just the weighted average of the expected returns on a and b, where the weights are the proportions of h_1 invested in a and b. As long as the correlation between the returns on a and b is less than 1, however, the standard deviation of the return on the portfolio is less than the weighted average of the standard

---

[12] Again the reader for whom the preceding analysis is not obvious should illustrate the results numerically. Thus, for example, let $E(\tilde{R}_a) = 0.20$, $E(R_b) = 0.10$, $\sigma(\tilde{R}_a) = 0.50$, and $\sigma(\tilde{R}_b) = 0.30$. Then examine the combinations of $E(\tilde{R}_p)$ and $\sigma(\tilde{R}_p)$ obtained for different values of x ($0 \le x \le 1$) in Equation (6.31) when $k_{ab} = 1$. In doing this, it is probably simplest to work with Equations (6.32) and (6.35) rather than (6.36). Next look at the case $k_{ab} = -1$, working now with Equations (6.32) and (6.38a). Finally, consider some value of k_{ab} in the interval $-1 < k_{ab} < 1$, using Equations (6.32) and (6.33) to determine the values of $E(\tilde{R}_p)$ and $\sigma(\tilde{R}_p)$ obtained as x is varied. In this case the simplest choice is of course $k_{ab} = 0$, though it may also be helpful to look at values of k_{ab} on either side of 0.

[13] The skeptical reader is encouraged to provide himself with a formal representation of the details of these arguments.

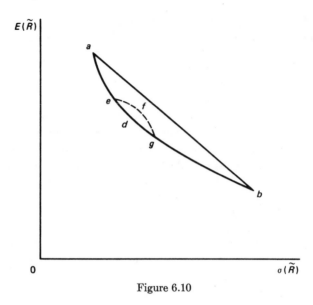

Figure 6.10

deviations of the returns on a and b. In essence, in general the process of mixing assets or portfolios to form new, more "diversified" portfolios is a dispersion-reducing activity, a point that we develop in more detail later.

It is important to note that this geometric analysis of weighted combinations applies to either assets or portfolios; that is, the points a and b could be individual assets or portfolios of assets. In fact, we could in principle consider all possible combinations of assets and portfolios and so develop a geometric representation of the set of feasible portfolios. From the efficient set theorem, however, we know that, as long as we are concerned with risk-averse investors, we can restrict attention to the efficient subset of feasible portfolios. Recall that an efficient portfolio has the following property: No portfolio with the same or higher expected return has lower standard deviation of return. Thus, in the $E(\tilde{R})$, $\sigma(\tilde{R})$ plane, efficient portfolios must lie along a positively sloping segment of the left boundary of the set of all feasible portfolios. A reasonable general representation of the left boundary of the feasible set is the curve $abcde$ in Figure 6.4. Only portfolios along the positively sloping segment bcd are efficient, however, because portfolios along ab and de do not satisfy the efficiency criterion. Although it can include many different portfolios, the efficient set bcd is drawn concave. This concavity is an implication of the earlier analysis of weighted combinations of assets and portfolios.[14]

---

[14] And again it is good practice for the reader to convince himself that this is true.

As drawn in Figure 6.4, the shape of the left boundary of the feasible set implies further assumptions about portfolio opportunities. In particular, there is no riskless asset available, and no two assets have perfectly negatively correlated returns. If there were a riskless asset or if returns on two assets had perfect negative correlation, the graph of the set of feasible portfolios would have to meet the vertical axis at some point. Moreover, the fact that the efficient set contains no linear segments implies that there are no efficient portfolios that are perfectly positively correlated. Although it is a little more difficult to see, Figure 6.4 also implicitly prohibits indefinite short selling of any asset or portfolio. If this were not the case, the top of the efficient set would be unbounded; that is, there would be an efficient portfolio for any arbitrarily high level of expected return.[15]

It is also an easy matter to introduce a riskless asset into the analysis. From the two-asset case discussed earlier we know that portfolios involving different proportions of a riskless asset and a risky asset or portfolio plot as a straight line. Thus, if there is a riskless asset f with the certain nonnegative return R_f, the new efficient set is determined by rotating a line with end point at R_f from right to left through the feasible set of risky portfolios, stopping when the line has been moved as far as possible, that is, when its slope is as large as possible, short of leaving the feasible set. From the concavity of the efficient set of risky portfolios, we know that following this procedure the eventual resting place of the line is along the efficient set of risky portfolios.

The situation in the presence of the riskless asset is represented in Figure 6.11. The line from R_f that just touches the efficient set at c represents the maximum leftward rotation of lines from R_f consistent with remaining in the feasible set. Portfolios between R_f and c along this line represent combinations of the riskless asset f and the portfolio c, where both f and c are held at nonnegative levels. It is clear that points below c along bcd no longer represent efficient portfolios, because there are combinations of f and c that have higher expected returns at the same levels of standard deviation. Similarly, if it is possible to borrow as well as lend at the rate R_f, points above c on bcd no longer represent efficient portfolios, because in this case there are feasible combinations of f and c, involving negative holdings of asset f, along the extension of $R_f c$ through c that represent portfolios with higher expected returns but no higher standard deviation than corresponding points along cd.

---

[15] For example, if indefinite short selling were allowed, portfolios with expected returns higher than $E(\tilde{R}_d)$ could be obtained by selling portfolio b short and using the proceeds of the short sale, along with initial investment funds h_1, to buy units of portfolio d. Although such portfolios need not be efficient, they illustrate that with indefinite short selling one could obtain portfolios with any level of expected return above $E(\tilde{R}_d)$.

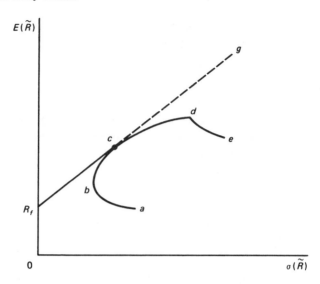

Figure 6.11   Portfolio Opportunities When There Is a Riskless Asset

Thus, when it is possible to lend but not to borrow at the riskless rate R_f, the efficient set of portfolios is represented by $R_f cd$ in Figure 6.11. When it is possible to both borrow and lend at the riskless rate R_f, the efficient set is the line from R_f through c and g in Figure 6.11. In this extreme and rather unrealistic situation, all efficient portfolios involve only combinations of f and c. The only difference between efficient portfolios is in the proportion of investment funds h_1 that is invested in the riskless asset f. Less risky efficient portfolios—those along $R_f c$—involve lending some funds at the rate R_f and investing remaining funds in the risky portfolio c. More risky efficient portfolios—those along the extension of $R_f c$ through c—involve borrowing at the riskless rate and investing both the borrowings and h_1 in the risky portfolio c.[16]

---

[16] In both Figs. 6.4 and 6.11 it is assumed that the individual who views the efficient set in this way feels that there is a trade-off between expected return and standard deviation of return in the market. In order to get more expected return, it is necessary to accept more standard deviation of return. It is not necessarily the case, however, that all individuals view the market in this way. An individual may feel that there is a portfolio that provides both highest expected return and minimum standard deviation from among the set of all feasible portfolios. In this case this portfolio would be the only member of the efficient set. (He may have this feeling because he believes that there are securities in this portfolio that are greatly "underpriced" relative to their "true worth.") In a market dominated by risk averters, however, we should not expect that this is the general view. Most investors would probably feel that there is some sort of trade-off between risk and return like that represented in Fig. 6.11.

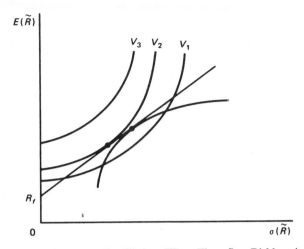

Figure 6.12   Consumer Equilibrium When There Is a Riskless Asset

The geometric representation of the optimal portfolio choice for a given value of c_1 is now very similar to the two-asset case discussed earlier. If the optimal portfolio is not at either of the end points of the efficient set, the optimum is a point of tangency between the highest attainable indifference curve and the efficient set.[17] Such a solution is shown in Figure 6.12 for the case in which there is a riskless asset and in Figure 6.5 for the case in which there is no riskless asset.

Thus the goal of the geometric analysis has now been attained: We have provided a rigorous justification for the picture of consumer equilibrium given in Figure 6.5. We can turn now to an algebraic analysis of the same problem.

*IV.C. Algebraic Representation of Consumer Equilibrium

With the geometric approach, to determine the combined optimal consumption-investment decision, in principle we must find the optimal

---

[17] We should note, for the mathematically more sophisticated, that the efficient set curve need not be differentiable everywhere, so that, strictly speaking, the representation of equilibrium in terms of a "tangency" could be incorrect. It can be shown, however, that the maximum number of points at which the efficient set curve is not differentiable cannot be greater than the number N of available assets. With infinitely divisible assets, the number of efficient portfolios is infinite; that is, the efficient set curve is continuous. Thus these nondifferentiable points do not greatly detract from our conclusions; in mathematical terms, they constitute a set of measure 0.

portfolio decision and its associated expected utility for each possible level of consumption c_1 and then choose the consumption level and its associated optimal portfolio that provides the global maximum of expected utility. With an algebraic approach, however, the problem can be solved in one step, and at least some insight into the interdependence between optimal consumption and investment decisions can be obtained.

Several equivalent mathematical statements of the consumption-investment problem are possible. For example, in the preceding analyses the decision variables were assumed to be period 1 consumption c_1 and the proportions x_i, $i = 1, 2, \ldots, N$, of total investment $h_1 = w_1 - c_1$ that are in each of the N available assets. The goal of the consumer is to choose values of c_1 and the x_i that

$$\max E[U(c_1, \tilde{c}_2)]$$

$$= \int_{-\infty}^{\infty} U(c_1, (w_1 - c_1)[1 + E(\tilde{R}_p) + \sigma(\tilde{R}_p)r])f(r)\ dr$$

$$= \int_{-\infty}^{\infty} U(c_1, (w_1 - c_1)[1 + \sum_{i=1}^{N} x_i E(\tilde{R}_i) + (\sum_{i=1}^{N}\sum_{j=1}^{N} x_i x_j \sigma_{ij})^{1/2}r])f(r)\ dr$$

$$(6.42)$$

subject to the constraints

$$0 \leq c_1 \leq w_1, \qquad (6.43)$$

$$\sum_{i=1}^{N} x_i = 1. \qquad (6.44)$$

But for current purposes it is more convenient to take a slightly different approach. In particular, we now view the decision variables as c_1 and the total investments $h_{1i} = (w_1 - c_1)x_i$ in each of the N assets. In these terms the goal of the consumer is to choose values of c_1 and the h_{1i}, $i = 1, 2, \ldots, N$, that

$$\max E[U(c_1, \tilde{c}_2)]$$

$$= \int_{-\infty}^{\infty} U(c_1, \sum_{i=1}^{N} h_{1i}[1 + E(\tilde{R}_i)] + [\sum_{i=1}^{N}\sum_{j=1}^{N} h_{1i}h_{1j}\sigma_{ij}]^{1/2}r)f(r)\ dr \quad (6.45a)$$

$$= \int_{-\infty}^{\infty} U(c_1, E(\tilde{c}_2) + \sigma(\tilde{c}_2)r)f(r)\ dr \qquad (6.45b)$$

subject to the constraint[18]

$$c_1 + \sum_{i=1}^{N} h_{1i} = w_1. \tag{6.46}$$

To solve the problem, we first form the lagrangian

$$Z = \int_{-\infty}^{\infty} U(c_1, \sum_{i=1}^{N} h_{1i}[1 + E(\tilde{R}_i)] + [\sum_{i=1}^{N} \sum_{j=1}^{N} h_{1i}h_{1j}\sigma_{ij}]^{1/2}r)f(r) \ dr$$

$$+ \lambda(w_1 - c_1 - \sum_{i=1}^{N} h_{1i}), \tag{6.47}$$

then differentiate partially with respect to c_1, h_{1i}, $i = 1, 2, \ldots, N$, and λ, and set these derivatives equal to 0, obtaining the necessary conditions for a maximum

$$\frac{\partial Z}{\partial c_1} = \frac{\partial E[U(c_1, \tilde{c}_2)]}{\partial c_1} = \lambda, \tag{6.48a}$$

$$\frac{\partial Z}{\partial h_{1i}} = \frac{\partial E[U(c_1, \tilde{c}_2)]}{\partial h_{1i}} = \lambda, \qquad i = 1, 2, \ldots, N, \tag{6.48b}$$

$$w_1 - c_1 - \sum_{i=1}^{N} h_{1i} = 0. \tag{6.48c}$$

---

[18] In going from Equation (6.42) to (6.45a) and (6.45b), we make use of the facts that

$$E(\tilde{c}_2) = \sum_{i=1}^{N} h_{1i}[1 + E(\tilde{R}_i)] = (w_1 - c_1)[1 + \sum_{i=1}^{N} x_i E(\tilde{R}_i)] = (w_1 - c_1)[1 + E(\tilde{R}_p)]$$

and

$$\sigma(\tilde{c}_2) = [\sum_{i=1}^{N} \sum_{j=1}^{N} h_{1i}h_{1j}\sigma_{ij}]^{1/2} = (w_1 - c_1)[\sum_{i=1}^{N} \sum_{j=1}^{N} x_i x_j \sigma_{ij}]^{1/2} = (w_1 - c_1)\sigma(\tilde{R}_p).$$

Remember also that if the distribution of the one-period portfolio return $\tilde{R}_p$ is normal, the distribution of period 2 consumption

$$\tilde{c}_2 = (w_1 - c_1)(1 + \tilde{R}_p)$$

must also be normal. And portfolios that are efficient in terms of $E(\tilde{R}_p)$ and $\sigma(\tilde{R}_p)$ must be efficient in terms of $E(\tilde{c}_2)$ and $\sigma(\tilde{c}_2)$.

In short, an optimal consumption-investment decision requires that the marginal expected utilities of period 1 consumption and period 1 investments in each of the N available assets be equal. This result, which is, after all, just a reexpression in terms of expected utility of a familiar economic principle, is really our sole insight into the interdependence of optimal consumption and investment decisions.

But the algebraic representation of the conditions of consumer equilibrium given by Equations (6.48) does allow us to rederive the properties of an optimal portfolio decision obtained geometrically earlier. In particular, the conditions (6.48) are now shown to imply the important efficient set theorem.

First, from Equation (6.45) note that

$$\frac{\partial E[U(c_1,\tilde{c}_2)]}{\partial h_{1i}}$$

$$= \int_{-\infty}^{\infty} \frac{\partial U(c_1,c_2)}{\partial c_2} \left[1 + E(\tilde{R}_i) + \frac{\partial \sigma(\tilde{c}_2)}{\partial h_{1i}} r \right] f(r) \ dr \tag{6.49a}$$

$$= \int_{-\infty}^{\infty} \frac{\partial U(c_1,c_2)}{\partial c_2} \left[1 + E(\tilde{R}_i) + \frac{\partial \sigma(\tilde{R}_p)}{\partial x_i} r \right] f(r) \ dr \tag{6.49b}$$

$$= \frac{\dfrac{\partial E[U(c_1,\tilde{c}_2)]}{\partial E(\tilde{R}_p)} [1 + E(\tilde{R}_i)] + \dfrac{\partial E[U(c_1,\tilde{c}_2)]}{\partial \sigma(\tilde{R}_p)} \dfrac{\partial \sigma(\tilde{R}_p)}{\partial x_i}}{w_1 - c_1}. \tag{6.49c}$$

In going from Equation (6.49a) to (6.49b), we make use of the fact that

$$\frac{\partial \sigma(\tilde{c}_2)}{\partial h_{1i}} = \frac{\sum_{j=1}^{N} h_{1j}\sigma_{ij}}{\sigma(\tilde{c}_2)} = \frac{(w_1 - c_1) \sum_{j=1}^{N} x_j\sigma_{ij}}{(w_1 - c_1)\sigma(\tilde{R}_p)} = \frac{\partial \sigma(\tilde{R}_p)}{\partial x_i}. \tag{6.50}$$

And in going from Equation (6.49b) to (6.49c), we simply make use of expressions (6.7) and (6.8) for the marginal expected utilities of $E(\tilde{R}_p)$ and $\sigma(\tilde{R}_p)$.

Next note that because λ is the same for all assets, Equation (6.48b) implies that for all i and j

$$\frac{\partial E[U(c_1,\tilde{c}_2)]}{\partial h_{1i}} = \frac{\partial E[U(c_1,\tilde{c}_2)]}{\partial h_{1j}},$$

which, with Equation (6.49c), reduces to

$$-\frac{\dfrac{\partial E[U(c_1,\tilde{c}_2)]}{\partial \sigma(\tilde{R}_p)}}{\dfrac{\partial E[U(c_1,\tilde{c}_2)]}{\partial E(\tilde{R}_p)}} = \frac{E(\tilde{R}_j) - E(\tilde{R}_i)}{\dfrac{\partial \sigma(\tilde{R}_p)}{\partial x_j} - \dfrac{\partial \sigma(\tilde{R}_p)}{\partial x_i}}. \tag{6.51}$$

The expression on the left in Equation (6.51) is just the marginal rate of substitution of $E(\tilde{R}_p)$ for $\sigma(\tilde{R}_p)$ along an indifference curve; that is, it is the slope of an indifference curve.[19] Because Equation (6.51) is an optimality condition, this slope is in fact the slope of the indifference curve at the point corresponding to the optimal feasible combination of $E(\tilde{R}_p)$ and $\sigma(\tilde{R}_p)$. We now show that the expression on the right in Equation (6.51) is just the slope of the efficient set at the point corresponding to the consumer's optimal portfolio choice. It then follows that Equation (6.51) is the familiar equilibrium tangency condition between an indifference curve and the efficient set (as shown, for example, in Figure 6.5).

Suppose that in the optimal consumption-investment decision the expected return on the portfolio is $E(\tilde{R}_p)^*$. The efficient portfolio with expected return $E(\tilde{R}_p)^*$ must be the solution to the problem: Choose x_i, $i = 1, 2, \ldots, N$, that[20]

$$\min \sigma(\tilde{R}_p) = [\sum_i \sum_j x_i x_j \sigma_{ij}]^{1/2} \tag{6.52a}$$

---

[19] For a given level of c_1, an indifference curve is defined by the set of combinations of $E(\tilde{R})$ and $\sigma(\tilde{R})$ with a given level of expected utility, say, V. The curve is implicitly defined by the function

$$F = E[U(c_1,\tilde{c}_2)] - V = 0.$$

The slope of the curve, which is the marginal rate of substitution of $E(\tilde{R}_p)$ for $\sigma(\tilde{R}_p)$, is then obtained from the differential of F as follows:

$$dF = \frac{\partial E[U(c_1,\tilde{c}_2)]}{\partial E(\tilde{R}_p)} dE(\tilde{R}_p) + \frac{\partial E[U(c_1,\tilde{c}_2)]}{\partial \sigma(\tilde{R}_p)} d\sigma(\tilde{R}_p) = 0,$$

$$\frac{dE(\tilde{R}_p)}{d\sigma(\tilde{R}_p)} = -\frac{\dfrac{\partial E[U(c_1,\tilde{c}_2)]}{\partial \sigma(\tilde{R}_p)}}{\dfrac{\partial E[U(c_1,\tilde{c}_2)]}{\partial E(\tilde{R}_p)}}.$$

[20] In the rest of this section, we simplify the notation by writing $\sum_i$ and $\sum_j$ for $\sum_{i=1}^{N}$ and $\sum_{j=1}^{N}$.

subject to the constraints

$$E(\tilde{R}_p) = E(\tilde{R}_p)^* = \sum_i x_i E(\tilde{R}_i), \tag{6.52b}$$

$$\sum_i x_i = 1. \tag{6.52c}$$

Forming the lagrangian

$$L = \sigma(\tilde{R}_p) + \lambda_1[E(\tilde{R}_p)^* - \sum_i x_i E(\tilde{R}_i)] + \lambda_2[1 - \sum_i x_i],$$

differentiating partially with respect to x_i, $i = 1, 2, \ldots, N$, λ_1, and λ_2, and setting these derivatives equal to zero, we obtain the necessary conditions for a minimum:

$$\frac{\partial L}{\partial x_i} = \frac{\partial \sigma(\tilde{R}_p)}{\partial x_i} - \lambda_1 E(\tilde{R}_i) - \lambda_2 = 0, \qquad i = 1, 2, \ldots, N. \tag{6.53a}$$

$$\frac{\partial L}{\partial \lambda_1} = E(\tilde{R}_p)^* - \sum_i x_i E(\tilde{R}_i) = 0. \tag{6.53b}$$

$$\frac{\partial L}{\partial \lambda_2} = 1 - \sum_i x_i = 0. \tag{6.53c}$$

Because λ_2 is the same for all assets, Equation (6.53a) implies that for any two assets i and j

$$\frac{\partial \sigma(\tilde{R}_p)}{\partial x_i} - \lambda_1 E(\tilde{R}_i) = \frac{\partial \sigma(\tilde{R}_p)}{\partial x_j} - \lambda_1 E(\tilde{R}_j), \tag{6.54}$$

or

$$\frac{1}{\lambda_1} = \frac{E(\tilde{R}_j) - E(\tilde{R}_i)}{\dfrac{\partial \sigma(\tilde{R}_p)}{\partial x_j} - \dfrac{\partial \sigma(\tilde{R}_p)}{\partial x_i}}. \tag{6.55}$$

The expression on the right of the equality in Equation (6.55) is identical with that on the right in Equation (6.51). Thus we are able to interpret Equation (6.51) once we give some meaning to λ_1 in Equation (6.55). But the Lagrange multiplier λ_1 is just the shadow price of the constraint (6.52b). It tells us how the minimum value of the standard deviation would change for "small" changes in $E(\tilde{R}_p)$ in the neighborhood of $E(\tilde{R}_p)^*$. Thus λ_1 is just the rate of exchange of $\sigma(\tilde{R}_p)$ for $E(\tilde{R}_p)$ at the point $E(\tilde{R}_p)^*$ in the efficient set. Its reciprocal $1/\lambda_1$, then, is just the slope of the efficient set at $E(\tilde{R}_p)^*$. Thus we have the desired result: Condition (6.51) implies that the optimal portfolio is at a point of tangency between an indifference curve and the efficient set.

Expression (6.55) is the "balance equation" for the efficient portfolio with expected return $E(\tilde{R}_p)^*$; that is, it tells us how the various available assets must be utilized in order to produce the efficient portfolio with expected return $E(\tilde{R}_p)^*$. The elements of Equation (6.55) are the partial derivatives

$$\frac{\partial E(\tilde{R}_p)}{\partial x_i} = E(\tilde{R}_i) \tag{6.56}$$

and

$$\frac{\partial \sigma(\tilde{R}_p)}{\partial x_i} = \frac{x_i \sigma^2(\tilde{R}_i) + \sum_{k \neq i} x_k \sigma_{ki}}{\sigma(\tilde{R}_p)}, \tag{6.57}$$

from Equation (6.50). Thus Equation (6.55) can be rewritten as

$$\lambda_1 = \frac{\dfrac{\partial \sigma(\tilde{R}_p)}{\partial x_j} - \dfrac{\partial \sigma(\tilde{R}_p)}{\partial x_i}}{\dfrac{\partial E(\tilde{R}_p)}{\partial x_j} - \dfrac{\partial E(\tilde{R}_p)}{\partial x_i}}$$

$$= \frac{\dfrac{(x_j \sigma^2(\tilde{R}_j) + \sum_{k \neq j} x_k \sigma_{kj}) - (x_i \sigma^2(\tilde{R}_i) + \sum_{k \neq i} x_k \sigma_{ki})}{\sigma(\tilde{R}_p)}}{E(\tilde{R}_j) - E(\tilde{R}_i)}. \tag{6.58}$$

In other words, for any pair of securities j and i, in forming the efficient portfolio with expected return $E(\tilde{R}_p)^*$, the values of the x's must be chosen so that the ratio of the difference between the marginal effects of assets j and i on the standard deviation of the return on the portfolio to the difference between the marginal effects of the two assets on the mean portfolio return is the same for all pairs of assets and equal to λ_1, the reciprocal of the slope of the efficient set at the point $E(\tilde{R}_p) = E(\tilde{R}_p)^*$.

From Equation (6.56) the marginal effect of an asset on the mean portfolio return is just the asset's expected return. From Equation (6.57), however, the marginal effect of an asset on the standard deviation of the portfolio return depends on the asset's variance $\sigma^2(\tilde{R}_i)$, the covariances of its return with those of other assets in the portfolio σ_{ki}, $k = 1, 2, \ldots, N$, $k \neq i$, the proportions in which the assets are held (the x_k) and the level of $\sigma(\tilde{R}_p)$. Moreover, in Equation (6.57) the variance $\sigma^2(\tilde{R}_i)$ is only one of the

N terms in the numerator; in general, the $N - 1$ covariance terms are much more important in the determination of $\partial\sigma(\tilde{R}_p)/\partial x_i$ than the term involving $\sigma^2(\tilde{R}_i)$. And this fact is of fundamental importance in later analyses.

In the case in which short selling is prohibited, so that the x_k must be nonnegative, Equation (6.58) must hold between any pair of assets that appear in the given efficient portfolio at a positive level. Assets would be excluded from the portfolio when their values of x in Equation (6.58) are negative; intuitively, at least for this particular efficient portfolio, the marginal effects of such assets on $\sigma(\tilde{R}_p)$ are too large relative to their marginal effects on $E(\tilde{R}_p)$.

Finally, it is interesting to note that when short selling of all assets is permitted, because Equation (6.58) must hold between every pair of assets, in general all assets are included in any efficient portfolio. Some assets are held long and others are sold short, but in general no asset is excluded from an efficient portfolio. On the other hand, when short selling is prohibited, most efficient portfolios do not involve holdings of all assets. For example, in this case the efficient portfolio with the highest possible level of expected return is generally just a single asset, and other efficient portfolios with high levels of expected return also involve zero holdings of many assets.

IV.D. Some Odds and Ends of the Mean–Standard Deviation Model

The main results of the mean–standard deviation version of the two-parameter consumption-investment model have now been presented. Thus we turn to a discussion of some peripheral points. All the issues to be considered should contribute to an understanding of the model, but for the most part this is all they have in common.

IV.D.1. The investment assets to be included in portfolio models

Having completed a formal analysis of the N-asset model in somewhat abstract terms, we can now consider the more mundane question of just which assets should be included. The answer is direct. In the two-period model consumption $\tilde{c}_2$ at period 2 is just the market value at that time of the portfolio chosen at period 1. A feasible portfolio, then, must imply a complete strategy for all activities that could possibly affect the market value of the individual's consumption ($=$ wealth) at the beginning of period 2. Thus a portfolio decision implies a complete set of simultaneous subdecisions concerning how the investment $h_1 = w_1 - c_1$ is allocated among, for example, common stocks, bonds, real estate, insurance policies, and any other activities relevant to $\tilde{c}_2$.

Moreover, it is important to emphasize that the subdecisions involved in a portfolio choice cannot usually be considered independently. For example, in an optimal decision resources cannot be allocated to common stocks or bonds without at the same time considering the insurance and real estate decisions. In the two-period model the individual chooses from among the available portfolios on the basis of their associated probability distributions of wealth $\tilde{w}_2$. It is the distribution of total wealth $\tilde{w}_2$ that matters. Thus a given subdecision, which comprises part of a portfolio choice, can be evaluated only in terms of its effects on the distribution of total terminal wealth, which in turn depends on many other subdecisions.[21]

There are two types of assets that warrant more detailed attention, however, although the problems that they create are somewhat more relevant in multiperiod than in two-period models. These assets are durable consumer goods—for example, homes, automobiles, and appliances—and human capital. With respect to durable consumer goods, there are no special problems if the services of these items can be purchased, or rented, on a period-by-period basis and if there are markets in which the goods can be sold at any time. In this case if the individual purchases a durable consumer item at the beginning of period 1, the market value of its services during period 1 is subtracted from its price and included in c_1. The remainder is then included in total investment h_1. The one-period return on the investment in the durable is then determined by its market price at the beginning of period 2. And it is worth mentioning that there are, of course, well-developed rental markets for housing and automobile services, and at least in major cities, rental markets for such durable items as refrigerators and automatic dishwashers are becoming more common. Moreover, there are primary and secondary markets in which these assets can be purchased and sold.

A thorough treatment of the optimal use of the consumer's human capital leads to much more difficult problems, however. We have avoided these in the two-period model by assuming that the consumer is paid at the beginning of period 1 for any labor services to be rendered during the period and that he sells no labor at period 2. In this case his labor income at period 1 is just one of the components of the total wealth w_1 that he uses to make his consumption-investment decision.

But suppose either that the consumer is paid at period 2 for labor sold at period 1 or that he sells additional labor services, and is paid for them, at

---

[21] This point is perhaps obvious to the readers of this book. But in the economics literature it is easy to find studies concerned, for example, with optimal insurance decisions of various types, as if these could be considered separately from the rest of the consumer's portfolio problem.

period 2. In either case the amount of labor income to be received at period 2 may not be completely certain. This creates no problems if there is a perfect market for human capital; that is, at period 1 the consumer can issue equity in, and not just borrow against, his future labor income, and there is a perfectly competitive market for shares in labor income of his type. In this case the market value of the consumer's human capital is just part of w_1, the total period 1 market value of all his resources, and he ends up holding shares in his own human capital only if these happen to be part of his optimal portfolio. If the consumer decides not to sell off all his human capital at period 1, the market value of whatever he holds is treated as part of his investment h_1. In short, with a perfect market for human capital, the latter turns out to be no different from any other wealth-producing asset that the consumer carries into period 1.

On the other hand if there is no market for human capital, the occupational income received at period 2 has no market value at the beginning of period 1. In this case there is no contribution to either w_1 or h_1 from the occupational income of period 2. This income, however, must be included as part of the total wealth $\tilde{w}_2$ provided by any feasible portfolio. In essence, the absence of a market for human capital constrains the individual to include his human capital in any feasible portfolio.

Finally, it is clear that the presence or absence of a market for human capital can affect the occupational decision itself. If there is a perfect market for human capital, the individual's attitudes toward risk do not affect his occupational decision, because he can sell the probability distribution on his income for period 2 and use the proceeds to purchase assets whose return distributions conform better to his own tastes. In this case, the best occupation is simply the one that maximizes the period 1 market value of his future income,[22] and the occupation decision can be made independently of the portfolio decision. If there is no market for human capital, however, the occupational decision is affected by the individual's attitudes toward risk, because the characteristics of the distribution of occupational income in period 2 affect the distribution of terminal wealth for every feasible portfolio.

This discussion of occupational decisions barely scratches the surface of this important area of economics. But our main interest is in the characteristics of optimal portfolio decisions and in the implications of these for the structure of equilibrium market prices of investment assets. Our discussion of occupational decisions and consumer durables is meant (1) to

---

[22] Even here we are oversimplifying, however. When we take account of the fact that the choice of occupation in part determines the individual's consumption of leisure, the occupational decision cannot be made on the basis of wealth alone.

provide a little more feeling for the framework in which the consumption-investment decision takes place and (2) to emphasize that an analysis concerned more directly with these variables would have to take into account that they also occur in the context of the overall consumption-investment decision. But because we are primarily interested here in the portfolio part of the decision, we have worked with assumptions that allow us to bypass the interesting problems that arise in the area of optimal occupational decisions.

IV.D.2. The effects of diversification: algebraic treatment

One of the conclusions in the geometric treatment of the N-asset model was that the process of mixing two assets or portfolios a and b in order to form a new portfolio is in general a dispersion-reducing activity; that is, the expected return on the new portfolio is just the weighted average of the expected returns on a and b, where the weights are the proportions of portfolio funds h_1 invested in a and b. When the correlation between the returns on a and b is less than 1, however, the standard deviation of the return on the new portfolio is less than the weighted average of $\sigma(\tilde{R}_a)$ and $\sigma(\tilde{R}_b)$. We now want to examine this conclusion in a slightly different way. Specifically, we are concerned with the behavior of the standard deviation of the return on the portfolio as the number of assets in the portfolio is increased.

Consider first the case in which an equal share of $h_1 = w_1 - c_1$ is invested in each of $K < N$ assets, that is, $x_i = 1/K$, $i = 1, \ldots, K$, and in which the returns on different assets are independent, so that $\sigma_{ij} = 0$, all i and j and $i \neq j$. The variance of the return on the portfolio is then

$$\sigma^2(\tilde{R}_p) = \sum_{i=1}^{K} x_i^2 \sigma^2(\tilde{R}_i) = \frac{1}{K^2} \sum_{i=1}^{K} \sigma^2(\tilde{R}_i).$$

Suppose now that, of all the assets in the market, the distribution of the return on asset g has the largest variance, $\sigma^2(\tilde{R}_g) = M$, and $M < \infty$. The variance on the return on a portfolio of K assets must then satisfy

$$\sigma^2(\tilde{R}_p) \leq \frac{KM}{K^2} = \frac{M}{K}. \tag{6.59}$$

Now this expression is smaller, the larger the value of K. In fact, if, simply to make a point, we assume that there are an infinite number of assets with independent returns in the market, it is possible to attain a portfolio whose variance of return is arbitrarily close to zero. In any case, it is clear from Equation (6.59) that in general the variance of the one-period return on the portfolio falls as the number of assets in the portfolio is increased. Thus increased diversification has the effect of making the one-period return on a portfolio more certain; the probability distribution on the return is more closely concentrated about its mean or expected value.

From a practical point of view, it is important to note that substantial reduction in the dispersion of portfolio return can be achieved with a relatively small amount of diversification. Expression (6.59) essentially implies that with equal weighting of assets whose returns are independent, the standard deviation of the return on a portfolio behaves like, or is proportional to, $1/\sqrt{K}$ as K, the number of assets in the portfolio, is increased. The function $1/\sqrt{K}$ is plotted in Figure 6.13. The function moves toward 0 more and more slowly as K is increased. For example, it is clear from the graph that increasing the size of the portfolio from 1 to 9 assets brings about a much larger decrease in dispersion than increasing K from 9 to 100.

Maintaining the assumption that equal amounts of h_1 are invested in each asset, let us now examine the effects of diversification on the variance of the one-period return on a portfolio when the returns on individual assets are dependent. With equal weighting

$$\sigma^2(\tilde{R}_p) = \sum_{i=1}^{K} \sum_{j=1}^{K} x_i x_j \sigma_{ij} = \frac{1}{K^2} \sum_{i=1}^{K} \sum_{j=1}^{K} \sigma_{ij}.$$

The double sum in this expression has K^2 terms; thus the variance of the one-period return on the portfolio is, in the case of equal weighting, just the average of the individual variances and covariances.

Now, however, let us rewrite $\sigma^2(\tilde{R}_p)$ in a slightly different way. Specifically, let us separate out those terms which involve the variances of the distributions of the one-period returns on individual assets:

$$\sigma^2(\tilde{R}_p) = \frac{1}{K^2} \sum_{i=1}^{K} \sigma^2(\tilde{R}_i) + \frac{1}{K^2} \sum_{i=1}^{K} \sum_{\substack{j=1 \\ j \neq i}}^{K} \sigma_{ij}.$$

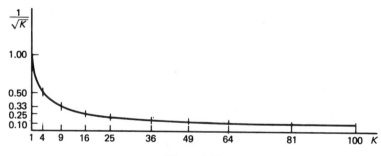

Figure 6.13

Again, if the variances of the one-period returns on individual assets, $\sigma^2(\tilde{R}_i)$, have a finite upper bound, then as the number of assets in the portfolio is increased, the first sum approaches 0; that is, in a portfolio of many securities, each weighted equally,

$$\sigma^2(\tilde{R}_p) \cong \frac{1}{K^2} \sum_{i=1}^{K} \sum_{\substack{j=1 \\ j \neq i}}^{K} \sigma_{ij}, \qquad K \text{ "large"}.$$

Now note that the average of the covariances between the returns of the assets in the portfolio is

$$\bar{\sigma}_{ij} = \frac{\displaystyle\sum_{i=1}^{K} \sum_{\substack{j=1 \\ j \neq i}}^{K} \sigma_{ij}}{K(K-1)}.$$

Thus we can write

$$\sigma^2(\tilde{R}_p) \cong \frac{1}{K^2} \sum_{i=1}^{K} \sum_{\substack{j=1 \\ j \neq i}}^{K} \sigma_{ij} = \frac{K-1}{K^2(K-1)} \sum_{i=1}^{K} \sum_{\substack{j=1 \\ j \neq i}}^{K} \sigma_{ij} = \frac{K-1}{K} \bar{\sigma}_{ij}.$$

As K is increased $(K-1)/K$ approaches 1, so that the variance of the distribution of the return on the portfolio approaches the average covariance between the one-period returns on the individual assets in the portfolio. Thus the dispersion in the distribution of the one-period return on a portfolio of many assets depends primarily on the relationships between the returns on the individual assets. The contribution of an individual asset to the dispersion of the portfolio return depends primarily on the relationships between this asset and other assets in the portfolio, rather than on the dispersion in the unconditional distribution of the return on the asset itself. When added to a large portfolio, an asset whose return has an extremely high variance may actually reduce the variance of the one-period return on the portfolio if the asset has low covariances with other assets.

Thus in a diversified portfolio the "riskiness" of an individual asset depends more on the covariability of the return on this asset with the returns on other assets than on the variance of the distribution on the return of the asset itself.[23] (And this is a result that reappears prominently in the next chapter.)

---

[23] Another way to explain this result is as follows: When the number of securities in the portfolio is increased by one, the number of terms involved in the variance of the portfolio return increases by $2K - 1$, or in other words, a row and a column are added to the variance-covariance matrix. Thus the variance of the return on the new asset is only one of $2K - 1$ new terms, and its contribution to portfolio variance is smaller, the larger the value of K.

IV.D.3. Quadratic utility functions

The main result concerning optimal portfolio decisions obtained thus far in this chapter is of course the efficient set theorem; that is, if the probability distributions of one-period returns on all portfolios are normal, the optimal portfolio for a risk-averse investor is mean–standard deviation efficient. We now show that the normality assumption is not necessary to obtain this result. If, alternatively, we are willing to assume that for any given value of c_1, the individual's utility function can be well approximated by a function that is quadratic in c_2, then the optimal portfolio for a risk averter is again efficient.

To prove this statement, it is again sufficient to show that with a quadratic approximation to the utility function, (1) for any given value of c_1, the consumer can rank the probability distributions of $\tilde{c}_2$ associated with different portfolios by looking only at the means and standard deviations of distributions of portfolio returns, and (2) given c_1, expected utility is an increasing function of expected portfolio return $E(\tilde{R}_p)$ and a decreasing function of standard deviation $\sigma(\tilde{R}_p)$.

For a given value of c_1, say, c_1', a quadratic approximation to the utility function $U(c_1',c_2)$ can be obtained from a Taylor series expansion, treating c_1 as a constant. If the expansion is taken about $c_2 = 0$, we get

$$U(c_1',c_2) = U(c_1',0) + \frac{\partial U(c_1',0)}{\partial c_2}\, c_2 + \frac{\partial^2 U(c_1',0)}{\partial c_2^2}\, \frac{c_2^2}{2} + \text{higher-order terms},$$

where $\partial U(c_1',0)/\partial c_2$ and $\partial^2 U(c_1,0)/\partial c_2^2$ are the first and second partial derivatives of U evaluated at the point $(c_1',0)$. If the higher-order terms in this expression are assumed to be negligible, we obtain the quadratic approximation

$$U(c_1',c_2) \cong V(c_1',c_2) = a_0 + a_1 c_2 - a_2 c_2^2, \qquad (6.60)$$

where, under the assumption that the individual is a risk averter,

$$a_0 = U(c_1',0) > 0, \quad a_1 = \frac{\partial U(c_1',0)}{\partial c_2} > 0, \quad a_2 = -\frac{1}{2}\cdot\frac{\partial^2 U(c_1',0)}{\partial c_2^2} > 0.^{24} \quad (6.61)$$

There is one major objection to quadratic utility functions. At some level of c_2 the slope of a quadratic with $a_2 > 0$ becomes negative, and this

[24] For a risk preferer a_2 would be negative.

Note that we are only approximating the utility function in the c_2 direction. Essentially, we are holding c_1 fixed and then developing a quadratic approximation for the projection of the utility function in the c_2 dimension. Note also that each term in Equation (6.61) generally depends on the chosen value of c_1, so that the constants in Equation (6.60) are different for different choices of c_1.

violates the assumption that marginal utility must always be positive. Negative marginal utility occurs when

$$\frac{\partial V(c_1', c_2)}{\partial c_2} = a_1 - 2a_2 c_2 < 0, \qquad a_2 > 0,$$

that is, when

$$c_2 > \frac{a_1}{2a_2}. \tag{6.62}$$

Because a quadratic function implies negative marginal utility of consumption beyond some point, the quadratic is always at best an approximation to the true utility function of a risk averter, and this is why we always treat it as such here.

The main attraction of a quadratic utility function is the ease with which comparisons of different probability distributions of period 2 consumption can be made. With the quadratic in Equation (6.60), the approximate expected utility of the probability distribution of $\tilde{c}_2$ associated with a particular portfolio decision is just

$$E[U(c_1', \tilde{c}_2)] \cong E[V(c_1', \tilde{c}_2)] = a_0 + a_1 E(\tilde{c}_2) - a_2 E(\tilde{c}_2^2), \tag{6.63}$$

where $E(\tilde{c}_2)$ and $E(\tilde{c}_2^2)$ are the mean and second moment of the distribution of $\tilde{c}_2$. Because

$$\sigma^2(\tilde{c}_2) = E(\tilde{c}_2^2) - E(\tilde{c}_2)^2,$$

the approximate expected utility given by Equation (6.63) can be restated as

$$E[V(c_1', \tilde{c}_2)] = a_0 + a_1 E(\tilde{c}_2) - a_2[\sigma^2(\tilde{c}_2) + E(\tilde{c}_2)^2]. \tag{6.64}$$

But the mean and variance of $\tilde{c}_2$ are related to those of the underlying portfolio return $\tilde{R}_p$ according to

$$E(\tilde{c}_2) = (w_1 - c_1')[1 + E(\tilde{R}_p)] \qquad \sigma^2(\tilde{c}_2) = (w_1 - c_1')^2 \sigma^2(\tilde{R}_p),$$

so that

$$E[V(c_1', \tilde{c}_2)] = a_0 + a_1(w_1 - c_1')[1 + E(\tilde{R}_p)]$$
$$- a_2(w_1 - c_1')^2[\sigma^2(\tilde{R}_p) + (1 + E(\tilde{R}_p))^2]. \tag{6.65}$$

Thus with the quadratic approximation to the consumer's utility function, given w_1 and $c_1 = c_1'$, differences between the approximate expected utilities associated with different portfolio choices can be determined from knowledge of only the means and variances, or standard deviations, of the portfolio return distributions, so that portfolios can be ranked on the basis of these two parameters. Moreover,

$$\frac{\partial E[V(c_1',\tilde{c}_2)]}{\partial \sigma(\tilde{R}_p)} = -2a_2(w_1 - c_1')^2 \sigma(\tilde{R}_p) < 0,$$

so that expected utility is indeed a declining function of $\sigma(\tilde{R}_p)$.

On the other hand, the approximate expected utility computed from V is not a monotonically increasing function of expected return $E(\tilde{R}_p)$. For a given value of $\sigma^2(\tilde{R}_p)$, $E[V(c_1',\tilde{c}_2)]$ declines with increases in expected return when

$$\frac{\partial E[V(c_1',\tilde{c}_2)]}{\partial E(\tilde{R}_p)} = a_1(w_1 - c_1') - 2a_2(w_1 - c_1')^2[1 + E(\tilde{R}_p)] < 0$$

or when

$$(w_1 - c_1')[1 + E(\tilde{R}_p)] > \frac{a_1}{2a_2}. \tag{6.66}$$

Thus, comparing (6.62) and (6.66), expected quadratically approximated utility declines with increases in $E(\tilde{R}_p)$ when $E(\tilde{c}_2) = (w_1 - c_1')[1 + E(\tilde{R}_p)]$ is in the downward sloping part of the quadratic utility function.

In short, with a quadratic approximation to the individual's utility function, expected utility rises with expected return $E(\tilde{R}_p)$ as long as $E(\tilde{c}_2)$ is within the range of values for which the quadratic is a monotone-increasing function of c_2. But this is precisely the range of values of c_2 for which the quadratic is a valid approximation to the consumer's utility function. Indeed, the implicit assumption underlying the use of a quadratic approximation to the true utility function is that in the approximate function negative marginal utility occurs at levels of consumption c_2 that are so high and so unlikely that their effect on the analysis is negligible. But this means that if the use of quadratics is valid for the consumer at hand, the optimal portfolio for $c_1 = c_1'$ must yield expected period 2 consumption within the range of the quadratic approximation that implies positive marginal utility of c_2.

Within this range the quadratically approximated expected utility is an increasing function of expected return and a decreasing function of standard deviation of return. It follows that the optimal portfolio for $c_1 = c_1'$ must be such that no portfolio with the same or higher expected return has lower standard deviation of return; that is, the optimal portfolio must be $E(\tilde{R})$, $\sigma(\tilde{R})$ efficient. And because this analysis applies to any given value of c_1, it applies to the optimal value, and thus the efficient set theorem holds:

When a risk averter's utility function is well approximated by a quadratic, his optimal portfolio is a member of the $E(\tilde{R})$, $\sigma(\tilde{R})$ efficient set.

But at least to us it seems that obtaining the efficient set theorem by means of quadratic approximations to utility functions is not so appealing as the approach based on the assumption that portfolio return distributions are all of the same two-parameter type, for example, normal. And our objection to the quadratic approach is not based on the fact that, strictly speaking, quadratics are not legitimate utility functions. All economic theory involves assumptions that amount to approximations of one sort or another, and this one seems no worse than most. Rather, our preference for the approach based on two-parameter portfolio return distributions comes from the fact that this distributional assumption can be tested directly on market data, whereas the assumption that utility functions can be well approximated by quadratics is at best tested only with extreme difficulty.

And we argue now that a class of two-parameter distributions does indeed seem to provide a good description of actual data on security returns. Moreover, we also contend that such results are not totally unexpected from a theoretical viewpoint; that is, there are also good theoretic arguments in support of two-parameter return distributions.

IV.D.4. Why normality?

The one-period return on a portfolio is just a weighted sum of the returns on the individual assets in the portfolio. Weighted sums of normal variables are themselves normally distributed; that is, the normal distribution is stable in the sense that it reproduces itself under weighted addition. Thus if distributions of asset returns are normal, distributions of portfolio returns are normal. Moreover, it is clear that stability, or invariance under addition, is a necessary property of any distribution assumed in the two-parameter portfolio model; that is, because assets are themselves portfolios, if all portfolio return distributions are to be of the same two-parameter type, the distributions must be stable or invariant under addition.

But the natural question then is: Why would one expect asset returns to have stable or, even more specifically, normal distributions? Suppose the one-period horizon in the consumption-investment problem is a year. The one-period return on an asset is just the change during the year in the market value of a dollar invested in the asset at the beginning of the year, that is, cash payments plus capital gains, all divided by the initial price. But the change in the market value of a unit of an asset over the entire one-year period is just the sum of the changes in market value from one trading point to the next during the year. For example, suppose that a particular asset j is traded at each of 100 equally spaced points in time during the year and the prices observed at these trades are p_{jt}, $t = 1, 2, \ldots, 100$. The one-period return on the asset for the year can then be written as either

$$\tilde{R}_j = \frac{p_{j,100} - p_{j,1}}{p_{j,1}}$$

or $\qquad \tilde{R}_j = \dfrac{(p_{j,100} - p_{j,99}) + (p_{j,99} - p_{j,98}) + \cdots + (p_{j,2} - p_{j,1})}{p_{j,1}}$.

If the price changes $p_{j,t+1} - p_{j,t}$ can be regarded as drawings from a distribution for which the variance exists, the central limit theorem would lead us to suppose that the sum of price changes in this expression would have a distribution that is approximately normal; that is, the central limit theorem tells us that under fairly general conditions, in the limit sums of identically distributed random variables approach a normal distribution if the variance of the elements of the sum exists. Thus the annual one-period return, which is just the sum of price changes between trading points multiplied by the constant $1/p_{j1}$, should have a distribution that is approximately normal.

But these limiting arguments that lead to the supposition of normal distributions for the one-period returns on assets or portfolios depend critically on the assumption that the variances of the distributions of price changes and one-period returns exist; that is, the expected values that define the variance are finite. There is much empirical evidence, however, that suggests rather strongly that this assumption may be inappropriate, at least for such important assets as common stocks and government bonds. See, for example, Blume [11], Fama [12], Mandelbrot [15], and Roll [17].

If the variances of price changes and one-period returns are infinite, the limiting arguments presented above lead to a much broader class of limiting distributions for asset and portfolio returns. Interestingly, all members of this class of limiting distributions have the stability property so critical for the two-parameter portfolio models, and in fact in the statistical literature these distributions are referred to as the "stable class."

Most important, the empirical evidence cited above suggests that observed distributions of asset and portfolio returns conform well to the two-parameter members of this stable class. Thus we now conclude this chapter by extending the two-parameter portfolio model to allow for two-parameter distributions that are stable but might have infinite variances. We find that the extended model has all the important properties of the two-parameter model based on normal return distributions.

V. THE TWO–PARAMETER MODEL WITH SYMMETRIC STABLE DISTRIBUTIONS OF PORTFOLIO RETURNS

Indeed, the development of the general two-parameter stable model will be much along the lines of that of the normal model. In particular, we first consider the characteristics of consumer tastes, and we show that with two-parameter stable return distributions, the consumer is able to rank distributions of portfolio returns on the basis of expected returns $E(\tilde{R}_p)$ and a measure of return dispersion $\sigma(\tilde{R}_p)$, which in the general stable model is no longer interpreted as the standard deviation. Moreover, we show that for a risk-averse consumer, expected utility is an increasing function of $E(\tilde{R}_p)$ and a decreasing function of $\sigma(\tilde{R}_p)$, so that the efficient set theorem holds; that is, the optimal portfolio must be $E(\tilde{R})$, $\sigma(\tilde{R})$ efficient, and a portfolio is efficient if no portfolio with the same or higher expected return $E(\tilde{R})$ has lower return dispersion $\sigma(\tilde{R})$. Even more specifically, we show that risk aversion and two-parameter stable portfolio return distributions imply indifference curves of $E(\tilde{R})$ against $\sigma(\tilde{R})$ that are positively sloping and convex, just as we saw in Figure 6.3 for the normal model.

Likewise on the opportunity side, we show that the efficient set of portfolios describes a positively sloping concave curve in the $E(\tilde{R})$, $\sigma(\tilde{R})$ plane, much like the curve bcd shown for the normal model in Figure 6.4. Thus the fundamental result for the two-parameter stable portfolio model is the picture of consumer equilibrium in Figure 6.5; that is, the optimum is represented by a point of tangency between a convex indifference curve and the concave efficient set curve. The results are obviously essentially identical with those obtained for the normal model. The primary difference is that in the two-parameter stable model, $\sigma(\tilde{R})$ is more generally interpreted as return dispersion rather than as standard deviation.

Before proceeding with the development of the stable model of consumer equilibrium, however, we must first discuss some of the relevant statistical properties of the stable class of distributions.

V.A. Properties of Stable Distributions: A Brief Review[25]

In the portfolio model to be presented below, it is assumed that all random variables have symmetric stable distributions. A symmetric stable distribution has three parameters that here are denoted α, $E(\tilde{y})$, and $\sigma(\tilde{y})$,

---

[25] The definition and original treatment of the class of stable distributions is due to Lévy [8]. A compact treatment of most of the available statistical theory is in Ref. 7. Derivations of the properties of these distributions summarized in this section are readily available in Ref. 7. The symmetric stable distributions are tabulated in Ref. 9, and procedures for estimating their parameters are discussed in Ref. 10.

where $\tilde{y}$ is the random variable.[26] The parameter α, which must be in the range $0 < \alpha \leq 2$, is called the "characteristic exponent," and it determines the type of a stable distribution. The stable distribution with $\alpha = 2$ is the normal; the symmetric stable distribution with $\alpha = 1$ is the Cauchy. The normal is the only stable distribution for which second- and higher-order absolute moments exist. When $\alpha < 2$, absolute moments of order less than α exist; those of order equal to or greater than α do not.

The absolute moment of order k is

$$E(|\tilde{y}|^k) \equiv \int_{-\infty}^{\infty} |y|^k f(y) \, dy,$$

where $f(y)$ is the density function of $\tilde{y}$. When we say that the absolute moment of order k does not exist, we mean that the integral that defines the moment does not exist; or more simply $E(|\tilde{y}|^k) = \infty$. It is a theorem of probability theory that the ordinary moment of order k defined as

$$E(\tilde{y}^k) \equiv \int_{-\infty}^{\infty} y^k f(y) \, dy$$

exists only if the absolute moment of order k exists. Thus the statements in the preceding paragraph imply that for stable distributions the variance

$$\sigma^2(\tilde{y}) = E(\tilde{y}^2) - E(\tilde{y})^2$$

exists only when $\alpha = 2$; the mean $E(\tilde{y})$ exists only when $\alpha > 1$. In our portfolio models we always assume that $\alpha > 1$, so that the expected value $E(\tilde{y})$ can be used as a measure of the location of the distribution of $\tilde{y}$.

The nonnegative parameter $\sigma(\tilde{y})$ defines the scale of a stable distribution. When $\alpha = 2$, $\sigma(\tilde{y})$ is the standard deviation divided by $\sqrt{2}$. When $\alpha < 2$, the standard deviation of the stable distribution does not exist, and $\sigma(\tilde{y})$ must be given some other interpretation. In Ref. 9 it is shown that when $1 < \alpha \leq 2$, which is the important range of values of α for portfolio models, $\sigma(\tilde{y})$ corresponds approximately to the semi-interquartile range (half the difference between the 0.75 and 0.25 fractiles) of the distribution of $\tilde{y}$.

The standardized variable

$$\tilde{r} = \frac{\tilde{y} - E(\tilde{y})}{\sigma(\tilde{y})} \tag{6.67}$$

[26] The stable class also includes asymmetric distributions. A fourth parameter, for skewness, is zero in the symmetric case. From a theoretical viewpoint the symmetry assumption reduces the generality of the model. But in fact the assumption seems to be justified by the data. See, for example, Blume [11], Fama [12], Kendall [13], Moore [16], and Roll [17].

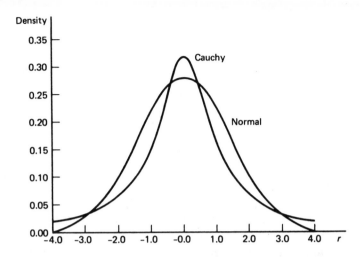

Figure 6.14   Cauchy and Normal Density Functions for the Standardized Variable r

provides an excellent means of studying the role of the characteristic exponent α in determining the type of a symmetric stable distribution. If $\tilde{y}$ is symmetric-stable with parameters α, $E(\tilde{y})$, and $\sigma(\tilde{y})$, then $\tilde{r}$ is symmetric stable with parameters α (unaffected by the transformation), $E(\tilde{r}) = 0$, and $\sigma(\tilde{r}) = 1$. Distributions with $\alpha < 2$ depart from the normal distribution ($\alpha = 2$) in the following ways: (1) For some range of $\tilde{r}$ close to $E(\tilde{r})$ a stable distribution with $\alpha < 2$ is more peaked (has higher densities) than the normal. (2) For $|\tilde{r}|$ "large," stable distributions with $\alpha < 2$ have higher tails than the normal distribution. (3) For some intermediate range of $|\tilde{r}|$, stable distributions with $\alpha < 2$ have lower densities than the normal distribution. These properties are illustrated in Figure 6.14, which presents the density functions of $\tilde{r}$ for the normal ($\alpha = 2$) and Cauchy ($\alpha = 1$) distributions.

By definition, stable random variables are stable or invariant under weighted addition; that is, let $\tilde{y}_1, \tilde{y}_2, \ldots, \tilde{y}_n$ be independent symmetric stable variables whose distributions have the same characteristic exponent α, but possibly different location and scale parameters $E(\tilde{y}_j)$, $\sigma(\tilde{y}_j)$, $j = 1, 2, \ldots, n$. Then if d_j, $j = 1, 2, \ldots, n$, are fixed weights, the sum

$$\tilde{y} = \sum_{j=1}^{n} d_j \tilde{y}_j$$

is symmetric stable with characteristic exponent α (unaffected by the weighted addition) and with location and scale parameters

$$E(\tilde{y}) = E(\sum_{j=1}^{n} d_j \tilde{y}_j) = \sum_{j=1}^{n} d_j E(\tilde{y}_j), \tag{6.68}$$

$$\sigma(\tilde{y}) = \sigma(\sum_{j=1}^{n} d_j \tilde{y}_j) = [\sum_{j=1}^{n} \sigma^{\alpha}(\tilde{y}_j) \mid d_j \mid^{\alpha}]^{1/\alpha}. \tag{6.69}$$

In short, the property of stability means that a weighted sum of independent stable variables, each distributed with the same value of α, is of the same type; that is, it is stable with the same value of α as the distributions of the individual summands.[27]

It is also well to note that the class of stable distributions provides a generalization of the normal "central limit theorem"; that is, if a weighted sum of random variables has a limiting distribution, the limiting distribution is a member of the stable class. In the case in which variances are assumed to exist, under fairly general conditions, distributions of weighted sums of random variables approach a normal distribution as the number of variables in the sum is increased; this is the central limit theorem as it applies to normal variables. The stable nonnormal distributions generalize the central limit theorem to the case in which the variances of the underlying variables do not exist.

Thus the entire stable class of distributions, which includes the normal as a special case, has the two properties that make the normal distribution so desirable in portfolio models. First, we soon see again that the stability property of these distributions is critical in ensuring that distributions of portfolio returns are all of the same two-parameter type. Second, the generalized central limit theorem provides some theoretical justification for the fact that observed return distributions seem to conform well to members of the stable class.

Finally, in our portfolio models it is assumed that distributions of returns on all assets and portfolios are symmetric stable with characteristic exponent $\alpha > 1$. The reason that α must be greater than 1 becomes clear later.[28] But we also assume that whatever the value of α, it is the same for

---

[27] The standardized, that is, $E(\tilde{r}) = 0$, $\sigma(\tilde{r}) = 1$, variable $\tilde{r}$ defined by (6.67) and expressions (6.68) and (6.69) for the location and scale parameters of weighted sums of stable variables are used extensively in later analyses. Setting $\alpha = 2$ in (6.68) and (6.69) and interpreting the σ's as standard deviations, one obtains the familiar expressions for the expected value and standard deviation of a weighted sum of independent normal, or other finite variance, variables.

[28] In fact the estimated values of α for returns on common stocks and United States Treasury bills have generally been well in excess of 1. From the evidence of Blume [11], Fama [12], and Roll [17], values of α in the neighborhood of 1.6 seem reasonable.

all assets and portfolios. This assumption is necessary to obtain two-parameter return distributions—only the values of $E(\tilde{R})$ and $\sigma(\tilde{R})$ vary from one portfolio to another—but it clearly reduces the generality of the model. Note, however, that the mean–standard deviation portfolio model in Sections II to IV assumed normality, that is, $\alpha = 2$, for all return distributions. In essence, we now generalize this model to allow the characteristic exponent α of return distributions to take any (given) value in the interval $1 < \alpha \leq 2$.

V.B. Representation of the Consumer's Tastes: The Efficient Set Theorem

The first step is to discuss the way in which consumer tastes can be characterized in a portfolio model with two-parameter stable return distributions. The arguments are almost identical with those for the normal model in Section II, so that the present discussion can be quite brief. In fact just the first few steps of the analysis are presented, and the remainder is summarized with reference to the results in Section II.

Again the individual is assumed to have a given quantity of initial wealth w_1 that he must allocate between consumption c_1 and a portfolio investment $w_1 - c_1 = h_1$, the return on which is the basis of his consumption in period 2. The individual is assumed to behave as if he wished to make a consumption-investment decision that maximized expected utility, computed from the utility function $U(c_1,c_2)$. He is assumed to be a risk averter, so that $U(c_1,c_2)$ is monotone-increasing and strictly concave in (c_1,c_2).

Consumption in period 2 is related to the one-period return $\tilde{R}_p$ on the individual's portfolio according to

$$\tilde{c}_2 = (w_1 - c_1)(1 + \tilde{R}_p).$$

But using the standardized variable

$$\tilde{r} = \frac{\tilde{R}_p - E(\tilde{R}_p)}{\sigma(\tilde{R}_p)}, \qquad (6.3)$$

$\tilde{c}_2$ can be written in terms of $E(\tilde{R}_p)$, $\sigma(\tilde{R}_p)$, and $\tilde{r}$ as

$$\tilde{c}_2 = (w_1 - c_1)[1 + E(\tilde{R}_p) + \sigma(\tilde{R}_p)\tilde{r}]. \qquad (6.4)$$

The expected utility associated with a choice of current consumption c_1 and portfolio p is then

$$E[U(c_1,\tilde{c}_2)] = \int_{-\infty}^{\infty} U(c_1, (w_1 - c_1)[1 + E(\tilde{R}_p) + \sigma(\tilde{R}_p)r])f(r)\,dr, \qquad (6.5)$$

where $f(r)$ is the density function of the variable r.

Because the distributions of $\tilde{R}_p$ for all portfolios are assumed to be symmetric stable with the same value of the characteristic exponent α, the standardized variable $\tilde{r}$, as defined by Equation (6.3), has a symmetric stable distribution with the same value of α. Thus with the definition of expected utility provided by Equation (6.5), the variable r and the density function $f(r)$ are the same for all portfolios. Differences between the expected utilities associated with different consumption-investment decisions depend entirely on c_1, $E(\tilde{R}_p)$, and $\sigma(\tilde{R}_p)$, so that consumption-investment alternatives can be ranked solely on the basis of these three variables. Formally, we can write

$$E[U(c_1,\tilde{c}_2)] = V(c_1,E(\tilde{R}_p),\sigma(\tilde{R}_p)). \qquad (6.6)$$

But except for the fact that the scale parameter $\sigma(\tilde{R}_p)$ is no longer the standard deviation, this analysis is identical with that in Section II, and in fact Equations (6.3) to (6.6) are reproduced directly from Section II. And the remainder of the analysis of the present model would go precisely as in the case of the model based on normally distributed portfolio returns. Again the analysis of expressions (6.7) and (6.8) in Section II would lead us to conclude here that

$$\frac{\partial EU(c_1,\tilde{c}_2)}{\partial E(\tilde{R}_p)} > 0 \qquad \text{and} \qquad \frac{\partial E[U(c_1,\tilde{c}_2)]}{\partial \sigma(\tilde{R}_p)} < 0;$$

that is, for a risk averter expected utility is an increasing function of expected portfolio return and a decreasing function of return dispersion. Again it follows that the optimal portfolio corresponding to any, and thus the optimal, choice of c_1 must be $E(\tilde{R})$, $\sigma(\tilde{R})$ efficient; that is, the optimal portfolio must be such that no portfolio with the same or higher expected return $E(\tilde{R})$ has lower return dispersion $\sigma(\tilde{R})$. But this is just the efficient set theorem. Finally, the analysis in Section II in the present model again implies that for any given c_1 indifference curves of $E(\tilde{R})$ against $\sigma(\tilde{R})$ are positively sloping and convex, just as shown in Figure 6.3 for the normal model.

In checking that these properties of consumer tastes when portfolio returns are symmetric stable are direct implications of the results for the normal model in Section II, note that the critical assumptions in the analysis in Section II are that (1) $U(c_1,c_2)$ is concave, which is equivalent to assuming risk aversion; (2) distributions of portfolio returns are symmetric; and (3) differences between distributions of portfolio returns can be completely summarized by two parameters, a measure of location $E(\tilde{R})$ and a measure of scale or dispersion $\sigma(\tilde{R})$. The fact that in the model based on normally distributed portfolio returns $\sigma(\tilde{R})$ was interpreted as the standard deviation was irrelevant. The important assumption was that differences between distributions of returns on portfolios can be completely summarized in terms of two parameters.

Or equivalently, the analysis of the properties of consumer tastes in Section II requires that one period returns on all assets and portfolios must be generated by two-parameter distributions of the same type. The assumption made here, that distributions of returns on all assets and portfolios are symmetric stable with the same value of the characteristic exponent α, reduces these to two-parameter distributions of the same type, and it is this which makes the analysis in Section II, with a change in the interpretation of the scale parameter $\sigma(\tilde{R})$, directly applicable to the more general stable model.

V.C. The Opportunity Set with Stable Return
Distributions

Without an exact description of his utility function we cannot, of course, determine which efficient portfolio the consumer chooses, but we do know that the optimal choice is a member of the efficient set. The next order of business, then, is to develop a representation of the efficient set for a market in which returns on all assets and portfolios conform to symmetric stable distributions. In order to do this, however, we must first discuss a model for describing how these returns are generated.

V.C.1. The market model

The one-period return on a portfolio is just a weighted average of the returns on the assets in the portfolio; that is,

$$\tilde{R}_p = \sum_{j=1}^{N} x_j \tilde{R}_j, \qquad (6.70)$$

where x_j is the proportion of investment funds $w_1 - c_1$ invested in asset j, N is the number of assets available, and

$$\sum_{j=1}^{N} x_j = 1.$$

The probability distribution of $\tilde{R}_p$ depends on the distributions of the $\tilde{R}_j$, the interrelationships among the $\tilde{R}_j$, and the set of x's chosen. In the models in this section it is assumed that the $\tilde{R}_j$ are symmetric stable random variables, so that $\tilde{R}_p$ is just a weighted sum of stable variables. There is ample empirical evidence that one-period returns on most assets are interdependent. See, for example, Kendall [13], King [14], and Blume [11]. But unfortunately a general statistical theory covering distributions of weighted sums of dependent stable variables is unavailable. The problem, then, is to develop a stochastic model in which the $\tilde{R}_j$ are dependent, but $\tilde{R}_p$ can nevertheless be expressed as a weighted sum of independent stable variables.

Assume that all interrelationships among the returns on individual assets arise from the fact that there is a common "market factor" $\tilde{M}$ that affects the returns on all assets; that is, the returns on individual assets are generated by the market model

$$\tilde{R}_j = a_j + b_j\tilde{M} + \tilde{\epsilon}_j, \qquad j = 1, 2, \ldots, N. \tag{6.71}$$

Here a_j and b_j are constants, and $\tilde{\epsilon}_j$ is a random disturbance whose distribution is assumed to have expected value equal to 0. It is assumed that $\tilde{\epsilon}_j$, $j = 1, 2, \ldots, N$, and $\tilde{M}$ are mutually independent, symmetric stable variables, all with the same characteristic exponent $\alpha > 1$.

Because $\tilde{M}$ affects the returns of all assets, Equation (6.71) does indeed allow for interdependence among the returns of different assets. Nevertheless, combining Equations (6.70) and (6.71),

$$\tilde{R}_p = \sum_{j=1}^{N} x_j a_j + \sum_{j=1}^{N} x_j b_j \tilde{M} + \sum_{j=1}^{N} x_j \tilde{\epsilon}_j, \tag{6.72}$$

so that the return on a portfolio is a weighted sum of the independent random variables $\tilde{M}$ and $\tilde{\epsilon}_j$, $j = 1, 2, \ldots, N$. Because these are assumed to be symmetric stable with the same characteristic exponent α, $\tilde{R}_p$ is also symmetric stable with the same value of α, and from Equations (6.68) and (6.69), $E(\tilde{R}_p)$ and $\sigma(\tilde{R}_p)$, the mean and dispersion of the distribution of $\tilde{R}_p$, are related to those of $\tilde{M}$ and the $\tilde{\epsilon}_j$ according to[29]

$$E(\tilde{R}_p) = \sum_{j=1}^{N} x_j a_j + \sum_{j=1}^{N} x_j b_j E(\tilde{M}) = \sum_{j=1}^{N} x_j E(\tilde{R}_j), \tag{6.73}$$

$$\sigma(\tilde{R}_p) = \left[\sigma^\alpha(\tilde{M}) \left| \sum_{j=1}^{N} x_j b_j \right|^\alpha + \sum_{j=1}^{N} \sigma^\alpha(\tilde{\epsilon}_j) \left| x_j \right|^\alpha\right]^{1/\alpha}. \tag{6.74}$$

[29] Fortunately, the empirical evidence, and especially Blume [11], indicates that our specification of the return-generating process, that is, the market model with $\alpha > 1$, is a good description of actual return data, at least for common stocks.

The market model was originally suggested by Markowitz [1] as a way of reducing the number of parameter inputs required in the normal or mean–standard deviation portfolio model. In the general mean–standard deviation model, from Equation (6.30), the variance of the return on a portfolio of N assets requires estimates of the N variances of the individual asset returns $\sigma^2(\tilde{R}_j)$ and $N(N-1)/2$ covariances; that is, there are $N(N-1)$ covariances, but $\sigma_{ij} = \sigma_{ji}$. But from Equation (6.74), with the market model, to measure portfolio dispersion we need only have estimates of $\sigma_{\tilde{M}}$, b_j and $\sigma(\tilde{\epsilon}_j)$,

Finally, there would be no problem in our models in allowing returns to be linear functions of any number of independent, symmetric stable variables. For example, in line with the work of King [14], we could postulate the "market-industry" model

$$\tilde{R}_j = a_j + b_j \tilde{M} + \sum_{k=1}^{K} c_{jk} \tilde{I}_k + \tilde{\epsilon}_j, \qquad j = 1, 2, \ldots, N.$$

Here the $\tilde{I}_k$ are industry factors, assumed to be mutually independent, independent of $\tilde{M}$ and the $\tilde{\epsilon}_j$, and distributed with the same value of α as $\tilde{M}$ and the $\tilde{\epsilon}_j$. But such a generalization of the return-generating process would complicate the algebra of the models to be presented without contributing additional insights. Thus we concentrate on the market model.

V.C.2. Diversification and the distribution of portfolio return

By way of introduction to the geometric discussion of the portfolio opportunity set to be presented in the next section, we now show that as long as the characteristic exponent α of the process generating asset returns is greater than 1, diversification is an effective tool for reducing the dispersion in the probability distribution of portfolio return. Consider a portfolio that includes only $n < N$ assets at a nonzero level; that is, some of the x_j in Equation (6.70) are zero. Without loss of generality, we label the n assets in the portfolio 1, 2, ..., n, so that

$$\sigma(\tilde{R}_p) = [\sigma^\alpha(\tilde{M}) \mid \sum_{j=1}^{n} x_j b_j \mid^\alpha + \sum_{j=1}^{n} \sigma^\alpha(\tilde{\epsilon}_j) \mid x_j \mid^\alpha]^{1/\alpha}. \qquad (6.75)$$

In general, how is return dispersion $\sigma(\tilde{R}_p)$ affected as n is increased and the proportions of initial wealth invested in individual assets are reduced? Any rearrangement of the x_j affects the weighted average $\sum x_j b_j$ and so also affects the first or "market" term in Equation (6.75). But the change in the average can go in either direction, and in any case it is not due to diversification per se. In essence, because the market factor $\tilde{M}$ affects the returns on all assets, increased diversification does not in general reduce its effects on the dispersion of the portfolio return.

On the other hand, when $\alpha > 1$, diversification, in general, systematically reduces the effects of the $\tilde{\epsilon}_j$ on the dispersion of the portfolio return. Con-

---

$j = 1, 2, \ldots, N$. By looking at the parameter requirements for a few values of N, for example, $N = 100$, the reader can easily convince himself that the market model does indeed substantially reduce the number of parameter inputs required in a portfolio analysis.

sider the simple case $x_j = 1/n$, $j = 1, 2, \ldots, n$. Then the last term in Equation (6.75) becomes

$$\sigma^\alpha(\tilde{\epsilon}_p) = \left(\frac{1}{n}\right)^\alpha \sum_{j=1}^n \sigma^\alpha(\tilde{\epsilon}_j).$$

Because the $\sigma^\alpha(\tilde{\epsilon}_j)$ are assumed to be bounded, as long as $\alpha > 1$ the value of $\sigma^\alpha(\tilde{\epsilon}_p)$ decreases as n is increased. In essence, the $\tilde{\epsilon}_j$ represent the effects of random factors, independent from asset to asset, and these effects become more and more offsetting as the portfolio is diversified. It must be emphasized, however, that this effect is only realized when $\alpha > 1$. When $\alpha = 1$, in general, diversification has no effect on $\sigma^\alpha(\tilde{\epsilon}_p)$; when $\alpha < 1$, increased diversification usually causes $\sigma^\alpha(\tilde{\epsilon}_p)$ to increase.

A numerical example makes these statements more concrete. For simplicity suppose that $\sigma^\alpha(\tilde{\epsilon}_j) = 1$ and $x_j = 1/n$ for all j. Then Table 1 shows the behavior of

$$\sigma^\alpha(\tilde{\epsilon}_p) = \left(\frac{1}{n}\right)^\alpha \sum_{j=1}^n \sigma^\alpha(\tilde{\epsilon}_j) = n^{1-\alpha}$$

for different values of α as n is increased. It is clear from the table that when $\alpha = 1$, diversification is ineffective in reducing the dispersion of the distribution of the return on the portfolio. When $\alpha = 1$, under the simple conditions assumed in this example $\sigma^\alpha(\tilde{\epsilon}_p) = 1$, regardless of the number of assets in the portfolio. When $\alpha < 1$, the table demonstrates that the return on a more diversified portfolio may actually have a higher degree of dispersion than the return on a less diversified portfolio. When $\alpha = 0.5$, $\sigma^\alpha(\tilde{\epsilon}_p)$ goes from 1.0 to 3.162 to 10.0 as n is increased from 1 to 10 and then to 100.

TABLE 1

Values of $\sigma^\alpha(\tilde{\epsilon}_p) = n^{1-\alpha}$ for Different α and n

			n		
α		1	10	100	1000
2.00		1	0.100	0.010	0.001
1.75		1	0.178	0.032	0.006
1.50		1	0.316	0.100	0.032
1.25		1	0.562	0.316	0.178
1.00		1	1.000	1.000	1.000
0.50		1	3.162	10.000	31.623

When $\alpha > 1$, diversification reduces the dispersion of the distribution of the return on the portfolio. Moreover, Table 1 demonstrates that diversification is more effective, the higher the value of α. As n is increased, $\sigma^\alpha(\tilde{\epsilon}_p)$ approaches the limiting value 0 at different rates, depending on the value of α. For example, when $\alpha = 2$, $\sigma^\alpha(\tilde{\epsilon}_p) = 0.100$ for a portfolio of 10 assets, whereas when $\alpha = 1.5$, a portfolio of 100 assets is required before $\sigma^\alpha(\tilde{\epsilon}_p)$ reaches this level.

In statistical terms all this means that when $\alpha > 1$ there is a law of large numbers at work that makes the return on a portfolio more certain as the number of assets in the portfolio is increased. The law becomes weaker as α moves away from 2 in the direction of 1, and when $\alpha = 1$ there is no law of large numbers at work. Finally, when $\alpha < 1$ the law of large numbers actually works in reverse, so that the return on the portfolio becomes less certain as the number of assets is increased.

An encouraging feature of Table 1 is the fact that for $\alpha > 1.25$, $\sigma^\alpha(\tilde{\epsilon}_p)$ moves relatively quickly toward its asymptotic value as the number of assets in the portfolio is increased. Because the available empirical work seems to indicate that, at least for the common stocks of large American companies and for United States government bonds, $1.25 < \alpha < 2.0$, an investor should be considerably heartened by the discussion in the previous paragraphs. When α is in this range, diversification is still an effective way to reduce the dispersion of the distribution of the return on a portfolio, although it is not so effective as in the case $\alpha = 2$ (the normal distribution).

V.C.3. The efficient set

We showed earlier that if distributions of portfolio returns are symmetric stable with the same value of α, the efficient set theorem holds; that is, the optimal portfolio for a risk averter must be such that no portfolio with the same or higher expected return $E(\tilde{R})$ has lower return dispersion $\sigma(\tilde{R})$.[30] We now want to show that the preceding analysis of the effects of diversification on dispersion of portfolio returns implies that, as in the mean–standard deviation model, when $\alpha > 1$ the efficient set curve is positively sloping and concave in the $E(\tilde{R})$, $\sigma(\tilde{R})$ plane, somewhat like the curve bcd in Figure 6.4.

From the discussion in Section IV.B, recall that the concavity of the efficient set curve in the mean–standard deviation portfolio model follows

[30] We should note that the efficient set theorem for symmetric stable return distributions was established before the introduction of the market model specification of the return-generating process. The efficient set theorem is a consequence of consumer risk aversion and two-parameter distributions of portfolio returns and does not require the more restrictive specification of the return-generating process provided by the market model.

from the fact that any portfolio p formed from two assets or portfolios i and j according to

$$\tilde{R}_p = x\tilde{R}_i + (1-x)\tilde{R}_j, \qquad 0 < x < 1, \tag{6.76}$$

has

$$E(\tilde{R}_p) = xE(\tilde{R}_i) + (1-x)E(\tilde{R}_j), \tag{6.77}$$

$$\sigma(\tilde{R}_p) \leq x\sigma(\tilde{R}_i) + (1-x)\sigma(\tilde{R}_j); \tag{6.78}$$

that is, the expected portfolio return is just the average of the expected returns on i and j, whereas the standard deviation of the portfolio return is equal to or less than the corresponding average of the standard deviations of $\tilde{R}_i$ and $\tilde{R}_j$, with Equation (6.78) holding as an equality only when either (1) one of i or j is riskless or (2) there is an exact linear relationship between $\tilde{R}_i$ and $\tilde{R}_j$. We now argue that these results also hold when returns are generated by the market model and the characteristic exponent $1 < \alpha \leq 2$, except that now we interpret $\sigma(\tilde{R}_p)$ more generally as return dispersion rather than as standard deviation.

First, from Equation (6.73) we see immediately that Equation (6.77) holds in the symmetric stable market model, so that we can concentrate our attention on Equation (6.78). But remember that in the mean–standard deviation model Equation (6.78) is just a representation of the fact that diversification is a dispersion-reducing activity. The analysis of the effects of diversification in the preceding section showed that this is also true in the symmetric stable market model as long as the characteristic exponent α of the return-generating process is greater than 1. It may be helpful, however, to illustrate this result again and from a viewpoint a little closer to the current context.

Thus suppose that $\tilde{R}_i$ and $\tilde{R}_j$ in Equation (6.76) are the returns on two individual assets. From Equation (6.72) note that when the returns on the components of a portfolio are generated by the market model, portfolio returns also follow the market model; that is,

$$\tilde{R}_p = a_p + b_p\tilde{M} + \tilde{\epsilon}_p,$$

where
$$a_p = \sum_{j=1}^{N} x_j a_j, \qquad b_p = \sum_{j=1}^{N} x_j b_j, \qquad \tilde{\epsilon}_p = \sum_{j=1}^{N} x_j \tilde{\epsilon}_j.$$

Thus with a two-asset portfolio

$$\sigma(\tilde{R}_p) = [\sigma^\alpha(\tilde{M}) \mid b_p \mid^\alpha + \sigma^\alpha(\tilde{\epsilon}_p)]^{1/\alpha} \tag{6.79a}$$

$$= [\sigma^\alpha(\tilde{M}) \mid xb_i + (1-x)b_j \mid^\alpha + (x^\alpha \sigma^\alpha(\tilde{\epsilon}_i) + (1-x)^\alpha \sigma^\alpha(\tilde{\epsilon}_j))]^{1/\alpha}. \tag{6.79b}$$

Similarly, the dispersion parameters of the distributions of $\tilde{R}_i$ and $\tilde{R}_j$ are

$$\sigma(\tilde{R}_i) = [\sigma^\alpha(\tilde{M}) \mid b_i \mid^\alpha + \sigma^\alpha(\tilde{\epsilon}_i)]^{1/\alpha}$$

and
$$\sigma(\tilde{R}_j) = [\sigma^\alpha(\tilde{M}) \mid b_j \mid^\alpha + \sigma^\alpha(\tilde{\epsilon}_j)]^{1/\alpha}.$$

Hence when asset and portfolio returns are generated by the market model, return dispersion arises from two sources, the market factor $\tilde{M}$ and the residual term $\tilde{\epsilon}$. The contribution of the market factor term to total return dispersion depends on the magnitude of the "sensitivity coefficient" b, and for the portfolio of assets i and j, $b_p = xb_i + (1 - x)b_j$ is just an average of the coefficients for the individual assets. In short, the market factor $\tilde{M}$ is common to the returns on both assets, and forming a portfolio does not in itself reduce the effects of $\tilde{M}$ on return dispersion. Rather, the effects of diversification come from the residual term $\tilde{\epsilon}_p$, where we have

$$\sigma(\tilde{\epsilon}_p) = [x^\alpha \sigma^\alpha(\tilde{\epsilon}_i) + (1 - x)^\alpha \sigma^\alpha(\tilde{\epsilon}_j)]^{1/\alpha} < x\sigma(\tilde{\epsilon}_i) + (1 - x)\sigma(\tilde{\epsilon}_j) \quad (6.80)$$

as long as $\alpha > 1$ and neither $\sigma(\tilde{\epsilon}_i)$ nor $\sigma(\tilde{\epsilon}_j)$ is identically 0.

The reader can convince himself that, as in the mean–standard deviation model, Equation (6.78) holds as an equality in the symmetric stable market model with $\alpha > 1$ when (1) either i or j is riskless, that is, $\sigma(\tilde{R}_i) = 0$ or $\sigma(\tilde{R}_j) = 0$, or (2) there is an exact linear relationship between $\tilde{R}_i$ and $\tilde{R}_j$. And the latter can happen only when $\sigma(\tilde{\epsilon}_i) = \sigma(\tilde{\epsilon}_j) = 0$, that is, the returns on both securities can be perfectly predicted from $\tilde{M}$, a case which, according to the empirical evidence of Blume [11], can be ignored. If either (1) or (2) holds, the combinations of $E(\tilde{R}_p)$ and $\sigma(\tilde{R}_p)$ obtained by varying x in Equation (6.76) lie along a straight line in the $E(\tilde{R}_p)$, $\sigma(\tilde{R}_p)$ plane between the points representing the assets i and j. Otherwise Equation (6.78) holds, and the $E(\tilde{R}_p)$, $\sigma(\tilde{R}_p)$ combinations obtained by varying x in Equation (6.76) lie to the left of the line between i and j. And this is all again precisely as in the mean–standard deviation model.[31]

V.C.4. Consumer equilibrium

In short, the fact that diversification is a dispersion-reducing activity implies that Equation (6.78) holds when returns are generated by the symmetric stable market model with $\alpha > 1$. Then using arguments identical with those used earlier in the mean–standard deviation model, we can show that Equations (6.77) and (6.78) together imply that the efficient set curve is positively sloping and concave in the $E(\tilde{R})$, $\sigma(\tilde{R})$ plane, somewhat like the curve bcd in Figure 6.4. We have already argued that the consumer's

---

[31] The analysis is somewhat more tedious, although not more difficult, when i and j themselves can be portfolios. In particular, the expression for $\sigma(\tilde{\epsilon}_p)$ is more complicated than Equation (6.80). But the reader can verify that the results are the same.

indifference curves of $E(\tilde{R})$ against $\sigma(\tilde{R})$ in the stable model have the same general properties as those of the mean–standard deviation model. Thus Figure 6.5 is again a relevant picture of consumer equilibrium; that is, again consumer equilibrium is represented by a point of tangency between a convex indifference curve and the concave efficient boundary.[32]

VI. CONCLUSIONS

Our discussion of the one-period two-parameter model of optimal consumption-investment decisions is now complete. We turn in the next chapter to a model of capital market equilibrium for which this consumption-investment model is the basic building block.

REFERENCES

The pioneering works on the mean–standard deviation portfolio model are

1. Markowitz, Harry, *Portfolio Selection: Efficient Diversification of Investments.* New York: John Wiley & Sons, Inc., 1959.
2. Tobin, James, "Liquidity Preference as Behavior towards Risk," *Review of Economic Studies*, vol. 25 (February 1958), pp. 65–86.
3. Tobin, James, "The Theory of Portfolio Selection," in *The Theory of Interest Rates*, F. H. Hahn and F. P. R. Brechling, eds. London: Macmillan & Co., Ltd., 1965, chap. 1.

The so-called market model in the present chapter was first suggested by Markowitz [1, pp. 96–100]. The mean–standard deviation version of the model was then studied in detail by

4. Sharpe, William F., "A Simplified Model for Portfolio Analysis," *Management Science*, vol. 9 (January 1963), pp. 277–293.

The model was then applied to the class of symmetric stable distributions by

5. Fama, Eugene F., "Portfolio Analysis in a Stable Paretian Market," *Management Science*, vol. 11 (January 1965), pp. 404–419.

Statistical background on the stable class of distributions, discovered by Lévy [8], is in

6. Feller, William, *An Introduction to Probability Theory and Its Applications*, vol. II. New York: John Wiley & Sons, Inc., 1966, chaps. 6 and 17.
7. Gnedenko, B. V., and A. N. Kolmogorov, *Limit Distributions for Sums of Independent Random Variables*, K. L. Chung, trans. Reading, Mass.: Addison-Wesley Publishing Company, Inc., 1954, chap. 7.
8. Lévy, Paul, *Calcul des Probabilités*. Paris: Gauthier-Villars, 1925, part II, chap. 6.

---

[32] The interested reader might also check that the algebraic results obtained for the mean–standard deviation model in Sec. IV.C also carry over easily to the symmetric stable model in this section.

9. Fama, Eugene F., and Richard Roll, "Some Properties of Symmetric Stable Distributions," *Journal of the American Statistical Association*, vol. 63 (September 1968), pp. 817–836.

10. Fama, Eugene F., and Richard Roll, "Parameter Estimates for Symmetric Stable Distributions," *Journal of the American Statistical Association*, vol. 66 (June 1971). pp. 331–338.

References 9 and 10 are particularly concerned with problems of estimation. Empirical work cited in this chapter on the distributions of security returns is in

11. Blume, Marshall E., "The Assessment of Portfolio Performance: An Application of Portfolio Theory." Unpublished Ph.D. dissertation, Graduate School of Business, University of Chicago, March, 1968. Many of the results in this thesis are summarized in Professor Blume's paper, "Portfolio Theory: A Step toward Its Practical Application," *Journal of Business*, vol. 43 (April 1970), pp. 152–173.

12. Fama, Eugene F., "The Behavior of Stock Market Prices," *Journal of Business*, vol. 38 (January 1965), pp. 34–105.

13. Kendall, M. G., "The Analysis of Economic Time-Series," *Journal of the Royal Statistical Society (Series A)*, vol. 96 (1953), pp. 11–25.

14. King, Benjamin F., "Market and Industry Factors in Stock Price Behavior," *Journal of Business*, vol. 39 (January 1966), pp. 139–190.

15. Mandelbrot, Benoit, "The Variation of Certain Speculative Prices," *Journal of Business*, vol. 36 (October 1963), pp. 394–419.

16. Moore, Arnold, "A Statistical Analysis of Common Stock Prices." Unpublished Ph.D. dissertation, Graduate School of Business, University of Chicago, 1962.

17. Roll, Richard, *The Behavior of Interest Rates: The Application of the Efficient Market Model to U.S. Treasury Bills*. New York: Basic Books, Inc., Publishers, 1970.

7

RISK, RETURN, AND MARKET EQUILIBRIUM

I. INTRODUCTION

In Chapter 6 a model of consumer equilibrium for the two-period consumption-investment problem was presented. In the present chapter the implications of this model for a theory of capital market equilibrium under uncertainty are considered. Specifically, we are concerned with the following questions: Given a market of risk-averse, expected utility–maximizing consumers, (1) what is the appropriate measure of the risk of an asset, and (2) what is the relationship in equilibrium between this measure of the asset's risk and its one-period expected return?

The asset-pricing model to be presented in the present chapter is the natural extension of the consumption-investment model in Chapter 6. The consumption-investment model is concerned with how the risk-averse, expected utility–maximizing consumer should allocate his initial wealth w_1 between consumption c_1 and a portfolio investment $h_1 = w_1 - c_1$ in the various assets available in the market. The asset-pricing model then draws the aggregate implications of the wealth allocation decisions of individual consumers for the equilibrium relationship between risk and expected return for assets and portfolios.

II. THE MARKET SETTING

The market setting in which equilibrium must be established is assumed to be as follows.

Perfect Markets. First, markets for consumption goods and investment assets are assumed to be perfect in the sense that all goods and assets are infinitely divisible; any information is costless and available to everybody; there are no transactions costs or taxes; all individuals pay the same price for any given commodity or asset; no individual is wealthy enough to affect the market price of any asset; and no firm is large enough to affect the opportunity set facing consumers. In short, as in most of the rest of this book, individual consumers and firms are assumed to be price takers in frictionless markets.

Firms. It is assumed that all production is organized by "firms." At the beginning of period 1 firms purchase, and pay for, the services of inputs—labor, machinery, and so on—and use these to produce consumption goods and services to be sold at the beginning of period 2. Firms finance their period 1 outlays for production by issuing shares in their period 2 market values (= sales of output), and these shares are the investment assets held by consumers. It is the process by which the period 1 market prices of such assets are determined that is the main concern here.

Consumers. The model of consumer equilibrium is that in Chapter 6. Briefly, at the beginning of period 1, consumers are assumed to have given quantities of resources—labor, which will be sold to some firm, and portfolio assets, that is, shares of firms, carried forward from previous periods—that must be allocated to current consumption c_1, measured in terms of some numéraire—for example, "dollars"—and a portfolio investment whose market value at the beginning of period 2 determines the level of consumption c_2 for period 2. Consumers are all risk-averse expected utility maximizers; that is, in his period 1 consumption-investment decision, each consumer behaves as if he were trying to maximize expected utility with respect to a utility of consumption function $U(c_1, c_2)$ that is monotone-increasing and strictly concave in (c_1, c_2).

Moreover, every consumer believes that, or better, behaves as if distributions of one-period returns on all portfolios can be fully described in terms of two parameters, expected return $E(\tilde{R}_p)$ and some measure of return dispersion $\sigma(\tilde{R}_p)$. From Chapter 6 we know that this implies that the consumer behaves as if distributions of returns on all portfolios are symmetric stable with the same value of the characteristic exponent α, for example, normal distributions when $\alpha = 2$. From the previous chapter we also know that the combination of consumer risk aversion and two-parameter return distributions implies the "efficient set theorem": that is, the optimal portfolio for a given consumer is $E(\tilde{R}_p)$, $\sigma(\tilde{R}_p)$ efficient, where portfolio efficiency requires that no portfolio with the same or higher expected return $E(\tilde{R}_p)$ has lower return dispersion $\sigma(\tilde{R}_p)$.

Market Equilibrium. Equilibrium at the beginning of period 1 is assumed to be reached through a process of tâtonnement with recontracting; that is, investors come to market with their resources and tastes, and firms bring their production opportunity sets. A tentative set of prices for consumption goods, labor, and shares is announced, firms make tentative production decisions, and investors offer their labor to firms and begin bidding for consumption goods and investment assets. Prices and decisions are tentative; it is agreed that no decisions are executed until an equilibrium set of prices, that is, a set of prices at which all markets can clear, has been determined.

Our treatment of this model concentrates on the nature of equilibrium in the capital market; that is, we take equilibrium in the markets for labor and consumption goods as given. And the order of presentation is a bit illogical. In particular, to emphasize that all prices and decisions are simultaneously determined and executed, it would be best, if possible, to consider first the characteristics of capital market equilibrium, that is, the relationship between risk and return, and then move on to partial equilibrium studies of the nature of optimal consumption-investment decisions by individuals and optimal production decisions by firms.

But the analysis cannot proceed in this way. The "risk structure" of equilibrium expected returns on shares can only be determined from properties of optimal consumption-investment decisions by individuals. Then the implications of the risk structure of equilibrium expected returns for optimal production decisions by firms can be considered. In short, although in our world everything happens at once, the analysis proceeds from partial equilibrium (consumer-investors) to market equilibrium to partial equilibrium (firms). Thus the first step is to discuss the appropriate measure of the risk of an individual asset and the relationship between risk and expected return from the viewpoint of an individual consumer. We then generalize these concepts to the level of the market.[1]

We concentrate initially on the case in which all portfolio return distributions are assumed to be normal. Or more accurately, consumers are assumed to behave as if all portfolio return distributions are normal. But we show later that the major results also hold when the two-parameter portfolio return distributions are symmetric stable with characteristic exponent $\alpha < 2$.

III. RISK AND EXPECTED RETURN FROM THE VIEWPOINT OF A CONSUMER

A consumer comes to market at period 1 with resources, that is, his labor and shares of firms purchased in earlier periods, whose value will not be known until a set of equilibrium prices has been determined. When a market equilibrium is reached, the market value of the consumer's resources or his wealth w_1 will be determined, and there will be an optimal allocation of w_1 between initial consumption c_1 and investment $h_1 = w_1 - c_1$. We show now how the risk of an asset to the consumer and the relationship between its risk and expected return can be obtained from what we already know about the properties of an optimal portfolio decision.

III.A. The Risks of Assets and Portfolios

The consumer invests at period 1 only to obtain consumption for period 2. His consumption for period 2 is the period 2 market value of his portfolio. Thus the consumer's sole concern in his period 1 investment decision is the probability distribution on period 2 portfolio market value that he obtains. It is logical, then, that the risk of an individual asset to the consumer must be measured by its contribution to the risk of his portfolio.

With normally distributed portfolio returns, we know that the consumer finds it possible to summarize the distribution of the period 2 market value of any portfolio in terms of two parameters—the expected one-period return on the portfolio, $E(\tilde{R}_p)$, and the standard deviation of the one-period return,

---

[1] A note for the more sophisticated: We use the term "market equilibrium" in recognition of the fact that we always work conditional on an assumed equilibrium in the markets for labor and consumption goods. A full general equilibrium model would allow for simultaneous determination of prices in these markets as well as in the capital market.

In essence, we examine the characteristics of capital market equilibrium, given a general equilibrium, that is, simultaneous equilibrium in all markets. And we further break the given general equilibrium down into partial equilibrium analyses of the consumer and the firm. Thus we look at the roles played by the consumer, the firm, and the capital market in a given general equilibrium.

$\sigma(\tilde{R}_p)$. In this context, it is relevant to think of $\sigma(\tilde{R}_p)$ as a measure of the risk of the portfolio p. Thus the risk of an individual asset in the portfolio p is measured by its contribution to $\sigma(\tilde{R}_p)$. Likewise in looking at the expected return on an asset, the consumer is only concerned with how it contributes to the expected return on the portfolio.

The mean and standard deviation of the return on the portfolio p are

$$E(\tilde{R}_p) = \sum_{j=1}^{N} x_{jp}E(\tilde{R}_j), \tag{7.1a}$$

$$\sigma(\tilde{R}_p) = \left[\sum_{i=1}^{N}\sum_{j=1}^{N} x_{ip}x_{jp}\sigma_{ij}\right]^{1/2}. \tag{7.1b}$$

Here $\tilde{R}_j$ is the return on asset j, and the tilde again indicates that the return is a random variable; $\sigma_{ij} = \text{cov}\,(\tilde{R}_i,\tilde{R}_j)$; and x_{jp} is the proportion of asset j in the portfolio p, so that[2]

$$\sum_{j=1}^{N} x_{jp} = 1.$$

The expected return on the portfolio p is just the weighted average of the expected returns on the individual assets in the portfolio. Thus the contribution of any asset to the expected portfolio return depends directly on the expected return on the asset.

Likewise, the standard deviation of the return on p is made up of a weighted average of the pairwise covariances between the returns on individual assets. To determine the contribution of an individual asset, say, asset i, to $\sigma(\tilde{R}_p)$, it is helpful to break Equation (7.1b) down as follows:

$$\sigma(\tilde{R}_p) = \frac{\sigma^2(\tilde{R}_p)}{\sigma(\tilde{R}_p)}$$

$$= \frac{\displaystyle\sum_{i=1}^{N}\sum_{j=1}^{N} x_{ip}x_{jp}\sigma_{ij}}{\sigma(\tilde{R}_p)}$$

$$= \sum_{i=1}^{N} x_{ip}\left(\frac{\displaystyle\sum_{j=1}^{N} x_{jp}\sigma_{ij}}{\sigma(\tilde{R}_p)}\right). \tag{7.2}$$

[2] This is a change in notation from Chap. 6, where x_j was used to represent the proportion of investment funds put into asset j. The usefulness of the additional portfolio subscript in the more complicated models in the present chapter should soon become apparent.

Thus the contribution of asset i to the risk or standard deviation of the return on portfolio p depends directly on $\sum_{j=1}^{N} x_{jp}\sigma_{ij}$, the weighted average of the pairwise covariances between the return on asset i and the return on each of the assets in the portfolio. If we measure the risk of asset i in the portfolio p as

$$\frac{\sum_{j=1}^{N} x_{jp}\sigma_{ij}}{\sigma(\tilde{R}_p)} \quad \text{(risk of asset } i \text{ in portfolio } p\text{)}, \tag{7.3}$$

then we see from expressions (7.2) and (7.3) that the portfolio's risk is just the weighted average of the risks of the individual assets.

Two points should be made here. First, note that when we take a portfolio viewpoint, the risk of an individual asset depends on the weights x_{jp} and on $\sigma(\tilde{R}_p)$, both of which vary from portfolio to portfolio. Thus the risk of an asset is not unique; it must always be measured with reference to some specific portfolio. Second, note that the risk of asset i depends on the variance of its return, $\sigma^2(\tilde{R}_i) = \sigma_{ii}$, and on the $N-1$ pairwise covariances of its return with the returns on other assets. Thus in a well-diversified portfolio, that is, a portfolio of many assets with no individual asset accounting for a large part of the total investment, the risk of an asset is likely to depend much more on these covariances than on the variance of the asset's return. But this result was already suggested in Chapter 6 (in the discussion of the "effects of diversification"), and we meet up with it again later.

The development of expressions (7.1) to (7.3) has given us a way to measure the risk of an individual asset. We now want to determine the relationship between risk and expected return that is relevant for a consumer. Again we see that the appropriate expected return–risk relationship can be obtained from what we already know about the properties of optimal portfolio decisions.

III.B. The Relationship between Risk and Expected Return

Because the consumer is assumed to be risk-averse and capable of summarizing distributions of one-period portfolio returns in terms of mean $E(\tilde{R}_p)$ and standard deviation $\sigma(\tilde{R}_p)$, we know that his optimal portfolio must be efficient. Suppose that in fact the situation is as shown in Figure 7.1; that is, the optimal portfolio is the efficient portfolio with expected return $E(\tilde{R}_e)$ and dispersion $\sigma(\tilde{R}_e)$. The fundamental idea in the analysis of risk from the viewpoint of the consumer is that because the consumer

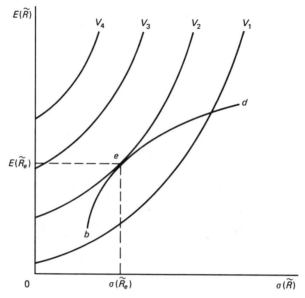

Figure 7.1   Consumer Equilibrium

holds the efficient portfolio e, the risk of any asset to him should be measured by its contribution to the total risk of e. We now show that for the consumer who chooses e the appropriate relationship between risk and expected return is that implicit in the condition that e is efficient.[3]

Reviewing briefly the results in Section IV.C in Chapter 6, the efficient portfolio e is given by the solution to the problem: Choose the proportions x_{jp}, $j = 1, 2, \ldots, N$, invested in the shares of each of the N available firms that

$$\min \sigma(\tilde{R}_p) = \left[\sum_{i=1}^{N} \sum_{j=1}^{N} x_{ip} x_{jp} \sigma_{ij}\right]^{1/2} \tag{7.4a}$$

subject to the constraints

$$E(\tilde{R}_p) = \sum_{j=1}^{N} x_{jp} E(\tilde{R}_j) = E(\tilde{R}_e), \tag{7.4b}$$

$$\sum_{j=1}^{N} x_{jp} = 1. \tag{7.4c}$$

---

[3] The next three paragraphs unavoidably involve the use of partial derivatives. The mathematically wary reader should nevertheless be able to follow the logic of the analysis from the verbal explanations.

The values of x_{jp} that provide the solution to this problem are x_{je}, $j = 1, 2, \ldots, N$, and the minimum value of $\sigma(\tilde{R}_p)$ is of course $\sigma(\tilde{R}_e)$. The x_{je} must satisfy Equations (7.4b), (7.4c), and the "balance equations"

$$E(\tilde{R}_j) - E(\tilde{R}_i) = S_e\left(\frac{\partial\sigma(\tilde{R}_e)}{\partial x_{je}} - \frac{\partial\sigma(\tilde{R}_e)}{\partial x_{ie}}\right), \qquad i, j = 1, 2, \ldots, N, \quad (7.5)$$

where S_e is the slope of the efficient set at the point e in Figure 7.1 and $\partial\sigma(\tilde{R}_e)/\partial x_{je}$ is $\partial\sigma(\tilde{R}_p)/\partial x_{jp}$ evaluated at the optimal values $x_{jp} = x_{je}$, $j = 1, 2, \ldots, N$.[4]

In words, the partial derivative $\partial\sigma(\tilde{R}_p)/\partial x_{jp}$ is the rate of change of the standard deviation of the portfolio return with respect to changes in the proportion of portfolio funds invested in asset j. Equivalently, it is the marginal effect of asset j on the dispersion or risk of the portfolio return. Thus (7.5) is a balance equation in the sense that it tells us how the values of the x's, the proportions invested in individual assets, must be chosen in order to balance properly the differences between the expected returns on assets and the differences between their marginal effects on the dispersion of the portfolio return.

It is, however, useful to transform Equation (7.5) into an expression involving the expected portfolio return $E(\tilde{R}_e)$ and standard deviation $\sigma(\tilde{R}_e)$. Thus first multiply both sides of Equation (7.5) by x_{ie}, and then sum over i to obtain

$$\sum_{i=1}^{N} x_{ie}[E(\tilde{R}_j) - E(\tilde{R}_i)] = S_e\left(\sum_{i=1}^{N} x_{ie}\frac{\partial\sigma(\tilde{R}_e)}{\partial x_{je}} - \sum_{i=1}^{N} x_{ie}\frac{\partial\sigma(\tilde{R}_e)}{\partial x_{ie}}\right).$$

Or because $\sum_{i=1}^{N} x_{ie} = 1$,

$$E(\tilde{R}_j) - E(\tilde{R}_e) = S_e\left(\frac{\partial\sigma(\tilde{R}_e)}{\partial x_{je}} - \sum_{i=1}^{N} x_{ie}\frac{\partial\sigma(\tilde{R}_e)}{\partial x_{ie}}\right). \qquad (7.6)$$

[4] That is, to solve the problem in Equation (7.4) we form the lagrangian

$$L = \sigma(\tilde{R}p) + \lambda_1\left[E(\tilde{R}_e) - \sum_{j=1}^{N} x_{jp}E(\tilde{R}_j)\right] + \lambda_2\left[1 - \sum_{j=1}^{N} x_{jp}\right],$$

differentiate partially with respect to λ_1, λ_2, and x_{jp}, $j = 1, 2, \ldots, N$, and set these derivatives equal to 0, thus obtaining Equations (7.4b), (7.4c), and

$$\frac{\partial L}{\partial x_{jp}} = \frac{\partial\sigma(\tilde{R}_p)}{\partial x_{jp}} - \lambda_1 E(\tilde{R}_j) - \lambda_2 = 0, \qquad j = 1, 2, \ldots, N.$$

Because the shadow price λ_1 is the same for all j and is in fact equal to $1/S_e$, this expression leads directly to Equation (7.5).

But note that, using Equation (7.1b) and the chain rule for differentiation,

$$\frac{\partial \sigma(\tilde{R}_e)}{\partial x_{ie}} = \frac{d\sigma(\tilde{R}_e)}{d\sigma^2(\tilde{R}_e)} \cdot \frac{\partial \sigma^2(\tilde{R}_e)}{\partial x_{ie}} = \frac{\sum_{j=1}^{N} x_{je}\sigma_{ij}}{\sigma(\tilde{R}_e)} . \tag{7.7}$$

Thus the marginal effect of asset i on the standard deviation of the portfolio return is what we have already found to be the risk of asset i, that is, its contribution to the risk (standard deviation) of the portfolio return. And, from Equation (7.2),

$$\sum_{i=1}^{N} x_{ie} \frac{\partial \sigma(\tilde{R}_e)}{\partial x_{ie}} = \sum_{i=1}^{N} x_{ie} \frac{\sum_{j=1}^{N} x_{je}\sigma_{ij}}{\sigma(\tilde{R}_e)} = \sigma(\tilde{R}_e). \tag{7.8}$$

Substituting Equation (7.8) into Equation (7.6), we obtain the new balance equation

$$E(\tilde{R}_j) - E(\tilde{R}_e) = S_e \left(\frac{\partial \sigma(\tilde{R}_e)}{\partial x_{je}} - \sigma(\tilde{R}_e) \right), \qquad j = 1, 2, \ldots, N. \tag{7.9}$$

Or equivalently, using Equation (7.7),

$$E(\tilde{R}_j) - E(\tilde{R}_e) = S_e \left(\frac{\sum_{k=1}^{N} x_{ke}\sigma_{jk}}{\sigma(\tilde{R}_e)} - \sigma(\tilde{R}_e) \right). \tag{7.10}$$

In words, to form the efficient portfolio with expected return $E(\tilde{R}_e)$, the proportions x_{ke} invested in individual assets must be such that the difference between the expected return on the asset and the expected return on the portfolio is proportional to the difference between the marginal effect of the asset on $\sigma(\tilde{R}_e)$ and the weighted average of these marginal effects, which weighted average is just $\sigma(\tilde{R}_e)$, and where the proportionality factor S_e is the slope of the efficient set at the point e.

But the balance equation (7.10) can also be interpreted as the relevant relation between the risk of an asset and its expected return for a consumer who chooses the portfolio e. In a market in which one-period returns on all portfolios are normal, a risk-averse consumer finds it possible to summarize the distribution of return for any portfolio in terms of two parameters, expected return $E(\tilde{R}_p)$ and standard deviation $\sigma(\tilde{R}_p)$. In this context it is valid to think of $\sigma(\tilde{R}_p)$ as measuring the risk of the distribution of $\tilde{R}_p$: For a given value of $E(\tilde{R}_p)$, the risk-averse consumer always prefers a lower value of $\sigma(\tilde{R}_p)$ to a higher value. If his optimal portfolio is the efficient portfolio with expected return $E(\tilde{R}_e)$, then $\sigma(\tilde{R}_e)$ measures this portfolio's risk. And the efficiency condition on the portfolio e given by Equation (7.10) can then be interpreted as the relationship between expected return and risk for an individual asset, measured relative to the efficient portfolio e; that is, the difference between the expected returns on an asset and on the portfolio is proportional to the difference between the risk of the asset and the risk of the portfolio.[5]

Before concluding this discussion of risk and the relationship between risk and expected return from the viewpoint of the consumer, we wish to make two points.

First, note that

$$\text{cov } (\tilde{R}_i, \tilde{R}_e) = \text{cov } (\tilde{R}_i, \sum_{j=1}^{N} x_{je}\tilde{R}_j) = \sum_{j=1}^{N} x_{je}\sigma_{ij}.$$

Thus, using Equation (7.7),

$$\frac{\sum_{j=1}^{N} x_{je}\sigma_{ij}}{\sigma(\tilde{R}_e)} = \frac{\partial\sigma(\tilde{R}_e)}{\partial x_{ie}} = \frac{\text{cov } (\tilde{R}_i, \tilde{R}_e)}{\sigma(\tilde{R}_e)} . \tag{7.11}$$

In short, we already knew that the risk of an asset i in the portfolio e can be interpreted either as the contribution of the asset to the risk of the portfolio—the first term in Equation (7.11)—or as the marginal effect of the asset on the risk of the portfolio—the second term in Equation (7.11). From (7.11) we now know that cov $(\tilde{R}_i, \tilde{R}_e)/\sigma(\tilde{R}_e)$ is an equivalent measure of the asset's risk, which can now be interpreted as being directly determined by the relationship between the return on the asset and the return on the portfolio.[6]

Finally, the risk of a portfolio is measured by the standard deviation of its return. Because the efficient set curve *bed* shown in Figure 7.1 is non-

---

[5] A note for the more sophisticated: If there are nonnegativity restrictions on the x's, Equation (7.10) applies only to assets that appear in the portfolio e at a nonzero level. But we should not expect to be able to use the portfolio e to measure the risks of assets that do not appear in e. Moreover, the risks of such assets are not really relevant to the consumer who chooses this portfolio.

[6] Recall that cov $(\tilde{R}_i, \tilde{R}_e)$ is a measure of the relationship between the return on asset i and the return on the portfolio e. For example, the correlation coefficient corr $(\tilde{R}_i, \tilde{R}_e)$ between $\tilde{R}_i$ and $\tilde{R}_e$ is

$$\text{corr } (\tilde{R}_i, \tilde{R}_e) = \frac{\text{cov } (\tilde{R}_i, \tilde{R}_e)}{\sigma(\tilde{R}_i)\sigma(\tilde{R}_e)} .$$

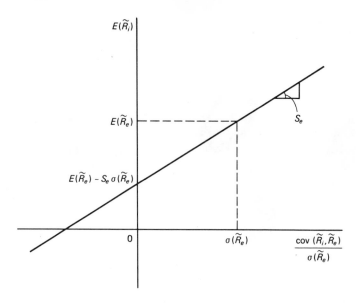

Figure 7.2   Expected Return–Risk Relationship for Individual Assets That Is
Relevant for the Consumer Who Chooses the Efficient Portfolio e

linear, as far as portfolios are concerned, the consumer faces a nonlinear
trade-off of expected return for risk. For any given efficient portfolio,
however, the risk of an asset is measured by its contribution to the standard
deviation of the return on the portfolio, and the relationship between the
expected return on an asset and its risk is always linear; that is, for any
given efficient portfolio e the values of $E(\tilde{R}_e)$, $\sigma(\tilde{R}_e)$, and S_e in the balance
equation (7.10) are the same for all assets. Thus in this equation the
relationship between the expected return on an asset and its risk is linear
and might, for example, be as shown in Figure 7.2. From Equation (7.10),
the slope of the expected return–risk line in Figure 7.2 is S_e; its intercept
on the vertical axis is $E(\tilde{R}_e) - S_e\sigma(\tilde{R}_e)$, the expected return on an asset
whose return has zero covariance with the return on e.

IV. RISK AND EXPECTED RETURN FOR THE MARKET

From the viewpoint of the individual risk-averse consumer—and he is,
after all, the one who bears the risk of his chosen portfolio—the preceding
analysis provides a complete description of appropriate procedures for
measuring the risks of assets and the relationship between risk and expected
return. The results of such an analysis, however, are likely to depend on the

particular consumer under consideration, because (1) the risk of an asset to the consumer is measured relative to the particular portfolio that is optimal for him and (2) his picture of the efficient set itself depends on subjective estimates of the parameters of the portfolio model that may be specific to him.[7]

But although risk is ultimately an individual matter, the goal of the asset-pricing model is to develop testable aggregate or market implications of the expected return–risk relations for individual consumers that arise naturally within the context of the two-parameter models of consumer equilibrium. We have the intuitive feeling that in a market of risk-averse investors, there must be some way of deriving expected return–risk relations that also have validity for the market as a whole.

IV.A. Homogeneous Expectations and Portfolio Opportunities

One approach to the problem of deriving meaningful aggregate relationships, and one that is common to most of the literature in this area, is to restrict the model further by assuming that expectations and portfolio opportunities are "homogeneous" throughout the market; that is, all consumers have the same set of portfolio opportunities, in terms of the assets that are available, and all view the probability distributions of returns associated with the various available portfolios in the same way.[8] In this case when market equilibrium is attained, all consumers face the same picture of the efficient set, and the expected return–risk relations derived for any given efficient portfolio are relevant for all investors who choose this portfolio. Moreover, consumers agree on the expected return–risk relations that apply to any particular efficient portfolio. Thus it seems valid to say that in this situation there are expected return–risk relations that make sense at the level of the market.

---

[7] But it is important to emphasize that the fact that consumers may face different pictures of the efficient set and may perceive risk-return relations differently in itself poses no problem for the determination of a market equilibrium. Market equilibrium simply requires a set of market-clearing prices; that is, equilibrium prices of shares must be such that when consumers make their consumption-investment decisions and firms make their production decisions, all desired exchanges of investment assets take place and the market is cleared of all outstanding units of all assets; that is, demand equals supply for each asset.

[8] See Sharpe [7], Lintner [8,9], Mossin [10], and Fama [11]. It may be helpful to think of the homogeneous expectations assumption as a way of concentrating on the pure effects of "objective" uncertainty on the pricing of investment assets.

IV.B. The Role of a Riskless Asset

But unfortunately the model still lacks empirical content. To test an equation like (7.10), it is necessary to know the exact composition, that is, the values of the x_{je}, of some efficient portfolio and the slope of the efficient set at the point corresponding to this portfolio. The assumption of homogeneous expectations and portfolio opportunities has not provided us, as uninvolved observers, with this information. One way out of this dilemma is to restrict the model even further by assuming that there is a riskless asset f, that is, $\sigma(R_f) = 0$, and all consumers can borrow or lend at the riskless rate R_f.

As we saw in Chapter 6, the presence of riskless borrowing-lending opportunities greatly simplifies the determination of the efficient set of portfolios. Consider portfolios of f and any risky asset or portfolio a that are formed according to

$$\tilde{R}_p = xR_f + (1 - x)\tilde{R}_a, \qquad x \leq 1. \tag{7.12}$$

The expected value and standard deviation of $\tilde{R}_p$ are

$$E(\tilde{R}_p) = xR_f + (1 - x)E(\tilde{R}_a),$$

$$\sigma(\tilde{R}_p) = (1 - x)\sigma(\tilde{R}_a).$$

Thus, as shown in Figure 7.3, the graph of $E(\tilde{R}_p)$ against $\sigma(\tilde{R}_p)$ for port-

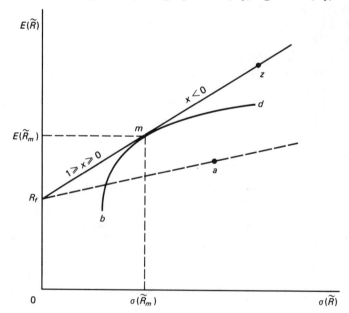

Figure 7.3   Portfolio Opportunities with Riskless Borrowing and Lending

folios formed according to Equation (7.12) is a straight line from R_f through a. Points between R_f and a on the line correspond to lending portfolios (that is, $0 \leq x \leq 1$), and points above a represent borrowing portfolios $(x < 0)$.

The efficient set in the presence of riskless borrowing-lending opportunities is now easily determined. Take a straight line from R_f and rotate it upward and to the left in Figure 7.3 until it can be moved no further without leaving the feasible set. This leads to the line from R_f through m. Except for m, points along bmd no longer represent efficient portfolios; at given levels of $E(\tilde{R})$ there are portfolios along $R_f mz$ that provide lower levels of $\sigma(\tilde{R})$. Portfolios along $R_f mz$ are formed according to

$$\tilde{R}_p = xR_f + (1 - x)\tilde{R}_m, \qquad x \leq 1. \qquad (7.13)$$

Thus when it is possible both to borrow and lend at the rate R_f, the only difference between any two efficient portfolios is in the proportion x invested in the riskless asset f. More risky efficient portfolios—those above m on the efficient set line in Figure 7.3—involve borrowing $(x < 0)$ and investing all available funds, including borrowings, in the risky combination m. Less risky portfolios—those along the line segment $R_f m$—involve lending $(1 \geq x \geq 0)$ some funds at R_f and investing remaining funds in m. The particular portfolio that a consumer chooses depends on his attitudes toward risk and expected return, but optimum portfolios for all investors are just combinations of f and m. There is no incentive for anyone to hold risky assets not included in m. Thus if Figure 7.3 is to represent market equilibrium, m must be the market portfolio; that is, m consists of all assets in the market, each entering the portfolio with weight equal to the ratio of its total market value to the total market value of all assets.[9] In addition, the riskless rate R_f must be such that net borrowings are 0; that is, at the rate R_f the total quantity of funds that people want to borrow is equal to the quantity that others want to lend.

The market portfolio m is efficient; thus the balance equation (7.9) must hold for m, so that

$$E(\tilde{R}_j) - E(\tilde{R}_m) = S_m\left(\frac{\partial \sigma(\tilde{R}_m)}{\partial x_{jm}} - \sigma(\tilde{R}_m)\right), \qquad j = 1, 2, \ldots, N. \qquad (7.14)$$

Noting from Figure 7.3 that $S_m = [E(\tilde{R}_m) - R_f]/\sigma(\tilde{R}_m)$, with some

[9] That is, for $j = 1, 2, \ldots, N$, in the market portfolio m,

$$x_{jm} = \frac{\text{Total market value of all outstanding shares in firm } j}{\text{Total market value of all outstanding shares of all firms}}.$$

excess return / risk

contribution to risk of asset j

rearrangement of terms, Equation (7.14) can be rewritten

$$E(\tilde{R}_j) = R_f + \left[\frac{E(\tilde{R}_m) - R_f}{\sigma(\tilde{R}_m)} \right] \frac{\partial \sigma(\tilde{R}_m)}{\partial x_{jm}}, \quad j = 1, 2, \ldots, N. \quad (7.15)$$

But this is more than a balance equation that helps determine the proportions x_{jm}, $j = 1, 2, \ldots, N$, necessary to form the efficient portfolio with expected return $E(\tilde{R}_m)$. There is no question of choosing the optimal proportions invested in each asset in forming this particular efficient portfolio; with homogeneous expectations and riskless borrowing-lending opportunities, in equilibrium market prices and expected returns on individual shares must be such that the optimal proportions are those associated with the market portfolio m. Thus in this case Equation (7.15) represents a condition on market prices and expected returns that must be met in equilibrium.

Moreover, the only risky assets that any consumer holds are shares in the market portfolio m. Thus it seems that for everyone who is actively in the market, the risk of an individual asset j is appropriately measured by $\partial \sigma(\tilde{R}_m)/\partial x_{jm}$, the marginal effect of the asset on the dispersion in the distribution of $\tilde{R}_m$, and Equation (7.15) is the appropriate relationship between risk and expected return. In this sense, then, Equation (7.15) is an expected return–risk relation for the market as a whole. Thus the assumptions of homogeneous expectations and riskless borrowing-lending opportunities have carried us to our goal: We have a picture of market equilibrium that implies a measure of risk for individual assets and a relationship between risk and equilibrium expected return that are relevant at both the level of the individual consumer and that of the market.

IV.C. Interpretation

These are the fundamental results of the present chapter, and it is useful to discuss them a bit more. We first reconsider briefly the measurement of risk and the relationship between risk and expected return. Then we examine the two key assumptions (1) that consumers have homogeneous expectations and (2) that there are riskless borrowing-lending opportunities.

IV.C.1. Risk and expected return in the market portfolio

From Equation (7.11) we know that

marginal contribution of risk for asset j

$$\frac{\partial \sigma(\tilde{R}_m)}{\partial x_{jm}} = \frac{\sum_{k=1}^{N} x_{km}\sigma_{kj}}{\sigma(\tilde{R}_m)};$$

that is, as for any portfolio, $\partial\sigma(\tilde{R}_m)/\partial x_{jm}$, the marginal effect of asset j on the standard deviation of the return on the market portfolio m, is also the contribution of asset j to the standard deviation or total risk of the return on m. And that is why we say that it measures the risk of j in m. Moreover, in the view of market equilibrium presented here, the only risky assets that consumers hold are shares in m; thus $\partial\sigma(\tilde{R}_m)/\partial x_{jm}$ measures the risk of j for any consumer and the market as a whole.

It is interesting to examine the role that the variance of the one-period return on asset j plays in the determination of its risk and thus of the risk premium in its expected one-period return. The risk of asset j in the market portfolio m can also be written

$$\frac{\partial\sigma(\tilde{R}_m)}{\partial x_{jm}} = \frac{\sum_{k=1}^{N} x_{km}\sigma_{kj}}{\sigma(\tilde{R}_m)} = \frac{x_{jm}\sigma^2(\tilde{R}_j) + \sum_{\substack{k=1\\k\neq j}}^{N} x_{km}\sigma_{kj}}{\sigma(\tilde{R}_m)}.$$

Thus $\sigma^2(\tilde{R}_j) = \sigma_{jj}$ is just one of the N terms that determine the risk of asset j, and N, the total number of assets in the market, is of course quite large. Moreover, recall that x_{jm}, the weight applied to the variance term, is the total market value of all outstanding units of asset j, divided by the total market value of all outstanding units of all assets, so that x_{jm} is likely to be very close to 0. Thus for most assets the variance term in the asset's risk is likely to be trivial relative to the weighted sum of covariances.

But such a result is hardly surprising. In Chapter 6 we showed that in a diversified portfolio the contribution of an individual asset to the standard deviation of the portfolio return depends almost entirely on the average covariance between the return on the asset and the returns on other assets in the portfolio and depends very little on the variance of the asset's return. In essence, the results of the present chapter concerning expected return–risk relationships simply say that in equilibrium an asset's risk is measured from a portfolio point of view.

Finally, from Equation (7.11) we know that there are in fact three equivalent ways of representing the risk of asset j in the market portfolio m:

$$\frac{\partial\sigma(\tilde{R}_m)}{\partial x_{jm}} = \frac{\sum_{k=1}^{N} x_{km}\sigma_{kj}}{\sigma(\tilde{R}_m)} = \frac{\text{cov}(\tilde{R}_j,\tilde{R}_m)}{\sigma(\tilde{R}_m)}; \qquad (7.16)$$

that is, the risk of asset j is directly determined by the covariance of its return with the return on m, and as usual, this covariance measures the relationship between the returns on j and m. With Equation (7.16),

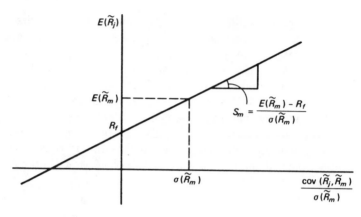

Figure 7.4   Relationship between Expected Return on an Asset and Its Risk When There Is Riskless Borrowing and Lending

Equation (7.15) can be rewritten

$$E(\tilde{R}_j) = R_f + \left[\frac{E(\tilde{R}_m) - R_f}{\sigma(\tilde{R}_m)}\right] \frac{\text{cov}(\tilde{R}_j, \tilde{R}_m)}{\sigma(\tilde{R}_m)}, \qquad j = 1, 2, \ldots, N; \quad (7.17)$$

that is, the equilibrium expected return on any asset j is the riskless rate of interest plus a risk premium that is proportional to the asset's risk. The proportionality factor $S_m = [E(\tilde{R}_m) - R_f]/\sigma(\tilde{R}_m)$ is the same for all assets, and it seems appropriate to interpret this factor as the market price per unit of risk.

Equations (7.17) and (7.15) give us a linear relationship between the expected return on an asset and its risk that might, for example, be as shown in Figure 7.4. It is important to recognize, however, that in two-parameter models the linearity of the relationship between the risk of an asset and its expected return does not depend on either homogeneous expectations or riskless borrowing-lending. Thus, as illustrated in Figure 7.2, Equation (7.10) is a linear expected return–risk relation, derived without either of these assumptions, that is relevant for an investor who chooses the efficient portfolio e. Rather, the role of homogeneous expectations and riskless borrowing-lending is to give a relationship between risk and expected return that is relevant for every investor and so is unambiguously interpreted as a market condition. We now examine each of these assumptions in a little more detail.

IV.C.2. Homogeneous expectations and the riskless asset: a closer look

We first reemphasize that the assumption of homogeneous expectations and portfolio opportunities plays no essential role in either the determination of a market equilibrium or the analysis of the details of consumer equilibrium. A market equilibrium requires a set of asset prices such that all desired exchanges of assets can take place and the market is cleared of all outstanding units of all assets. In short, market equilibrium simply requires a set of asset prices such that supply equals demand for every asset.

Given a set of market-clearing prices, it does not matter to the consumer whether the picture of the efficient set facing him is based on expectations, that is, parameter estimates, that he has in common with everybody in the market or whether the picture results from his personal estimates of expected returns, variances, and covariances on the assets and portfolios available to him. In either case he goes about making an optimal consumption-investment decision in the same way, and as long as he is risk-averse and assumes that portfolio return distributions are normal, his optimal portfolio is always some mean–standard deviation efficient portfolio.

Moreover, once he chooses some efficient portfolio e, from his point of view Equation (7.10) is the relevant relationship between expected return and risk; that is, the fact that the means, variances, and covariances in this expression are personal estimates rather than market expectations does not change the fact that the risk of an individual asset j is measured by his estimate of its effect on the dispersion of the distribution of the return on his portfolio.

In essence, the risk of an individual asset to an investor is always measured relative to the portfolio that he holds, regardless of whether his expectations or his portfolio opportunities are the same as everyone else's. The assumption that expectations and portfolio opportunities are homogeneous throughout the market just simplifies the analysis in that one picture of the efficient set represents market equilibrium for all investors.

With homogeneous expectations and portfolio opportunities, all consumers can agree on the relationship between the expected return on an asset and its risk, measured vis-à-vis any particular efficient portfolio e. But the efficient set is continuous, so that in the absence of a riskless asset, for any given asset j there are an infinite number of risk measures and expected return–risk relationships, one for each different efficient portfolio; that is, for a given asset j, Equation (7.10) must hold for every efficient portfolio. The expected return $E(\tilde{R}_j)$ on asset j and the set of covariances σ_{ij}, $i = 1, 2, \ldots, N$, are the same from portfolio to portfolio, but the set of weights x_{ie}, $i = 1, 2, \ldots, N$, is different, as are the expected return $E(\tilde{R}_e)$, the standard deviation $\sigma(\tilde{R}_e)$, and S_e, the slope of the efficient set at the point e.

Thus in the absence of opportunities to borrow and lend at a riskless rate, the concept of an expected return–risk relationship for the market as a whole is not unambiguous; in this case there are many different efficient portfolios of risky assets and thus many different equilibrium expected return–risk relationships for any given asset. From the viewpoint of an individual investor it is sensible to talk about the risk of an asset and the equilibrium relationship between risk and expected return; with convex indifference curves, his choice of an optimal efficient portfolio is unique. From the viewpoint of the market, however, all we can say is that in equilibrium the trade-off of $E(\tilde{R})$ for $\sigma(\tilde{R})$ along the efficient set must be such that when all consumers make optimal portfolio decisions, the market is cleared of all outstanding units of all assets.

With both homogeneous expectations and riskless borrowing-lending, however, in equilibrium the only risky assets held by any investor are shares in the market portfolio m, so that Equation (7.17) is a relationship between expected return and risk that has unambiguous meaning at the level of the market. Thus it seems clear that the characteristics of consumer and market equilibrium when there is riskless borrowing-lending have much appeal, if only for their simplicity. Nevertheless, admittedly at least the assumption of indefinite riskless borrowing opportunities is somewhat artificial; the borrowings must be repaid from risky portfolio investments, so that, strictly speaking, there is always some chance of at least partial default.

But one must keep the proper perspective. The goal of the asset-pricing model is to develop testable aggregate or market implications of the expected return–risk relations for individual consumers that arise naturally within the context of the two-parameter models of consumer equilibrium. The general idea is that if consumers are trying to choose efficient portfolios, the pricing of investment assets must somehow reflect expected return–risk relations that are appropriate when assets are viewed as components of efficient portfolios. The assumptions of homogeneous expectations and riskless borrowing-lending opportunities are just one specific and straightforward way to give precise form to this general idea. As in any economic model, the value of such assumptions cannot be judged in the abstract but rather depends only on how well the testable implications of the assumptions stand up in the future to the market data that they are meant to explain.

Moreover, if all the implications of this specific model of market equilibrium are not upheld in empirical tests, it does not follow that there is no other model of market equilibrium based on two-parameter portfolio models that can provide a more adequate explanation of the data. For example, intuition tells us that if the pricing of investment assets is in line with portfolio considerations, the market portfolio must be a member of the efficient set. Thus even if we do not assume that there is riskless borrowing and lending, Equation (7.14) is nevertheless a relevant representation of the relationship between risk and expected return. In the absence of riskless borrowing and lending, however, the expected return–risk line given by Equation (7.14) is not as shown in Figure 7.4; that is, because there is no riskless rate, we cannot interpret the intercept and slope of the line in terms of such a rate.

In most general terms, all that we ultimately expect from two-parameter models of market equilibrium is vindication for the two major implications of the two-parameter portfolio models. First, if people are generally risk-averse and make portfolio decisions according to the two-parameter model, then along the set of efficient portfolios, and presuming that we had some way to identify efficient portfolios, we should on average observe a positive trade-off of risk for return. Second, prices of individual investment assets should reflect the presumed attempts of investors to hold efficient portfolios; that is, in any given efficient portfolio we should on average observe a linear relationship between the risk of an asset and its return, where the asset's risk is measured by its contribution to the total risk in the return on the portfolio.

V. EQUILIBRIUM EXPECTED RETURN AND THE MARKET VALUE OF A FIRM

The geometric exposition of the model of market equilibrium is most conveniently carried out in terms of one-period returns on assets and portfolios. In the return form of the model, with homogeneous expectations and riskless borrowing-lending, everyone faces the same picture of the portfolio opportunity set, and this is especially useful in the derivation of an equilibrium relationship between expected return and risk that has clear-cut meaning for the market as a whole.

But of course what are determined in the capital market at period 1 are the prices of investment assets, that is, the prices of the shares of firms. It will now be shown that the expected return–risk relation (7.17) is easily transformed into a pricing equation that relates P_j, the equilibrium market value of firm j at period 1, to its expected period 2 value $E(\tilde{V}_j)$ and to the "risk" of $\tilde{V}_j$.

Because firms are assumed to issue only shares, the return $\tilde{R}_j$ and expected return $E(\tilde{R}_j)$ on the shares of firm j are

$$\tilde{R}_j = \frac{\tilde{V}_j - P_j}{P_j} \quad \text{and} \quad E(\tilde{R}_j) = \frac{E(\tilde{V}_j) - P_j}{P_j}. \qquad (7.18)$$

Thus

$$\tilde{V}_j = P_j(1 + \tilde{R}_j).$$

Likewise, P_m and $\tilde{V}_m$, the market values at periods 1 and 2 of the market portfolio or "market wealth" are

$$P_m = \sum_{j=1}^{N} P_j \quad \text{and} \quad \tilde{V}_m = \sum_{j=1}^{N} \tilde{V}_j.$$

And the relationship between P_m and $\tilde{V}_m$ is

$$\tilde{V}_m = P_m(1 + \tilde{R}_m). \tag{7.19}$$

With these expressions, the covariance between the period 2 values $\tilde{V}_j$ and $\tilde{V}_m$ can be obtained from the covariance between the one-period returns $\tilde{R}_j$ and $\tilde{R}_m$ as follows:

$$\text{cov}\,(\tilde{V}_j, \tilde{V}_m) = \text{cov}\,[P_j(1 + \tilde{R}_j), P_m(1 + \tilde{R}_m)]$$

$$= P_j P_m \,\text{cov}\,(\tilde{R}_j, \tilde{R}_m). \tag{7.20}$$

And, from Equation (7.19),

$$\sigma(\tilde{V}_m) = P_m \sigma(\tilde{R}_m). \tag{7.21}$$

Finally, from Equations (7.20) and (7.21),

$$\frac{\text{cov}\,(\tilde{R}_j, \tilde{R}_m)}{\sigma(\tilde{R}_m)} = \frac{\text{cov}\,(\tilde{V}_j, \tilde{V}_m)}{P_j \sigma(\tilde{V}_m)}. \tag{7.22}$$

The equilibrium market value P_j implied by the equilibrium expected return–risk relation (7.17) is now easily obtained. Substituting Equations (7.18) and (7.22) into (7.17), we get

$$\frac{E(\tilde{V}_j) - P_j}{P_j} = R_f + \left[\frac{E(\tilde{R}_m) - R_f}{\sigma(\tilde{R}_m)}\right] \frac{\text{cov}\,(\tilde{V}_j, \tilde{V}_m)}{P_j \sigma(\tilde{V}_m)}.$$

This in turn implies the pricing equation

$$P_j = \frac{E(\tilde{V}_j) - S_m[\text{cov}\,(\tilde{V}_j, \tilde{V}_m)/\sigma(\tilde{V}_m)]}{1 + R_f}, \tag{7.23}$$

where $S_m = [E(\tilde{R}_m) - R_f]/\sigma(\tilde{R}_m)$, or equivalently, $S_m = [E(\tilde{V}_m) - P_m(1 + R_f)]/\sigma(\tilde{V}_m)$.

To interpret Equation (7.23), first note that

$$\frac{\text{cov}\,(\tilde{V}_j, \tilde{V}_m)}{\sigma(\tilde{V}_m)} = \frac{\text{cov}\,(\tilde{V}_j, \sum_{k=1}^{N} \tilde{V}_k)}{\sigma(\tilde{V}_m)} = \frac{\sum_{k=1}^{N} \text{cov}\,(\tilde{V}_j, \tilde{V}_k)}{\sigma(\tilde{V}_m)},$$

so that
$$\sigma(\tilde{V}_m) = \frac{\sum\limits_{j=1}^{N} \sum\limits_{k=1}^{N} \text{cov}\ (\tilde{V}_j, \tilde{V}_k)}{\sigma(\tilde{V}_m)} = \sum_{j=1}^{N} \frac{\text{cov}\ (\tilde{V}_j, \tilde{V}_m)}{\sigma(\tilde{V}_m)}. \tag{7.24}$$

Thus cov $(\tilde{V}_j, \tilde{V}_m)/\sigma(\tilde{V}_m)$ is the contribution of the period 1 production decision of firm j to $\sigma(\tilde{V}_m)$, the standard deviation of aggregate period 2 wealth. If we interpret $\sigma(\tilde{V}_m)$ as aggregate risk, then cov $(\tilde{V}_j, \tilde{V}_m)/\sigma(\tilde{V}_m)$ measures the risk of firm j.

Next note that, using Equation (7.24) and the fact that $E(\tilde{V}_m) = \sum\limits_{j=1}^{N} E(\tilde{V}_j)$, if we sum over j in Equation (7.23), we get

$$P_m = \frac{E(\tilde{V}_m) - S_m\sigma(\tilde{V}_m)}{1 + R_f}. \tag{7.25}$$

Thus in the two-parameter model, two dimensions, the mean and standard deviation of total period 2 wealth, are priced in the capital market at period 1. The period 1 price of a unit of mean is $1/(1 + R_f)$; the price of a unit of standard deviation is $-S_m/(1 + R_f)$. And from Equation (7.23), the period 1 market value of firm j is just the sum of the market values of (1) the contribution, $E(\tilde{V}_j)$, of the firm's period 1 production decision to expected period 2 market wealth and (2) cov $(\tilde{V}_j, \tilde{V}_m)/\sigma(\tilde{V}_m)$, which is the contribution of the firm to the standard deviation or risk of aggregate period 2 wealth.

To look at these results in a slightly different way, note that the means, covariances, and standard deviations in the pricing equations (7.23) and (7.25) result entirely from the period 1 production decisions of firms. Given the production decisions of firms, all the capital market determines at period 1 are the two prices $1/(1 + R_f)$ and $-S_m/(1 + R_f)$, from which, by way of Equation (7.23), the market values of all firms are obtained.

In aggregate, then, the objects being cleared from the capital market at period 1 are total expected market wealth and risk, $E(\tilde{V}_m)$ and $\sigma(\tilde{V}_m)$. And the units that firm j contributes to both are indistinguishable from those contributed by other firms. This shows up clearly in the pricing equation (7.23), where the market price per unit of expected value, $1/(1 + R_f)$, and the market price per unit of risk, $-S_m/(1 + R_f)$, are the same for all shares. The important implication of all this is that in the two-parameter model no firm is unique in terms of the objects that it brings to the capital market for sale.

This does not mean, of course, that the consumer has no incentive to diversify. Rather, the essence of the model is that risk itself is always meas-ured relative to an efficient portfolio. It is important always to keep in mind that all the expected return–risk results of the present chapter follow from the fact that in the two-parameter portfolio model the risk-averse consumer's optimal portfolio is efficient.

Finally, it is a simple matter to convert Equation (7.23) for the equilibrium period 1 market value of firm j into a pricing equation for individual shares. Let n_j be the number of shares outstanding in firm j, let p_j be the period 1 price of a share, and let $\tilde{v}_j$ be its period 2 value. Then

$$P_j = n_j p_j,$$

$$E(\tilde{V}_j) = n_j E(\tilde{v}_j),$$

$$\operatorname{cov}(\tilde{V}_j, \tilde{V}_m) = n_j \operatorname{cov}(\tilde{v}_j, \tilde{V}_m),$$

so that, from Equation (7.23), we easily obtain

$$p_j = \frac{E(\tilde{v}_j) - S_m[\operatorname{cov}(\tilde{v}_j, \tilde{V}_m)/\sigma(\tilde{V}_m)]}{1 + R_f}. \tag{7.26}$$

We could interpret Equation (7.26) in the same terms as Equations (7.23) and (7.25). Rather than going over old ground, however, let us take a slightly different approach, which likewise applies equally well to Equations (7.23) and (7.25). In particular, note that $p_j(1 + R_f)$ is the market value for certain at period 2 of p_j dollars invested in the riskless asset at period 1. Thus the numerator in Equation (7.26), which is equal to $p_j(1 + R_f)$, is the certainty equivalent of $\tilde{v}_j$; it is the expected market value $E(\tilde{v}_j)$ less an adjustment for the risk of $\tilde{v}_j$. Cov $(\tilde{v}_j, \tilde{V}_m)$ is indeed the appropriate measure of the risk of a share of firm j, because it measures the contribution of a share to $\sigma(\tilde{V}_m)$; that is, $\sigma(\tilde{V}_m) = \sum_{j=1}^{N} n_j \operatorname{cov}(\tilde{v}_j, \tilde{V}_m)/\sigma(\tilde{V}_m)$. The period 1 price of a share is thus the present value, computed at the riskless rate, of the certainty equivalent of the distribution of the share's period 2 value.

It is well to note that we now have at least three comparable measures of the risk of a firm: cov $(\tilde{R}_j, \tilde{R}_m)/\sigma(\tilde{R}_m)$, cov $(\tilde{v}_j, \tilde{V}_m)/\sigma(\tilde{V}_m)$, and cov $(\tilde{V}_j, \tilde{V}_m)/\sigma(\tilde{V}_m)$. The first measures the contribution of firm j to the risk or standard deviation of the rate of return on the market portfolio and so can be interpreted as the risk of the rate of return on firm j and on its shares. The second measures the contribution of a share in firm j to $\sigma(\tilde{V}_m)$, the risk of period 2 market wealth, and so can be interpreted as the risk of the period 2 value of a share. Likewise cov $(\tilde{V}_j, \tilde{V}_m)/\sigma(\tilde{V}_m)$ can be interpreted as the risk of the period 2 market value of firm j or more simply as the total risk of the firm.

VI. OPTIMAL PRODUCTION DECISIONS BY FIRMS

Two of the three steps in the analysis have now been completed. We examined the nature of optimal consumption-investment decisions by consumers, given a market equilibrium. Then we considered the implications of consumer decisions for the risk structure of equilibrium expected returns in the market. The final step is to investigate the implications of optimal consumer decisions and the risk structure of equilibrium expected returns for the characteristics of optimal production or, if you like, investment decisions by firms. In essence, we are now concerned with the fact that outstanding quantities of investment assets (shares in firms) as well as their prices must be determined in the market at the beginning of period 1.

But before proceeding with our analysis of the firm, it is well to note again that, although of necessity we examine separately the characteristics of equilibrium from the viewpoints of the consumer and of the firm, the reader should keep in mind that the production decisions of firms, the consumption-investment decisions of consumers, and the structure of market prices for investment assets are all determined simultaneously in the market at period 1. All these are implied as soon as we say that a market-clearing set of prices has been attained. In the partial equilibrium analyses of consumers and firms, we are looking at those parts of the market or general equilibrium which represent the positions of these microentities.

The first step in the analysis of the firm is to discuss the firm's objective function (the goal of its production decisions). Then this objective function is combined with the results of the asset-pricing model to produce simple production decision rules. The assumptions of homogeneous expectations and riskless borrowing-lending opportunities are maintained throughout.

VI.A. The Firm's Objective Function

At the beginning of period 1 the firm is faced with a production opportunity set, to be defined more precisely below, and it must decide on a production plan that is in the best interests of the shareholders. But this implies two further problems: (1) Which shareholders should the firm be concerned with, current or prospective, and (2) what are the best interests of the shareholders?

There is really nothing that the firm can do for prospective shareholders. When the portfolio decisions of consumers are executed at the beginning of period 1, anyone who decides to hold the shares of the firm during the period pays the equilibrium price and receives the equilibrium trade-off between risk and expected return. Thus when we speak of shareholder interests in the firm's production decision, we refer to those who hold the firm's shares before the market is cleared at the beginning of period 1. But what are the best interests of these shareholders as far as the activities of the firm are concerned?

The shares of firms that the consumer holds before his current portfolio decisions are executed are just part of the resources that he brings to the market. In addition, the assumption of perfect commodity and capital markets presumes that no firm is large enough to have an effect on the opportunity set, that is, the types of goods and assets available and their prices, facing consumers.[10] Thus given that there are no transactions costs and the only consideration in his portfolio decision is maximum expected utility, the choice of optimum portfolio is independent of the assets that happen to comprise the investor's initial resources. It follows that of the factors—initial wealth, utility function, and opportunity set—involved in the consumption-investment decision, the only one that the firm can affect with its production decision is w_1, the market value of initial wealth. Here the best interests of the consumer are clear—more initial wealth is better than less.[11] Or in other words, the firm should choose the production plan that maximizes the wealth of those who come to market with its old shares at the beginning of period 1. And this is equivalent to maximizing $P_j - I_j$, where P_j is the market value of firm j at period 1 and I_j is the "investment" that the firm must make to generate the market value P_j.[12]

We emphasize, however, that the maximize shareholder wealth rule is critically dependent on the perfect market assumption that the firm's production decisions do not affect the equilibrium picture of the efficient

---

[10] For the more sophisticated, we should note that among financial economists the conditions under which the capital market of the two-parameter model can be perfect in this sense have been a subject of substantial debate. Because the issues are rather esoteric, we do not go into them here. The interested reader is referred to Ref. 13.

[11] A more formal proof is as follows. If the individual's initial wealth is increased, one possible, although probably suboptimal, strategy is to use the additional wealth to increase consumption in period 1, leaving the portfolio decision unchanged. Because the marginal expected utility of c_1 is positive, the expected utility for such a strategy must be higher than that associated with the consumption-investment decision that is optimal for the lower level of wealth. Thus an optimal reallocation at the higher wealth level must do at least as well.

[12] In the simplest case the firm just issues new shares at period 1 in the amount I_j, so that $P_j - I_j$ is the value of its old shares. But the reader who understood the discussion of the effects of financing decisions in Chap. 4 will realize that the simplest case is also the general case; that is, $P_j - I_j$ is the contribution of the production decision to the wealth of the old shareholders regardless of how the production decision is financed.

The reader should also recognize that this discussion of the firm's objective function is just an application of the general discussion in Chap. 4 to the specific market context of the two-parameter model.

set. If the firm's activities affect the combinations of $E(\tilde{R})$ and $\sigma(\tilde{R})$ that are available in equilibrium, it affects its shareholders' expected utilities by its effects on their period 1 wealth levels and on the portfolio opportunity set. In principle, both would have to be considered in an optimal production decision, although in practice it is not at all clear how this would be done.

For example, if we dropped the assumption of homogeneous expectations, it would be easy to imagine situations in which some shareholders, who are more optimistic about the investment prospects of the firm than the market as a whole, may want the firm to invest more, although this causes the period 1 market value of their shares to be lower. For these shareholders, the expansion of their perceived opportunity sets, that is, the combinations of $E(\tilde{R})$ and $\sigma(\tilde{R})$ that they perceive to be available, can be more than sufficient to compensate for the loss in wealth that they suffer if the firm invests more than is implied by value maximization.[13]

With perfect markets and homogeneous expectations, however, the maximize shareholder wealth rule has unambiguous meaning, and we now examine its implications in a little more detail.

VI.B. Optimal Production Decisions:
Single-Activity Firms

Given equilibrium values of the capital market prices R_f and S_m, the most direct way for firm j to proceed in maximizing the excess of value over cost, $P_j - I_j$, is to make use of the pricing equation (7.23); that is, the firm looks at the outlays I_j at period 1 that are required in order to generate different combinations of expected period 2 value $E(\tilde{V}_j)$ and risk cov $(\tilde{V}_j, \tilde{V}_m)/\sigma(\tilde{V}_m)$ and then uses Equation (7.23) to determine the period 1 production decision that maximizes $P_j - I_j$.

But although this is the most generally valid description of the path to optimal production decisions, we promised in Chapter 4 eventually to give a less restrictive discussion of the concepts of "risk class" and "cost of capital" than provided in that chapter. Thus we now see what meaning we can give these concepts within the context of the two-parameter model.

For simplicity we initially assume that the firm is only engaged in one "type" of activity, so that its production decision involves choosing the optimal scale of operations. What we mean when we say that the firm is

---

[13] A note for the more sophisticated: The economics literature in general has little to say about the problem of optimal decision making when members of the group affected by the decision disagree about the characteristics of the opportunity set. It is surprising, then, that nonfinance economists tend to slight the finance literature for the apparent dependence of its uncertainty models on the assumption of homogeneous expectations. In fact, almost all uncertainty models in economics take this condition as given. It is just that financial economists are more careful to make the assumption explicit.

engaged in one type of activity is that the value of cov $(\tilde{R}_j,\tilde{R}_m)/\sigma(\tilde{R}_m)$, the risk of the return on its shares, is the same for any production decision that it might make.[14] From Equation (7.17) this assumption implies that the expected return on the market value of the firm is the same for all production decisions; that is, the equilibrium expected return on the market value of the firm is

$$E(\tilde{R}_j) = R_f + \left[\frac{E(\tilde{R}_m) - R_f}{\sigma(\tilde{R}_m)}\right] \frac{\text{cov } (\tilde{R}_j,\tilde{R}_m)}{\sigma(\tilde{R}_m)} . \qquad (7.17)$$

Thus if cov $(\tilde{R}_j,\tilde{R}_m)/\sigma(\tilde{R}_m)$ is the same for all production decisions, $E(\tilde{R}_j)$ is the same for all production decisions.

If $E(\tilde{V}_j)$ is the expected market value of firm j at period 2, in equilibrium the market value of the firm at period 1, P_j, must be such that

$$\frac{E(\tilde{V}_j) - P_j}{P_j} = E(\tilde{R}_j).$$

Or equivalently

$$P_j = \frac{E(\tilde{V}_j)}{1 + E(\tilde{R}_j)}, \qquad (7.27)$$

where the value of $E(\tilde{R}_j)$ is given by Equation (7.17).

If I_j is the investment at period 1 that is required in order to generate the expected market value $E(\tilde{V}_j)$, the one-period expected return on I_j is the value of ρ_j^* that satisfies

$$I_j = \frac{E(\tilde{V}_j)}{1 + \rho_j^*} . \qquad (7.28)$$

It follows easily from Equations (7.27) and (7.28) that additional investment will contribute positively to $P_j - I_j$ as long as

$$\rho_j^* > E(\tilde{R}_j). \qquad (7.29)$$

[14] The more sophisticated reader should be able to show that the assumption that cov $(\tilde{R}_j,\tilde{R}_m)/\sigma(\tilde{R}_m)$ is the same for all production decisions implies that the firm produces mean and risk in fixed proportions; that is, the ratio of the firm's total risk to its expected period 2 value,

$$\frac{[\text{cov } (\tilde{V}_j,\tilde{V}_m)/\sigma(\tilde{V}_m)]}{E(\tilde{V}_j)},$$

is the same for all possible values of $E(\tilde{V}_j)$. Hint: The result can be obtained from Equations (7.22) and (7.23).

Thus the equilibrium expected return $E(\tilde{R}_j)$, as defined by Equation (7.17), can be interpreted as the minimum required expected one-period return or cost of capital for the firm's production activities, which have the risk level implied by cov $(\tilde{R}_j,\tilde{R}_m)/\sigma(\tilde{R}_m)$. And it is clear that the value of cov $(\tilde{R}_j,\tilde{R}_m)/\sigma(\tilde{R}_m)$ determines the firm's risk class in the sense that two firms with the same value of this risk parameter have the same equilibrium expected return and thus the same cost of capital.

We leave it to the reader to show that this definition of a risk class is much less restrictive than that in Chapter 4, where in order to be in the same risk class, the period 2 market values of two firms were assumed to be perfectly correlated and, per dollar of expected value, the distributions of the period 2 values of the firms were assumed to be identical. At this point, the reader should also be able to convince himself that the less restrictive definition of a risk class obtained in the present chapter is the consequence of a more detailed specification of the market context than provided in the general models in Chapter 4.

The production condition in expression (7.29) is easily given a familiar geometric interpretation. Let the boundary of the set of production activities available to firm j be expressed by the transformation function

$$T(E(\tilde{V}_j),I_j) = 0,$$

which tells the maximum amounts of expected market value at the beginning of period 2, $E(\tilde{V}_j)$, that can be obtained with different amounts of investment I_j at the beginning of period 1. For simplicity assume that $E(\tilde{V}_j)$ is a strictly concave function of I_j. Thus if the investment I_j is considered an outlay $-I_j$, the transformation function looks something like the curve OT in Figure 7.5. $P_j - I_j$ is maximized by pushing investment I_j to the point at which the slope of the transformation curve is $-(1 + E(\tilde{R}_j))$, that is, where the marginal expected one-period return on investment is equal to

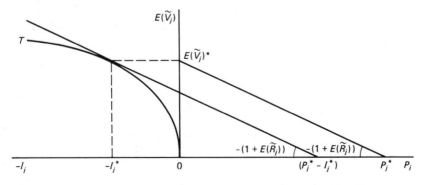

Figure 7.5   Optimal Production Decisions for a Single-Activity Firm

$E(\tilde{R}_j)$, the cost of capital for the firm's productive activities. The optimal investment is I_j^*, which leads to expected market value $E(\tilde{V}_j)^*$ at period 2, which in turn has current market value $P_j^* = E(\tilde{V}_j)^*/[1 + E(\tilde{R}_j)]$. The picture is obviously quite similar to that obtained in Chapter 2 in the analysis of optimal production-investment decisions in a world of perfect certainty and perfect capital markets (see Figure 2.7).

VI.C. Optimal Production Decisions:
Multiple-Activity Firms

In many cases the firm itself is a portfolio of productive activities, each of which produces some probability distribution of market value at the beginning of period 2. The last step in our analysis of optimal production decisions is to develop production criteria that can be applied activity by activity.

Let $\tilde{V}_{kj}$ be the period 2 market value of activity k in firm j, so that $\tilde{V}_j$, the total period 2 value of the firm, is

$$\tilde{V}_j = \sum_{k=1}^{m(j)} \tilde{V}_{kj}, \tag{7.30}$$

where $m(j)$ is the number of activities. It is always possible to define "implicit" or "indirect" period 1 prices P_{kj} for activities such that

$$P_j = \sum_{k=1}^{m(j)} P_{kj}. \tag{7.31}$$

The prices are implicit or indirect, because consumers must buy shares of firm j; they cannot deal directly in the firm's individual production activities. Nevertheless it will now be shown that, like the explicit prices P_j, the implicit prices P_{kj} satisfy Equation (7.23), where the measure of risk is $\mathrm{cov}\,(\tilde{V}_{kj}, \tilde{V}_m)/\sigma(\tilde{V}_m)$, and that optimal production decisions require evaluating each activity in accordance with its own risk and its own equilibrium expected return.

First note that, from Equation (7.30),

$$E(\tilde{V}_j) = \sum_{k=1}^{m(j)} E(\tilde{V}_{kj}) \tag{7.32}$$

and $\quad \mathrm{cov}\,(\tilde{V}_j,\tilde{V}_m) = \mathrm{cov}\,(\sum_{k=1}^{m(j)} \tilde{V}_{kj},\tilde{V}_m) = \sum_{k=1}^{m(j)} \mathrm{cov}\,(\tilde{V}_{kj},\tilde{V}_m). \tag{7.33}$

With Equations (7.31) to (7.33), the equilibrium period 1 market value of firm j, as given by Equation (7.23), can be rewritten

$$P_j = \sum_{k=1}^{m(j)} P_{kj} = \frac{\sum_{k=1}^{m(j)} E(V_{kj}) - S_m \sum_{k=1}^{m(j)} [\text{cov }(V_{kj},V_m)/\sigma(\tilde{V}_m)]}{1 + R_f}$$

Or equivalently

$$P_j = \sum_{k=1}^{m(j)} P_{kj} = \sum_{k=1}^{m(j)} \left\{ \frac{E(\tilde{V}_{kj}) - S_m[\text{cov }(\tilde{V}_{kj},\tilde{V}_m)/\sigma(\tilde{V}_m)]}{1 + R_f} \right\}. \quad (7.34)$$

Thus the period 1 market value of the firm is just the sum of the implicit market values of its production activities, with the implicit market value of an activity obtained by applying the pricing equation (7.23) to the expected period 2 value of the activity, $E(\tilde{V}_{kj})$, and to its risk cov $(\tilde{V}_{kj},\tilde{V}_m)/\sigma(\tilde{V}_m)$. Or in other words, the period 1 value of the firm is just as if the firm sold each of its production activities separately.

But there is nothing at all strange in this result. Remember that in the two-parameter model the objects being cleared from the capital market at period 1 are total expected market wealth at period 2,

$$E(\tilde{V}_m) = \sum_{j=1}^{N} E(\tilde{V}_m) = \sum_{j=1}^{N} \sum_{k=1}^{m(j)} E(\tilde{V}_{kj}),$$

and the total dispersion or risk of market wealth,

$$\sigma(\tilde{V}_m) = \frac{\sum_{j=1}^{N} \text{cov }(\tilde{V}_j,\tilde{V}_m)}{\sigma(\tilde{V}_m)} = \frac{\sum_{j=1}^{N}\sum_{k=1}^{N} \text{cov }(\tilde{V}_{kj},\tilde{V}_m)}{\sigma(\tilde{V}_m)}$$

For all firms the price of a unit of period 2 expected market value is $1/(1 + R_f)$; the price of a unit of risk is $-S_m/(1 + R_f)$. Because the contributions of a firm to total expected market wealth and dispersion of market wealth are just the sums of the expected values and risks of each of its production activities, the market value of the firm is just the sum of the implicit market values of its separate activities, where these implicit prices are just as if the firm sold shares directly in each activity.

The pricing equation (7.34) provides a way for the firm to evaluate directly the contribution of individual production activities to its period 1 market value. And the optimal scale for each activity is, of course, determined by balancing period 1 costs against contributions to market value. But as in the case of single-activity firms, if the risk of the return on the market value of an activity is independent of the scale of the activity, there is a cost of capital that can be used to determine the activity's optimal scale.

First, note that, from Equations (7.30) and (7.31), the one-period return on the shares of firm j can be written in terms of the returns on its separate production activities:

$$\tilde{R}_j = \frac{\tilde{V}_j - P_j}{P_j} = \frac{\sum\limits_{k=1}^{m(j)} \tilde{V}_{kj} - \sum\limits_{k=1}^{m(j)} P_{kj}}{\sum\limits_{k=1}^{m(j)} P_{kj}} = \sum\limits_{k=1}^{m(j)} \frac{P_{kj}}{\sum\limits_{k=1}^{m(j)} P_{kj}} \left(\frac{\tilde{V}_{kj} - P_{kj}}{P_{kj}} \right)$$

or
$$\tilde{R}_j = \sum\limits_{k=1}^{m(j)} x_{kj} \tilde{R}_{kj}, \qquad (7.35)$$

where $x_{kj} = P_{kj}/P_j$ is the proportion of the total market value of firm j at period 1 that is accounted for by the production activity k, and $\tilde{R}_{kj} = (\tilde{V}_{kj} - P_{kj})/P_{kj}$ is the one-period return on the period 1 value of activity k. It follows that

$$E(\tilde{R}_j) = \sum\limits_{k=1}^{m(j)} x_{kj} E(\tilde{R}_{kj}). \qquad (7.36)$$

With Equations (7.35) and (7.36), the covariance between the one-period return on the firm's shares and the one-period return on the market portfolio m is

$$\mathrm{cov}\,(\tilde{R}_j, \tilde{R}_m) = \mathrm{cov}\,\left(\sum\limits_{k=1}^{m(j)} x_{kj} \tilde{R}_{kj}, \tilde{R}_m \right)$$

$$= \sum\limits_{k=1}^{m(j)} x_{kj}\,\mathrm{cov}\,(\tilde{R}_{kj}, \tilde{R}_m),$$

so that
$$\frac{\mathrm{cov}\,(\tilde{R}_j, \tilde{R}_m)}{\sigma(\tilde{R}_m)} = \frac{\sum\limits_{k=1}^{m(j)} x_{kj}\,\mathrm{cov}\,(\tilde{R}_{kj}, \tilde{R}_m)}{\sigma(\tilde{R}_m)}. \qquad (7.37)$$

We know that in equilibrium the expected return on the shares of firm j must satisfy the expected return–risk relation (7.17); that is,

$$E(\tilde{R}_j) = R_f + S_m \frac{\mathrm{cov}\,(\tilde{R}_j, \tilde{R}_m)}{\sigma(\tilde{R}_m)}.$$

But with Equations (7.36) and (7.37), this can be rewritten

$$E(\tilde{R}_j) = \sum_{k=1}^{m(j)} x_{kj}E(\tilde{R}_{kj}) = R_f + S_m \sum_{k=1}^{m(j)} x_{kj} \frac{\text{cov }(\tilde{R}_{kj},\tilde{R}_m)}{\sigma(\tilde{R}_m)},$$

or $\quad E(\tilde{R}_j) = \sum_{k=1}^{m(j)} x_{kj}E(\tilde{R}_{kj}) = \sum_{k=1}^{m(j)} x_{kj}\left[R_f + S_m \frac{\text{cov }(\tilde{R}_{kj},\tilde{R}_m)}{\sigma(\tilde{R}_m)}\right].$

In words, the expected return on the firm's shares is just the weighted average of the $E(\tilde{R}_{kj})$, the expected returns on its individual activities, and the values of each of the $E(\tilde{R}_{kj})$ must satisfy the equilibrium relationship between risk and expected return.

In essence, the firm is just a portfolio of production activities, and market relationships between risk and expected return hold for each activity. And with a perfect capital market, the equilibrium expected returns $E(\tilde{R}_{kj})$, $k = 1, 2, \ldots, m(j)$, are the required expected one-period returns or costs of capital for the firm's production activities. The steps required to show this are identical with those which led to expression (7.29) for the case of a single-activity firm; thus we leave formal derivation to the interested reader.

Thus although in the capital market consumers must deal directly in the shares of firm j, nevertheless the implicit market values of the firm's separate production activities and the optimal production criteria for these activities are as if consumers could deal directly in the activities themselves.

VI.D. Optimal Production Decisions: Some Comments

Three important points in the analysis of optimal production decisions should be mentioned.

First, although the market value at period 1 of each of the firm's production activities depends only on the expectation and risk of the distribution of the period 2 market value of the activity, this does not imply independence among production activities in either revenues or costs. In fact, the constraints on the firm's production opportunities are most simply represented by its transformation function

$$T^j(E(\tilde{V}_{1j}),E(\tilde{V}_{2j}),\ldots,E(\tilde{V}_{m(j),j}),I_{1j},I_{2j},\ldots,I_{m(j),j}) = 0,$$

which tells the maximum expected market values at period 2 that can be generated by different outlays at period 1. The general functional form of T^j allows for interdependence among the levels of any of the variables. (A realistic example of such dependencies would be the case in which the outlays I_{kj} necessary to generate a given level of $E(\tilde{V}_{kj})$ depend on the other production activities that a firm undertakes.) Nevertheless when the optimal levels of current outlays for all activities have been chosen, the resulting period 2 expected market value of each activity is priced in accordance with its risk.

Second, it is important to note that in the analysis of optimal production decisions the risk of a particular production activity is measured by the contribution of the activity to the dispersion in the market value of the market portfolio. The risk of the activity to the firm itself, however this might be measured, is of no consequence; the market evaluates the activity and its risk in the same way, regardless of the particular portfolio of activities that the firm happens to hold. Moreover, optimal investment decisions imply no incentive for the firm to diversify. Although consumers all hold efficient portfolios, in a perfect market consumers can combine the shares of different firms and obtain efficient portfolios with no transactions costs, so that in itself diversification on the part of an individual firm is of no particular value to them.

Third, it is interesting to examine the role of utility functions in the analysis of optimal production decisions. The utility functions of individual consumers combine in the market to determine the trade-off between $E(\tilde{R})$ and $\sigma(\tilde{R})$ along the efficient set. The properties of the efficient set lead directly to the equilibrium expected return–risk relations that in turn are the basis of optimal investment criteria for the firm. But although the firm's optimal investment decisions must take direct account of market expected return–risk relations, its investment decisions do not directly involve utility functions. In fact, just as in a world of perfect certainty, with a perfect market the notion of a utility function for a firm is completely inappropriate in determining an optimal production plan. From the viewpoint of the shareholders, the goal of the firm is simply to maximize the period 1 market value of their shares.

*VII. ALGEBRAIC TREATMENT OF CAPITAL MARKET EQUILIBRIUM

So far the development of the theory of capital market equilibrium has been, to whatever extent possible, geometric. In the present section the model is reconsidered from a completely algebraic viewpoint. The main purpose is to verify the completeness of the geometric analysis; that is, we must verify that in the geometric development we have imposed a sufficient number of conditions to determine the variables of interest.

The procedure is to present first the necessary conditions of consumer equilibrium. Then the equilibrium conditions for firms are discussed. Finally, the equilibrium conditions for consumers and firms are combined with market-clearing constraints to complete the picture of capital market equilibrium.

VII.A. Consumer Equilibrium

The goal of the consumer is to make a consumption-investment decision at the beginning of period 1 that maximizes the expected utility of consumption in periods 1 and 2, subject to the constraint that period 1 consumption plus the market value of portfolio investments is equal to the market value of his resources at the beginning of period 1. There are, however, many equivalent ways in which this problem can be stated. For example, as has been the practice in the present chapter and the last, we can think of consumer i as choosing optimal values of period 1 consumption $c_1{}^i$ and proportions x_{jp}, $j = 1, 2, \ldots, N$, of investment funds $(w_1{}^i - c_1{}^i)$ allocated to the shares of each of the N firms.[15] Or, as in Section IV.C in Chapter 6, we can think of the consumer as choosing $c_1{}^i$ and total dollars $h_{1j}{}^i$, $j = 1, 2, \ldots, N$, invested in the shares of individual firms, so that $\sum_{j=1}^{N} h_{1j}{}^i = w_1{}^i - c_1{}^i$. Finally, the consumer's decision problem can also be stated in terms of the variables $c_1{}^i$ and $n_j{}^i$, $j = 1, 2, \ldots, N$, where $n_j{}^i$ is the number of shares of firm j that appear in the portfolio that is optimal for consumer i at the beginning of period 1. This last approach is the most convenient for present purposes.

The individual's consumption in period 2, $\tilde{c}_2{}^i$, is related to the one-period return on his portfolio, $\tilde{R}_p$, as follows:

$$\tilde{c}_2{}^i = (w_1{}^i - c_1{}^i)(1 + \tilde{R}_p).$$

Because we assume that the one-period returns on all portfolios have normal distributions, $\tilde{R}_p$ can be written

$$\tilde{R}_p = E(\tilde{R}_p) + \sigma(\tilde{R}_p)\tilde{r},$$

where $\tilde{r}$ is the unit normal variable; that is, the distribution of $\tilde{r}$ is normal with mean equal to 0 and standard deviation equal to 1. Thus $\tilde{c}_2{}^i$ can be rewritten

$$\tilde{c}_2{}^i = (w_1{}^i - c_1{}^i)(1 + E(\tilde{R}_p) + \sigma(\tilde{R}_p)\tilde{r})$$

or
$$\tilde{c}_2{}^i = (w_1{}^i - c_1{}^i)(1 + \sum_{j=1}^{N} x_{jp}E(\tilde{R}_j) + \sigma(\sum_{j=1}^{N} x_{jp}\tilde{R}_j)\tilde{r}), \qquad (7.38)$$

---

[15] In the present section we often have to deal with more than one consumer at a time. Thus the superscript i is used to refer to a particular consumer i, and there are assumed to be I consumers in the market.

where
$$x_{jp} = \frac{n_j{}^i p_j}{\sum\limits_{j=1}^{N} n_j{}^i p_j} = \frac{n_j{}^i p_j}{w_1{}^i - c_1{}^i}, \qquad j = 1, 2, \ldots, N, \qquad (7.39)$$

are the proportions of investment funds, $w_1{}^i - c_1{}^i$, invested in each of the N available assets. Thus, substituting Equation (7.39) into Equation (7.38), we can express $\tilde{c}_2{}^i$ in terms of the numbers of shares of each firm purchased, $n_j{}^i$, as

$$\tilde{c}_2{}^i = \sum_{j=1}^{N} n_j{}^i p_j + \sum_{j=1}^{N} n_j{}^i p_j E(\tilde{R}_j) + \sigma\left(\sum_{j=1}^{N} n_j{}^i p_j \tilde{R}_j\right)\tilde{r}.$$

The decision facing consumer i can then be stated as follows: Choose the values of $c_1{}^i$ and $n_j{}^i$, $j = 1, 2, \ldots, N$, that

$$\max E[U(c_1{}^i, \tilde{c}_2{}^i)]$$

$$= \int_{-\infty}^{\infty} U\left(c_1{}^i, \sum_{j=1}^{N} n_j{}^i p_j + \sum_{j=1}^{N} n_j{}^i p_j E(\tilde{R}_j) + \sigma\left(\sum_{j=1}^{N} n_j{}^i p_j \tilde{R}_j\right)\tilde{r}\right)f(r)\, dr$$

subject to the constraint

$$w_1{}^i = c_1{}^i + \sum_{j=1}^{N} n_j{}^i p_j.$$

The necessary conditions for a maximum are determined by first forming the lagrangian expression

$$L = E[U(c_1{}^i, \tilde{c}_2{}^i)] + \lambda^i\left(w_1{}^i - c_1{}^i - \sum_{j=1}^{N} n_j{}^i p_j\right),$$

then differentiating L partially with respect to $c_1{}^i$, $n_j{}^i$, $j = 1, 2, \ldots, N$, and λ^i, and setting the partial derivatives equal to 0, obtaining

$$\frac{\partial E[U(c_1{}^i, \tilde{c}_2{}^i)]}{\partial c_1{}^i} = \lambda^i, \qquad (7.40a)$$

$$\frac{\dfrac{\partial E[U(c_1{}^i, \tilde{c}_2{}^i)]}{\partial n_j{}^i}}{p_j} = \lambda^i, \qquad j = 1, 2, \ldots, N, \qquad (7.40b)$$

$$w_1{}^i - c_1{}^i - \sum_{j=1}^{N} n_j{}^i p_j = 0. \qquad (7.40c)$$

Equations (7.40a) and (7.40b) are, of course, just the usual conditions that the marginal expected utilities per dollar allocated to period 1 consumption and investments in each of the N available assets must be equal. We can perhaps see this more easily by combining (7.40a) and (7.40b) to obtain the new system of equations

$$\frac{\partial E[\tilde{U}(c_1{}^i, \tilde{c}_2{}^i)]}{\partial n_j{}^i} = \frac{\partial E[\tilde{U}(c_1{}^i, \tilde{c}_2{}^i)]}{\partial c_1{}^i}, \qquad j = 1, 2, \ldots, N, \quad (7.41a)$$

$$w_1{}^i - c_1{}^i - \sum_{j=1}^{N} n_j{}^i p_{j1} = 0. \tag{7.41b}$$

This also shows that one of the $N + 1$ equations (7.40a) and (7.40b) is redundant; given values of N of the $N + 1$ variables $c_1{}^i$ and $n_j{}^i$, $j = 1, 2, \ldots, N$, the budget constraint (7.40c) allows us to determine the value of the Nth variable.

VII.B. Equilibrium for the Firm

Recall that with homogeneous expectations and perfect capital markets, the objective of the firm, assumed to operate in the best interests of its shareholders, is to maximize the difference between the market value of the firm at period 1, P_j, and the outlays required by the production decision made at period 1. For simplicity, we assume now that a share in firm j represents a claim to \$1 of $E(\tilde{V}_j)$, the expected market value of the firm at period 2. Thus $E(\tilde{V}_j) = n_j$, where n_j is the number of shares in firm j implied by the production decision of period 1. As in Section VI.B, we also assume that the firm is engaged in only one type of production activity, and the production decision involves choosing the optimal scale at which to operate this activity. Equivalently, the firm must choose the optimal number of units of period 2 expected market value to generate, but whatever the level of $E(\tilde{V}_j)$ chosen, each unit or share has the same set of covariances cov $(\tilde{v}_j, \tilde{v}_i)$, $i = 1, 2, \ldots, N$, with the shares of other firms. Finally, the firm is a perfect competitor; that is, it takes its share price p_j as given.[16]

In this context the decision problem facing the firm can be stated as follows: Choose a value of n_j that

$$\max (P_j - I(n_j)),$$

or equivalently

$$\max (n_j p_j - I(n_j)),$$

---

[16] At this point, the reader can easily convince himself that these conditions are indeed equivalent to those imposed in Sec. VI.B. In particular, they imply that cov $(\tilde{R}_j, \tilde{R}_m)/\sigma(\tilde{R}_m)$ is independent of the scale of $E(\tilde{V}_j)$. In short, the firm is in a given risk class, and its only decision is to choose the optimal scale of activity.

where $I(n_j)$ are the outlays required at period 1 to generate $E(\tilde{V}_j) = n_j$ units, or shares, of period 2 expected market value. Thus the necessary condition for a maximum is

$$\frac{dI(n_j)}{dn_j} = p_j, \qquad j = 1, 2, \ldots, N. \qquad (7.42)$$

This is hardly a new result. First note that

$$p_j = \frac{E(\tilde{v}_j)}{1 + E(\tilde{R}_j)} = \frac{\$1}{1 + E(\tilde{R}_j)}, \qquad (7.43)$$

where $E(\tilde{R}_j)$ is the equilibrium expected return on a share of firm j. Note also that

$$E(\tilde{v}_j) = \$1 = \frac{dE(\tilde{V}_j)}{dn_j}. \qquad (7.44)$$

In words, increasing the number of shares by one increases the period 2 expected market value of the firm by \$1. Thus using Equations (7.43) and (7.44), Equation (7.42) can be rewritten

$$\frac{dI(n_j)}{dn_j} = \frac{dE(\tilde{V}_j)/dn_j}{1 + E(\tilde{R}_j)};$$

that is, production should be pushed to a point at which the incremental outlay yields a one-period expected return equal to the equilibrium expected return on the firm's shares, which can thus be regarded as the firm's cost of capital. But this is, of course, precisely the condition on optimal production decisions represented in Figure 7.5.

VII.C. Market Equilibrium

Given the share prices p_j, $j = 1, 2, \ldots, N$, Equations (7.42) provide N equations in the N unknowns n_j, $j = 1, 2, \ldots, N$. Thus the numbers of shares supplied to the market by firms are determined. Similarly, given the share prices p_j, Equations (7.41) provide $N + 1$ equations for the $N + 1$ unknowns c_i^i and n_j^i, $j = 1, 2, \ldots, N$. Because there are I sets of such equations, one for each of the $i = 1, 2, \ldots, I$ consumers in the market, the numbers of shares in firms demanded by consumers are also determined. To determine the share prices themselves, we simply add the market-clearing constraints,

$$\sum_{i=1}^{I} n_j^i p_j = n_j p_j, \qquad j = 1, 2, \ldots, N. \qquad (7.45)$$

In words, the demand for the shares of each firm by consumers must be equal to the quantity supplied by the firm. And here we have N equations in the N unknown prices $p_j, j = 1, 2, \ldots, N$.

But the more sophisticated reader may be troubled by the fact that any market equilibrium model can only determine relative prices. (And relative prices, the rates of exchange of goods for each other, are, after all, the only prices that have economic meaning.) In fact, only relative prices are implied in our model. In the total system represented by Equations (7.41), (7.42), and (7.45) we have precisely enough equations to determine the quantities of shares issued by firms and the prices of these shares, the number of shares of each firm demanded by each consumer, and the value of optimal period 1 consumption $c_1{}^i$ for each consumer. But in concentrating on the determination of equilibrium in the capital market, we have implicitly taken equilibrium in the goods market, that is, prices of period 1 consumption goods, as given. Thus the equilibrium prices of shares determined in the capital market are conditional on or relative to the assumed prices for consumption goods.

VIII. MARKET EQUILIBRIUM WITH SYMMETRIC STABLE RETURN DISTRIBUTIONS

The last step in the discussion of market equilibrium is to generalize the two-parameter mean–standard deviation model in the preceding sections to the case in which portfolio return distributions can be symmetric stable with characteristic exponent $1 < \alpha \leq 2$. In short, we extend the model of capital market equilibrium in the present chapter to the two-parameter symmetric stable portfolio model presented at the end of the last chapter. Because the analysis and conclusions are so similar to those for the two-parameter normal model, the discussion here can be brief, and in fact we just present the first few steps.

The first step is to review briefly some of the building blocks of the symmetric stable model.

VIII.A. The Market Model Return–Generating Process

In the symmetric stable portfolio model in Chapter 6, the returns on investment assets—the shares of the N firms—are assumed to be generated by the "market model"

$$\tilde{R}_j = a_j + b_j \tilde{M} + \tilde{\epsilon}_j, \qquad j = 1, 2, \ldots, N. \tag{7.46}$$

Here a_j and b_j are constants, and $\tilde{\epsilon}_j$ is a random disturbance with expected value equal to 0. It is assumed that $\tilde{M}$ and the $\tilde{\epsilon}_j, j = 1, 2, \ldots, N$, are mutually independent, symmetric stable variables, all with the same characteristic exponent α, which is assumed to be greater than 1.

With asset returns generated according to Equation (7.46), the return on any portfolio p is

$$\tilde{R}_p = \sum_{j=1}^{N} x_{jp}\tilde{R}_j = \sum_{j=1}^{N} x_{jp}a_j + \sum_{j=1}^{N} x_{jp}b_j\tilde{M} + \sum_{j=1}^{N} x_{jp}\tilde{\epsilon}_j, \qquad (7.47)$$

so that the return on a portfolio is a weighted sum of the independent random variables $\tilde{M}$ and the $\tilde{\epsilon}_j$. Because these are assumed to be symmetric stable with the same characteristic exponent α, $\tilde{R}_p$ is also symmetric stable with the same value of α; and $E(\tilde{R}_p)$ and $\sigma(\tilde{R}_p)$, the expected value and dispersion of the distribution of $\tilde{R}_p$, are related to those of $\tilde{M}$ and the $\tilde{\epsilon}_j$ according to

$$E(\tilde{R}_p) = \sum_{j=1}^{N} x_{jp}E(\tilde{R}_j) = \sum_{j=1}^{N} x_{jp}[a_j + b_jE(\tilde{M})], \qquad (7.48)$$

$$\sigma(\tilde{R}_p) = [\sigma^\alpha(\tilde{M}) \mid \sum_{j=1}^{N} x_{jp}b_j \mid^\alpha + \sum_{j=1}^{N} \sigma^\alpha(\tilde{\epsilon}_j) \mid x_{jp} \mid^\alpha]^{1/\alpha}. \qquad (7.49)$$

Now, however, we interpret $\sigma(\tilde{R}_p)$ as return dispersion rather than as standard deviation. For the purpose of concreteness, remember that with symmetric stable distributions $\sigma(\tilde{R}_p)$ corresponds approximately to the semi-interquartile range of the distribution of $\tilde{R}_p$.

In the two-parameter model based on normally distributed portfolio returns all the major results on the measurement of risk and the relationships between expected return and risk derive from the efficient set theorem, that is, from the fact that the optimal portfolio for a risk averter must be $E(\tilde{R})$, $\sigma(\tilde{R})$ efficient. But from Chapter 6 we already know that, interpreting $\sigma(\tilde{R})$ as return dispersion, the efficient set theorem also holds in the two-parameter stable model. And we now use this fact, precisely as in the normal model, to develop expected return–risk relations both for the individual consumer and for the market as a whole.

VIII.B. Consumer Equilibrium and the Measurement of Risk

Suppose that Figure 7.1 now represents the picture of equilibrium for a given consumer in the two-parameter symmetric stable portfolio model.[17]

[17] From Chap. 6 remember that in the symmetric stable portfolio model, the consumer's indifference curves for $E(\tilde{R})$ against $\sigma(\tilde{R})$ are positively sloping and convex with expected utility increasing upward and to the left in the $E(\tilde{R})$, $\sigma(\tilde{R})$ plane, and the efficient set curve is positively sloping and concave. Thus Fig. 7.1 is indeed an appropriate representation of consumer equilibrium.

As in the normal model, the basic presumption again is that, because the consumer chooses the efficient portfolio e, for him the risks of individual assets and the relationship between expected return and risk must be measured relative to e. And we now see that, precisely as in the normal model, these concepts are embedded in the implications of efficiency for properties of e.

The efficient portfolio with expected return $E(\tilde{R}_e)$ is the solution to the problem: Choose values of $x_{jp}, j = 1, 2, \ldots, N$, that

$$\min \sigma(\tilde{R}_p) = \left[\sigma^\alpha(\tilde{M}) \mid \sum_{j=1}^{N} x_{jp}b_j \mid^\alpha + \sum_{j=1}^{N} \sigma^\alpha(\tilde{\epsilon}_j) \mid x_{jp} \mid^\alpha\right]^{1/\alpha} \quad (7.50a)$$

subject to

$$E(\tilde{R}_p) = \sum_{j=1}^{N} x_{jp}E(\tilde{R}_j) = E(\tilde{R}_e) \qquad (7.50b)$$

and

$$\sum_{j=1}^{N} x_{jp} = 1. \qquad (7.50c)$$

With the usual lagrangian methods, we could easily determine that the solution to this problem must satisfy Equations (7.50b), (7.50c), and the old familiar balance equation

$$E(\tilde{R}_j) - E(\tilde{R}_i) = S_e \left(\frac{\partial \sigma(\tilde{R}_e)}{\partial x_{je}} - \frac{\partial \sigma(\tilde{R}_e)}{\partial x_{ie}}\right), \quad i,j = 1, 2, \ldots, N, \quad (7.5)$$

where S_e is the slope of the efficient set at the point e, and $\partial \sigma(\tilde{R}_e)/\partial x_{je}$ is $\partial \sigma(\tilde{R}_p)/\partial x_{jp}$ evaluated at the optimizing values $x_{jp} = x_{je}, j = 1, 2, \ldots, N$. Multiplying both sides of Equation (7.5) by x_{ie} and summing over i, we obtain the new balance equation

$$E(\tilde{R}_j) - E(\tilde{R}_e) = S_e \left(\frac{\partial \sigma(\tilde{R}_e)}{\partial x_{je}} - \sum_{i=1}^{N} x_{ie}\frac{\partial \sigma(\tilde{R}_e)}{\partial x_{ie}}\right), \qquad j = 1, 2, \ldots, N. \qquad (7.6)$$

As the equation numbers indicate, so far things are precisely as in the two-parameter normal model. The next and critical step in the development of the normal model was to show that

$$\sum_{i=1}^{N} x_{ie} \frac{\partial \sigma(\tilde{R}_e)}{\partial x_{ie}} = \sigma(\tilde{R}_e), \qquad (7.8)$$

so that Equation (7.6) could be rewritten

$$E(\tilde{R}_j) - E(\tilde{R}_e) = S_e\left(\frac{\partial\sigma(\tilde{R}_e)}{\partial x_{je}} - \sigma(\tilde{R}_e)\right), \qquad j = 1, 2, \ldots, N. \quad (7.9)$$

This balance equation can then be interpreted as the relevant relationship between expected return and risk for the consumer who chooses the efficient portfolio e; that is, in the two-parameter world, the risk of the portfolio e is measured by its return dispersion $\sigma(\tilde{R}_e)$. But $\partial\sigma(\tilde{R}_e)/\partial x_{je}$ is just the contribution of asset j to $\sigma(\tilde{R}_e)$; thus, it measures the risk of asset j in the efficient portfolio e. Then Equation (7.9) can be interpreted as the relationship between the expected returns and risks of individual assets vis-à-vis the portfolio e: It says that the portfolio e is formed in such a way that the difference between the expected return on any asset and the expected return on the portfolio is proportional to the difference between the risk of the asset and the risk of the portfolio, where the proportionality factor is S_e, the slope of the efficient set at the point e.

But the balance equation (7.9) and this interpretation of it as an expected return–risk relation apply equally well to the two-parameter stable model. To establish this, we need only show that Equation (7.8) holds in this model, so that (7.9) follows from (7.5), which has already been shown to hold in the stable case. But Equation (7.8) itself follows directly from

$$\frac{\partial\sigma(\tilde{R}_e)}{\partial x_{ie}} = \sigma(\tilde{R}_e)^{1-\alpha}\left[\sigma^\alpha(M)\frac{b_i}{\dfrac{1}{N}\sum\limits_{j=1}^{N} x_{je}b_j}\;|\sum\limits_{j=1}^{N} x_{je}b_j|^\alpha + \sigma^\alpha(\tilde{\epsilon}_i)\frac{|x_{ie}|^\alpha}{x_{ie}}\right]. \quad (7.51)$$

Thus the major lines of the analysis of risk and the relationship between expected return and risk for the individual consumer are the same in the two-parameter stable model and in the model based on normally distributed portfolio returns. The only differences between the models are that in the general stable case the return dispersion $\sigma(\tilde{R})$ can no longer be interpreted as standard deviation and the risk measure $\partial\sigma(\tilde{R}_e)/\partial x_{ie}$ can no longer be interpreted as a weighted sum of covariances.

And it is important not to overstate the differences between the models. Remember that the normal distribution itself is the symmetric stable distribution with characteristic exponent $\alpha = 2$. If asset returns are normally distributed and generated by the market model in Equation (7.46), the analysis of this section applies to the normal model, and in particular Equation (7.51) measures the risk of an asset relative to the efficient portfolio e. The special nature of Equation (7.51) arises from the special nature of the market model and not from any assumption of nonnormality.

Thus in the normal model, from Equation (7.7),

$$\frac{\partial \sigma(\tilde{R}_e)}{\partial x_{ie}} = \frac{\sum_{j=1}^{N} x_{je}\sigma_{ij}}{\sigma(\tilde{R}_e)} = \frac{\sum_{j=1}^{N} x_{je} \operatorname{cov}(\tilde{R}_i, \tilde{R}_j)}{\sigma(\tilde{R}_e)}.$$

But when share returns are generated by the market model,

$$\operatorname{cov}(\tilde{R}_i, \tilde{R}_j) = \operatorname{cov}(a_i + b_i\tilde{M} + \tilde{\epsilon}_i, a_j + b_j\tilde{M} + \tilde{\epsilon}_j)$$

$$= b_i b_j \sigma^2(\tilde{M}), \qquad i \neq j,$$

$$= b_i^2 \sigma^2(\tilde{M}) + \sigma^2(\tilde{\epsilon}_i), \qquad i = j,$$

so that

$$\frac{\partial \sigma(\tilde{R}_e)}{\partial x_{ie}} = \frac{\sigma^2(\tilde{M}) b_i \sum_{j=1}^{N} x_{je} b_j + x_{ie}\sigma^2(\tilde{\epsilon}_i)}{\sigma(\tilde{R}_e)}.$$

But this is just Equation (7.51) for the case $\alpha = 2$.

Perhaps the major difference between the normal and nonnormal two-parameter portfolio models is best described as follows. With normally distributed asset returns, arbitrary relationships among these returns can be expressed quite generally in terms of covariances. On the other hand, with nonnormal symmetric stable asset returns, the absence of a general statistical theory for deriving portfolio return distributions from the distributions of dependent asset returns requires us to posit a model like the market model, wherein the returns on securities are dependent, yet the return on a portfolio can be expressed as a weighted sum of independent symmetric stable variables.

VIII.C. Risk and Return for the Market

The development of expression (7.9) gives us a theory for the measurement of risk and the relationship between risk and expected return that is relevant at the level of the individual consumer. As in the normal model, to generalize these concepts to the level of the market, we must further restrict the market context. And the restrictions that we impose are precisely those of the normal model. In particular, we assume the existence of (1) riskless borrowing-lending opportunities and (2) homogeneous expectations. And the results are again precisely as in the normal model.

Thus, with riskless borrowing-lending, portfolios of the riskless asset f and any risky asset or portfolio a that are formed according to

$$\tilde{R}_p = xR_f + (1 - x)\tilde{R}_a, \qquad x \leq 1, \tag{7.12}$$

have expected return and dispersion

$$E(\tilde{R}_p) = xR_f + (1 - x)E(\tilde{R}_a),$$

$$\sigma(\tilde{R}_p) = (1 - x)\sigma(\tilde{R}_a).$$

Thus, as shown in Figure 7.3, the graph of $E(\tilde{R}_p)$ against $\sigma(\tilde{R}_p)$ for portfolios formed according to Equation (7.12) is a straight line from R_f through a. Points between R_f and a on the line correspond to lending portfolios—that is, $0 \le x \le 1$—and points above a represent borrowing portfolios—that is, $x < 0$.

As in the normal model, the efficient set of portfolios will be given by the line from R_f through m and z in Figure 7.3. Thus all efficient portfolios will be combinations of the riskless asset f and the single portfolio of risky assets m. And with homogeneous expectations, Figure 7.3 will be the picture of portfolio opportunities facing every investor, so that the risky component of every investor's optimal portfolio is the portfolio m. It follows that market equilibrium requires that m be the market portfolio.

Applying Equation (7.9) to m and noting from Figure 7.3 that $S_m = [E(\tilde{R}_m) - R_f]/\sigma(\tilde{R}_m)$, we get the familiar result,

$$E(\tilde{R}_j) = R_f + \left[\frac{E(\tilde{R}_m) - R_f}{\sigma(\tilde{R}_m)}\right]\frac{\partial\sigma(\tilde{R}_m)}{\partial x_{jm}}, \quad j = 1, 2, \ldots, N. \quad (7.15)$$

Since the only risky assets held by consumers are shares in the market portfolio m, for all consumers, and thus for the market as a whole, the risk of an asset and the relationship between its risk and its expected return are appropriately measured relative to the market portfolio. This is done in Equation (7.15), in which the equilibrium expected return on asset j is the riskless rate of interest R_f plus a risk premium that is proportional to $\partial\sigma(\tilde{R}_m)/\partial x_{jm}$, the asset's contribution to the total risk, that is, dispersion of return, of the market portfolio.

The analysis of the nature of optimal production decisions for the two-parameter stable model of this section is identical to the analysis of optimal production decisions in the normal model, and so does not even bear any repeating.

IX. CONCLUSIONS

One-period, two-parameter models of consumer, firm, and market equilibrium have now been presented. It should be clear, however, that the properties of consumer equilibrium are the underpinnings of all three models. And, in particular, all of the major results derive from the fact that with two-parameter portfolio return distributions, the optimal portfolios for risk-averse consumers are $E(\tilde{R})$, $\sigma(\tilde{R})$ efficient.

In the next chapter we conclude the book with a discussion of some multiperiod models.

REFERENCES

The basic building block for the portfolio and thus the asset-pricing models is the development of the expected utility hypothesis in

1. Von Neumann, John, and Oskar Morgenstern, *Theory of Games and Economic Behavior*, 3d ed. Princeton, N.J.: Princeton University Press, 1953.

The pioneering works in portfolio analysis are

2. Markowitz, Harry, *Portfolio Selection: Efficient Diversification of Investments*. New York: John Wiley & Sons, Inc., 1959.
3. Tobin, James, "Liquidity Preference as Behavior towards Risk," *Review of Economic Studies*, vol. 25 (February 1958), pp. 65–86.

Later contributions are

4. Tobin, James, "The Theory of Portfolio Selection," *The Theory of Interest Rates*, F. H. Hahn and F. P. R. Brechling, eds. London: Macmillan & Co., Ltd., 1965, chap. 1.
5. Sharpe, William F., "A Simplified Model for Portfolio Analysis," *Management Science*, vol. 9 (January 1963), pp. 277–293.
6. Fama, Eugene F., "Pòrtfolio Analysis in a Stable Paretian Market," *Management Science*, vol. 11 (January 1965), pp. 404–419.

The mean–standard deviation version of the asset-pricing model was first presented by

7. Sharpe, William F., "Capital Asset Prices: A Theory of Market Equilibrium under Conditions of Risk," *Journal of Finance*, Vol. 19 (September 1964), pp. 425–442.

and then slightly later by

8. Lintner, John, "Security Prices, Risk, and Maximal Gains from Diversification," *Journal of Finance*, vol. 20 (December 1965), pp. 587–615.
9. Lintner, John, "The Valuation of Risk Assets and the Selection of Risky Investments in Stock Portfolios and Capital Budgets," *Review of Economics and Statistics*, vol. 47 (February 1965), pp. 13–37.
10. Mossin, Jan, "Equilibrium in a Capital Asset Market," *Econometrica*, vol. 34 (October 1966), pp. 768–783.

Some clarification of the Sharpe-Lintner models is provided in

11. Fama, Eugene F., "Risk, Return, and Equilibrium: Some Clarifying Comments," *Journal of Finance*, vol. 23 (March 1968), pp. 29–40.

The two-parameter models are extended to the class of symmetric stable distribution in

12. Fama, Eugene F., "Risk, Return, and Equilibrium," *Journal of Political Economy,* vol. 78 (January–February 1971).

The problem of optimal production decisions in the two-parameter model is treated by

13. Fama, Eugene F., "Perfect Competition and the Market Value Rule in the Two-Parameter Model," manuscript, December, 1971.

MULTIPERIOD MODELS

I. INTRODUCTION

This concluding chapter of the book is organized around the general theme of multiperiod models of consumer (investor) and capital market equilibrium. The analyses very soon take us to the boundaries of current knowledge in finance and for this reason are not likely to provide the reader with a very good sense of closure. But the primary goal of the book, after all, is to give an accurate picture of the current status of the theory of finance. And the vitality of the area encourages an impression of semi-maturity, with much of the best yet to come, rather than an image of full growth.

The chapter covers two topics. First we consider multiperiod models of consumer and capital market equilibrium, attempting to relate these as much as possible to the two-period models in the preceding chapters. Then the implications of a perfect capital market for the nature of the process generating prices of investment assets through time are discussed.

Although multiperiod models is the organizing theme of the chapter, the two major topics are only semirelated. The orientation of the first—multiperiod models of consumer and market equilibrium—is theoretical, and unfortunately the analysis requires a slightly higher level of mathematics than has been the case up to now.[1] The primary goal is to provide multiperiod extensions of the two-period models in the preceding chapters. As elsewhere in the book, the analysis is presented so that the reader who cannot follow all the mathematics can nevertheless pick up the major ideas from the verbal discussions.

On the other hand, the orientation of the second major topic—the so-called efficient markets model—is primarily empirical. Most of this book is based on the assumed existence of a perfect capital market. In presenting the efficient markets model, although the empirical work is not discussed, we contend that the available empirical evidence supports many of the major implications of a perfect market, and that among the various areas of economics, the theory of finance ranks high in terms of degree of correspondence between theory and empirical evidence.

II. MULTIPERIOD CONSUMPTION–INVESTMENT DECISIONS

II.A. The Problem

The simplest version of the multiperiod consumption-investment problem, and the only version that is treated here, considers a consumer with wealth w_1, defined as the market value of his assets at the beginning of period 1, which must be allocated to consumption c_1 and a portfolio investment $w_1 - c_1$. The portfolio yields an uncertain wealth level $\tilde{w}_2$ at the beginning of period 2 that must be divided between consumption c_2 and investment $w_2 - c_2$. Consumption-investment decisions must be made at the beginning of each period, until the consumer dies and his wealth is distributed among his heirs. The consumer's objective is to maximize the expected utility of lifetime consumption.[2]

---

[1] Indeed, following the practice in earlier chapters, perhaps all Sec. II should be asterisked.

[2] The simple multiperiod model to be presented here could easily be extended in several directions. For example it would not be difficult—indeed the major complications are notational—to extend the model to take account of the fact that the consumer has an asset, his "human capital," that generates income in many periods but which cannot be sold outright in the market at the beginning of any period. Such an extended model could allow the ways that the consumer employs his human capital during any period—his choice of occupation(s) and the division of his time between labor and leisure—to be at his discretion. But such complications would only confuse our attempts to bridge the gap between the two-period models in the preceding chapters and the multiperiod models to be considered here.

The goal is to present a general multiperiod consumption-investment model but one that nevertheless leads to interesting hypotheses about observable aspects of consumer behavior. The main result is the proposition that if the consumer is risk-averse, that is, his utility function for lifetime consumption is strictly concave, and markets for consumption goods and portfolio assets are perfect,[3] the consumer's observable behavior in the market in any period is indistinguishable from that of a risk-averse expected utility maximizer who has a two-period horizon.

With this result it is then possible to provide a multiperiod setting for hypotheses about consumer behavior derived from two-period wealth allocation models, and these have been studied extensively, both here and elsewhere. Two-period models assume, of course, that consumers have two-period horizons, but in most cases their behavioral propositions require only that consumers behave as if they were risk-averse two-period expected utility maximizers, and this is the case in the multiperiod model to be presented here. Thus perhaps the major contribution of the present analysis is in providing a means for bridging the gap between two-period and multiperiod models.

The multiperiod model that we present covers much more general types of two-period models than just the two-parameter models in the preceding chapters. But we later consider in detail the adjustments to the multiperiod model that are necessary to provide a multiperiod setting for the major propositions about consumer behavior and the nature of market equilibrium associated with the two-period two-parameter models. Indeed we show that a multiperiod model in which the optimal portfolio for any period is "efficient" in terms of distributions of one-period returns requires few assumptions beyond those already made in the two-period models.

II.B. The Wealth Allocation Model

But first the multiperiod model must itself be developed. Let Φ_t, the "state of the world," signify the set of information—current and past prices, and so on—available at the beginning of period t. Thus Φ_{t-1} is a subset of Φ_t. For simplicity we assume that in any period or state the number of investment assets available is N—although there would be no problems in letting N depend on Φ_t—and the one-period returns from t to $t + 1$ on these assets are represented as $R_j(\Phi_{t+1}), j = 1, 2, \ldots, N$, so that a value of Φ_{t+1} implies the values of the returns.[4] Thus if $h_j, j = 1, 2, \ldots, N$,

---

[3] That is, as always, (1) consumption goods and portfolio assets are infinitely divisible, (2) reallocations of consumption and investment expenditures are costless, and (3) the consumer is a price taker in all markets.

[4] Note that the random variable is now considered to be the state of the world at $t + 1$, Φ_{t+1}. And the returns are random variables because they depend on Φ_{t+1}.

are the dollars invested in each asset at t, the consumer's wealth at $t + 1$ is

$$w_{t+1} = \sum_{j=1}^{N} h_j [1 + R_j(\Phi_{t+1})]. \tag{8.1}$$

If for simplicity we assume that the consumer will die for certain[5] at the beginning of period $\tau + 1$ and if the state of the world at $\tau + 1$ is $\Phi_{\tau+1}$, the consumer's utility for lifetime consumption is assumed to be given by the function

$$U_{\tau+1}(C_{\tau+1} \mid \Phi_{\tau+1}) = U_{\tau+1}(c_{1-k}, \ldots, c_1, \ldots, c_{\tau+1} \mid \Phi_{\tau+1}),$$

where in general

$$C_t = (c_{1-k}, \ldots, c_1, \ldots, c_t) \tag{8.2}$$

is consumption from the beginning of his life, period $1 - k$, to period t, and the consumption $c_{\tau+1}$ is in the form of a bequest. The goal of the consumer in his consumption-investment decisions is to maximize the expected utility of lifetime consumption.

The consumer must make an optimal consumption-investment decision for period 1, taking into account that decisions must also be made at the beginning of each future period prior to $\tau + 1$ and that these future decisions will depend on future events. Dynamic programming, with its "backward optimization," provides a natural approach; that is, to solve the decision problem for period 1, the consumer first determines optimal decisions for all contingencies for the decision problem to be faced at period τ. Then he determines optimal decisions for $\tau - 1$, under the assumption that he always makes optimal decisions at τ. And so on, until he works his way back to the decision at period 1, which is then based on the assumption that optimal decisions are made at each future period for any possible contingency.

Formally, optimal decisions at period τ for all w_τ and Φ_τ can be summarized by the function

$$U_\tau(C_{\tau-1}, w_\tau \mid \Phi_\tau)$$

$$= \max_{c_\tau, h} \int_{\Phi_{\tau+1}} U_{\tau+1}\left(C_\tau, \sum_{j=1}^{N} h_j [1 + R_j(\Phi_{\tau+1})] \mid \Phi_{\tau+1}\right) dF_{\Phi_\tau}(\Phi_{\tau+1}) \tag{8.3}$$

subject to

$$0 \leq c_\tau \leq w_\tau \quad \text{and} \quad \sum_{j=1}^{N} h_j = w_\tau - c_\tau,$$

---

[5] The model is easily extended to allow for an uncertain period of death. Indeed the major complications are notational. (See, for example, Ref. 1.)

where $F_{\Phi_\tau}(\Phi_{\tau+1})$ is the distribution function of $\Phi_{\tau+1}$, given state Φ_τ at τ, and the notation

$$\max_{c_\tau, h}$$

is read "maximize with respect to a feasible choice of c_τ and h_j, $j = 1, 2, \ldots, N$."[6]

$U_\tau(C_{\tau-1}, w_\tau \mid \Phi_\tau)$ is the maximum expected utility at τ of lifetime consumption as a function of realized past consumption $C_{\tau-1}$ and wealth w_τ, given that the state of the world is Φ_τ. When period τ actually comes along, $C_{\tau-1}$, w_τ, and Φ_τ will be known, but in earlier periods this will not be the case. And just as $U_{\tau+1}(C_{\tau+1} \mid \Phi_{\tau+1})$ serves as the input or objective function for the decision at period τ, $U_\tau(C_{\tau-1}, w_\tau \mid \Phi_\tau)$ now serves as the objective function for the decision problem at period $\tau - 1$; that is, optimal decisions for all $w_{\tau-1}$ and $\Phi_{\tau-1}$ can be summarized by the function

$U_{\tau-1}(C_{\tau-2}, w_{\tau-1} \mid \Phi_{\tau-1})$

$$= \max_{c_{\tau-1}, h} \int_{\Phi_\tau} U_\tau(C_{\tau-1}, \sum_{j=1}^{N} h_j[1 + R_j(\Phi_\tau)] \mid \Phi_\tau)\, dF_{\Phi_{\tau-1}}(\Phi_\tau)$$

subject to

$$0 \le c_{\tau-1} \le w_{\tau-1} \quad \text{and} \quad \sum_{j=1}^{N} h_j = w_{\tau-1} - c_{\tau-1}.$$

Again $U_{\tau-1}(C_{\tau-2}, w_{\tau-1} \mid \Phi_{\tau-1})$ is the maximum expected utility of lifetime consumption if the consumer is in state $\Phi_{\tau-1}$ at $\tau - 1$, his wealth is $w_{\tau-1}$, his past consumption was $C_{\tau-2}$, and optimal consumption-investment decisions are made first at $\tau - 1$ and then at τ in whatever state of the world occurs at τ. And $U_{\tau-1}(C_{\tau-2}, w_{\tau-1} \mid \Phi_{\tau-1})$ in turn becomes the objective function for the decision problem at $\tau - 2$.

In fact for $t = 1, 2, \ldots, \tau$, the entire process of backward optimization can be summarized by the recursive relation

$U_t(C_{t-1}, w_t \mid \Phi_t)$

$$= \max_{c_\tau, h} \int_{\Phi_{t+1}} U_{t+1}(C_t, \sum_{j=1}^{N} h_j[1 + R_j(\Phi_{t+1})] \mid \Phi_{t+1})\, dF_{\Phi_t}(\Phi_{t+1}) \quad (8.4)$$

[6] Stieltjes integrals are used here, so that $\Phi_{\tau+1}$ can be either a discrete or continuous random variable. For practical purposes, and speaking somewhat less than rigorously, this means that when $\Phi_{\tau+1}$ is a discrete variable, the integral in Equation (8.3) is interpreted as a sum over all possible values of $\Phi_{\tau+1}$, and $dF_{\Phi_\tau}(\Phi_{\tau+1})$ is the probability of the value $\Phi_{\tau+1}$. On the other hand, when $\Phi_{\tau+1}$ is a continuous random variable, it is most convenient to interpret Equation (8.3) as an ordinary Riemann integral, with $dF_{\Phi_\tau}(\Phi_{\tau+1})$ just a shorthand way of writing $f_{\Phi_\tau}(\Phi_{\tau+1})\, d\Phi_{\tau+1}$, where $f_{\Phi_\tau}(\Phi_{\tau+1})$ is the density function for $\Phi_{\tau+1}$ given state Φ_τ at τ.

subject to

$$0 \leq c_t \leq w_t \quad \text{and} \quad \sum_{j=1}^{N} h_j = w_t - c_t.$$

The function $U_t(C_{t-1}, w_t \mid \Phi_t)$ provides the maximum expected utility of lifetime consumption if the consumer is in state Φ_t at period t, his wealth is w_t, his past consumption was C_{t-1}, and optimal consumption-investment decisions are made at the beginning of period t and all future periods.

As stated in Equation (8.4), the multiperiod consumption-investment problem exemplifies a common feature of dynamic programming models. In general it is possible to represent the decision problem of any period t in terms of a derived objective function, in this case U_{t+1}, which is explicitly a function only of variables for $t + 1$ and earlier periods but which in fact summarizes the results of optimal decisions at $t + 1$ and subsequent periods for all possible future events. Thus the recursive relation (8.4) represents the multiperiod problem as a sequence of two-period problems, although at any stage in the process the objective function used to solve the two-period problem summarizes optimal decisions for all future periods.

Representing the multiperiod consumption-investment problem as a sequence of two-period problems in itself says nothing about the characteristics of an optimal decision for any period. The main result here is the following.

Theorem 1. If the utility function for lifetime consumption $U_{\tau+1}(C_{\tau+1} \mid \Phi_{\tau+1})$ has properties characteristic of risk aversion, specifically, if for all $\Phi_{\tau+1}$, $U_{\tau+1}(C_{\tau+1} \mid \Phi_{\tau+1})$ is monotone-increasing and strictly concave in $C_{\tau+1}$, then for all t the derived functions $U_t(C_{t-1}, w_t \mid \Phi_t)$ also have these properties.[7]

The proof of the theorem is presented in a later section. We now turn to a study of its implications.

II.C. Implications: Bridging the Gap between Two-Period and Multiperiod Models

Although at this point its importance is far from obvious, it is the concavity of the functions $U_t(C_{t-1}, w_t \mid \Phi_t)$ for all t and Φ_t, as stated in Theorem

---

[7] The monotonicity of $U_{\tau+1}$ says that the marginal utility of consumption in any period is positive. Strict concavity implies that for $0 < \alpha < 1$,

$$U_{\tau+1}(\alpha C_{\tau+1} + (1 - \alpha)\hat{C}_{\tau+1} \mid \Phi_{\tau+1}) > \alpha U_{\tau+1}(C_{\tau+1} \mid \Phi_{\tau+1}) + (1 - \alpha)U_{\tau+1}(\hat{C}_{\tau+1} \mid \Phi_{\tau+1}),$$

where $C_{\tau+1}$ and $\hat{C}_{\tau+1}$ are any two consumption vectors that differ in at least one element. Geometrically, as always, concavity says that a straight line between any two points on the function $U_{\tau+1}$ lies below the function. As in the case of the more familiar utility of money function, the concavity of $U_{\tau+1}$ implies risk aversion.

1, that now allows us to bridge the gap between two-period and multiperiod wealth allocation models.

II.C.1. The utility of money function

A foretaste of the discussion can be obtained by using the multiperiod model to derive the familiar utility of wealth function, most often discussed in the literature in connection with the expected utility model. If the state of the world at period 1 is Φ_1 and the consumer's past consumption has been $\hat{C}_0$, then for $t = 1$ expression (8.4) yields

$$U_1(\hat{C}_0, w_1 \mid \Phi_1) = \max_{c_1, h} \int_{\Phi_2} U_2(C_1, \sum_{j=1}^{N} h_j[1 + R_j(\Phi_2)] \mid \Phi_2) \, dF_{\Phi_1}(\Phi_2)$$

subject to

$$0 \leq c_1 \leq w_1 \quad \text{and} \quad \sum_{j=1}^{N} h_j = w_1 - c_1.$$

But $\hat{C}_0$ is known at period 1; thus we might just as well write

$$v_1(w_1 \mid \Phi_1) = U_1(\hat{C}_0, w_1 \mid \Phi_1).$$

v_1 is the relevant utility function for timeless gambles taking place at period 1, that is, gambles in which the outcome is known before the consumption-investment decision of period 1 is made (see Chapter 5). From Theorem 1, v_1 has the characteristics of a risk averter's utility of wealth function; that is, it is monotone-increasing and strictly concave in w_1. Thus, although he obtains his utility of wealth function by a complicated process of backward optimization and although his utility of wealth function in fact shows the expected utility of lifetime consumption associated with a given level of wealth at period 1, the consumer's behavior in choosing among timeless gambles is indistinguishable from that of a risk averter making a once and for all decision. Or in other words, our analysis provides a multiperiod setting for the more traditional discussions of utility of wealth functions for risk averters, most of which abstract from the effects of future decisions.

II.C.2. Two-period and multiperiod models: general treatment

More generally, when it comes time to make a decision at the beginning of any period t, $t = 1, 2, \ldots, \tau$, past consumption, equal, say, to $\hat{C}_{t-1}$, is known, so that the decision at t can be based on the function

$$v_{t+1}(c_t, w_{t+1} \mid \Phi_{t+1}) = U_{t+1}(\hat{C}_{t-1}, c_t, w_{t+1} \mid \Phi_{t+1}).$$

Thus, for given wealth w_t and state of the world Φ_t, the consumer's problem at t can be expressed as

$$\max_{c_t, h} \int_{\Phi_{t+1}} v_{t+1}(c_t, \sum_{j=1}^{N} h_j[1 + R_j(\Phi_{t+1})] \mid \Phi_{t+1}) \, dF_{\Phi_t}(\Phi_{t+1}) \qquad (8.5)$$

subject to

$$0 \le c_t \le w_t \quad \text{and} \quad \sum_{j=1}^{N} h_j = w_t - c_t.$$

From Theorem 1, U_{t+1} is monotone-increasing and strictly concave in (C_t, w_{t+1}); it follows that v_{t+1} is monotone-increasing and strictly concave in (c_t, w_{t+1}). Thus although the consumer faces a τ period decision problem, the function $v_{t+1}(c_t, w_{t+1} \mid \Phi_{t+1})$, that is relevant for the consumption-investment decision of period t, has the properties of a risk averter's two-period utility of consumption-terminal wealth function. Although the consumer must solve a multiperiod problem, given v_{t+1} his observed behavior in the market is indistinguishable from that of a risk-averse expected utility maximizer who has a two-period horizon.[8]

In itself this result says little about consumer behavior. Its value derives from the fact that it can be used to provide a multiperiod setting for more detailed behavioral hypotheses usually obtained from specific two-period models. But by design the multiperiod model is based on less restrictive assumptions than most two-period models,[9] so that adapting it to any specific two-period model requires additional assumptions. As we now show, however, these are mostly restrictions already implicit or explicit in the two-period models. Little generality is lost in going from a two-period to a multiperiod framework.

---

[8] But we must keep in mind that, although $v_{t+1}(c_t, w_{t+1} \mid \Phi_{t+1})$ is only explicitly a function of variables for periods t and $t + 1$, it shows the maximum expected utility of lifetime consumption, given optimal consumption-investment decisions in periods subsequent to t. Thus v_{t+1} depends both on tastes, as expressed by the function $U_{\tau+1}(C_{\tau+1} \mid \Phi_{\tau+1})$, and on the consumption-investment opportunities that will be available in future periods.

The notion of summarizing market opportunities in a utility function should not cause concern. Indeed this is done when utility is written, as we do throughout, as a function of total consumption; then we are implicitly summarizing the consumption opportunities, in terms of goods and services and their anticipated prices, that will be available in each period. We return to this point later, when the utility function $U_{\tau+1}(C_{\tau+1} \mid \Phi_{\tau+1})$ for dollars of consumption is derived from a more basic utility function for consumption goods.

[9] In particular, we have essentially assumed only that markets for consumption goods and portfolio assets are perfect and that the consumer is a risk averter in the sense that his utility function for lifetime consumption is strictly concave.

II.C.3. A multiperiod setting for two-period two-parameter portfolio models

Given the concavity of v_{t+1}, (8.5) is formally equivalent to the consumption-investment problem of a risk-averse consumer with state-dependent utilities and a two-period horizon.[10] As such it can be used to provide a multiperiod setting for a wide variety of two-period models, such as the two-period states of the world model analyzed in Chapter 4.

But the theories of wealth allocation and capital market equilibrium most thoroughly discussed here and elsewhere in the literature of finance are the two-period two-parameter models in Chapters 6 and 7. The remainder of this section is concerned with using our model to provide a multiperiod setting for the results of these two-period models.

The two-parameter portfolio models start with the assumption that one-period returns on assets and portfolios conform to two-parameter distributions of the same general "type," in particular, symmetric stable distributions with the same value of the characteristic exponent α. Thus, the distribution for any asset or portfolio can be fully described once its expected value and a dispersion parameter, such as the standard deviation—in the normal case, $\alpha = 2$—or the semi-interquartile range—in the general case, $1 < \alpha \leq 2$—are known. It is then shown that if investors behave as if they tried to maximize expected utility with respect to two-period utility functions $v_{t+1}(c_t, w_{t+1})$ that are strictly concave in (c_t, w_{t+1}), optimal portfolios are efficient in terms of the two parameters of distributions of one-period returns.[11] The fact that optimal portfolios must be efficient then leads to a theory of risk and the relationships between expected return and risk, first for the individual consumer and then, with the additional assumptions of homogeneous expectations and riskless borrowing-lending opportunities, for the market as a whole.

But these two-period two-parameter models assume somewhat more about the utility function v_{t+1} than our multiperiod model has so far provided. In particular, in the multiperiod model the function $v_{t+1}(c_t, w_{t+1} \mid \Phi_{t+1})$, which is relevant for the consumption-investment decision of period t, is strictly concave in (c_t, w_{t+1}), but utility can be a function of the state Φ_{t+1}; that is, utility can be state-dependent. Thus to provide a multiperiod setting for the two-period two-parameter models, it is sufficient to determine conditions under which v_{t+1} is independent of Φ_{t+1}.

[10] The term "state-dependent utilities" refers to the fact that the function $v_{t+1}(c_t, w_{t+1} \mid \Phi_{t+1})$ allows the utility of a given combination (c_t, w_{t+1}) to depend on Φ_{t+1}. The term "state preference" is also used.
[11] Recall that a portfolio is efficient only if no portfolio with the same or higher expected return has lower return dispersion.

State-dependent utilities in the derived functions v_{t+1} have three possible sources. First, tastes for given bundles of consumption goods can be state-dependent. Second, as shown later in Theorem 2, utilities for given dollars of consumption depend on the available consumption goods and services and their prices, and these are elements of the state of the world. Finally, the investment opportunities available in any given future period may depend on events occurring in preceding periods, and such uncertainty about investment prospects induces state-dependent utilities. Thus the most direct way to exclude state-dependent utilities is to assume that:

1. The consumer behaves as if the consumption opportunities, in terms of goods and services and their prices, and the investment opportunities— distributions of one-period portfolio wealth relatives—that will be available in any future period can be taken as known and fixed at the beginning of any previous period.
2. The consumer's tastes for given bundles of consumption goods and services are independent of the state of the world.[12,13]

To see that (1) and (2) do indeed rule out state-dependent utilities, note that if the utility of lifetime consumption $U_{\tau+1}$ is independent of $\Phi_{\tau+1}$, that is, if we can write $U_{\tau+1}(C_{\tau+1})$ instead of $U_{\tau+1}(C_{\tau+1} \mid \Phi_{\tau+1})$, and if there is only one possible set of consumption goods and prices and one possible set of distributions of one-period portfolio wealth relatives that can be available in the market at period τ, then from Equation (8.3) the maximum expected utility of lifetime consumption generated by the consumption-investment decision of period τ depends only on $C_{\tau-1}$ and w_τ; that is, we can write $U_\tau(C_{\tau-1},w_\tau)$ instead of $U_\tau(C_{\tau-1},w_\tau \mid \Phi_\tau)$. And with these assumptions, that is, (1) and (2), on opportunities and tastes, the same result holds for all earlier periods; that is, the maximum expected utility of lifetime consumption associated with a given (C_t,w_{t+1}) is independent of Φ_{t+1}, so that Φ_{t+1} can be dropped from $U_{t+1}(C_t,w_{t+1} \mid \Phi_{t+1})$ and thus from $v_{t+1}(c_t,w_{t+1} \mid \Phi_{t+1})$. For given wealth w_t, the decision problem facing the consumer at the

[12] It is important to note that some such assumptions are implicit in the two-period two-parameter models themselves, because they do not allow for the effects of state-dependent utilities on the consumption-investment decision.

[13] These assumptions are in fact somewhat more extreme than are strictly necessary to provide a multiperiod setting for the two-parameter model. The primary result of the two-period two-parameter models is the efficient set theorem: The optimal portfolio for a risk averter must be efficient. This result continues to hold with state-dependent utilities as long as, speaking roughly, any uncertainty about the future consumption goods and prices that will be available in the market is independent of any uncertainty about the future investment opportunities that will be available. It is not clear to us, however, that these are in fact much weaker assumptions than those in the text.

beginning of any period t can then be written as

$$\max_{c_t,h} \int_{\Phi_{t+1}} v_{t+1}(c_t, \sum_{j=1}^{N} h_j[1 + R_j(\Phi_{t+1})]) \, dF_{\Phi_t}(\Phi_{t+1})$$

subject to

$$0 \le c_t \le w_t \quad \text{and} \quad \sum_{j=1}^{N} h_j = w_t - c_t.$$

Because Theorem 1 applies directly to this simplified version of the multiperiod model, at any period t the function $v_{t+1}(c_t, w_{t+1})$ is monotone-increasing and strictly concave in (c_t, w_{t+1}) and is thus formally equivalent to the utility function used in the standard treatments of the two-period two-parameter portfolio models. If distributions of one-period security and portfolio wealth relatives are of the same two-parameter type, it follows directly that we have a multiperiod model in which the consumer's behavior each period is indistinguishable from that of the consumer in the traditional two-period two-parameter portfolio models. From here it is a short step to develop a multiperiod setting for period by period application of the major results of the two-period two-parameter models of market equilibrium. In particular, all that we need are the assumptions of homogeneous expectations and riskless borrowing-lending opportunities.

But all this, of course, depends somewhat on the rather restrictive assumptions (1) and (2), which have the effect of making deterministic the evolution through time of market consumption and investment opportunities. What would happen if we allowed the investment opportunities to be available at $t + 1$ to depend, but not perfectly, on the opportunities available at t, which in turn are somewhat uncertain in earlier periods?[14] Or what would be the effects of allowing prices of consumption goods at $t + 1$ to depend, but again with some uncertainty, on the prices to be observed at t? And suppose that uncertainty about prices of consumption goods is related to the uncertainty in investment returns? All these questions would seem to take us out of context of the two-period two-parameter models, but in the current state of the art, we do not really know much about the characteristics of consumer and market equilibrium that they imply. And here, at the moment, is where things must be left.

---

[14] For example, we might assume, and perhaps not unrealistically, that the levels of equilibrium expected returns on investment assets that will be available at $t + 1$ depend, but with some uncertainty, on the levels that will be available at t, which in turn depend on those of $t - 1$, and so on.

II.C.4. Theorems and proofs

Thus we conclude our presentation of multiperiod consumption-investment models with a proof of Theorem 1 and an additional theorem relating the concavity of the consumer's utility function for consumption expenditures to the concavity of his underlying utility function for consumption goods and services.

Theorem 1. If $U_{t+1}(C_t, w_{t+1} \mid \Phi_{t+1})$ is monotone-increasing and strictly concave, henceforth m.i.s.c., in (C_t, w_{t+1}), then $U_t(C_{t-1}, w_t \mid \Phi_t)$ is m.i.s.c. in (C_{t-1}, w_t).

Proof. The proof of the proposition relies primarily on straightforward applications of well-known properties of concave functions (see Ref. 6). We first establish Lemma 1.

Lemma 1. If $U_{t+1}(C_t, w_{t+1} \mid \Phi_{t+1})$ is m.i.s.c. in (C_t, w_{t+1}), the expected utility function

$$\int_{\Phi_{t+1}} U_{t+1}(C_t, w_{t+1} \mid \Phi_{t+1}) \, dF_{\Phi_t}(\Phi_{t+1})$$

$$= \int_{\Phi_{t+1}} U_{t+1}\left(C_t, \sum_{j=1}^{N} h_j[1 + R_j(\Phi_{t+1})] \mid \Phi_{t+1}\right) dF_{\Phi_t}(\Phi_{t+1}) \quad (8.6)$$

is strictly concave in $(C_t, h_1, h_2, \ldots, h_N)$.

Proof. For any given value of Φ_{t+1},

$$w_{t+1} = \sum_{j=1}^{N} h_j[1 + R_j(\Phi_{t+1})]$$

is a linear and thus concave, although not strictly concave, function of the h_j. Because by assumption $U_{t+1}(C_t, w_{t+1} \mid \Phi_{t+1})$ is m.i.s.c. in (C_t, w_{t+1}), $U_{t+1}(C_t, \sum_{j=1}^{N} h_j[1 + R_j(\Phi_{t+1})] \mid \Phi_{t+1})$ is strictly concave in $(C_t, h_1, h_2, \ldots, h_N)$.[15] Integrating over Φ_{t+1} in Equation (8.6) preserves this concavity.

The remainder of the proof of Theorem 1 is then as follows. Let c_t^*, h_j^*, $j = 1, 2, \ldots, N$, and $\dot{c}_t^*$, $\dot{h}_j^*$, $j = 1, 2, \ldots, N$, be the optimal values of

---

[15] If $f(x_1, x_2, \ldots, x_N) = f(X)$ is m.i.s.c. in X and if $x_i = g_i(y_1, y_2, \ldots, y_a) = g_i(Y)$, $i = 1, 2, \ldots, N$, is concave, although not necessarily strictly concave, in Y, then $f(g_1(Y), g_2(Y), \ldots, g_N(Y)) = f(G(Y))$ is strictly concave in Y. (See, for example, Ref. 5, p. 52.)

c_t and the h_j in Equation (8.4) for any two vectors (C_{t-1}, w_t) and $(\dot{C}_{t-1}, \dot{w}_t)$ that differ in at least one element. For $0 < \alpha < 1$, let

$$\hat{C}_{t-1} = \alpha C_{t-1} + (1 - \alpha)\dot{C}_{t-1},$$

$$\hat{w}_t = \alpha w_t + (1 - \alpha)\dot{w}_t,$$

$$\hat{c}_t = \alpha c_t^* + (1 - \alpha)\dot{c}_t^*,$$

$$\hat{h}_j = \alpha h_j^* + (1 - \alpha)\dot{h}_j^*, \qquad j = 1, 2, \ldots, N.$$

To establish the concavity of $U_t(C_{t-1}, w_t \mid \Phi_t)$, we must show that

$$U_t(\hat{C}_{t-1}, \hat{w}_t \mid \Phi_t) > \alpha U_t(C_{t-1}, w_t \mid \Phi_t) + (1 - \alpha)U_t(\dot{C}_{t-1}, \dot{w}_t \mid \Phi_t). \quad (8.7)$$

From Lemma 1, for $0 < \alpha < 1$,

$$\int_{\Phi_{t+1}} U_{t+1}(\hat{C}_{t-1}, \hat{c}_t, \sum_{j=1}^{N} \hat{h}_j[1 + R_j(\Phi_{t+1})] \mid \Phi_{t+1})\, dF_{\Phi_t}(\Phi_{t+1})$$

$$> \alpha \int_{\Phi_{t+1}} U_{t+1}(C_{t-1}, c_t^*, \sum_{j=1}^{N} h_j^*[1 + R_j(\Phi_{t+1})] \mid \Phi_{t+1})\, dF_{\Phi_t}(\Phi_{t+1})$$

$$+ (1 - \alpha) \int_{\Phi_{t+1}} U_{t+1}(\dot{C}_{t-1}, \dot{c}_t^*, \sum_{j=1}^{N} \dot{h}_j^*[1 + R_j(\Phi_{t+1})] \mid \Phi_{t+1})\, dF_{\Phi_t}(\Phi_{t+1})$$

$$= \alpha U_t(C_{t-1}, w_t \mid \phi_t) + (1 - \alpha)U_t(\dot{C}_{t-1}, \dot{w}_t \mid \Phi_t). \quad (8.8)$$

Because the consumption-investment decision implied by $\hat{c}_t$, $\hat{h}_j$, $j = 1$, $2, \ldots, N$, is feasible but not necessarily optimal for the wealth level $\hat{w}_t$,

$$U_t(\hat{C}_{t-1}, \hat{w}_t \mid \Phi_t)$$

$$\geq \int_{\Phi_{t+1}} U_{t+1}(\hat{C}_{t-1}, \hat{c}_t, \sum_{j=1}^{N} \hat{h}_j[1 + R_j(\Phi_{t+1})] \mid \Phi_{t+1})\, dF_{\Phi_t}(\Phi_{t+1}),$$

which, with Equation (8.8) implies Equation (8.7).[16]

---

[16] It is assumed that $\hat{c}_t$, $\hat{h}_j$, $j = 1, 2, \ldots, N$, is a feasible consumption-investment decision for the wealth level $\hat{w}_t$, or equivalently, that the set of feasible values of c_t, h_j, $j = 1, 2, \ldots, N$, is convex. But this is a weak assumption that is met, for example, when the constraints on c_t and the h_j are equations, such as $\sum_{j=1}^{N} h_j = w_t - c_t$, or linear inequalities, such as $0 \leq c_t \leq w_t$ or $\underline{h}_j \leq h_j \leq \bar{h}_j$, where $\underline{h}_j$ and $\bar{h}_j$ are lower and upper bounds on the quantity invested in asset j.

The monotonicity of $U_t(C_{t-1}, w_t \mid \Phi_t)$ in (C_{t-1}, w_t) follows straightforwardly from the monotonicity of $U_{t+1}(C_t, w_{t+1} \mid \Phi_{t+1})$ in C_t. Thus the proposition is established.

Finally, as noted earlier (footnote 8, page 328 and also in the last section in Chapter 5), when utility is written, as we have done throughout, as a function of consumption dollars, we are implicitly summarizing the consumption opportunities, in terms of goods and services and their anticipated prices, that will be available in each period. We now show how a "cardinal" utility function for consumption dollars can be derived from a cardinal utility function for consumption commodities.

Let $q(\Phi_t) = (q_1, q_2, \ldots, q_{K(\Phi_t)})$ be the quantities of $K(\Phi_t)$ available commodities consumed during t in state Φ_t, and let $p(\Phi_t) = (p_1, p_2, \ldots, p_{K(\Phi_t)})$ be the corresponding price vector. In any period or state one of the available consumption commodities is always "dollar gifts and bequests," which has price \$1 per unit. At the horizon $\tau + 1$, dollar gifts and bequests, denoted $w_{\tau+1}$, is the only available consumption good. Let

$$Q_\tau = (q(\Phi_{1-k}), \ldots, q(\Phi_1), \ldots, q(\Phi_\tau))$$

represent lifetime consumption of commodities, and let $V(Q_\tau, w_{\tau+1} \mid \Phi_{\tau+1})$ be the consumer's utility of lifetime consumption, given state $\Phi_{\tau+1}$ at $\tau + 1$, and where $\Phi_{1-k} \subset \cdots \subset \Phi_1 \subset \cdots \subset \Phi_{\tau+1}$. The utility function for dollars of consumption can then be defined as

$$U_{\tau+1}(C_{\tau+1} \mid \Phi_{\tau+1}) = \max_{Q_\tau} V(Q_\tau, w_{\tau+1} \mid \Phi_{\tau+1})$$

$$\text{s.t.} \quad C_{\tau+1} = \left(\sum_{i=1}^{K(\Phi_{1-K})} p_i(\Phi_{1-k}) q_i(\Phi_{1-k}), \ldots, \sum_{i=1}^{K(\Phi_\tau)} p_i(\Phi_\tau) q_i(\Phi_\tau), w_{\tau+1} \right)$$

$$= (c_{1-k}, \ldots, c_\tau, c_{\tau+1}). \tag{8.9}$$

The role of $\Phi_{\tau+1}$ in $U_{\tau+1}$ is twofold. First, psychological attitudes toward current and past consumption, or "tastes," may depend on the state of the world. Second, even if tastes for consumption commodities are not state-dependent, so that $\Phi_{\tau+1}$ can be dropped from V, the utility of any stream of dollar consumption expenditures depends on the history of the set of available consumption commodities and their prices, both of which are subsumed in $\Phi_{\tau+1}$.

A utility function $U_{\tau+1}(C_{\tau+1} \mid \Phi_{\tau+1})$ that has the properties required by Proposition 1 can then be obtained from $V(Q_\tau, w_{\tau+1} \mid \Phi_{\tau+1})$ as follows.

Theorem 2. If $V(Q_\tau, w_{\tau+1} \mid \Phi_{\tau+1})$ is m.i.s.c. in $(Q_\tau, w_{\tau+1})$, then $U_{\tau+1}(C_\tau, w_{\tau+1} \mid \Phi_{\tau+1})$ is m.i.s.c. in $(C_\tau, w_{\tau+1})$.

Proof. Let Q_τ^* be the optimal value of Q_τ in Equation (8.9) for $(C_\tau, w_{\tau+1})$, and let $\dot{Q}_\tau^*$ be optimal for $(\dot{C}_\tau, \dot{w}_{\tau+1})$, where the vectors $(C_\tau, w_{\tau+1})$ and $(\dot{C}_\tau, \dot{w}_{\tau+1})$ differ in at least one element. For $0 < \alpha < 1$, let

$$(\hat{Q}_\tau, \hat{w}_{\tau+1}) = \alpha(Q_\tau^*, w_{\tau+1}) + (1 - \alpha)(\dot{Q}_\tau^*, \dot{w}_{\tau+1}),$$

$$(\hat{C}_\tau, \hat{w}_{\tau+1}) = \alpha(C_\tau, w_{\tau+1}) + (1 - \alpha)(\dot{C}_\tau, \dot{w}_{\tau+1}).$$

Then the strict concavity of V implies that

$$V(\hat{Q}_\tau, \hat{w}_{\tau+1} \mid \Phi_{\tau+1}) > \alpha V(Q_\tau^*, w_{\tau+1} \mid \Phi_{\tau+1}) + (1 - \alpha) V(\dot{Q}_\tau^*, \dot{w}_{\tau+1} \mid \Phi_{\tau+1}).$$

Or equivalently

$$V(\hat{Q}_\tau, \hat{w}_{\tau+1} \mid \Phi_{\tau+1}) > \alpha U_{\tau+1}(C_\tau, w_{\tau+1} \mid \Phi_{\tau+1}) + (1 - \alpha) U_{\tau+1}(\dot{C}_\tau, \dot{w}_{\tau+1} \mid \Phi_{\tau+1}).$$

Because $\hat{Q}_\tau$ is a feasible but not necessarily an optimal allocation of $\hat{C}_\tau$, an optimal allocation must have utility at least as high as that implied by $\hat{Q}_\tau$, so that

$$U_{\tau+1}(\hat{C}_\tau, \hat{w}_{\tau+1} \mid \Phi_{\tau+1}) > \alpha U_{\tau+1}(C_\tau, w_{\tau+1} \mid \Phi_{\tau+1}) + (1 - \alpha) U_{\tau+1}(\dot{C}_\tau, \dot{w}_{\tau+1} \mid \Phi_{\tau+1}),$$

and the concavity of $U_{\tau+1}$ is established.

To establish the monotonicity of $U_{\tau+1}$ in C_τ, simply note that if the dollars available for consumption in any period are increased, consumption of at least one commodity can be increased without reducing consumption of any other commodity, so that utility must be increased. An optimal reallocation of consumption expenditures must do at least as well.

III. EFFICIENT CAPITAL MARKETS

Most of the models presented in this book are based on the assumption of a perfect capital market, that is, a market in which all available information is freely available to everybody, there are no transactions costs, and all market participants are price takers. Our uncertainty models of market equilibrium have in addition usually assumed homogeneous expectations; that is, market participants agree on the implications of available information for both current prices and probability distributions on future prices of individual investment assets.

Such a market has a very desirable feature. In particular, at any point in time market prices of securities provide accurate signals for resource allocation; that is, firms can make production-investment decisions, and consumers can choose among the securities that represent ownership of firms' activities under the presumption that security prices at any time "fully reflect" all available information. A market in which prices fully reflect available information is called efficient.

In keeping with the policy of this book, we only discuss here the theoretical foundations of the efficient markets model. But the model has been subjected to a substantial amount of empirical testing, and we contend that the model stands up well to the data. If true, this is important support for theoretical models based on a perfect market. Indeed we believe the available (mid-1971) evidence indicates that although the theoretical models we build in this book are abstracted substantially from real-world considerations, we nevertheless have reason to hope they might do quite well in describing actual market phenomena.

III.A. Expected Return or Fair Game Models

The definitional statement that in an efficient market prices fully reflect available information is so general that it has no testable implications. To make the model testable, the process of price formation must be specified in more detail. We must define somewhat more exactly what is meant by the phrase *fully reflect*.

One possibility would be to posit that equilibrium prices, or expected returns, on securities are generated by the two-parameter model in Chapter 7 and Section II in the present chapter. In general, however, the models and especially the empirical tests of capital market efficiency have not been so specific. Most of the available work is based only on the assumption that the conditions of market equilibrium can, somehow, be stated in terms of expected returns. In general terms, like the two-parameter model such theories would posit that, conditional on some relevant information set, the equilibrium expected return on a security is a function of its "risk." And different theories would differ primarily in how risk is defined.

All members of the class of such "expected return theories" can, however, be described notationally as follows:

$$E(\tilde{p}_{j,t+1} \mid \Phi_t) = [1 + E(\tilde{R}_{j,t+1} \mid \Phi_t)]p_{jt}, \qquad (8.10)$$

where E is the expected value operator; p_{jt} is the price of security j at time t; $p_{j,t+1}$ is its price at $t + 1$, with reinvestment of any intermediate cash income from the security; $R_{j,t+1}$ is the one-period percentage return; Φ_t is a general symbol for whatever set of information is assumed to be fully reflected in the price at t; and the tildes indicate that $p_{j,t+1}$ and $R_{j,t+1}$ are random variables at t.

The process of price adjustment summarized in Equation (8.10) is as follows. At time t the market uses all the available information Φ_t to assess the probability distribution of $\tilde{p}_{j,t+1}$, which in turn implies an expected future price $E(\tilde{p}_{j,t+1} \mid \Phi_t)$. This assessment of the distribution of $\tilde{p}_{j,t+1}$, along with some model of equilibrium expected returns, then determines $E(\tilde{R}_{j,t+1} \mid \Phi_t)$. The equilibrium expected return $E(\tilde{R}_{j,t+1} \mid \Phi_t)$ then combines with $E(\tilde{p}_{j,t+1} \mid \Phi_t)$ to determine the equilibrium price at t, p_{jt}. And this is the sense in which the information Φ_t is fully reflected in the formation of p_{jt}.

But we should note right off that, as simple as it is, the assumption that the conditions of market equilibrium can be stated in terms of expected returns elevates the purely mathematical concept of expected value to a status not necessarily implied by the general notion of market efficiency. The expected value is just one of many possible summary measures of a distribution of returns, and market efficiency per se, that is, the general notion that prices fully reflect available information, does not imbue it with any special importance. Thus, the results of tests based on this assumption depend to some extent on its validity as well as on the efficiency of the market. But some such assumption is the unavoidable price that one must pay to give the theory of efficient markets empirical content.

The assumptions that the conditions of market equilibrium can be stated in terms of expected returns and that equilibrium expected returns and current prices are formed on the basis of, and thus fully reflect, the information set Φ_t have a major testable implication—they rule out the possibility of trading systems based only on information in Φ_t that have expected profits or returns in excess of equilibrium expected profits or returns. Thus let

$$x_{j,t+1} = p_{j,t+1} - E(\tilde{p}_{j,t+1} \mid \Phi_t). \qquad (8.11)$$

Then
$$E(\tilde{x}_{j,t+1} \mid \Phi_t) = 0, \qquad (8.12)$$

which, by definition, says that the sequence $\{x_{jt}\}$ is a "fair game" with respect to the information sequence $\{\Phi_t\}$. Or equivalently, let

$$z_{j,t+1} = R_{j,t+1} - E(\tilde{R}_{j,t+1} \mid \Phi_t). \qquad (8.13)$$

Then
$$E(\tilde{z}_{j,t+1} \mid \Phi_t) = 0, \qquad (8.14)$$

so that the sequence $\{z_{jt}\}$ is also a fair game with respect to the information sequence $\{\Phi_t\}$.

In economic terms, $x_{j,t+1}$ is the excess market value of security j at time $t + 1$: It is the difference between the observed price and the expected value of the price that was projected at t on the basis of the information Φ_t. And similarly, $z_{j,t+1}$ is the return at $t + 1$ in excess of the equilibrium expected return projected at t. Let

$$\alpha(\Phi_t) = [\alpha_1(\Phi_t), \alpha_2(\Phi_t), \ldots, \alpha_N(\Phi_t)]$$

be any trading system based on Φ_t that tells the investor the amounts $\alpha_j(\Phi_t)$ of funds available at t that are to be invested in each of the N

available securities. The total excess market value at $t + 1$ that is generated by such a system is

$$V_{t+1} = \sum_{j=1}^{N} \alpha_j(\Phi_t)[R_{j,t+1} - E(\tilde{R}_{j,t+1} \mid \Phi_t)],$$

which, from the fair game property in Equation (8.14), has expectation

$$E(\tilde{V}_{t+1} \mid \Phi_t) = \sum_{j=1}^{n} \alpha_j(\phi_t) E(\tilde{z}_{j,t+1} \mid \Phi_t) = 0.$$

One should not get lost in the algebra here, however. In intuitive terms, all that we have come to is the rather obvious conclusion that if all the information in Φ_t is used by the market in assessing expected future returns and prices, there is no way an investor can use Φ_t as the basis of a trading system with expected returns in excess of equilibrium expected returns.

We turn now to two special cases of this fair game efficient markets model, the submartingale and the random walk, that play an important role in the empirical literature.[17]

III.B. The Submartingale Model

Suppose we assume in Equation (8.10) that for all t and Φ_t

$$E(\tilde{p}_{j,t+1} \mid \Phi_t) \geq p_{jt},$$

or equivalently

$$E(\tilde{R}_{j,t+1} \mid \Phi_t) \geq 0. \tag{8.15}$$

This is a statement that the price sequence $\{p_{jt}\}$ for security j follows a submartingale with respect to the information sequence $\{\Phi_t\}$, which is to say nothing more than that the expected value of next period's price, as projected on the basis of the information Φ_t, is equal to or greater than the current price. If Equation (8.15) holds as an equality, so that expected returns and price changes are zero, the price sequence follows a martingale.

A submartingale in prices has one important testable implication. Consider the set of "one security and cash" mechanical trading rules, by which we mean systems that concentrate on individual securities and that define the conditions under which the investor would hold a given security, sell it short, or simply hold cash at any time t. Then the assumption in

---

[17] Although we refer to the model summarized by Equation (8.10) as the fair game model, keep in mind that the fair game properties of the model are implications of the assumptions that (1) the conditions of market equilibrium can be stated in terms of expected returns and (2) the information Φ_t is fully utilized by the market in forming equilibrium expected returns and thus current prices.

Equation (8.15) that expected returns conditional on Φ_t are nonnegative directly implies that such trading rules based only on the information in Φ_t cannot have greater expected profits than a policy of always buying and holding the security during the future period in question.[18]

III.C. The Random Walk Model

In the early treatments of the efficient markets model in the finance literature, the statement that the current price of a security fully reflects available information was assumed to imply that successive price changes, or more usually, successive one-period returns, are independent. In addition, it was usually assumed that successive changes, or returns, are identically distributed. Together the two hypotheses constitute the random walk model.[19] Formally, the model says that

$$f(R_{j,t+1} \mid \Phi_t) = f(R_j), \tag{8.16}$$

which is the usual statement that the conditional and marginal probability distributions of an independent random variable are identical. In addition, the density function f must be the same for all t.

Expression (8.16) says much more, of course, than the general expected return model summarized by Equation (8.10). For example, if we restrict Equation (8.10) by assuming that the expected return on security j is constant over time, we have

$$E(\tilde{R}_{j,t+1} \mid \Phi_t) = E(\tilde{R}_j),$$

[18] Note that the expected profitability of one security and cash trading systems vis-à-vis buy-and-hold is not ruled out by the general expected return or fair game efficient markets model. The latter rules out systems with expected profits in excess of equilibrium expected returns, but because in principle it allows equilibrium expected returns to be negative, holding cash, which always has zero actual and thus expected return, may have higher expected return than holding some security.

And negative equilibrium expected returns for some securities are quite possible. For example, in the two-parameter model, a security whose returns on average move opposite to the general market is particularly valuable in reducing dispersion of portfolio returns, and so its equilibrium expected return may well be negative.

[19] The statistically sophisticated reader will recognize that the terminology is loose. Prices follow a random walk only if price changes are independent, identically distributed; and even then we should say "random walk with drift," because expected price changes can be nonzero. If one-period returns are independent, identically distributed, prices do not follow a random walk, because the distribution of price changes depends on the price level. But although rigorous terminology is usually desirable, our loose use of terms should not cause confusion; and our usage follows that of the efficient markets literature.

This says that the mean of the distribution of $R_{j,t+1}$ is independent of the past information, whereas the random walk model in Equation (8.16) in addition says that the entire distribution is independent of the past information.[20]

It is best to regard the random walk model as an extension of the general expected return or fair game efficient markets model in the sense of making a more detailed statement about the economic environment. The fair game model just says that the conditions of market equilibrium can be stated in terms of expected returns, and thus it says little about the details of the stochastic process generating returns. A random walk arises in the context of such a model when the environment is, fortuitously, such that the evolution of investor tastes and the process generating new information combine to produce equilibria in which return distributions repeat themselves through time.

A detailed review of the empirical literature on the efficient markets model is available elsewhere [11]; thus we do not discuss the evidence here. (This is, of course, also in keeping with the policy of preceding chapters.) We wish to suggest, however, that there is much evidence in support of the position that perfect markets models, like those developed in this book, have substantial value in describing real-world economic phenomena.

REFERENCES

Much of the discussion of multiperiod consumption-investment decisions in Section II is taken from

1. Fama, Eugene F., "Multiperiod Consumption-Investment Decisions," *American Economic Review*, vol. 60 (March 1970), pp. 163–174.

   Other works on multiperiod models are

2. Hakansson, Nils, "Optimal Investment and Consumption Strategies under Risk for a Class of Utility Functions," *Econometrica*, vol. 38 (September 1970), pp. 587–607.
3. Mossin, Jan, "Optimal Multiperiod Portfolio Policies," *Journal of Business*, vol. 41 (April 1968), pp. 215–229.
4. Phelps, Edmund, "The Accumulation of Risky Capital: A Sequential Utility Analysis," *Econometrica*, vol. 30 (October 1962), and reprinted in *Risk Aversion and Portfolio Choice*, D. Hester and J. Tobin, eds. New York: John Wiley & Sons, Inc., 1967, pp. 139–153.

---

[20] The random walk model does not say, however, that past information is of no value in assessing distributions of future returns. Indeed because return distributions are assumed to be the same through time, past returns are the best source of such information. The random walk model does say, however, that the sequence, or the order, of the past returns is of no consequence in assessing distributions of future returns.

Properties of convex and concave functions used in proving Theorems 1 and 2 can be found in

5. Eggleston, H. G., *Convexity*. New York: Cambridge University Press, 1958.
6. Iglehart, Donald L., "Capital Accumulation and Production for the Firm: Optimal Dynamic Policy," *Management Science*, vol. 12 (November 1965), pp. 193–205.

Consumption-investment models involving state-dependent utilities can be found in

7. Arrow, Kenneth J., "The Role of Securities in the Optimal Allocation of Risk-Bearing," *Review of Economic Studies*, vol. 31 (April 1964), pp. 91–96.
8. Diamond, Peter, "A Stock Market in a General Equilibrium Model," *American Economic Review*, vol. 57 (September 1967), pp. 759–776.
9. Hirshleifer, Jack, "Investment Decision under Uncertainty: Applications of the State-Preference Approach," *Quarterly Journal of Economics*, vol. 80 (May 1966), pp. 252–277.
10. Hirshleifer, Jack, "Investment Decision under Uncertainty: Choice-Theoretic Approaches," *Quarterly Journal of Economics*, vol. 79 (November 1965), pp. 509–536.

References for two-period two-parameter consumption-investment models and models of capital market equilibrium are at the end of Chapters 6 and 7.

The discussion of the efficient markets model in Section III draws heavily from

11. Fama, Eugene F., "Efficient Capital Markets: A Review of Theory and Empirical Work," *Journal of Finance*, vol. 35 (May 1970), pp. 383–417.

In addition to providing extensive references, this paper contains a detailed summary of the empirical literature. The first rigorous treatments of the efficient markets model are in

12. Mandelbrot, Benoit, "Forecasts of Future Prices, Unbiased Markets, and Martingale Models," *Journal of Business*, vol. 39 (Special Supplement, January 1966), pp. 242–255.
13. Samuelson, Paul A., "Proof that Properly Anticipated Prices Fluctuate Randomly," *Industrial Management Review*, vol. 6 (Spring 1965), pp. 41–49.

INDEX